An American Woman in Pakistan

. . . Memories of Mangla Dam

Irene Aylworth Douglass

An American Woman in Pakistan: Memories of Mangla Dam

Published by Wheatmark®
1760 East River Road, Suite 145, Tucson, Arizona 85718 U.S.A.
www.wheatmark.com

ISBN: 978-1-60494-981-0 (paperback)
ISBN: 978-1-60494-999-5 (ebook)
LCCN: 2013941838

rev201301
rev201302

This book is dedicated to the late Guy F. Atkinson, the company he founded, and the dedicated employees and loyal families who followed their men to projects wherever the opportunity for achievement and adventure took them.

Acknowledgments

I AM GRATEFUL TO MY late in-laws, Grace and Ambrose Aylworth, who saved the stacks of tissue-thin air letters I wrote them from Pakistan. Years later, I discovered those letters which gave me a sequence of events, some things long forgotten. The first draft of the book came easily with letters to jog my memory and help me recall events.

Thanks to Jim Aylworth, my ex-husband and long-time friend, who took us on the adventure of our young lives. Jim's research assistance and recollections were invaluable in this endeavor.

Over the years, my writing groups have been a catalyst. Rita Jamison, my writing teacher, urged me to write of my experiences in Pakistan. Her continued support and friendship has been encouraging.

Jeri Chase Ferris, who has published over a dozen books, believed this was a story that needed to be told. She helped outline the book and guided me through the revisions with patience and insight. I am grateful for her gracious gift of knowledge, professionalism, and friendship.

Fida Shaw and I reconnected after fifty years, confirming my belief that people appear in life at exactly the right time. Fida reviewed my Urdu words and references to Muslim culture to ensure the correct usage. I appreciate his review and suggestions.

I want to thank all who assisted me in this effort.

Contents

Pakistan

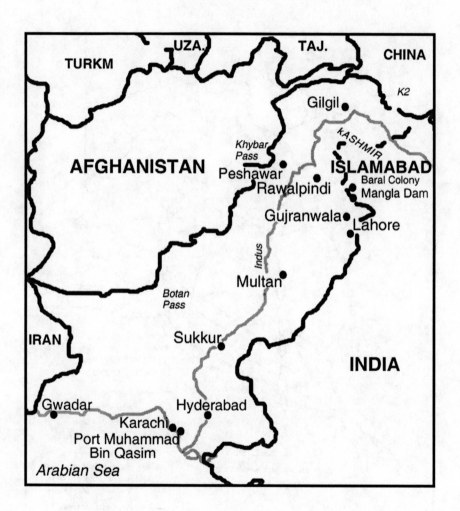

Indus River Settlement Plan

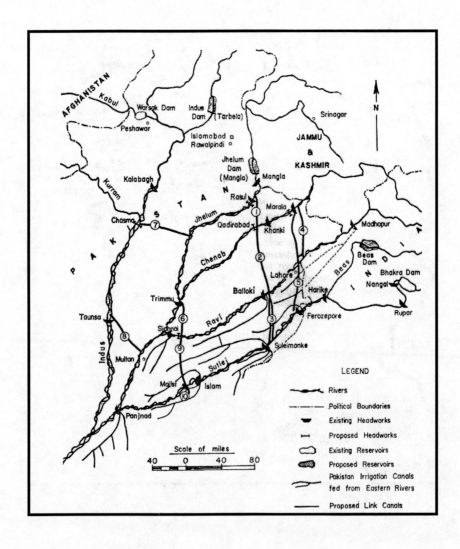

Introduction

OVER THE CENTURIES, EUROPEAN EXPLORERS found the treasures of India irresistible. The exotic spices, silk and exquisite cotton fabrics, some with delicate hand embroidery, and precious stones attracted traders to merchandise prized in Europe. The dangers of the long journey seemed of little consequence with the promise of the great wealth the India trade would provide them. Traders followed the paths pioneered by Alexander the Great, Marco Polo, and Genghis Khan as they trekked along the Silk Road and funneled through the Khyber Pass to reach the riches of this land of myth and magic. Other explorers came by sea to ports along the Arabian Sea and the Bay of Bengal.

Many traders established colonies that hugged the shores of India and brought missionaries dedicated to converting the Hindus, Sikhs, and Buddhists to Christianity. They built schools, clinics, and hospitals. None took over the country as completely as did the East India Company and the British, whose rule (or "Raj") in India spanned two centuries of domination that made India a part of the British Empire, the undisputed crown jewel of the vast British Empire on which "the sun never sets."

Pathways and dirt roads suitable for oxcarts and foot traffic provided the primary means of travel between the self-sufficient villages. Transporting goods over any distance on land made railroads the most feasible means of transportation. The Khyber Mail Express from Karachi to the Khyber Pass became the luxury train on the vast railway system. The Grand Trunk Road stretched fifteen hundred miles from Calcutta to the Khyber Pass.

The partition of India and Pakistan in 1947 created the new Muslim country of East and West Pakistan, separated by hundreds of miles of India. Over twelve million people were relocated in a bloody aftermath of the partition. The Hindus moved from Pakistan to supposedly equal land in India; Muslims in India were relocated to the new country of Pakistan. They did not go without violence. Tribes fighting tribes brought danger to each mile of the chaotic relocation. Trains transporting displaced persons were often stopped just short of the station, and all aboard were shot. Trains arrived at the station carrying dead bodies, not new citizens. Sikhs fought Muslims, Muslims fought Hindus, and women in particular were never safe. Reports of rapes and pillaging were rampant with the Punjab suffering the most casualties. In the end, over one million people were reportedly killed.

The division of India also meant dividing its roads, its railways, the equipment to maintain them, and the water supply flowing from the Himalayas. Dividing the extensive infrastructure of the vast country was difficult, but none more complicated than dividing the waters of the rivers that sustained the fertile agriculture, especially in the Punjab where runoff from the mighty Himalayas flowed to nourish or curse the breadbasket of the continent. The equitable distribution of water in the subcontinent became a priority, and the Indus Basin Project that had been long discussed came to fruition.

Leaders governing the new countries realized the benefits the Indus Basin Project would bring. They recognized the need to harness the vast amount of water that flowed from the Himalayas each year. With the coming of the monsoons, a majority of the water flowed to the sea, leaving farmers without sufficient water for irrigation. The vast Punjab was a virtual breadbasket of fertile land, capable of enormous production, which could become a reality with sufficient stored water to balance the years of droughts and pounding monsoon rains. The solution, according to the best hydraulic engineers of the time, was to build dams with reservoirs large enough to contain the runoff from the mountains for use during the dry seasons. The existing system of using water from miles of canals along the rivers helped, but it was inadequate to sustain the farmers in years when droughts occurred.

A treaty signed in September 1960 formalized the Indus Basin Project (also called the Indus Basin Settlement Plan), and a special fund created by an international agreement between the governments of Australia, Canada,

Germany, New Zealand, Pakistan, India, the United Kingdom, and the United States provided the financing for the project through the World Bank.

This treaty included plans for an extremely large dam, Mangla—which was actually two dams, Mangla and Jari—and a sizable barrier for the reservoir called the Sukian Dike, a major project in itself. Later, Tarbela Dam on the Indus River would be built, along with a network of eight new link canals and six barrages to complete the Indus Basin Project.

One primary goal of the project was to resolve the long-standing water dispute that had often brought India and Pakistan to the brink of war. The treaty gave the waters of the three eastern rivers—Ravi, Beas, and Sutlej—to India. The three western rivers—Chenab, Jhelum, and Indus—went to Pakistan. The Indus Basin Project was the most ambitious and imaginative water development project ever undertaken in the world. The terms of the Indus Basin Project also prohibited India from taking the upstream waters away from Pakistani farmers, which had been a legitimate complaint.

By 1961, the publicity about the first dam to be built, Mangla Dam, excited the world's construction company leaders when bids were to be tendered later that year. News of the project attracted the attention of the Guy F. Atkinson Construction Company's management in South San Francisco. Mr. Guy, as his employees affectionately called him, was in his eighties but still very much involved in the operations of the company when tendering a bid was under consideration. Mr. Guy's son, George H. Atkinson, was the CEO of the company. They each made trips to Pakistan to see the location and gather enough information for submitting a bid on Mangla Dam. Company engineers traveled to Pakistan to determine the scope of the work, evaluate the terrain, and decide what kind of equipment and personnel would be needed.

[handwritten margin note: Warsak was first]

The Atkinsons also decided that, to be competitive in this large bid and assure the success of the project, they needed partners with strong financial and construction experience. They assembled a team that consisted of the Guy F. Atkinson Company, Chicago Bridge and Iron Company, S.J. Groves & Sons Company, Charles L. Harney, Inc., C.J. Langenfelder & Sons, Inc., the Ostrander Construction Company, R.A. Trippeer, Inc., and Walsh Construction Company. Together, these firms qualified for the bonding capacity required by the World Bank.

With this prestigious consortium in place, details of construction were broken down into three phases, with the diversion of the Jhelum River from its ancient bed around Mangla Fort, a historic landmark, as the first priority. This first phase anticipated diverting the river in September 1966. If they could move the enormous amount of earth and accomplish that in the window of time between early September and mid-October, between the summer and winter monsoons, the contractors planned to divert the river a full year earlier than the date specified in the contract. The early diversion and completion would earn the company a sizable bonus. With this goal, schedules were revised and geared to divert the river by September 1965. All work revolved around that date.

The remote location of the job, eight hundred miles north of Karachi, the nearest seaport, and 130 miles north of Lahore, made replacement parts for the huge earthmoving equipment critical. A huge three-acre warehouse was built to house spare parts, extra tires, and all the miscellaneous supplies that weren't available on the local market. Huge earthmoving equipment was shipped from the states and in a variety of sizes to move and haul the earth as necessary. Instead of using traditional drill and blast techniques, the tunnel-boring machine, a custom-fabricated, behemoth drilling rig, was selected to expedite this critical phase of the work. The TBM, or Mole, would drill five lateral tunnels that would be thirty-six feet in diameter and over fifteen hundred feet long. These tunnels would divert the river's waters.

The company's policy was consistent with other jobs done over the years: to complete the work as rapidly as possible to save overhead and the cost of financing while maintaining the highest industry standards which had earned the Atkinson Company its exemplary reputation. With the team of partners and a plan in place for completing the construction a full year ahead of the scheduled completion date, management's goal was to earn the early completion bonus. Early diversion of the river would save a full year of operating costs.

On December 15, 1961, the bids for the first phase of the Indus Basin Project, the construction of Mangla Dam, were opened in London. Only four companies in the world qualified to tender a bid. The consortium sponsored by the Guy F. Atkinson Company was the low bidder at 354 million dollars.

News of the Atkinsion Consortium's successful bid spread like wildfire to the company's far-flung personnel. For some men, this job offered a chance to secure their retirement with one more big job. Other employees couldn't imagine living so far from families or moving so far from the United States, so they would not go under any circumstances. Regardless of their personal opinions on how they would answer if called, all were proud of the company's huge undertaking and successful award of the contract.

Early in 1962, the first Americans arrived in West Pakistan to begin the construction on houses so the workers' families could come. Part of the bid had included creating a comfortable town with many American conveniences. The company's first consideration was the family. As some of the old-timers were fond of saying, "If Mama's happy, everyone's happy."

To entice a man to bring his family to Pakistan for a thirty-month contract, management knew a good community, a school, and health-care facilities were important. When completed, Baral Colony was undoubtedly "the most elaborate construction camp in the world."

Before the families could come, however, the 240-acre plateau across the river that had been chosen for the American town had to be developed. The water and sewer systems, along with the roads, came first. The town was laid out, and construction of the following structures began in late spring of 1962: fifty-eight one-bedroom houses, sixty-four one-bedroom duplex units, seventy-eight two-bedroom houses, 133 three-bedroom houses, twenty-four four-bedroom houses, thirty-two one-bedroom apartment units, thirty-eight two-bedroom apartment units, five twenty-one-man bachelor units, one eighty-bed hospital, one auditorium, two churches, one theatre, and one bowling alley. Later, a nine-hole golf course was added by popular demand.

The plans for the town included a large central complex with a shopping center, a bachelor's mess, a public restaurant and bar, meeting rooms and offices, barber and beauty shops, laundry and dry cleaning services, a post office, a photography shop, camp offices, and space for airline representatives. Recreational facilities—playing fields with night lighting, a squash court, a gymnasium, two large swimming pools, and a wading pool—were provided in the town area. Outside the town, Thill Colony would be constructed to house six thousand Pakistani workers, their mess hall, mosque, and a school for their children.

Company management saw the need for fresh vegetables, and decided to develop a twenty acre site near the river. American crews sent drilling rigs to provide wells, an agricultural specialist arrived from the States, and an extensive garden flourished, providing fresh vegetables for Baral Colony and for a large portion of the Pakistani labor camps mess halls. Chickens raised on the farm provided eggs and poultry.

Imported foods and meats, as well as canned goods and government-controlled alcoholic beverages supplied the balance of the town's needs.

By fall of 1962, as the monsoons of late summer slowed to a halt, the town was ready for the first occupants. In October, a small migration of Americans left their homes in the United States to live in Pakistan and to build Mangla Dam, one of the world's largest compacted earth-filled dams, the largest at the time of completion in 1967.

◇◇◇◇◇

WE WERE ONE OF THE first families to arrive on October 18, 1962. We would not enjoy Baral Colony for the first year. My husband's assignment took us to Lahore, where, at twenty-two, I was one of youngest wives of the nearly five hundred American families. We had the unique experience of living in Lahore and later at Baral Colony.

Come with me to the far side of the world and peek into the shops and streets of a land that time forgot. Shop with me in the bazaars to see what life was like for women in *purdah* in Pakistan. Americans were a novelty.

Even if I had worn a veil or a burqua, my five-foot-nine frame would have given me away. Read along as I answer the question people have always asked me: "What was it like to live in Pakistan?"

The Far Side of the World

"LADIES AND GENTLEMEN, WE'VE LANDED in Karachi, West Pakistan. Local time is two in the morning."

The announcement awakened me. I stretched and yawned. Today must be October 18. We had left home eight days ago. I felt like we had been traveling forever. I looked out the aircraft's window into the darkness of this unknown country that would be our home for the next two years. Dim lights flickered from the only building visible. The flight, half-empty since our refueling stop in Calcutta, allowed each of us a row of seats where my sons and I had slept since darkness finally descended after we left Calcutta. This day of flying began in Hong Kong and our flights had chased the sun westward in its journey. I unfastened my seat belt and roused four-year-old Mark and seventeen-month-old Kevin. During the past week, our world had consisted of airplanes, bland meals brought by flight attendants, and the engine's roar droning the lower chord of harmony to every voice and sound. I tried to remember what life was like outside the cabin of an airplane.

We disembarked into a blast of heat that felt like a furnace door was open. If the night was this hot, what would the days be like? I looked around, hoping my cablegram from Hong Kong had brought my husband,

Jim, to meet us. I walked down the steps, holding Mark's hand and carrying Kevin, the diaper bag, and my purse. As I followed the other passengers toward the halo of light from the terminal building, my legs felt weak. The ground seemed to rise and fall as I walked.

"Are you Irene Aylworth?" a voice called from the darkness.

"Yes, I'm Irene."

A man about my height appeared out of the darkness, his face still hidden in the shadows, and stood before me. "I'm Roger, Mangla Dam Contractor's liaison in Karachi. I'll help you through customs. Here, let me carry your bag." He took the heavy diaper bag from my arm.

"Thanks for meeting us. I expected Jim. I cabled him from Hong Kong and told him our baby was sick."

"Jim called and said to tell you he couldn't get away. He'll meet you in Lahore."

I was disappointed but not surprised. Jim had written that his company's office in Lahore had only one other American employee. There was no one to replace him. I followed Roger across the tarmac. My legs felt wobbly, and my head throbbed from the incessant sound of the jet engines.

"How was your trip?" Roger asked. "Were you in San Francisco during that Columbus Day storm?"

"Yes, San Francisco was hit hard. The rains let up shortly after we departed. Our flight to Honolulu was smooth. My baby broke out with measles on the flight to Tokyo." I turned up Kevin's jacket collar to hide the blotches.

Roger's eyes widened at my news. "Wow! Sorry to hear that. From the news we got, the storm devastated the Northwest Coast and did terrible damage."

We followed him into the low-roofed terminal. Overhead ceiling fans provided some relief from the heat by stirring the heavy, humid air. Dark-skinned men called to one another in a strange language, Urdu I'd read it was called. What were they saying?

Roger led us to an office off the main lobby. I sank into a straight chair and held Kevin on my lap. Mark climbed into the wooden swivel chair behind the desk and twisted it around and around, a simple diversion for a small child.

"If you give me your baggage claim checks, I'll pick up your luggage.

You'll have to sign the custom forms. I can do everything else. Do you have anything to declare?"

Before I could answer, Roger left to retrieve our luggage. Two porters followed him. I thought of the rupees I'd bought in Hong Kong. Did I need to declare them? I would ask him later.

I sat in that shabby office at the Karachi airport. What in the world was I doing here? Nothing I had seen or read described heat like this and in the middle of the night. The air weighed on me like a heavy blanket that I wanted to toss aside. An overseas assignment had sounded like an exotic adventure. I didn't expect the storm, the measles, or this unbearable heat. I loved to travel, and I had agreed to Jim's dream of being a soldier of fortune and exploring the world. It had not occurred to me that traveling alone with two small children would be a problem. I felt mature and capable. After all, I was twenty-two years old.

Just the week before, my mom took the boys and me to the airport in Reno, Nevada. Since Jim's departure in April, we lived in a small house that we had rented near my mom's home. He had to go ahead with the other men to begin the project in West Pakistan, where he would be a purchasing agent on the Mangla Dam project. The men went first to build the town before the families could come.

I felt a little longing for home when I thought of our little cottage with the fragrance of lilacs in the spring, aromatic roses, and freshly cut grass last summer. My neighbors were friendly, and one shared an amazing spiced carrot cake along with news over the fence. The days were pleasantly warm, and the nights were cool, so Nevada was a more comfortable climate for me to wait than to suffer through another humid summer in South Dakota where Jim had worked on another company job the previous two years, Oahe Dam. Mom and my sisters lived in Reno, and I saw them frequently while I passed the long months with my class at the university and got our shots that were required for travel to Pakistan. Six months was a long time to wait.

Now we were on our way, six months after Jim's departure, excited to embark on a new adventure in a country halfway around the world. Mom and my sisters drove up as the Bekins van pulled away with our furniture and household items that would go into storage. The important basic household items and clothing I'd packed to ship to Pakistan were sent separately, itemized with the required customs papers, to be shipped by sea. That shipment would take eight to ten weeks to reach us at our new home.

Mom's coat whipped around her legs as she walked around the Cadillac and looked at the mountains. Worry wrinkled her face. The wind tossed my hair as I reached for the suitcases.

"A big storm is coming in. I don't like you flying in this kind of weather." Mom's voice trembled. "I'm sure the company could reschedule your flights after this storm passes. You can stay in your old room." She looked at me with fear in her eyes.

Six months had crept by like a sluggish snail since Jim had left in April. I didn't want to wait one more day. Life felt like it had been on hold, and I was ready to start living again. My excitement at our bold decision to move to a Muslim country halfway around the world mingled with fear of the unknown. My only hesitation was that I'd leave behind my family, friends, and everything familiar.

"Let's go," I told Mom as we loaded the suitcases into the cavernous trunk of her car. I climbed in. "It's less than an hour's flight to San Francisco. The storm will pass."

Storm clouds gathered in pewter swirls around Mount Rose. The low clouds obscured Slide Mountain's tip as we drove south to the Reno airport. As we unloaded the luggage and fought the wind that propelled the tumbleweeds across the airstrip where they clung to a galvanized fence like giant puff balls, we checked my luggage and went to the boarding gate. I embraced my mom, hugged my sisters, and blinked back tears. The time had come to leave.

"Bye, Mom. Remember to write, and I will, too. I promise."

My sister Alice, her blonde hair swirling in the fierce wind, hugged me as we both brushed away tears. I kissed her. Then I turned to Marie, my younger sister who had tied her chestnut-colored hair in a ponytail, and kissed her. I smiled at the three of them, knowing I wouldn't see them for two years, and boarded the plane. I carried Kevin and held Mark's hand as we walked up the steps and into the aircraft.

I found our seats near the front of the small airplane. Mark chose the window seat, and I held Kevin on my lap. I fastened Mark's seat belt and then my own. I held Kevin against me as the plane taxied down the runway.

The propeller-driven plane bucked and pitched as it took off to the south, climbing and fighting strong Washoe Zephyr winds as it angled upward past Rattlesnake Mountain, then turned west over Lake Tahoe, and headed toward San Francisco. The plane fought for altitude as it flew toward the Sierras on our westward flight. High winds buffeted the sides and top of the aircraft, bouncing us up and down. The winds off the mountains became worse as they brought cold air and moisture from the higher elevations. I had grown up in Truckee Meadows where Reno nestled in the mountain-rimmed valley. We were used to some wind and breezes that cooled the heat of the valley, but the Washoe Zephyrs were powerful winds that brought far stronger storms. As a child, they had kept me awake as they whistled under my bedroom windowsill.

"Attendants, take your seats. Sorry, folks, there will be no beverage service on this flight," the captain said over the loudspeaker as we continued to roller-coaster our way over the Sierra.

Twice, the plane made sharp drops, causing my stomach to hit my throat with a squeamish feeling. I'd never been airsick, but this wasn't like any other flight. Briefcases, overcoats, cameras, and parcels flew from the overhead compartments, littering the aisle of the airplane. The man across the aisle and the woman beside him crossed themselves then sat with eyes closed and hands clutching the armrests.

"Mommy, I'm scared," Mark cried.

I hugged him, stroked his head, and pulled him close to me. Another woman across the aisle clasped her rosary. Her lips moved silently.

"I am, too, sweetheart. But remember, if we aren't scared, we can't be brave. A big storm is coming. That's why there's so much wind." I didn't want my son to feel my fear.

"I don't like storms," he said.

"I don't either. It will be better as soon as we get over the mountains." Kevin squirmed in my lap. I struggled to hold him securely against me.

The flight from Reno was supposed to take fifty minutes, as the schedule said, but on this flight, the pilot fought against fierce headwinds that challenged our progress the whole way to San Francisco. We didn't know it at the time, but Hurricane Frieda, also called the Columbus Day Storm, was battering the northern coast of California and the Pacific Northwest. We were in the midst of the storm's fury. When we were past the mountains, the plane's pitch and roll felt more like a corduroy road.

The pilot landed in San Francisco with three bounces, and we taxied to the gate ninety minutes after leaving Reno.

The man across the aisle smiled at me when we rolled to a stop. "I thought we were going to crash."

The woman behind him spoke, "Weather like this could stop me from ever flying again. I was terrified."

I squared my shoulders and tried not to worry about the flights ahead of us.

We disembarked with the other passengers, still shaken but grateful that we had arrived safely. We claimed our luggage and found a van waiting to take us to the Guy F. Atkinson Construction Company's office in South San Francisco, a short drive from the airport.

"You can leave your luggage in the van until you meet with Mr. Doyle. Then I'll take you to Letterman Hospital for the yellow fever shots," said the driver. The last shot we needed to travel to Pakistan was a yellow fever inoculation. The army hospital was the only place on the West Coast with the vaccine. The driver turned on the windshield wipers as the rain began.

"The Columbia Service Company office is on the second floor," the driver said.

We found the office of Mr. Bob Doyle, the man who made all the travel arrangements for the families. Mr. Doyle quickly reviewed our itinerary as two other families arrived. During the years of Mangla Dam's construction, 860 employees and 1578 dependents were processed through this small office adjacent to the company's main office. Mr. Doyle explained how I'd find the vans arranged for us, and the hotel reservations. We said farewell and looked around the parking lot. We found the driver and left for the Letterman Army Hospital at the Presidio of San Francisco. After we got our shots, the driver then drove us to the El Rancho Motel near the airport, where we'd be staying until our departure. We checked in,and found our motel room carpet soaked. Housekeeping brought us a stack of towels to spread over the wet carpet since they had no other vacant room for us. The rain pounded the peninsula all afternoon.

That night, Jim's uncle, Chuck Robinson, and his bubbly wife, Peggy, picked us up and drove us to Peggy's favorite Japanese restaurant in San Francisco, usually a fifteen-minute drive.

"Damn wind!" Chuck swore as he navigated his car through hubcap-deep rivers of rainwater that slowed traffic to a crawl and high winds that buffeted the Bayshore Freeway. It took forty-five minutes to reach the restaurant. Chuck cursed the storm several times along the way. Peggy caught us up on Chuck's job and Jim's family news in an effort to distract him.

The San Francisco Giants were scheduled to play the New York Yankees in the first game of the 1962 World Series that evening, but as we passed Candlestick Park, little traffic moved around the ballpark. The storm had forced a rare two-day postponement of the 1962 World Series.

The next morning, we took the motel's van to the airport through the unabated rain. We were scheduled to leave on Pan American's Flight One around the world, westbound. Pan Am also had a Flight Two that circled the world, traveling eastbound. A familiar face appeared in the crowd. It was Frank Robinson, the oldest of Jim's four uncles, his mother's brother.

"Frank, did you drive all this way in the storm?"

His home in Menlo Park wasn't far in good weather, but people who didn't need to go out in this mess didn't.

"I wanted to make sure you and the boys got off all right. Grace was worried." He hugged me and bent down to shake hands with the boys. "Hello, Mark. My, you have grown. This must be your little brother I haven't met." He looked at Kevin.

I detected a tear on his tanned cheek. A few minutes later, Jim's Aunt Isabel, a spry septuagenarian, arrived, wearing her matching coat and hat and sensible walking shoes, the perfect image of a well-dressed San Franciscan. Auntie Belle, as the family called her, was the model of San Francisco's popular humor columnist, Herb Caen's Little Old Lady: well-dressed and conversant on all the latest construction and politics in the city. She had taken a bus from downtown to the airport, viewing the storm as a mild inconvenience. None of Jim's three uncles or maiden Aunt Isabel had children, so they indulged Jim as a child, and now his sons were their proxy grandchildren.

Uncle Frank looked at Kevin's harness that attached to a strap over my arm. Friends had suggested it, and at first, I rejected the idea of a leash on a child. But since Kevin was a child who loved to explore and I couldn't risk letting him get lost in the crowds, I weighed his safety against the practicality of the device.

"I brought the boys a few toys from Woolworth's." Isabel handed them each a package.

Jim's relatives were more concerned about our journey than I realized, and now these two dear people traveled through this storm to see us off. Their company was comforting as I pushed the doubts from my mind that had crept in about our decision. Was this really an adventure or folly to go so far from home? Only time would tell.

When our flight was called, a Pan Am employee held a huge umbrella over our heads as he escorted us around the puddles that dotted the tarmac. The winds threatened to wrest the umbrella from his hands. We climbed the steps of Pan Am's Flight One and waved good-bye to Aunt Isabel and Uncle Frank, hoping they could see us through the rain.

Mr. Doyle had told me there were bassinets for children Kevin's age. Smaller infants occupied all four. Kevin was tall and weighed twenty-seven pounds. This flight was full, and Kevin's ticket, a 10 percent fare for children under two years of age, did not include a seat for him.

That would be safer anyway. I can hold him if there's turbulence like we had on the last flight.

We found our seats and buckled Mark into the middle seat next to a gray-haired woman in the window seat. The jet gained speed on the runway and sprayed an arc of water as high as the windows as we took off. During those minutes when all I could see was water out the windows, I thought we might be going into the bay, but we climbed higher and higher. Blue skies replaced the storm clouds, and the rest of the flight to Hawaii was smooth. Hurricane Frieda's fury was spent.

"Down, Mom."

Kevin became restless and wanted to explore. I tried to keep him busy with picture books and snacks the flight attendant produced. The man seated across the aisle smiled and struck up a conversation. He had a ready smile and was soon teasing Kevin.

"Are you going to Hawaii on vacation?" He turned to talk to me.

"No, we only have one night in Honolulu."

I'd love to spend more time in the tropical paradise I'd seen only in photographs.

"Where are you headed?" he asked.

"Pakistan. My husband is working on a dam project there. How about you?"

"I flew this plane to San Fran earlier today. I'm deadheading back to Honolulu, my home base. You've got a lot of flying ahead of you."

He watched Kevin squirm on my lap. The airline attendant started serving meal trays. The pilot got up and offered to take Kevin for some exercise just as the flight attendant offered me a tray. Without the pilot's help, it would have been impossible to find a place for the tray or to eat with Kevin on my lap. The pilot walked Kevin the length of the aircraft several times, giving me a chance to check on Mark, eat, and relax. Kevin's walk tired him enough to doze in my arms after I fed him part of Mark's dinner tray.

I asked the flight attendant for a blanket and pillow. Our new pilot friend held Kevin while I fashioned a makeshift bed on the floor under the seat ahead of mine. Right after I laid him down, he dozed off. I placed my foot between his head and the aisle to prevent anyone from kicking him as they passed by. Kevin was fretful and warm, but he slept the last two hours of the flight to Honolulu.

Mark had become friends with a gray-haired woman next to him, a widowed grandmother on her way to serve as a Peace Corps volunteer in Asia. She read to Mark and engaged him in conversation when I was busy with Kevin. She and the pilot were two kind strangers whose care and assistance made the trip easier for me.

We landed in Honolulu and checked into a motel near the beach for our scheduled stop that Saturday night. Our motel was also the location of a wild party that continued most of the night on either side of our room. The group of young people enjoyed their loud music, so I slept little that night. The next morning, I took the boys to the beach. We walked to the white sand beach fringed with palm trees where the boys ran barefoot in the sand and teased the waves that broke on the shore. All too soon, it was time to gather our things and return to the airport.

This leg of our trip was a seven-hour flight to Tokyo. The ticket agent in Honolulu arranged to give us the two seats behind the bulkhead. Kevin still wouldn't have a seat, but the ticket agent said these seats had more space. We'd no sooner departed from Honolulu when Kevin became restless and fussy. His head felt hot. There was no doubt his temperature was rising. I gave him baby aspirin and frequently asked the flight attendant for juice and water. The seat I had wasn't right up against the window, but it had a space of a foot wide between the seat and the aircraft wall, a perfect spot to make a bed for Kevin. I padded the outside of the aircraft with extra blankets to keep him warm. This space worked better for a child his size than an infant sized bassinet I'd seen on the first flight.

As passengers boarded for the next departure, I recognized three wives with their children whose husbands worked for Jim's company. They'd all spent a few days visiting Japan and were full of tales of their experiences. All three were excited because their husbands had arranged to join them in Hong Kong. Their plans sounded wonderful.

When Kevin's head continued to feel hot, I fished the baby thermometer from the diaper bag. His temperature registered 102 degrees. By the time we landed in Hong Kong, red spots appeared on his tummy and chest. This was probably measles, I deduced. What would I do with a sick child in Hong Kong? Would they quarantine us? How much would that delay our trip?

When we landed in Hong Kong, a van driver and escort sent by the company met the other women, their five children, and me. The van driver took us to the Park Hotel for a rest stop scheduled by Mr. Doyle. The measles had struck five days after we left Reno. I was afraid of the possibility of being quarantined. Once in our room, I called the desk and asked for a doctor. He arrived a short time later and examined Kevin. He advised aspirin, plenty of fluids, and rest. I sent a cablegram to Jim in Lahore to let him know we might have to stay longer than the two nights scheduled. I also suggested I'd like him to meet us for the rest of the trip.

The next day, Kevin alternated between sleeping and being fretful. We went to the hotel's dining room for breakfast, where I selected a table away from other people. One of the company wives I'd talked to on the flight stopped by to chat. She was sympathetic when she heard of Kevin's measles.

"My older ones have had them, so don't worry," the mother of four reassured me, making me feel better. "Why don't you hire an *amah* so you can see some of Hong Kong while you're here? I hired one for this afternoon through the desk clerk. They are screened and reliable."

To miss seeing some of Hong Kong would be a shame, so I took her suggestion and arranged for an *amah* for two hours. Kevin would probably sleep while I went out for a short time. An older Chinese *amah* arrived at our room that afternoon just after Kevin had fallen asleep. She spoke English well and started a game with Mark. Her warm manner put me at ease, and I felt comfortable leaving them for a while. I set out to explore the neighborhood around our hotel.

Kowloon, an island located across from the mainland, teemed with people. Chinese people had fled the countryside when the Japanese invaded before the Second World War. Some fled to Taiwan; many crowded into

Hong Kong. The city expanded skyward when land became scarce. High-rise apartments with laundry drying on balconies held as many people as towns might have in the interior of China.

I passed a beauty salon and decided to have my hair done. The long trip and rain left me feeling bedraggled, and I wanted to look good when I saw Jim. The beauty shop receptionist showed me right in. A man arranged the drape and proceeded with minimal conversation. I pantomimed my wishes to him, and he went to work. Hong Kong was experiencing a water shortage, so he shampooed my hair using a scant amount of water. He used a little more for a rinse before the second shampoo. I was concerned he'd leave shampoo in my hair, but for the final rinse, he turned on the faucet over the shampoo bowl. Working fast, he rinsed all the shampoo from my hair, using a minimum of water, and quickly turned off the water. He styled and set my hair, but he put me under a dryer where I scanned the photographs in a Chinese magazine. Then he combed my hair into a very chic style. He then pulled a hose from the ceiling with a spray attachment that he used to spray a cloud of something over my newly coifed head. The product smelled like shellac and fixed my hair in a clutch of chemicals that would last for days. When I paid for my elegant hairdo, I was pleased it cost a fraction of what I would have paid at home.

The sheer quantity of merchandise, fabrics, radios, and souvenirs kept my head swiveling to take it all in. I stepped into a fabric store to inquire about a lovely bolt displayed in the window. The owner soon opened one bolt after another, spreading each on the counter for my inspection. Confused by too many choices when I wasn't in the mood to shop, I thanked him and continued on my way. As I walked, I soaked up the smells of spices, incense, and sweat from the bustling crowd of Oriental people. At the foreign exchange office, I changed one hundred dollars into Pakistan rupees, as Jim had suggested. The nine hundred and fifty rupee wad of bills was too large to fit into my wallet. I rolled them in my handkerchief and tucked them in the bottom of my purse.

My errand completed, I returned to the hotel. As I got off the elevator and walked toward our room, a lovely young Chinese woman in a scooped-neck dress stepped out of a room down the hall. She straightened her dress and tucked a roll of bills into her bra as I passed her. She looked my age, in her early twenties, and she was obviously finding lucrative diversions in the same hotel.

By the morning of the third day, Kevin felt much better and his spots were fading. I had planned to change our flights if he were still sick, but his fever was down. As he chased Mark around the room, laughing and apparently feeling better, I decided to keep the flights we had scheduled. When we checked in at the airport, I turned up the collar of his jacket to hide the remaining red blotches.

He wasn't contagious anymore without a fever.

We boarded a Lufthansa jet in Hong Kong. This next flight would be a long one and take us to Karachi, West Pakistan. We flew all that day, following the sun across the sky. It was the longest day I can remember. It was still daylight when we stopped for refueling in Bangkok, and night finally fell as we watched the sun sink in the sky in Calcutta. We all slept and awakened in Karachi, West Pakistan's southern port city on the Arabian Sea. After one more flight to Lahore, we would be with Jim at last.

What in the world was I going to do in this heat? Why I had agreed to come to Pakistan when I could barely stand the heat during those two years in South Dakota? Jim assured me we would have air-conditioning. But where was it? Not in this airport in the middle of the night.

My thoughts flashed back to that warm spring day in Pierre. Jim burst in the door as I prepared dinner, probably excited to tell me about his job on the Oahe Dam project, which he liked. His excitement could barely be contained. The grin, which I learned to recognize as his "transfer grin," covered not only the lower part of his face but also sparked a twinkle in his brown eyes. His news was not about Oahe, but something that would change our lives.

"The company's bid won the contract to build Mangla Dam in West Pakistan. This is the largest nonmilitary contract ever awarded. When it's completed, Mangla Dam will be the largest volume, compacted earth dam ever built." Jim paced back and forth with hands thrust into his pockets. "I never thought they'd ask me to go since I've only been with the company for two years. But today I got a call from the main office offering me a job. They'd like me to leave in two weeks." He paused for my reaction.

Trying to grasp his news, I turned off the burner on the stove and looked at him in disbelief. What was he talking about? Pakistan? Leave in two weeks?

"This is the chance of a lifetime," he continued.

I sat down. My knees felt weak at his news.

"Can you imagine a contract for three hundred and fifty-four million dollars?" He was elated.

"How can we leave that soon?" I asked.

He said something about leaving in two weeks.

"I've heard there are shots required before you can travel to Asia."

Rumors and gossip about the gigantic new project had started before Christmas. Some employees decided "no way." Others were eager to take on the assignment for the increase in salary and the opportunity to travel. Others saw a chance to have one more high-paying job to build a bigger nest egg for their retirement.

"The men have to go first to build the town," Jim said. "The dam site is out in the middle of nowhere. It will take six months to build the houses, hospital, schools, and commissary before the town will be ready for families. The men will live in bachelor quarters until then." He paced back and forth, running his fingers through his crew cut to emphasize his point. He was too excited to sit still.

"How long would we be there?" I was still trying to absorb this news.

"The contracts are for thirty months with three weeks paid vacation at the completion of the contract. We could travel through Europe for a few weeks on our way back home." Jim loved to travel.

During his years in the navy as a Seabee, he'd been stationed in Trinidad. He dreamed of being a soldier of fortune and seeing the world. I yearned to travel, too, and I sure didn't want to put a damper on his dreams.

"How much would they pay you?"

The figure he named was double his present salary. "We'd be able to save most of the money since the cost of living there will be much lower. The company's rental housing will cost less than stateside prices. All our medical and dental care and all our travel expenses will be paid."

As Jim continued, he curbed his enthusiasm as he tried to portray a realistic picture for me. I could see he wanted to go.

"This isn't going to be a Sunday school picnic. Pakistan is a Third World country. They're Muslim, and it's halfway around the world. With your fair hair, you may be an object of curiosity. They may not have seen many Americans."

Like many Americans in the early 1960s, we were swept up in our new President Kennedy's plea to "ask not what your country can do for you, but what you can do for your country." The Peace Corps had become a magnet, drawing people to volunteer in underdeveloped countries around the world. We both liked the idealism of that project, but we had two small children and needed a salary. We were fortunate that Jim's GI Bill and our frugality had allowed him to graduate from college without the burden of student loans. Jim felt the Pakistan project would give us the best of both worlds, an increase in salary and the chance to help people in a country less fortunate than ours. The opportunity to travel was a bonus.

"That's fantastic. Let's go." I readily jumped on the adventure bandwagon. "Where will the boys and I live until we can come? Six months from now would be October!" Another of South Dakota's humid, hot summers seemed unbearable.

"You can stay here or go anywhere you would like in the States. The company will pay to move you," he said.

My hometown of Reno, where my mom and younger sisters lived, came to mind. The University of Nevada, where I had started college before marrying Jim, would give me a start.

Only our family doctor's good sense had kept Jim from departing on the next plane. Dr. Lindbloom gave Jim the immunization shots as quickly as feasible, keeping a week between some injections for full efficacy. Although Jim was thirty-one years old, he often felt rules should be bent for him. The doctor insisted that immunizations had to be done as directed. We found ourselves in a whirlwind of parties given by neighbors and Jim's coworkers. Then we were on our way just two weeks after his bombshell news. Our household effects would be shipped to Reno where we would rent a house until it was time to leave for Pakistan. The boys and I would get our shots during the summer.

We left Pierre, where we'd lived for two years. We traveled through South Dakota, Wyoming, a corner of Utah, and Nevada in three days. There was no time for sightseeing. The challenge of the unknown drew Jim like a magnet, and we were both too excited to care about anything but getting on with this next stage of our lives. We rented a small house with two bedrooms and a fenced yard not far from my mom's home and the university. When Jim left a few days later, his Reno friends, Betty and Don Hilts, gave us a farewell party.

I had urged Jim to take the assignment. I wanted to help him further his career. I told myself I could take care of two children and myself for six months. Even so, on the day of his departure, I was having second thoughts.

How could he leave us alone for so long? Could I really manage our boys by myself for that long? The reality of the uncertainty ahead of us hit me as we stood at the airport in Reno.

Jim's flight to San Francisco was called, and he turned to hug me. "I'll see you in six months. If you need anything, you can call Betty and Don or my parents." He kissed the boys, turned to kiss me again, and boarded the aircraft.

I secretly hoped he would run back and tell me he could not leave us. His jaw set with determination, he waved before he disappeared into the bowels of the aircraft. My heart felt heavy. In spite of my determination not to show emotion, my tears flowed. Betty held me while Don distracted Mark and Kevin. How could I have agreed to such a long separation?

Unpacking and making curtains for the house kept me busy for a few weeks. I signed up for a summer class at the University of Nevada, "Political History of the Far East." Betty took care of the boys on the mornings I had class. The lectures covered Japan, China, and some of Indochina, but they never made it to the political scene in Pakistan and India, which I wanted to learn more about. I knew from the news that Field Marshall Mohammad Ayub Khan was the president of Pakistan. News magazines showed him to be a tall, burly man with a mustache. He sometimes wore a suit and tie or occasionally donned a turban and long tunic-style coat.

The radio brought me music and news of the world. John F. Kennedy was president. I admired his wife Jackie and devoured any articles or news of her style and the magic the couple brought to the White House. I bought patterns and sewed dresses in her classic simple style. Wonderful photos of her trip to India and Pakistan appeared in popular magazines. I studied all the photographs and dreamed of a similar trip to India when Jim could take a vacation. Perhaps we too could see the Taj Mahal and the Jaipur Palace and ride on an elephant. What fun that would be! India was just over the border from West Pakistan, so these marvels weren't far from the dam Jim's company was going to build. Pictures in *Life* showed Jackie visiting President Ayub Khan of Pakistan and attending the Lahore Horse Show. The picture of him giving her a beautiful Arabian horse captivated me. My dreams fed my imagination as the long months crept by.

The magazine pictures did not convey the heat. Now I sat in the dingy airport in Karachi, where the temperature in the middle of the night had to be over one hundred degrees. I shifted in my seat and looked around the waiting area. My suit jacket was rumpled, but I couldn't take it off. My blouse was stained with juice Kevin had spilled on it during the flight. The air felt heavy and oppressive, very different from Nevada's dry heat. Even the flies were lethargic as they circled the slow-moving ceiling fans.

Roger reappeared. "Do you have anything to declare?" He was handing me a customs declaration to sign. Reflexively, I signed my name and wrote my passport number.

Roger took the customs declaration and left to retrieve our luggage, followed by two porters.

After he left, I remembered the rupees I'd bought in Hong Kong. Did I need to declare them? I'd ask him later. How could anyone think in this heat?

Two Pakistanis, clad in long shirts and baggy harem-like pants, which I later learned were called *shalwar kameez*, carried our luggage. Both wore long scarves wound around their heads as a turban. Each sported a mustache, as did most other men I saw. They trailed behind Roger as he walked us to a white Ford sedan. The driver opened the trunk for the two men carrying the luggage to stow our suitcases. He drove us a short distance from the airport through darkened streets and stopped in front of a nondescript hotel.

"You're scheduled to stay two nights in Karachi," Roger told me.

"I know, but with a sick child, I really don't feel like spending time here. Couldn't we go to Lahore tomorrow instead of waiting another day?"

I was weary of flying and wanted this trip to end. I was eager to see Jim. The past six months had seemed like an eternity.

Roger nodded. "The Lahore flight leaves at eight thirty in the morning. If I can get you space, you'll have to be ready to go at about seven."

"We'll be ready."

I sighed. The shorter stay in Karachi seemed sensible. I'd catch up on sleep later. Two men carried our luggage into the hotel room. Roger tipped them, and they disappeared into the dark, humid night.

The dismal room held two wood-framed beds with crisscrossed rope supporting thin mattresses. The beds, called *charpoys*, looked nothing like our American beds, but at least were horizontal and appeared to be clean. The crisply ironed sheets were turned down and ready for us. I examined the ropes supporting the thin mattresses. Kevin crawled up and stretched out while Mark explored our room.

What strange beds.

The boys' pajamas were in the first suitcase. I helped them remove their rumpled clothes and felt their foreheads as I kissed them good night. Kevin's head felt about the same as Mark, so I hoped his fever was gone. As I straightened up, the room swayed. I felt like I was still on the airplane.

Strange scratching noises echoed in the small room. I checked all the walls and peered beneath the beds, but I didn't see anything. Perhaps I was imagining the noises. My head felt so dizzy. The terrazzo floors felt cool on my feet when I kicked off my shoes. Suddenly, I felt very thirsty but remembered Jim's warning in one of his infrequent letters.

"Don't drink the tap water. Don't even brush your teeth with it, or you will be really sick."

The old telephone in the room looked like something from a World War II movie. I picked it up and asked the operator for boiled water. A knock at the door came within minutes of my request. A turbaned *bearer* handed me a tray with glasses and an insulated carafe. "*Pani* for you, memsahib." I tipped him with a few American coins. He bowed and thanked me in British-accented English. The water he poured into the glass was steaming hot. Evidently, the hotel staff wanted guests to know that the water had been boiled. I had to wait for it to cool before I brushed my teeth.

When I straightened out the diaper bag, I discovered the package of rupees that I'd purchased in Hong Kong. *Oh, dear. I forgot about the rupees.*

Then I remembered the two large salami rolls I'd bought at Jim's request from his favorite Italian deli. They were wrapped in butcher paper and plastic then stowed among my clothing in another suitcase. Was there pork in salami? Should I have declared them? Jim's favorite snack wasn't available in Pakistan, and he requested some in the last letter he wrote.

Later, I learned I'd selected a perfect place to smuggle something into a Muslim country, the diaper bag. Muslim men never change diapers, nor would they touch one. This was a chore for women or low caste servants. My rupees were safe.

Stretching out on the second *charpoy*, I heard the scratching noises again. I checked under the beds, in the bathroom, and on the ceiling. All I could see were the whitewashed walls. Finally, I showered, sipped some water that had cooled enough to drink, turned off the light, and fell into an exhausted sleep.

Tomorrow, we would see Jim!

Our Home in Lahore

THE TELEPHONE WOKE ME. IT seemed like I had just closed my eyes.

"I'll pick you up in a half hour so you can make the early flight to Lahore. They'll serve breakfast on board," Roger said.

I quickly got ready and dressed the children. Roger appeared with two *bearers* who took our luggage to the waiting car. The trip back to the airport took much longer this morning with teeming masses of people crowding the roadways. Men on bicycles, clad in white, made the roadway look like a churning river of fabric. Our driver kept one hand on the horn most of the way. Careening down the left side of the road in the British way unnerved me. The traffic was unlike anything I had ever seen with bicycles, motorbikes, oxcarts, taxis, horse-drawn carts, and trucks all fighting for the same space. Dust, the odor of horse manure, and smoke from the cooking fires filled the air.

We boarded the flight to Lahore. The airline's breakfast consisted of spicy Pakistani food neither of the boys would eat. A banana, crackers, and juice would have to do. The hot tea tasted aromatic and delicious though I wasn't used to tea that was half milk.

Mark was eager to see his father again. He looked out the window, obviously worried. "Do we have to fly over the mountains again?"

He remembered the flight from Reno to San Francisco a week ago. I didn't want another flight like that one either. I found a map in the seat pocket, opened it, and pointed to Karachi and the Arabian Sea.

"This is the city we just left, Karachi, right here near the ocean. We might see some desert over that way." I pointed to my left and the Sind Desert on the western part of the map. "If you look way up there, those are the highest mountains in the world, the Himalayas. They get a lot of snow, and when it melts, water flows down from the mountains. Five rivers bring the water from the mountains to the flat farmland that they call the Punjab. We will meet Daddy here." I pointed to Lahore. "It's on the Ravi River."

Lahore was about seven hundred miles north of Karachi. I wasn't sure how much of my geography lesson Mark understood, but he nodded with relief. There were no more mountains to fly over.

"What is that green part?" Mark pointed to the middle of India on the map.

"That's called India, and the green part is probably jungles," I said.

His brown eyes widened, pondering the jungles we'd read about in books. He loved books with action, and I could see he was no doubt imagining monkeys, lions, and tigers roaming the land.

A man sitting across the aisle from me smiled and greeted the boys. He had watched Mark's questions and our study of the map. Obviously, we looked different than other passengers, and I later learned that a woman traveling alone wasn't common.

"What business is your husband in?" His curiosity rose.

"He works on the Mangla Dam project."

He looked impressed and reached into his vest pocket. "May I present my business card to you to give your husband? I can help provide many materials they may need for the project."

Apparently, he knew about Mangla Dam's construction. I thanked him and tucked his card into my purse.

We landed in the Lahore airport on October 18, 1962, eight calendar days since we'd left home. We had lost one day when we crossed the international date line. Would I recognize Jim after six long months? Would he look different? Has this experience changed him? Then, there he was, grinning broadly from behind the chain-link fence as we walked across the tarmac. He followed, matching our steps until we reached a gate where he rushed through to greet us.

Jim looked very thin and tanned, and he beamed with pleasure when he saw the boys. He scooped Kevin into his arms. Mark clung to his father's pants leg and held him fast so he couldn't get away again. Jim apparently had found a Pakistani barber to copy the flat top haircut he'd worn since his days in the Seabees. Kevin squirmed to get down and walked back to me.

"They sure have grown. Look at Kevin walk," Jim said in amazement as he gave me a welcoming hug and a quick kiss.

He led us to a waiting white sedan. The driver opened the car door with a sweeping bow of greeting then supervised the loading of the baggage into the trunk. Jim gave me a hasty hug and another quick, nondemonstrative kiss as he ushered the boys and me into the backseat. He sat in the passenger seat next to the driver. I knew public demonstrations of affection were not proper in a Muslim country, but I didn't care. I wanted to feel his arms around me, and I was disappointed.

We drove along a wide, divided road with a few sparse trees lining it, which made driving on the left side less frightening than it had been in Karachi. It felt to me that the traffic pattern was all wrong. We passed sprawling homes on the outskirts of Lahore with expansive grounds and a carpet of pale green grass in front of gated walls.

The traffic resembled the chaos we'd seen that morning in Karachi. Herds of goats and sheep, marked with orange, pink, or green dye on their ears or rumps, vied for space on the broad avenues with motor vehicles, motorcycles, and carts pulled by muscular oxen. A smart stepping sorrel mare caught my eye. The tassels on her bridle swished in time with her trot. Her bells announced her approach as she pulled a two-wheeled vehicle with passengers facing backward and the driver in front. A fringed canopy shaded the riders.

How charming. I watched the horse trot by.

"Those are *tongas*, the local equivalent of a taxi." Jim continued to describe the neighborhood and landmarks along the way.

Damn. I've traveled halfway around the world, and you sit up front like a tour guide showing me the sights? Couldn't you let me know you're happy to see us?

We drove another ten minutes. Then our driver turned into the entrance of a four-story building. A man opened the spike-topped wrought iron gate and nodded for us to enter. Brick columns every eight feet with an iron fence between them, also topped by iron spikes, supported the fence around the sprawling compound. On the corner, just outside the compound fence, was a tiny mosque. The building had two long wings on either side, forming a big U-shaped structure. An oval driveway circled the entry area between the wings with a section of pale green grass in the center. The driver stopped at an entrance at the left front corner of the building.

"This is WAPDA Flats, where we will live." Jim continued in his tour guide mode. "We're at the corner of Racecourse Road and Jail Road. The racetrack is a half-mile down that way on Racecourse Road." He pointed past the intersection. "The Water and Power Development Authority of West Pakistan built WAPDA Flats to accommodate expatriates who came to work on the Indus Basin Project."

The driver opened the car door. Jim helped us out of the car as the sound of chanting came over a loudspeaker, filling the air with a wailing minor key sound.

"That's the midday call to prayer for devout Muslims." The voice echoed with words I couldn't understand. "You'll hear the *muezzin* chanting it five times a day."

Jim led us up the short flight of stairs on the left front entrance of the building. He showed us through a breezeway with stairs leading to the upper floors and stopped at the door of an apartment with the number two on a brass plate.

"It's called a flat since it's all on one level. I was living on the third floor, but I moved my stuff down here. I thought it would be easier for you and the boys not to have to climb two flights of stairs."

He unlocked the door, and we stepped into our new home. My eyes took a moment to adjust to the dim light inside after the glaring midday sun. The entry hall was at least eight feet wide, and the high ceilings gave the flat a spacious, cavernous look. Doors from each of the rooms connected to the central hall. A large wooden credenza hugged the long wall of the entry.

The living room was through an archway to the right and furnished with a sofa, two matching chairs, and a dining table with eight chairs at one end of the room. Soft area rugs covered the terrazzo floors. The rust and brown upholstered furniture was a simple boxy style, and all the fabrics matched the draperies and carpets. The windows looked out on the oval driveway of the main entrance. The apartment looked like a designer had a hand in coordinating the selections.

"I like the colors in this room," I told Jim. "It's better furnished than I imagined it would be."

"I thought you might like it." Jim grinned at my approval.

We walked through the rooms of our new home, and I began to envision moving in our household items, deciding where the few things I'd shipped would go. The built-in china cabinet was well stocked with dishes and glassware, more than enough for our needs. All the floors were highly polished terrazzo, and the walls were whitewashed. The apartment was larger and better furnished than I had expected.

Jim called me to the master bedroom, which was almost as large as the living room/dining room. High ceilings and a fan slowly moved the air around. Two large windows and French doors opened to a small terrace overlooking the side gate and Jail Road. I pulled back a curtain to find a large stall shower in the master bath, which also had a pedestal sink and a toilet. The second bedroom's French doors opened onto a terrace overlooking the central courtyard where we had arrived. This bedroom also had its own bathroom with a toilet, a pedestal sink, and a large footed bathtub.

It will work well to bathe the boys.

"They don't have king-sized beds here, so I pushed the twins together." Jim smiled.

All the beds were Western style with box springs and mattress, not the small *charpoys* we had slept on at our hotel in Karachi. That was a relief. The *charpoy* was horizontal but offered little additional comfort.

I looked around, hoping I'd find a radio, knowing I would probably not find a television. "Are we going to have a telephone?"

"I doubt it. Getting a phone installed took John Ziemer three months, and that was faster than normal because he's our office manager. By the time I applied and went through all the red tape, we'd probably be transferred to Mangla."

We knew from the beginning that Jim's assignment in Pakistan would take us to be where he was needed most. Now, it was in Lahore, but as the project progressed, we would be transferred to the construction site at Mangla, north of Lahore at the base of the mountains.

Jim led me through a swinging door to the left of the front entrance. The kitchen's austerity was a stark contrast to the comfort of the other rooms. A wide sink hung on the wall. A drainpipe directed water from the sink to a hole in the concrete. A wooden shelf at right angles to the sink served as a drain board, slanting into the sink. The only work surface was a wooden table with one drawer. The four-burner apartment-sized stove looked adequate, but I wasn't sure about the refrigerator that looked as older than I was.

"Pakistanis don't make their kitchens very fancy since only the servants use them," Jim said. "Here's the *godown* or pantry."

On the far side of the interior kitchen was a small, bright room containing a tall metal cabinet with a locking mechanism. It had the only window in the flat with a view of the playground. One wall contained two open shelves. Ragged holes in the wall looked like the right spacing for another shelf to fit.

"Last night, I had a disaster. In the middle of the night, I heard a loud crash and thought the Indians and Pakistanis were at it again. Shooting. The shattering of glass sounded like we had been bombed. I checked all the windows. None was broken, but when I got to the pantry, I found the shelf had pulled out of the wall. All the baby food crashed to the floor and broke. I ordered more this morning." Jim looked chagrined.

"You really didn't need to order baby food." I picked up Kevin and asked him to open his mouth. "Show Daddy your teeth, Kevin." He opened wide and grinned at his father. "Kevin can eat anything you can, Jim. I just cut his food in small bites. He hasn't eaten baby food in months."

Not only had Jim missed seeing Kevin's first steps, that six-month absence represented one-third of Kevin's life. He had missed watching Kevin learn to walk and many changes in both our sons. Our younger son had changed from a baby into a toddler.

"He was still nursing when I left in April." Jim looked amazed at his son.

The doorbell rang. Jim opened the door and greeted a petite, dark-haired American lady. She looked past Jim and reached her hands out to greet me with a hug and a warm smile.

"I want you to meet Dorothy Ziemer," Jim said. "Her husband John manages the Lahore office, and they live directly above us on the fourth floor."

I was happy to see another American.

"Welcome to Lahore. Come on upstairs when you can. When I heard about Jim's disaster with the food, I fixed lunch for you. Margaret Platt may join us. She's packed and leaving today for the job site," Dorothy said.

I recognized the name. Margaret Platt wrote me a letter a few months ago at Jim's request. Her informative letter suggested items I might want to bring from home. Her information was the only guideline I had. The company had not given us any direction at all.

"We'll be upstairs in a few minutes," Jim told Dorothy as she departed.

Jim showed the boys their room while I surveyed the built-in closets. I unpacked a few personal items while Jim put the boys' suitcases in their room. As I added the plastic bag of rinsed diapers to the laundry basket, I remembered the stash of nine hundred rupees I'd bought in Hong Kong. I bent over, and again, I felt my surroundings reel as if I were still on the airplane. I searched through my suitcase for a clean blouse, unpacked Jim's chubs of salami, and put them in the refrigerator. I added some lipstick, and I was ready to go.

We climbed the three flights of stairs to the Ziemer's fourth-floor apartment. I was perspiring from the effort. The stairwell was located in the open-air breezeway under the roof but not within reach of the air-conditioning. Our apartment entrance was in the same breezeway. Stairs ascended to the upper floors and out the back to the driveway and playground. After the climb, I saw the wisdom of the ground-floor apartment Jim had selected for us.

"The company keeps the other two apartments on the second and third floors for visitors. That's why they retain two servants, Alam, the *bearer*, and Afsar, the *homal*, to keep those quarters clean and ready for anyone who might need them." Jim smiled. "You'll meet them after lunch."

The Ziemer's flat was identical to ours, but brighter with more light streaming in the windows on the fourth floor. It also looked homier with their personal things added to the basic furniture. I could envision making ours look better with a few touches. Our household shipment would arrive in the next month or two. Until then, we could do quite well with the pans, linens, and furnishings the company provided. I could find some decorative items in the local stores like the lovely brass items Dorothy displayed in their apartment.

"We thought it would be safer for the boys to be on the first floor and closer to the playground. Jim's been on the third floor since April," Dorothy said.

How strange we had waited six months to move into the building where Jim had lived since last April. Why couldn't we have come earlier?

Dorothy's lunch was perfect for the boys—peanut butter and jelly sandwiches, chicken noodle soup, fresh fruit, and milk. We liked it, too, and we were happy to see familiar food.

"The milk is a problem here. We use Carnation instant powdered milk made with boiled water. I add a little evaporated milk for more flavor," Dorothy said.

The boys tried it but didn't drink more than a few sips of the milk. It didn't taste like the cow's milk they were accustomed to at home.

"The bread is delicious," I said. "It's just like my mom used to make."

"That's another problem. Local bread is terrible, and the flour is dirty when you buy it on the local market. I bake our bread," she said. "I save my nylon stockings and cut them into squares to sift the local flour before I use it."

That sounded like a lot of work to bake bread.

We had almost finished lunch when Margaret Platt arrived, breathless. Dorothy offered her lunch, but she declined.

"I just wanted to say good-bye to you, Dorothy, and welcome to Irene and the boys. I'm eager to get on the road to Mangla and join Errol at our new house." Errol Platt was the business manager, one of the three top executives on the Mangla Dam project. "Errol said the house is finished and beautiful. I can hardly wait to see it and get settled."

Margaret was a contrast to Dorothy's petite, Doris Day personality. Margaret's bright blue eyes sparkled. Her skin was a pale ivory, and her voluptuous figure and striking beauty made her someone people noticed right away. I was pleased to have a chance to meet the woman who had taken the time to write me. I thanked her for the informative letter, which I followed as my only instructions on what to bring, buying buttons, polyester thread, and extra zippers and elastic for repairs as she suggested. I secreted several pair of nylons in our shipment that she said were unheard of in local stores.

"Good-bye until we see you at Mangla. *Inshallah*," Margaret said.

"What does *Inshallah* mean?"

"If God be willing. I'm sure we'll see you there soon." Margaret waved and departed.

We finished lunch, thanked Dorothy, and walked back downstairs to our flat. Two Pakistani men were in our apartment when we returned. Jim introduced us.

"This is Alam, the *bearer*, and Afsar, the *homal*," Jim said.

They both smiled, put their hands together, touched their head and chest, and then bowed in greeting. They grinned at the boys. Alam and Afsar finished dusting and tidied up the apartment while we had lunch. Alam was the older of the two and looked more serious. Afsar was slightly taller and had curlier hair.

The same scratching noises I'd heard last night at the motel were in the entry hall.

"What is that noise?"

"Those are little gecko lizards. They're harmless and welcome since they eat insects." Jim pointed to a small white lizard that ran up the wall.

The lizard was nearly invisible on the whitewashed walls. No wonder I couldn't find out what the noise was last night. The minute Kevin and Mark saw the lizard, they gave chase, following it with their eyes when it climbed higher than their reach.

"See, kids. Lizard."

"Izzy izzy," Kevin repeated.

We put the boys to bed for a nap. I wasn't sure about Kevin sleeping in the twin bed. His crib was in our shipment. Jim pushed the bed against the wall, and we laid a folded blanket on the terrazzo floor beside the bed just in case he fell off. I was ready for a nap, too. It was still the middle of the night back home. The long days of traveling caught up with me. I pulled the covers down on our bed, hoping that Jim had the day off and would join me.

"Sorry. I have to get back to work." He gave me a lingering hug. "Tonight, we'll ask Alam to stay with the boys. We're going out to dinner with the Ziemers and the Richmonds. I didn't think you'd want to cook on the first night. We'll meet them at Falletti's Hotel dining room at seven."

He kissed me and left. As I slipped between the starched white sheets, my body relaxed, and within minutes, I was asleep. Several times, I was aware of the door opening and closing while I slept. Once I saw Alam peeking through a crack in the door. I was unnerved having a strange man in the house while I slept, but fatigue overcame me, and I fell asleep again.

The call to prayer awakened me. My watch said it was five o'clock. The sound of chains clanking mingled with the wailing chant. I peered through the curtains and saw a group of men walking down the street Jim said was called Jail Road. Armed guards walked beside and behind the men whose chains I'd heard scraping the pavement. The men must be prisoners being taken to jail.

Now that I was wide awake, I got up and assessed my hair. My two-dollar Hong Kong hairdo sprayed with shellac, or something equally tenacious, held my hair so it hadn't moved even through my airplane naps and part of a night in Karachi. My bouffant flip just needed a little brushing to look fine. I showered, dressed, and looked in on the boys. They were still asleep. I was relieved that Kevin's forehead felt cool to my touch. The measles had finally run their course.

"*Memsahib* like tea?" Alam startled me as he appeared silently in the doorway.

"Yes, please. I'd like that very much."

Alam appeared to be in his mid-thirties. He was quite handsome with raven hair and trimmed mustache. He spoke good English. Afsar, the *homal* (cleaning man), spoke very little English. He smiled, lowered his eyes, and bowed his head, touching his hands and palms together to his head, his lips, and then his heart in a *salaam* (greeting). He backed away as he left the room.

Jim came home just as I finished my tea. His brow furrowed as he explained a complication in the evening's dinner plans.

"We are still having dinner with the Ziemers and Richmonds, but we have a problem. Four newly hired men went to the dam site, took one look around, and quit on the spot. They'll be meeting us at the hotel for dinner. That way I can keep an eye on their drinking and get them safely on the late plane to Karachi."

"Does that mean you have to work tonight, too?" I was surprised and a bit annoyed.

"I had a phone call from George Archibald, the project manager, with orders to personally see that they get on that plane. I have to be sure that they are sober enough to board the flight. Pakistani airlines are strict about that."

Alam agreed to stay with the boys that evening, though it was not a part of his job. I gave him a few instructions, and I was relieved when I learned he had three children of his own. My sons had always been fine with babysitters at home. Since they had so little sleep last night and this afternoon's nap was about the time they'd go to bed if we were in America, they might sleep while we went to dinner. That would make Alam's job easier, and I didn't think we'd be gone very long. Dorothy left snacks and food for their dinner. She was wonderful to anticipate our needs and make the first days easy for me. Jet lag was something I'd never experienced.

Ghulam, the same driver who had picked us up at the airport earlier today, drove us to the hotel Down the street from the apartment building, open-air cafés and tea shops lined the road. Strings of lights strung between the trees cast eerie shadows of silhouetted figures that appeared and disappeared. In the dim light, we saw men sitting on *charpoys* drinking tea and eating food around charcoal-fueled fires. Young men walked together in pairs, arm in arm or holding hands. Sounds of Oriental music wafted through the air from a radio.

We turned left down a dark road until Ghulam came to a break in the wall along the right side of the road. He made a sharp turn into a hidden driveway. The brick gatepost had a brass nameplate that read *Oberoi Falleti's Hotel.*

"Is this where we are going for dinner?" I asked.

The driveway cut through the darkness to a building set back from the road. "This is Falletti's Hotel. It's part of the hotel chain called Oberoi Hotels, which are popular in India and Pakistan," Dorothy said. "They're comparable to our Hiltons or Sheratons, and the food in their dining room is good."

"Falletti's sounds like it's Italian," I said.

"The man who built the hotel was Italian from Naples. He was traveling through India. He came to Lahore and fell in love with a courtesan he met here. He stayed in Lahore for the rest of his life and built this hotel," John Ziemer said. John had dark, straight hair, neatly trimmed, and a formal manner befitting the office manager for Lahore.

"What a romantic story," I said.

"The gardens were his passion, and he liked to attract artists and poets, so he built the hotel with a landscape comparable to those found in Italy." John sounded respectful to the Italian who followed his heart.

A circular driveway, bordered with low hedges, brought us to the front steps. An elderly turbaned doorman opened our car door and bowed, all in one fluid motion. His walnut-colored face looked as if it had been chiseled from fine-grained wood. The fragrance of gardenias and roses wafted toward us as we walked to the front door. Another turbaned *bearer* bowed as he held the front door open. A dining room steward greeted us in the same fashion and led us through the large room where the aroma of garlic and unfamiliar spices lingered in the air. The large dining room's far wall of French doors opened to a formal garden surrounding the terrace with white lights outlining the tree branches. Above the French doors, dormer windows allowed sparrows to fly in and out at will, perching on the table and helping themselves to crumbs.

"The Richmonds are already here," Dorothy said. "Come and meet Bill and Rosita."

Rosita Richmond, a handsome Filipina who looked younger than Bill, was seated at the head of the table. Mrs. Richmond spoke rapidly in Urdu to the closest server, who took the towel draped over his arm and flicked away the small birds. Bill Richmond, dressed in a tropical weight business suit, appeared to be in his seventies. Company management had coaxed him out of retirement with a job to help the three managers of the Mangla Dam project.

"Yes, that's our goal. If we can achieve the diversion before the monsoons come in the fall of 1965, we can finish the dam a full year ahead of schedule," Bill said. "That would earn us a handsome bonus for early completion."

Four men arrived and huddled in a group at the far end of the long table. As the ladies and I sat down, they took their seats, stone faced and unfriendly. I wanted to ask them what they had seen that was so terrible they were leaving after seeing the location of the project. But Jim had admonished me to ask no questions.

The waiters brought appetizers with exotic-smelling spices consisting of little bits of dough around spicy, small meatballs and tiny vegetable tartlets. Next was a salad of sliced tomatoes

"Don't risk the salad," Jim said.

I wasn't terribly hungry and was already feeling full after a few appetizers. The main course was steak sliced in thin strips, roasted carrots, and potatoes. The waiters served from the right side, holding a spoon and a fork in one hand and placing the food with precision on the plates. I pushed the food around and listened to the music reverberating through the wall from the next room. The band was playing familiar American songs. I recognized the melody of "Cherry Pink and Apple Blossom White," "Memories are Made of This," and other familiar American songs. What a pleasant surprise to hear familiar music.

I resisted the urge to make small talk with the men across from Jim. By breaking their contract before the thirty months were completed, these men would probably be required to pay their own transportation back to the States. Had they found conditions so deplorable that they decided to leave regardless of the financial penalty? Was it too remote for their families? I wondered in silence and watched our gracious hostess, Mrs. Richmond.

Rosita Richmond came from a wealthy family and grew up with servants. She only had to lift an eyebrow or make a small gesture to convey her desires to the table servers, and they jumped at her slightest movement. The service was seamless and silent. She and Dorothy were friends from a previous project the company had in the Philippines. They had enjoyed living in the same building in Lahore these past few months, enjoying their reunion. Rosita and Bill were leaving for their new home at the job site tomorrow, so this dinner was a welcome for me, and a farewell for Bill and Rosita. Rosita was exotic and beautiful in a classic Oriental way, her long greying hair twisted in a chic bun on her head.

"If you don't watch the bread on your plate, the birds will get it," Jim told me with a grin.

The table *bearer* kept his towel ready to discourage the invaders. Service was prompt and attentive, but the guarded conversation and silence from the far end of the table made the evening seem long. I excused myself and went to the restroom. On the way, I looked through the arched doorway into the cabaret where several Pakistani and European couples were dancing. The singer sang "You're My Kind of Girl," and looked right at me. "She walks like an angel walks. She talks like an angel talks."

I loved hearing the popular American music. Couples danced the cha-cha, the Twist, and ballroom dances that were the rage at home. I was reluctant to leave the music.

Back at the table, the four men looked uncomfortable, and two of them scowled through most of the dinner. Jim and John Ziemer stood and said farewell to Bill and Rosita Richmond as they said goodnight.

Jim walked Dorothy, John, and me to the sedan where John's driver, Ghulam, waited for us.

"I won't be long," he said and left for the airport with the four men.

You might as well put the boys and me on that plane, too. I fly halfway around the world with our children, and you can't even spend the first night with us.

I was annoyed, irritated, and very tired.

Alam met me at the door. Afsar, the *homal*, came out of the room where the boys were just waking up. I said good night to Dorothy. I liked her, and I was pleased I had a chance to meet Margaret and Rosita. My first day in Lahore had been a busy one.

I inspected the rooms and opened cabinet doors in the dining room where a china service for twelve and three sizes of glasses neatly lined the shelves. The company had also provided a set of pots and pans, from a large stainless steel-covered roaster to several sizes of saucepans and a large soup pot. The pantry was stocked with crackers, oatmeal, and a variety of canned vegetables and fruit. In the small refrigerator was water, boiled by Jim for the required twenty minutes and stored in Beefeater's gin bottles. There wasn't much food since Jim had eaten all of his meals out. He said he ordered food from the commissary, and it would take a few days to arrive in Lahore.

Jim returned after midnight. At the airport, he had a trouble with the men's ticketing, but that was solved, and they were now on the flight to Karachi and then on to the U.S. I was reading a magazine when Jim came in and put his arms around me. I was happy to be together again and in our new home. Everything was going to be all right as soon as I adjusted to the local time.

Our bed had been turned down while we were at dinner.

Jim, weary and tired from the long day, held me close. "Welcome to Lahore. I'm glad you and the boys are here I couldn't very well expect Bill to take those men to the airport. He's in his seventies, and not in the best of health."

I tried to listen and see Jim's viewpoint, but I was still feeling neglected.

We snuggled and I tried to stay awake as he spoke. I kept nodding off as he told me about Lahore. "The Moguls built some amazing monuments and gardens I know you're going to enjoy. Lahore is probably the most beautiful city in Pakistan. That's why they call it the Paris of the East," Jim spoke as I dropped off to sleep.

Stranger in a Strange Land

SUNLIGHT STREAMED THROUGH OUR BEDROOM window as I opened my eyes and heard the plaintive call to prayer accompanied by the scraping sound of the chains on the paved roadway. The grating of the chains sent chills thorough me as I awakened the first morning in Lahore. It took a few moments for me to remember the corner mosque. I looked out and saw a group of prisoners walking toward Gulberg Road, the opposite way they were walking yesterday at five o'clock. *Will the guards let the prisoners stop and pray?*

I wasn't sure what time it was, but this was the day we would have arrived if I hadn't cancelled one night in Karachi.

"Good morning, sleepyhead. We have to register you at the police station today, so I took the morning off." Jim bent down to hug me.

I stretched and yawned. He had taken time off work to be with us. I regretted my anger of the night before when he had to work late. After all, we did surprise him by arriving a day earlier than scheduled.

While I got ready, Mark showed his dad how he could dress himself. Then I took care of dressing Kevin. Breakfast consisted of oatmeal and canned fruit with the powdered milk Jim had ordered. The boys didn't like the taste of the powdered milk. I would have to find an alternative for them.

After breakfast, Jim handed me a key to the apartment. "Are you ready to go for a ride?"

Mark was eager to go anywhere with Jim. Kevin looked at me for a decision.

I nodded. "Sure we are. Let's go."

The company pickup was a white Ford and, like all company trucks, had "ManDamCo," the abbreviation for Mangla Dam Contractors, stenciled on a green oval logo on the door. This truck's identifying number, 62519, was lettered in the logo. All project vehicles were bought and shipped from the United States, so they were all equipped with American left-hand drive.

"First, let's get you legal for Pakistan and register you with the police."

We merged into traffic. Lahore's streets teemed with people, cars, and motorcycles zipping around horse-drawn *tongas* and oxcarts. I'd never seen so many varieties of vehicles all competing for space on the road. Traffic flowed on the left-hand side of the roads, but as faster cars, trucks, and motorcycles passed slow-moving horse-drawn *tongas* or ox-pulled carts, the middle of the road was the most popular traffic lane.

Police headquarters was an imposing building where we showed our passports, immunization cards, and Jim's proof of employment to a stern-faced officer sitting behind a desk. He reviewed our documents and took our fingerprints and a Polaroid photograph. Next, we were registered as foreigners and issued police identity cards, which we were required to carry at all times. The officer handed the documents back to us, smiling.

"Welcome to Pakistan," he said. "Fine *babas*." He nodded at our children. We thanked him and left.

Next, Jim drove us downtown along a wide, tree-lined boulevard with businesses and retail stores called Shahrah-E-Quaid-E-Azam, after Mohammad Ali Jinnah, the founder of Pakistan. The wide boulevard had two lanes in each direction, a wide center island, and a lane near the curb where cars were parked. Jim pulled into the parking lane and into a diagonal spot.

"Everyone calls it the Mall," Jim said. "And here's the company's office."

Tucked between a car dealership and the U.S. Aid office was the Mangla Dam Contractors office, abbreviated to ManDamCo. Jim parked the truck and walked us to the office where a counter divided a small waiting area with two chairs from the work area beyond. A swinging half-door allowed entry to the work area. Several desks lined the walls with John Ziemer at one, a brass nameplate with Jim's name on another, and two men working at the other two desks. They stood to greet me, and Jim introduced me.

"This is Jamal Farouki."

A tall man smiled and held out his hand. He stood over six feet tall with a barrel chest, mustache, and straight hair combed back that made him look like a Pakistani version of Errol Flynn. He had a rakish grin and a confident manner.

"I'm pleased to meet you," he said. "My wife and I would be honored if you could join us for dinner at the Punjab Club when you are settled."

I thanked him and looked at Jim, wondering if the Punjab Club was as exclusive as he made it sound.

Next, I met Freddie, a slim, young man with a light tan complexion and wavy hair. Jim had mentioned in the truck that Freddie's mother was Pakistani and his father was British. Children of mixed marriages were called Anglo Pakistani or Anglos. These two men with their fluency in Urdu were important to the American's office operation. Although many people in Pakistan spoke English, some small business owners did not, so Urdu-speaking employees were necessary.

"Pleased to meet you," the younger man said shyly.

Then Jim led us out a side door and over a wooden bridge above the car dealer's shop area to two restrooms, which were available only to the building's tenants.

"If you're out shopping, you might want to remember these are available for you. It's not always easy to find a suitable public restroom." Jim showed me where the key was kept.

He checked his messages and gave some instructions to Freddie and Jamal, and we returned to the truck. A small boy with a delicate bronze complexion had been watching us. He rushed to open the pickup truck's door for me. His luminous brown eyes peered from beneath a shock of raven hair, all the while smiling.

"Welcome, *memsahib*. Very nice *babas*." He grinned at Mark and Kevin. "You need *homal*. I, Majid, be your best *homal*."

He looked no older than ten and seemed to be looking for a job. I wondered what Alam, the company *bearer* and the company *homal*, would say if I showed up with a small boy to take over some of their duties.

"That Majid," Jim muttered. "He hangs around the office and can be a real pest." We drove a few blocks and stopped at a red sandstone building.

"I have to mail some company letters. You might want to pick up some stamps and aerograms to write letters home." Corresponding with Jim's parents had been my job since we were first married.

Next to the entrance of the post office, a gray-bearded man sat on a blanket and leaned against the wall. He held a slanted board on his knees, writing and talking to the man who bent in front of him and appeared to be telling him something. The seated man looked up and questioned him. Then he bent again to his task. Three men waited in line behind the first one.

"What are those people doing, Jim?" I nodded toward the small group focused on the seated man.

"That's a scribe. He writes letters for those who can't write and reads for them," Jim said. "There's a very high illiteracy rate in this country, so those who cannot read use scribes to communicate."

We lined up at the post office window. The man ahead stepped aside, urging us forward. So did the next one, saying, "Please, *memsahib*." One by one, they stepped aside. "Memsahib, you go, please." Within minutes, we were at the front of the line. Their kindness touched me. Our errand at the post office took little time.

Further along the Mall, the wide boulevard narrowed to a two-lane road, at the end of which sat an iron cannon on a triangular island in the middle of the road.

"They call that Kim's gun, or Zam-Zama from the book by Rudyard Kipling. When the war ended years ago, warring tribesmen melted down their weapons and had them cast into this cannon, symbolizing peace between the tribes."

Jim parked the truck in front of Tollinton's Market. "Until the commissary at the job is up to speed, we'll have to live off the land. This market isn't what you're used to, but it's the best there is. It's not a supermarket by any means, but you may find a few things we can eat. I ordered staples, canned fruits and vegetables, and I heard that pork chops just arrived from the States, so I ordered them, too. You won't find pork in a Muslim country."

We stepped inside the market, out of the heat and hot sun. It took a few minutes for my eyes to adjust to the darkness in the market, which extended far back from the street. The main gallery held a kiosk that displayed a variety of merchandise. A radio blared singsong music. The mixture of odors unrelated to food was something I hadn't expected. The floors were dusty concrete, and a woman was sweeping with a broom of long straws. Dust swirled in her path. She and the kiosk's attendant were the only other women in the building.

Jim led me out a side door to a yard where crates of live chickens were for sale. Meat cutters squatted in the shade or leaned on the large blocks where they cut the meat, carcasses of animals hanging above their heads. The heat was already intense, and it was only ten in the morning. I decided to pass on any of those unappetizing products. Further along, men offered fish for sale in large containers dripping with melting ice.

"Here, *memsahib*, nice fresh beef for you. I have undercut." The butcher held up a tapered loin of beef shaped like a large fish.

He wiped a long scimitar-like knife with a bloodstained cloth that had once been white. Nothing he had looked anything like I'd found in American markets or looked appetizing to me.

We returned to the main gallery. Something in the kiosk caught Jim's attention, and he steered me to the center island. American brand merchandise was displayed behind a dirty glass case. Soaps, hand lotion, canned ham, Spam, Vienna sausages, cigarette lighters, candy, and batteries were all offered for sale. But there was only one of each.

"They sure didn't waste much time getting stuff from the commissary to the black market." Jim pointed to a box of Tide stamped on the top in blue ink with the words "Mangla Dam Contractors."

I had read about the black market, but I did not really know what it meant, yet here I was shopping in one. Bottles of American hand creams, jars of jam, steak sauce, and other items priced roughly the same as we would pay in the States were openly sold in this public market. We selected a Danish canned ham. The eggs looked safe enough. I hesitated and then added one loaf of bread wrapped in waxed paper for sandwiches. Cokes were priced at only a quarter of a rupee, or about five cents. The deposit on the classic glass bottles was one rupee and a quarter, nearly thirty cents. I chose four bottles and added it to our purchases. The vegetable stalls looked more promising. I gathered some potatoes, onions, and carrots I recognized.

"How much?" I asked the vendor holding two potatoes in my hand.

"Two rupees for five *seer*," he replied.

I looked at Jim, puzzled and wondering what a *seer* was.

"A *seer* is two pounds," Jim explained.

That was forty-two cents for ten pounds, certainly a reasonable price. The produce was dirty, but I could wash it before I cooked them.

Kevin pulled Jim back outside for another look at the chickens. Mark stayed with me. We selected apples and oranges, salad ingredients, and five pounds of potatoes. The vendor wrapped it all in a wrinkled, much-used paper bag.

Outside, Jim and Kevin were looking at the colorful caged chickens, gray-black Bantam hens, Rhode Island Reds, and the others more exotic and beautifully plumed species.

On the sidewalk on our way back to the pickup, a thin waif of a boy scooted along the walkway on his hands, dragging his twig-like legs behind him. He looked to be about eight years old and was dressed in dirty, ragged clothing. His deep-set eyes fixed on me, a pleading look on his dark face.

"*Baksheesh, memsahib! Baksheesh!*" He extended his bony arm, palm upward, asking for alms.

His palms bore heavy callouses from using his hands to scoot along the sidewalk. At the hips, his legs turned sideways. His thin shoulders slumped like an old man's. Jim stopped me from giving the boy money and propelled me by the elbow into the truck.

"Don't give money to beggars. If you do, it is perpetuating their begging and their practice of maiming of children," he said.

"But that poor child can't walk at all. He must have been born that way," I said.

"Possibly," Jim said. "But more likely, the parents purposely crippled him to make him a beggar. Gypsies often cripple one of their children on purpose to make them look pitiful so they can get alms or *baksheesh*. Muslim people are very charitable, and giving alms to the poor is part of their religion. Many tithe, giving 10 percent of their income to the beggars. The wealthy give even more. However, some dishonest or lazy people prey on the charitable quality of the Muslims. Many of those children make enough in a day's begging to support the whole family."

I was stunned. What kind of parents would do that to a child? This was something too shocking to believe. Sending children out to beg was one thing, but to purposely mutilate a child was beyond my comprehension. I looked at my two young healthy sons and thanked God for our life in America. How could a parent do such a thing to an innocent child?

I kept my arms around them as we rode back to WAPDA Flats in silence.

Back at the apartment, Jim opened a message that had been handed to him at the office.

"One of the businessmen I've worked with wants to welcome you and the boys by bringing dinner over tonight. He owns a trucking company and is more reliable than any others I've used here to get materials to the job. Pakistanis are very hospitable people, and to refuse would be an insult. His note says he will be here around by six with dinner. You won't have to cook for another night. Just be careful. The Pakistani food is very spicy, so eat plenty of rice to neutralize the heat of the spices. And his wife won't be able to join us because she keeps strict *purdah*."

"What's *purdah*?"

"Pakistani women who observe *purdah* wear a veil or long garment called a *burqua*. They don't go out in public or show their faces to any man other than close relatives. Only their husbands, their father, sons, and brothers are allowed to see them without the veil. It is a strict Muslim custom from the old school. Some younger women are breaking away from it, but Mr. Khan tells me his wife is very traditional." Jim carried our purchases into the kitchen.

As we unpacked the food, Jim held up the lettuce and strawberries I'd bought. "You can't eat these. The seeds of strawberries are ideal breeding ground for amoebic dysentery. The same with the lettuce. Don't even think of eating green salad. The apples and oranges are fine. Just wash and peel them. The potatoes, you always peel and cook, so they are safe. Some people eat tomatoes by pouring boiling water over them and then peeling them. Even that's not too smart, so it's best not to eat them unless you cook them, like you do for spaghetti sauce." Jim tossed the lettuce and strawberries into the garbage chute, which was built into the kitchen wall.

Obviously, Jim was right. I had not considered the danger of food that harbored the dysentery bacteria. It seemed that dangerous microbes hid in places I hadn't even considered.

In the hot weather, businesses closed, and servants took a long rest during the heat, and so did we, still recovering from the time change and jet lag. Resting during the hot part of the day was the sensible custom. The servants reappeared in late afternoon.

When the boys awoke from their naps, I took them outside to see if any other children had appeared. Within a short time, the heat was too oppressive, and I was wilting in the unfamiliar humidity so we went back inside to read stories. Since we expected Mr. Khan, I put out a stack of dishes on the dining room sideboard in preparation for dinner. I wasn't sure how many were coming. It was thoughtful of Mr. Khan to bring dinner for us. I would have liked to meet his wife. I had so many questions about the women and their custom of covering themselves, all new and strange to me. But as Jim had said, he was also showing Jim appreciation for the business they did together, so his visit was not only social. Perhaps Pakistani women didn't entertain or accompany their spouses at functions related to business.

Jim arrived shortly before Mr. Assam Khan. At six o'clock on the dot, Mr. Khan arrived with two servants carrying containers of food. Jim introduced us, and soon Mr. Khan's servants filled our dining room table with large bowls of food. The exotic spices of curry, cardamom, and garlic wafted through our flat, aromatic and enticing. My appetite perked up, and I tried every dish. This was an exotic and welcome meal.

First, the servant passed a plate of ravioli-sized pastries called *samosas*. The crust was tan, and mashed, spiced potatoes filled the inside of some. A ground meat mixture filled others. The curry was spicy but perfect with a spoonful of aromatic rice Mr. Khan said was called *basmati* rice.

Mark managed a fork well for a four-year-old, but Kevin, at seventeen months old, was more comfortable with his fingers. He reached for a *samosa* with his left hand. Jim's mother was left-handed, and Kevin seemed to favor his left as well, but his age, it was still too early to tell.

"We teach our children to use only the right hand for eating since many foods are eaten with just the fingers. It is a custom from our nomadic ancestors," Mr. Khan said.

"But if the child is naturally left-handed, how do you change them?" Jim's mother, Grace, and I had discussed her trauma when her teachers forced to change to using her right hand.

"It is a matter of survival in our culture. No one is allowed to touch the communal food with his left hand," he said.

What difference did it make?

Mr. Khan's dinner turned out to be an exotic feast, introducing me to flavors and spices I'd never tried before. Mr. Khan hovered over us, making sure we took plenty of each new dish, such as the cauliflower seasoned with turmeric and garlic, giving it a rust-colored hue. The dessert was a custard pudding that dissipated the heat from the spicy dishes and provided a tasty finish for the meal. The boys loved the custard, but I wondered where the milk came from.

Assam Khan's gracious welcome went beyond the legendary Muslim hospitality. Food and drink (nonalcoholic for devout Muslims) is always offered to even casual guests but not always such a bountiful repast. I had boiled a pot of water for the tea I knew would be the preferred drink, which I offered with the powdered milk we had made. Mr. Khan added it to their tea, along with spoons of sugar. Jim had told me that businessmen insisted on having a cup of tea before the discussions of business matters could begin. Even though Jim did not care for the sweetened milk tea, he drank it with the business men. After Jim became better acquainted with the merchants, they learned of his preference for Coke or lemon squash and offered that instead of sweetened milk tea. The important thing was the ritual of relaxing over a beverage and making small talk before discussions of business.

"Mr. Khan, I can't thank you enough for this delicious meal. It is exceeded only by your kindness," I said as he was departing.

How would we be able to reciprocate when his wife kept strict *purdah* and could not come to our home?

When we were finally alone, Jim explained the usage of right hand and left hand. "If a thief is caught, the ancient punishment was to cut off his right hand. Since the left hand is used for toilet functions and the right hand to eat, the punishment for stealing is harsh."

"So the punishment for stealing is actually a death sentence." Now I understood Mr. Khan's advice to teach Kevin to eat with his right hand.

◇◇◇◇◇

THE NEXT MORNING WHILE IT was still cool, I took Mark and Kevin out to the playground at the front corner of the apartment complex. I held their hands as we crossed the driveway that circled the building that delivery vehicles and residents used. Besides a double teeter-totter and a huge swing set with three wooden seat swings attached to heavy chains, a tall fortress-like slide was the main attraction. Perched high on pillars, a round concrete platform had two slides reached by a ladder attached to the side of the platform. Each item of playground equipment had the potential for injury if children weren't supervised.

An American woman smiled and walked over to greet me. "Hello. I'm Marge Hansen. You must be Jim's wife. He told us you and the boys were coming." She was knitting while watching the children. "This is Carl." She indicated her small son with a mop of curly blond hair. "We had our family nearly raised when he came along." She held her knitting and needles in her hands, the yarn bag draped over her shoulder. She did appear older than most mothers of toddlers.

We chatted as the boys sized each other up. Carl and Mark appeared to be about the same age and soon took off running in an impromptu game of tag. Kevin watched and kicked the ankle-deep sand around, filling his shoes and waiting for his chance to join the game. I was delighted to learn Marge had a teenage daughter and hoped I had found a babysitter.

"Does she babysit?" I asked.

Marge's reply surprised me. "Oh, no. None of the American children babysit. That would take a job away from a Pakistani. We need to support their economy by hiring servants. That's how so many people make their living. With unemployment at nearly forty percent, we feel we must support the local economy. You will find that keeping house here is much more difficult than in the States. I don't know what I'd do without our cook to do the cooking and shopping."

"You have a cook, too?"

"Yes, and a *bearer* and a *dhobi* to do the laundry twice a week and an *ayah* to watch Carl, or I could never go out."

This was all new to me, and I wondered why it took so many people to run their home, an apartment a little larger than ours. I wanted to learn more about the servant and babysitter situation, but Marge changed the subject.

"Do you play bridge?"

I nodded. "Yes, I do, but it has been awhile."

Construction wives played bridge on a regular basis, and I'd learned the game to fill in when my friends didn't have enough players. I was still a novice.

"When you find an *ayah*, you'll have to come to the American Women's Club. They have monthly luncheons and bridge," Marge said. "You'll meet

European and American women. There's quite an international community here."

"I'd like that," I said.

"Mama, look."

Above my head, I could see Kevin climbing the ladder to the highest part of the slide. The concrete platform had sides about waist high for a toddler. From the platform, two metal slides, one straight and one with two bumps, descended to the ground. The platform could hold several children, but the child had to step over a wide gap at the top of the ladder to reach the platform. The gap was over a foot wide, and if Kevin missed that step, the drop to the ground was ten feet. I held my breath, not wanting to frighten my son, but terrified he'd miss the step to the platform and fall through that chasm.

"Stop, Kevin. Stay and let me help you." I hurried up the ladder and held his arm while he stepped across to the relative safety of the platform.

"Wait here. I'll catch you." I put his hand on the vertical barrier of the platform, backed down the ladder, and stood at the bottom of the slide Kevin had his eye on. When he saw me in position, Kevin pushed off, laughing as he slid down the slide, over the bumps and into my waiting arms.

"More, Mom!" He ran for the ladder.

I followed him up the ladder again, holding his shirt. After three trips, perspiration covered me, and sand filled my shoes. I was ready to retreat to the coolness of the apartment. I said good-bye to Marge and took the boys inside.

At lunchtime, I cut into the loaf of bread we had bought, where I discovered bits of paper that looked like confetti, a thick black hair, and wood shavings, possibly sawdust.

How disgusting. How could they sell something so full of dirt and hair?

I was angry I had not paid more attention to Dorothy's advice that the local bread would not do. I opened a can of soup instead and made cheese and cracker sandwiches for our lunch. After lunch, we climbed the three flights upstairs to see Dorothy.

"Hi. Come in. How are you?" She smiled down at Mark and Kevin.

"We went to the playground. I met a new friend. His name is Carl. Kevin went down the big slide," Mark told her in his matter-of-fact manner. He liked Dorothy.

"I thought Carl might like to be your friend," Dorothy told him. "Come sit down."

"Dorothy, do you have a recipe for bread? I didn't bring a cookbook with me and don't remember how my mom made it. I watched her when I was younger, so I remember about the kneading and letting it rise," I said.

"Well, you're well on your way if you know that much." She chuckled. "Here's my cookbook, and if you want to borrow some yeast and flour, I have plenty."

"Wonderful. I'm sure Jim must have ordered flour, sugar, and staples. I'll order more with our commissary order. I couldn't find a measuring cup in the apartment. Do you have one I could borrow for today?"

"I don't have one either. I'll show you a great substitute." She went to her pantry and returned with an empty peanut butter jar. "There are marks on the side that work fine to measure when you don't have anything else." She pointed to raised measurements that I had never noticed on peanut butter jars before. Dorothy handed me the jar which was a perfect substitute.

The boys were ready for a nap, so I copied the recipe and mixed the bread ingredients before I rested that afternoon. I could nap while the bread dough rose. First, however, I found the supply of blue aerograms, thin, tissuelike paper that was a letter that could then be folded into an envelope. This cost much less to mail than regular paper and envelopes. I wrote the addresses of my mom and Jim's parents.

The bread rose as I wrote one letter. I punched it down and moved it to the pantry where afternoon sun streamed in the window. By the time I finished writing the letters, the dough was spilling over the sides of the bowl. The pantry was a perfect incubator for the yeast. After punching the dough down again, I shaped the dough into loaves and filled the pans. I boiled a new supply of drinking water for twenty minutes. At least I could write letters and take care of other chores during the process of baking bread. I put the pans into the hot oven to bake. My first efforts at baking bread filled the apartment with the delicious, yeasty fragrance as the boys woke from their naps. Now we could go outside to play.

"Hi, Carl. Want to play?"

Mark recognized Carl and ran to join him with Kevin at his heels. Marge wasn't in sight, so one of the Pakistani women chatting in the shade must have been Carl's *ayah*. Kevin headed for the slide, and I followed him up the ladder again.

◇◇◇◇◇

"WE AREN'T GOING TO HAVE servants," Jim stated flatly when I brought up the issue after the boys were in bed that night. "We don't need them. You would be spoiled when we return home. We have to put up with Alam and Afsar since the company pays them. When there aren't any guests in the two vacant flats, they can help you, but we can't afford to spend money on servants."

He didn't want to discuss it further. I was annoyed at his attitude and didn't see that spending a few rupees to make life easier would be a strain on our budget. I was still exhausted from the trip and didn't have an immediate response to Jim's unilateral decision. Perhaps he didn't realize it wasn't always possible to take children everywhere. And what would we do for babysitters at night if none of the American teenagers were available?

I didn't like taking them to bazaars where they would be exposed to germs and diseases in the crowds. Although Alam had stayed with the boys that first night, his babysitting was not a service I could expect. A *bearer* did not take care of children or change a diaper. An *ayah*, or nanny, was the caregiver of children. If the child required diaper changes, a Muslim man would not perform that chore just as he would not clean the toilets. Sweepers, who were usually Christians did those "unclean" chores. I had read that, when Christian missionaries came to India, people from the untouchable caste converted to Christianity because it gave them a spiritual path out of their low caste status. The *homal* was a Muslim who performed the chores that Alam directed, so some adjustments to the old rules of division of labor must have been made to accommodate small households where a sweeper wasn't part of the staff.

Alam, as the *bearer*, ran the household and directed the other servants. Besides answering the door, delivering messages, serving the food at the table, and removing the dishes to the kitchen, a *bearer* would also shop or do errands. The division of labor was complicated, and I was beginning to understand who would perform what chores. We were fortunate that WAPDA Flats rent included the *malis* (gardeners) and the *chowkidar* (watchman) at the gate. If we had one of those lovely bungalows I saw in

Gulberg, we would need a whole staff of people to keep it clean and take care of the maintenance.

A few days later, I mentioned to Jim that the wages for a full-time *ayah* would be the same as four evenings out. "We were spending around twenty dollars per month on babysitters at home. Without one, we'll never be able to go out."

Jim finally acquiesced. "I guess if the American teenagers won't babysit and we want to go out, we need to get an *ayah* while we're in Lahore. However, when we move to Baral Colony, there will be American teenagers. Surely we'll find someone available to babysit, and we won't need the *ayah*."

Jim's company had made it clear that we would be in Lahore for an indefinite time, but their plan for Jim was to send him to the Mangla Dam job site when needed. We had been assigned a two-bedroom house at Baral Colony, which was completed and ready for us when the transfer came. This seemed like a reasonable compromise to solve our servant problem, which was really a Jim problem, according to Marge's assessment when I told her of his decision.

"Go ahead and find an *ayah* if it will cost the same as a babysitter," he said.

Jim understood the division of labor as it related to the job, but he was now seeing the difficulty of keeping house and observing the customary labor division. Now if only he'd realize I wasn't a nonstop machine like he was. Jim's nervous energy made the long hours tolerable for him, but not for me, especially in the unbearable heat.

I was pleased he finally accepted the situation. Now how could I find a good *ayah*?

◇◇◇◇◇

OUR FIRST WEEKS PASSED IN a time warp waking and sleeping at the wrong times. The days in Pakistan are exactly the opposite as time on the West Coast of the United States. Turning what had been our days into nights and nights into days was hard enough for me, but even more difficult for Mark and Kevin. The days and nights blurred together as Kevin would awaken at two in the morning, ready to rouse his brother and play. I shortened their naps. Now we had progressed from their staying awake until midnight to a nine o'clock bedtime. They liked to visit with Jim when he came home for dinner around eight o'clock.

"How would you like to make a trip to Mangla?" Jim asked after dinner one night nearly two weeks after our arrival. "Today, some parts for the equipment arrived that are needed at the job early Monday morning. The fastest way is for me to take them. Saturday's a holiday, so it's a good time for me to get away. I think you'd enjoy seeing some of the country and take a look at the dam site. We can check on the progress of our house."

I liked the idea of seeing the job site and our new house at Baral. "That sounds great. Let's go."

4

Our First Trip to Mangla Dam

EARLY SATURDAY MORNING, WE STARTED off in Jim's company pickup with our overnight suitcase wedged between boxes of parts we were delivering. We settled on the wide seat of the pickup with Mark and Kevin between us with Mark claiming the seat next to Jim. The pickup, like all the vehicles for the job, had been ordered from the States, so the steering wheel was on the left.

Traffic in Pakistan moved on the left side of the road, a holdover from the British days. From my seat on the right, where the driver should have been, oncoming traffic looked close and dangerous.

"How far is it?"

"One hundred and thirty miles," Jim replied.

That should be about two and a half hours based on driving times in the States.

I envisioned straight highways with miles of wilderness between here and the project site. They said the dam would be built in a remote part of Pakistan, so I expected remote meant that there were few people. How wrong that idea turned out to be.

People crowded the streets, off work today in honor of Revolution Day, a national holiday. We drove past areas of Lahore I hadn't yet seen, the

53

Badshahi Mosque and the campus of Punjab University with wide walkways and a park like campus. Each corner had some kind of monument to commemorate past Mogul leaders. Families strolled and played with their children in the public parks. We chuckled at sight of one man who had his wife and two children on a small motor scooter. Before long, we passed another scooter with a couple and three children aboard. It seemed whole families used scooters for transportation. The streets were crowded with all kinds of traffic, but the *tongas*, horse-drawn, high-wheeled carts, captured my attention with passengers who faced backward. They were close enough to the truck that we could hear the harness jingling and smell the horse's sweat. Chaotic noises, the honking lorries, and shouting vendors hawking their wares engulfed us.

One busy intersection had several roads converging in a large, open space where *tongas* parked, waiting for passengers from the nearby bazaar. A *tonga* going the opposite direction passed us, and a woman darted into the street. Jim slammed on the brakes to avoid hitting her as she bent over and scooped up the horse's droppings. She cast a wary look at Jim, but she was focused on completing her chore.

"What is she doing picking up horse manure?"

"She'll pat it to dry on the outside of her house and use it for fuel to cook dinner. Wood is scarce so dried dung is used for fuel. A few weeks ago, right on this section of road, one woman killed another when she took droppings from the first one's territory," Jim said. "They stake out areas like a miner might stake his claim."

I was shocked. What a different world we were living in now.

Traffic circles diverted vehicles in a clockwise path at major intersections Jim maneuvered the pickup well in the heavy traffic, but I was still uncomfortable driving on the left side of the highway. At one traffic roundabout, a turbaned man perched on a low fence post, squatting on his haunches like a bird. I had wondered what the men wore under their *dhotis* (long, skirt like garments tied at the loins). This man's position left no question of what they wore beneath the *dhoti*, nothing.

From my copilot's seat, my right foot reached involuntarily for the brake pedal whenever someone cut in front of us.

"They call this gate the Kashmiri Gate since it faces Kashmir," Jim said. "The old city was the crossroads of culture when it became a favorite of the Moguls."

The Old City of Lahore was enclosed by high walls with entry possible only through the arched gates. Buildings with red tile roofs and carved façades of lacelike marble walls gave us the feeling that we were riding into stories from the *Arabian Nights*. The cutwork marble panels allowed women who lived within to peer out without being seen through the lacy dividers.

We crossed a bridge spanning the Ravi River, one of the five tributaries of the Indus, and turned north at a sign directing traffic to Rawalpindi. It had taken us almost an hour to drive across the city of Lahore.

"This is the Grand Trunk Road, called the Backbone of India," Jim said. "A Pathan King named Sher Shaw Sari built this road centuries ago. Later, the Moguls added to it, and in the nineteenth century, the British paved it. The GT Road, as they call it, cuts a swath across the subcontinent of India from Calcutta on the East Coast to the Northwest frontier capital of Peshawar, the gateway to the Khyber Pass. Every ten miles there is a *serai*, or rest area. The Moguls liked to travel in style, stop to rest, or stay overnight at a place where there was water for them and their animals. These stops were an extension of life in the city's bazaars, a good place to exchange news and learn about road conditions."

Rows of shade trees lined the road and created a shady canopy, throwing a patchwork of dappled light and dark shadows on the pavement. Traffic on the GT Road was frightening but interesting. Brightly painted trucks, donkeys laden with produce, and horse-drawn *tongas* all competed for space. Oxcarts loaded twice the height of the oxen hid the driver beneath his load like a giant mushroom. Bleating flat-tailed sheep and goats, with ears or rumps painted with bright colors of pink, green, or purple indicating the owner, trotted along close together. An occasional camel caravan moseyed along with their wide loads cascading over the sides of the tall, ungainly animals, who gazed contemptuously at the mayhem below.

After a few miles, traffic slowed to a crawl. We could proceed only at the pace of the slowest animal. I was mesmerized as we crawled along in the colorful parade of traffic. The boys identified each animal we passed. The trucks now blared their horns, drivers shouted at the slow-moving vehicles, and the squeal of tires of impatient motorists screeched as they accelerated to pass the slow line ahead. There was little choice but to be patient and wait for a chance to pass.

My job as copilot in the right seat was to warn Jim of oncoming traffic so he could pass.

"Is it clear?" he asked, finally becoming impatient at our slow progress. "No. Wait for the next truck to pass."

Passing with the driver on the left side of the road was a harrowing experience. I reached for the brakes reflexively and held the door handle to brace myself when he accelerated.

The flat, fertile farmland of the Punjab surrounded us and stretched as far as we could see. Waterwheels operated by oxen walking in a circle pumped water into tin can-sized containers. As the wheel turned, the can emptied the water into a wooden trough, which emptied the water into a ditch, where it flowed to the crops. We felt like we were in a time warp as we saw farming methods that were unchanged in the centuries when men had first learned to coax crops from the earth. *Dhoti*-clad men cut the grain, swinging their handheld scythes. Their women worked beside them, gathering and threshing the grain into a cloth spread on a tamped earth circle. Nothing we saw along the roadsides indicated we were in the twentieth century. There were no power or telephone lines parallel to the road. It felt like we were watching life as it was lived during biblical times.

When Jim saw an opportunity to pass, he called to me from his side of the truck, "Is it clear on the right?"

I looked ahead. "No. Wait!" He eased back into the left lane of north-bound traffic. "You can go after the next truck passes."

Jim pulled into the right lane of the road, passing a whole herd of sheep, three oxcarts, and a camel caravan. He swung the pickup back into the left lane just before a truck bore down on us in the right lane.

"Circus truck." Mark pointed as we passed another truck painted in a rainbow of colors.

"Fruck." Kevin tried to repeat "truck" but didn't get it out quite right. He pointed to the truck Mark saw.

"The road's clear," I said.

He didn't pass as many animals or vehicles this time, but that didn't mean we had no close calls. We were now speeding along at twenty-five to thirty miles per hour.

We stopped at a town called Gugranwalla, about fifty miles north of Lahore, and walked around to stretch our legs. The boys were happy to get out and explore. People stared at us. Some pointed at Mark's blond hair, rarely seen in this country. Americans were obviously a novelty. I had worn a full skirt, well below my knees, and a blouse with sleeves. Still, the women we saw were covered, peeking out behind their scarves to look at us.

Jim stopped at a little shop and bought us Cokes. The shopkeeper opened the glass Coke bottle and wiped it with his shirtsleeve. I accepted it, and I was pleased to find it cool but not as cold as the refrigerated drinks we expected.

"Should we take it with us?" I held up the Coke bottle.

"We'd have to pay a rupee each for the bottles," Jim said. "Glass bottles are expensive here. Let's drink what you want and leave the bottles with him."

Cokes cost about a quarter of a rupee, but the bottle deposit was one rupee, the equivalent of a dollar.

We explored the town and stopped to watch young boys sitting on the ground. They were listening to a man who appeared to be their teacher. He asked questions, and the boys scratched marks in the dirt tamped smooth in front of them. The man walked around the boys, bending down to check their work. This appeared to be an outdoor classroom with no desks, books, chalkboard, or walls. The children were absorbed in their lessons.

"I have to go to the bathroom," Mark said.

"Well, son, let's go find a tree." Jim led him about twenty feet behind the Coke seller's shop.

The ditch beside us looked and smelled like an open sewer. Mark stood there, transfixed by a massive black water buffalo grazing in the field, the first time he had ever seen such a large-horned animal.

"Daddy, I can't go with that animal right there."

"He won't bother you. Just stand here by this tree."

"No, Daddy, I can't."

"I'll stand between you and the water buffalo," Jim said.

But it was to no avail. Mark was not going to go with that animal anywhere near him. We drove a few miles to a place where there were no water buffalo or other fearsome creatures in sight. Jim walked Mark to the lone tree.

"When you see a gas stations or a café, let's stop. I need a restroom, too," I said as they got back in the pickup.

"Gas stations don't have restrooms. Most people go outside."

Not me. I hoped it wouldn't be too much farther to the job site and a ladies' restroom.

Jim finally stopped and pulled into an area with gas pumps and pointed to the side door of a small building behind the gas station. I opened the door, wary of what I'd find. The smell of urine was strong, and as my eyes adjusted to the darkness inside, I could barely make out two cleated parallel steps on either side of a trough in the concrete floor that led to an opening in the outside wall. This was not the same as a Western toilet, but this was my only choice.

An hour later, we stopped again to give the boys a chance to walk around. Men turned the pole that supported a wooden Ferris wheel that held two children on each of the four seats. The contraption looked like a smaller version of a large Ferris wheel we had ridden in carnivals. The children laughed with delight as they rose in the air and then descended with more speed on their downward ride. My sons watched with curiosity when the children on the ride waved at us. The boys were shy, and the homemade wheel didn't look safe to me. I was happy the boys were content to watch.

A fruit stand near the Ferris wheel offered fragrant yellow mangos for sale. The young man at the stall picked up a mango, tossed it back and forth, squeezed it, and carved a small circle in the mango's narrow end with his pocketknife. He tilted his head back and sucked the juice and pulp from the fruit.

"Look, *memsahib*, mango easy to eat."

Perhaps if I washed and peeled them, mangos would be safe to eat. They were sold everywhere, and their fragrance was enticing. Villagers gathered around and continued to look at us with curiosity. I smiled but felt uncomfortable at the attention.

We drove north past the town of Jhelum. The towering mountains of the Himalayas puncturing the distant skyline became clearer as we were nearing our destination. Jim turned to the right at a tiny village called Dina. The mountains in front of us blocked the eastern view, and swirling white clouds hid their peaks.

"We had to put in a rail spur from the main line to the job site to bring in equipment and supplies." Jim pointed out the shiny new tracks running parallel to the freshly paved asphalt road.

We were almost to the base of the foothills when Jim turned up a hill and stopped in front of an old fort overlooking the river.

"This is Mangla Fort, a historic landmark, which is as far east as Alexander the Great is said to have made it into India in 325 BC," Jim said. "As you can see, it's in bad repair. We'll have to restore it as well as build the dam without damaging the fort. The dam will start at the bottom of this hill and curve across to the opposite bank." Jim pointed to the serpentine curve of the river below. "So this is where the dam will go, right across the Jhelum River. See that, kids? That's where we will build the dam." Jim pointed across the river, his arm sweeping a wide curve to show me where the dam would be. "That's Azad Kashmir across the river, the disputed territory Pakistan and India are still fighting over. The Vale of Kashmir is just over those hills."

Earthmoving machinery crawled like hungry beasts on the other side of the river, scooping up large shovels full of reddish-brown soil and dumping them into waiting trucks. We watched one truck as it was filled and pulled out. Another quickly took its place to be loaded.

The curve of the river around the fort was a natural place to block the river's flow with a dam. Looking upstream, the valley narrowed and then widened as it disappeared into the foothills.

"How will an earth dam hold all that water?" I asked.

"The dam will be three hundred and eighty feet high. There's also going to be another dam called Jari about twelve miles upstream and a long barrage called Sukian Dike to fill those low spots in the hills you see to the right. We have to raise the sides of the lake or reservoir before we can fill it," Jim said. "Imagine this valley as one big lake, which is what the Mangla Reservoir will be when we finish."

"See that far embankment where the machines are moving earth? That was a village. It took months to move the people so we could get started. That village sat right where we need to build the spillway, so the Pakistani government paid them to leave. Even with the promise of more than they could earn in three years, the people were reluctant to leave their family's ancestral home."

I felt sorry for the people who valued their family heritage and had to leave. Progress had its price and was too often at the expense of tradition. *What a sad compromise.*

Jim drove back to the main road and climbed a steep hill to the wide plateau opposite Mangla Fort. The security guard on duty examined our police identity cards and Jim's employee identification card and then waved us through. Jim made a sharp left turn at the top of the hill. Spread before us was the American town under construction.

"This is Baral Colony." Jim pointed to the beginnings of the new town.

This 240 acres had been chosen for the American and British colony. The town was laid out on a grid that could have been a housing project in any American suburb. The homes were brick construction with a modern, flat concrete roof. Some appeared to be occupied. Roads had been graded but not yet paved, so dust swirled with the breeze off the mountains, and each passing vehicle left a cloud of dust behind. A water truck drove by, spraying the billows of dust and replacing the dust with mud imprints of tire treads.

"The ditches on either side of the road are for water runoff. You've never seen water like they have in the monsoon season." On each side of the road was a ditch about two feet deep and two feet wide.

Jim turned into a cul-de-sac and showed us three homes that were larger than others and built farther apart. "This is where George Archibald, the project general manager, lives." Jim pointed to the first house. "Joe McNabb, the construction manager, and his wife Helen are next, and the one on the far left is Margaret and Errol Platt's home. Errol is the business manager of the project. You met Margaret in Lahore. She and Adeline moved from Lahore the day you arrived nearly two weeks ago."

Their houses on the edge of the bluff overlooked the river, which we could see as it snaked around the plateau on the other bank. The old Mangla Fort faced the emerging new town, a stark contrast of ancient fortification and modern construction. A brick wall on the edge of the plateau enclosed the town.

"Why do they have a fence around the town?" I looked at the eight-foot-tall brick wall with a three-strand section of barbed wire angled outward on the top.

"That is to keep out the camel caravans, goat herds, and salesmen who would be knocking at the doors of every home." Jim laughed. "This way, visitors have to show a pass and give the name of the person they are visiting. It's for everyone's protection."

Jim drove back toward the main street and stopped at a house, still on G Street. "This is the house we've been assigned." Jim parked the pickup.

The house looked much like the others on the street, perhaps a bit smaller than some since our two sons allowed us to have a two-bedroom house. Looking through the windows, I could see some of the walls were painted a soft blue.

"This will be a fine house for us," Jim said.

I looked at the dusty, bleak beginnings of what would soon become a community. The town appeared to be well thought out, and I could see that it would have every convenience. This was a smaller version of an American suburb, far from the excitement I had found in Lahore. Construction women were used to this kind of environment and accustomed to making the best of life in remote areas, which was where dams were always built. I would have to also acclimate myself when we lived here. On the Oahe Dam project in South Dakota, we were lucky to have the Sears' and Penney's catalogs to make up for the lack of stores. Here we would have to pay import duty of a 300 percent tax to the government of Pakistan on everything we ordered.

"This house got the Danish furniture," Jim said. "I wrote you how we had every furniture, carpet, and drapery plant in all of Pakistan working to full capacity to furnish the houses. Well, after three months, the local companies were so far behind schedule that it was obvious they couldn't deliver the furniture and carpets in time. The houses were nearly complete, and families were scheduled to arrive in October. The company had to prove to the local government that local factories couldn't complete the contracts on time and got permission to order furniture from Denmark."

We walked around the house with a large yard full of dirt and rocks.

Jim must have noticed my concern. "The company will plant grass in front. We can have a patio and barbecue pit built. We just have to pay for the labor, and the company will furnish the materials. Look, boys, this will be your yard."

"Where are the swings?" Mark looked around the tufts of weeds.

The yard was bleak, but I could envision flowerbeds and lawn to add color. We waved to a family we had met on the Oahe Dam project in South Dakota. They lived down the same street as our house. Their children were close to the same ages as ours. The yard would give the boys space to play outdoors. I was sure we'd make friends, and I would like it fine once we were transferred to this American colony.

"The large apartment building on the corner is the bachelor quarters." Jim pointed across the road. "And that's the mess hall for the single workers. We can stop here for lunch."

I was hungry and glad he suggested eating. The shopping center came next with spaces for a post office and smaller shops that occupied the block across the road from the apartments. There would soon be a theater, a restaurant and bar, a bowling alley with a snack bar, and sports courts for tennis and squash. By spring, two swimming pools would be added to create a country club atmosphere in the small town.

The Mangla International School was completed and would be open for the following week. Classes would span the age groups from kindergarten through high school. Because of the diverse population of workers, the school would have to meet the academic requirements of the Americans, British, and Pakistani schools. Few offshore jobs included high school, so this was a wonderful feature for families.

Despite the dust, I could see what a wonderful town this would be. What an enormous undertaking this had been to build so many homes in six months, rows and rows of brick houses, all complete and some occupied. The company knew the town and schools had to be good to attract and keep top-level employees. Old-timers would say, "If Mama is happy, everyone is happy." Management had taken heed of this old folk wisdom.

"When I arrived in April, there was nothing here. Now in six months, we have a town," Jim said with pride. "The hospital is up the hill above the town." He pointed to a higher plateau nestled in the curve of the foothills. "Until it's completed, they're operating a clinic out of one of the temporary buildings." We stopped in front of the bachelor's mess hall. "Are you guys ready for some lunch?"

We found a table and filled our trays with sandwiches. Soon, several men brought their trays over to join us. They began talking to Mark and Kevin. I realized this had been a "man camp" for six months, and the men missed their families. Our boys were a rare treat for them to enjoy until their children arrived.

"How is the training program going?" Jim asked the man next to me.

"Very well. You can imagine, with the high unemployment rate here, we had thousands of men apply. We selected only those who had some kind of skill. We found that, if a man has learned rudimentary carpentry work, he could be trained to do mechanics. If he's driven a truck or bus, he can be trained to drive heavy equipment. These men never saw equipment like we have here. We put them through a few weeks of classroom work with Urdu interpreters. Then we use a sandbox with Tonka model trucks so they learn the mechanics of backing a rig or pushing a shovel with a bulldozer. They're smart, but few have any education."

"How long before you can have one driving a rig?"

"Depends on the man, but usually within a month to six weeks, he's driving with a supervisor aboard. We put them to work in areas that are not ready to excavate but have plans to work in the future, so the training time is still productive."

"That's a good idea," I said. "Where have these men come from?"

"From a lot of places. Some of the ones with more mechanical ability are Waziri from the tribal area. They've had trucks to haul goods into the hills and they learned to repair them."

I was tired and felt ill from some intestinal upset. Jim checked at the bachelor's quarters, but no rooms were available for us to spend the night. We discovered that every available bed in the town was full of new arrivals. Margaret's husband, Errol Platt, came to our rescue and put us up in the servant's quarters just completed next to his house. Margaret Platt sent out blankets and pillows for our comfort.

The small concrete blockhouse was clean and had two single *charpoys* like the ones we had in the motel in Karachi and the most essential accommodation, a bathroom. The top half of the walls were open, screened to protect against insects, but the breeze blew around our snug beds. Kevin crawled in with me, and Mark slept with Jim. It wasn't perfect, but it was a far better option than returning to Lahore tonight.

That night, I slept little. Mark and Kevin were now suffering from stomach problems, too. The Platts hosted a party that evening for the new arrivals and invited us to join them. We heard the guests laughing and music playing but didn't feel well enough for a party. As the voices of the guests could be heard saying farewell, Jim dressed and went over to ask Margaret if she had anything for the diarrhea we were experiencing. She sent medication back with Jim. The night sounds of skittering insects, unseen animals foraging for food, and a roar that sounded like a distant mountain lion interrupted my slumber the few times I dropped off.

The next morning, Jim delivered the parts to the warehouse while the crew loaded the pickup with a few boxes to be returned to Lahore. Our return trip included a couple of rest stops that Sunday and took a little over four hours.

We had just returned to Lahore when John Ziemer rang the doorbell. He gestured for Jim to step out into the hall, where they spoke in hushed tones. Jim looked serious. His brow was furrowed with concern when he told me John's news.

"The American consul general called a special meeting with the managers all American companies working in Pakistan. President Kennedy demanded that Soviet Premier Khrushchev remove the Soviet missiles in Cuba that have been confirmed to be aimed at the United States. Kennedy has told them to remove the missiles immediately. If they don't, the United States will force their removal, even if we have to go to war." Jim grimaced as he pulled me into his arms. "We were ordered to prepare for evacuation by land or air, gather as much local cash as you can, and pack one suitcase per family."

We were shocked. Be ready for immediate evacuation?. The idea terrified me. We felt helpless. Looking back on that moment, I realize we were pawns in the chess game of world events.

The American Consulate's orders said, "Be prepared to be airlifted or walk out of the country. Gather as much cash in local currency as you can. Pack one suitcase per family."

How could I pack clothing for four, plus diapers for Kevin, in one suitcase? When we left the States, we had six suitcases, one filled with cloth diapers. I selected a change of clothing for each of us, a stack of cloth diapers, and stored them in my closet where they would be clean and ready.

Alam asked the next morning if he could return the suitcase to the storage *godown*.

"No, thanks, Alam. I'll keep it here for now."

Domestic Challenges

MARK AND KEVIN RETURNED FROM our trip with colds as well as the intestinal upset. I was worried, and I was relieved to find Marge at the playground the next morning.

"Can you recommend a family doctor?" I asked.

"Dr. Selzer is wonderful. He's in Gulberg, not far from here. He's good with children, kind and gentle. We're pleased we found him." Marge gave me his address and telephone number. "If you don't call first, he'll see you anyway, but you may have to wait a little while."

She saw the concern on my face. Kevin was barely over the measles, and his cold worried me.

Dr. Selzer's office was through a side entrance of a sprawling bungalow surrounded by lovely gardens. Jim parked and carried Kevin while I took Mark's hand. We didn't have to wait long when a white-haired man with blue eyes and a well-trimmed beard greeted us. Marge had also told me that Dr. Selzer was rumored to have fled his native Germany in the late 1930s as the Nazis took over. He'd walked all the way to India along the Silk Road. When he reached Lahore, he stopped and settled down. He later married a Pakistani woman and made Lahore his home.

"I am Dr. Selzer. How can I help you?" he asked in a thick German accent.

"The boys both have colds. This is Mark. Kevin just got over the measles," I said. "The boys and I've had diarrhea since Saturday when we drove to Mangla."

"Let me see what is the problem," Dr. Selzer said, his voice soft as he looked at Mark.

He took Mark's temperature, listened to his chest with his stethoscope, and felt the glands in his neck. He was gentle, getting Mark's agreement before continuing each step of the exam.

"Now, would you open your mouth and say aaahhh for me?" he asked.

Mark complied, opening wide as the doctor put a tongue depressor on his tongue and said "aaahhh," following the doctor's directions. Then he turned to Kevin and examined him in the same methodical manner.

"This medicine should help." He handed me a prescription. "How are their appetites?"

"Good except for the intestinal upset over the weekend," I said. "We took some anti-diarrhea pills that helped. They aren't drinking as much milk as usual. They don't like powdered milk."

"Are you boiling the water?"

"Yes, for twenty minutes. We use only boiled water for cooking."

"That's good. Don't eat any vegetables you cannot peel and cook. The same applies to fruits. The dysentery bacteria are in the fields where they are grown. There is a dairy with water buffalo milk your children may like. Water buffalo are impervious to TB, so it is safer than cow's milk. The dairy will deliver the milk, but you must pasteurize it before you drink it. Boil it for twenty minutes, let it cool, and strain it."

He handed me a note with the address of the dairy. This sounded like a good substitute for cow's milk. I liked this gentle, older man and felt we could trust him.

"The colds will run their course in a few days. Give the children plenty of fluids and rest."

Jim paid the doctor, who wrote out and handed him a receipt. The company would reimburse us for doctor visits since they paid our medical care.

◇◇◇◇◇

THE NEWS OF THE CUBAN Missile Crisis spread through the American community in Lahore and among our neighbors at WAPDA Flats. Jim and I yearned for news so we'd know what was going to happen to us. The American Consulate was vague about how we would leave the country if it came to an evacuation. The border with India was close. Less than twenty miles east of Lahore was Amritsar, India. To the west, the Sind Desert and mountains made travel by land to Afghanistan doubtful. An airlift, possibly to Tehran, seemed the best option should it come to that. The Himalayas to the north had been a barrier to invaders and explorers for centuries. The Silk Road and the Khyber Pass was the route most travelers took to reach India, and that led closer to Russia. The seaport of Karachi was seven hundred miles to the south.

I hoped we wouldn't be evacuated as we were getting acquainted. Sleep came slowly that night as I pondered the possibilities, none of them good.

◇◇◇◇◇

EVEN WITH THE WORLD EVENTS so unsettling, life went on. Laundry was an immediate priority. Jim explained how he handled it before our arrival. Laundry would now be my job.

"I had Alam send my laundry out with a local *dhobi*," Jim said. "They take the clothes to the canal to wash them. He's done a pretty good job, but the local soap is full of lye and harsh on the fabric. If you look at my clothes, some things are wearing out from pounding them with rocks or whatever they do to get them clean. They iron everything, even underwear and socks."

I inspected Jim's shirts, pants, and underwear. After six months of the *dhobi* (laundryman) working with them, many were threadbare. Now I saw why Jim had asked me to bring a new supply of shorts and undershirts. Twice each week, the *dhobi* picked up and returned Jim's laundry.

Some of Jim's shirts were patterned with tan scorch marks where the iron had been too hot. My inspection of Jim's wardrobe indicated the *dhobi* had ironed Jim's seersucker shirt with vigor, but in spite of his best efforts, he could not smooth the wrinkles. How frustrating that fabric must have been to him.

From the very first day, I'd washed my underwear and lingerie by hand in our bathroom sink and hung it to dry behind the shower curtain. No way would I go through the counting and receipt process Jim had told me about with my intimate apparel. My brassieres and stockings couldn't be replaced here, and I knew they would last longer with hand laundering.

When the *dhobi* arrived with Jim's clean laundry, I watched as Alam gave the clothing to the *dhobi* to be counted. After checking each garment, he wrote the number of each item in English with the description of the garment beside it in a beautiful, flowing Urdu script. Then the *dhobi* handed Alam a "chit" or piece of paper that was the laundry list. Alam checked each item as he wrote. This first week, I gave the *dhobi* the boy's soiled clothes and Kevin's diapers.

"Alam, where does the *dhobi* wash the clothes?" I asked.

"*Dhobi* take clothes to canal. Wash in canal water and then rinse in bluing solution. Make white clothes very white. Then he dry on branches or rocks."

"Where does he iron the clothes?" I was puzzled how this could be done with no power beside the canal.

"*Dhobi* have charcoal, put in iron, and use board or rock to iron clothes. Come back clean and ironed very nice. You see, *memsahib*." Alam proudly showed me Jim's pressed garments and underwear.

So everything was ironed on a board at canal side using a charcoal iron, some probably still damp, using a heavy, charcoal-heated iron like I'd seen in the bazaars. If the garment happened to be the first one ironed after fresh charcoal was added, it might be returned with pinpoint burn holes caused by the tiny sparks that escaped from the iron's ventilation holes. That explained the burn marks on many of Jim's shirts and pants.

The rest of the laundry was a problem. The boy's play clothes had to be changed twice a day, and all of Kevin's diapers had to be laundered. Jim wore khaki shirts and pants, and our sheets and towels added more laundry. The servants' uniforms were also our responsibility to have laundered. Washing machines were not common, and Laundromats were unknown in Pakistan in the early sixties.

Dorothy came to the rescue. She found a *dhobi* we could share. He was available to come to our homes to do the laundry twice a week.

"He likes to do the laundry in the bathtub," Dorothy said.

That sounded better to me. He could do our laundry in the morning when the boys were outside playing, and during the afternoon when the boys napped, he would do Dorothy's smaller quantity of laundry in her guest room bathtub. It sounded like a lot of work for the poor man, but he was eager and willing to take the job. The charge for our family was eighty rupees a month, or about sixteen dollars in American money, for our family's gargantuan amount of laundry. Dorothy and John would pay a little less with a smaller workload for the *dhobi*.

The first day the *dhobi* arrived, he washed and wrung the clothes in the bathtub. Then he piled the wet laundry in a basket, balanced it on his head, and climbed the four flights of stairs to the rooftop. There he draped the clothes on the rooftop clotheslines. By the time the last load was hung up to dry, some of the first items were dry and ready for pressing. He eyed the two twenty-volt electric iron I'd bought in the bazaar with no small amount of suspicion. He used the iron only when I refused to allow his charcoal iron inside the apartment. This arrangement suited Dorothy and me better than having our clothing taken to the canal. Our *dhobi* took great pride in handing the finished laundry to Alam, clean, ironed, and folded to perfection. Dorothy found a jewel for a *dhobi*. We both liked him very much.

Jim came home one day, excited with the news that a British family in the complex had been transferred back to England. Anyone leaving Pakistan had no trouble selling all their household effects since there were few consumer goods available to buy at any price.

"They have a wringer washing machine to sell." Jim was excited at his find. "They're asking two hundred dollars for it, and it's a two twenty-volt with the correct plug to work at WAPDA Flats."

Jim was more excited about the washing machine than I was. I'd disliked the wringer washer I had to use when he was in college. That old machine's wringer gobbled nylon and silky items, and I lost more than one favorite item of clothing. I soon learned to wring silky items by hand. When the pump died, I had to bail the water to empty the machine each time I did laundry, seventeen buckets per load. I despised that wringer washer.

"Jim, the *dhobi* is doing fine, and two hundred dollars sounds like too much money for an old washing machine."

I hated to change what was working so well. Did Jim think I'd take over the laundry with a wringer washer? Then I'd be the one to carry that mountain of wet clothing up to the roof to the clotheslines, bring it back down, and iron everything. I could see he was trying to diminish the need for servants, and this acquisition was aimed at the *dhobi* who did such a good job.

"Jim, I don't think it's a good idea, but if the *dhobi* can save some time by using the machine, maybe it will work. I lost the disputes I had with that wringer washer we had to use when you were in college. It shredded my favorite bathrobe in its wringer."

Jim bought the washer. He and Rashid, the driver of the delivery truck to Mangla, brought the machine into the apartment. The only place for it was in a corner of the boy's room where I hid it with a sheet. I had doubts about the machine based on my previous experience.

The first laundry day after we bought the machine, Jim waited for the *dhobi*. Then with Alam interpreting, he gave him instructions on how it worked. Alam translated with gestures copied from Jim's hand motions, how to work the agitator, the wringer, and the pump. Jim was sure this modern machine would probably make our *dhobi* the envy of the whole compound. He wouldn't have to kneel over the tub, wring the sheets by hand, and scrub spots by rubbing the fabric together. Jim was proud to provide our *dhobi* with such advanced technology.

Satisfied that the *dhobi* and Alam had the new machine under control, I left with the boys to ride with Jim to the Mall. When we returned about two hours later, Alam greeted me with a long face. I was beginning to know Alam better, and I'd learned to check out his mood before asking him for anything.

"*Dhobi* very frightened, *memsahib*. He says he finished if he has to use that machine. He touch machine and get bad shock. Hurt him and scare him. He no work for *memsahib* if he must use machine. He wants to wash clothes old way, in bathtub where he no get shock. Machine bad. Too much scare him."

I'd experienced an occasional shock from our one ten in the States and could only imagine how much worse the two twenty would be. I felt sorry for the *dhobi* and took his side.

"Jim, the machine has got to go. If he's afraid of it, I certainly won't use it either."

Jim sent word to his coworkers at Mangla that we had a washing machine for sale. Within days, the Eilers were delighted to buy the machine from us. They used it with no ill effects. Perhaps their *bearer* was more familiar with electricity, or they converted it to one hundred and ten volts at Mangla.

◇◇◇◇◇

THE SECOND WEEK OF NOVEMBER, I opened the door to find Jerome Fernandez, the Pan Am station manager in Lahore, at our front door. He handed me a U.S. newspaper with big headlines on the front page:

CUBAN MISSILE CRISIS RESOLVED
KHRUSHCHEV ORDERS MISSILES REMOVED

The showdown between President Kennedy and Nikita Khrushchev ended as the American president backed down the formidable Soviet leader. The possibility of war was averted. The evacuation we had feared for many tense days would not be necessary. I sighed with relief as I unpacked our suitcase.

Although the crisis was over, repercussions of the Cuban Missile Crisis lingered. Every day, Jim came home with news of more anti-American demonstrations, mobs of young men and college students protesting against America. My impression had been that we were popular overseas, so the protests came as a shock to me. One day, angry, shouting men surrounded a sedan with four women returning to WAPDA Flats while the terrified occupants tried to remain calm, all the while yelling, "Americans, go home!" and the angrier "American bastards, go home!" They rocked the car back and forth, shaking the occupants and pounding on the hood and trunk of the sedan. Only when their leader shouted and waved for the men to follow him did they stop and go down the road with their anger. Street noises were common, but these young men were different from the sounds of business and traffic.

I watched as the women's car drove into our compound, and the women got out, shaken but unhurt. Marge and I walked over to see if they needed our help. They were trembling and wanted to talk about their experience.

"Their faces were contorted with rage," one said.

"What did we do to provoke them? I thought they were going to roll the car over."

"They're radicals and want us to know they hate Americans."

"Thanks, we're fine, just a little unnerved," the older one answered for the others.

"Come on inside, ladies. Let's make a cup of tea or something stronger if you like."

Alam watched the demonstration from the compound and came over to see if the women were safe. He shook his head. "Pathans tell all people Americans bad."

Demonstrations continued around Lahore, often around the Punjab University. Perhaps there was some Russian sympathy from the young men when the Cuban Missile Crisis didn't end as they hoped.

◇◇◇◇◇

EACH TIME THE DOORBELL RANG, I wondered who would show up next. Peddlers of all kinds made their way past the *chowkidar*. We were just two apartments in from the street corner, so our apartment door was one of the first they saw. I learned to let Alam answer the door and determine the business of the caller. It was one of the duties a *bearer* was expected to perform, and Alam relished the job that he handled with dignity.

One day, after a knock at the door and muttered words in Urdu, Alam introduced me to a tall, thin woman in a flowing *sari*. She bowed when I greeted her, touching her hands together, lowering her head, and bringing the hands to her forehead and then her chest in the traditional greeting. A few strands of gray streaked her long, dark hair, and her wrinkled skin hung over her bony hands.

"This is Miriam. Is good *ayah*, *memsahib*," Alam said. "Is Christian. Speaks good English."

I am sure he thought having a Christian *ayah* for our children would please me. After what I had learned about the untouchables and their conversion to Christianity as a means of salvation, I wasn't sure being Christian was important. Did he know this woman before she came, or did his rapid exchange with her in Urdu outside the door give him the assurance of her qualifications? I wasn't sure. I asked her for references. She reached inside her *sari* and produced a folded letter. I was reading the letter when Kevin and Mark burst into the room. She reached out her arms to Kevin, who readily walked over to her. Mark eyed this strange woman with suspicion and climbed into my lap.

I read the letter and asked her a few questions. She appeared to be acceptable, and without a telephone, I had no way to verify her recommendation letter. Alam said she was a good *ayah*. I plunged into an offer of employment.

"I will give you a trial for two weeks. If everything works out, we will pay ninety rupees a month," I said.

Marge had told me about one hundred was average. I had learned to start low in any price negotiations.

"One hundred twenty," she countered. "I speak English many years, *memsahib*."

"One hundred," I countered. Marge said most *ayahs* spoke some English for that price.

"All Americans pay at least one hundred ten rupees."

She made me feel a little cheap. We were only talking about twenty-four dollars a month at one hundred and twenty rupees.

"Okay, one hundred ten." I was weary of negotiating.

Her English was very good. The fact that she spoke English better than Alam might be helpful.

Three days after she started work, she complained about going home in the dark, and the days were getting shorter as fall progressed. The electric stove scared her, so she wouldn't heat anything I left for the boy's lunch. She could make sandwiches, but that was the extent of her cooking ability. Larger homes would have a cook to prepare the food. Mark ignored her directions. At four, he liked to make his own decisions.

I talked to him that night. "Mark, if I am not home and Daddy is working, you have to mind Miriam. She is like a babysitter."

He nodded, but I wondered if he would accept her authority.

The next day, I went out to the playground to see how she was doing with the boys. Kevin climbed the ladder, and Miriam tried to follow him as I'd asked to help him across that chasm. Her thin sandals and thin, voluminous *sari* impeded her ability to walk up the ladder. Kevin got far ahead of her and stepped across the gap between the ladder and the platform before she arrived at the top. I held my breath while he stepped across.

The next night, I told her she could go home early so she didn't have to walk in the dark. Part of her job, bathing and putting the boys to bed, would revert to me. Ah, well, this was something I liked to do, and I was just as glad to see her leave.

We'll see how this works out.

If our plans included going out, she would have to go home in the dark. If we were out very late, maybe Jim would drive her, or she could spend the night. I was willing to give her a chance in spite of our first few bumps in the road.

I was in our bedroom fixing a hem when Miriam came in with Kevin.

"*Memsahib*, how much money is *sahib* making?" she asked unexpectedly.

Caught off guard at such a personal question, I caught my breath and thought for a moment. Even if I had to give an answer, I wouldn't have known how to explain Jim's salary. Our base pay was in American dollars. We drew Pakistani rupees each month to cover all our living expenses, which was subject to an income tax of about 40 percent levied by the Pakistani government. What we didn't need to live on went into our bank account in the States.

"We don't discuss personal information like that even with our close friends." After our negotiation on her wages, she would probably ask for a raise. "It's time to take the boys outside to play."

The weather was warm, and Mark and Kevin loved that playground with the treacherous slide.

"Please watch Kevin on the slide," I called after her.

The following day, Marge came to the door, out of breath. "Dorothy is coming to the American Women's Club luncheon today, and we need a fourth for bridge. Can you come? We need to leave in an hour, and we'd love to have you join us. I have a car and driver today."

I now had the *ayah* to watch the boys, so I decided to go. "I'd love to go." I hurried to get ready.

We gathered in the oval driveway in the middle of the complex and got into the waiting car. Sheila Baxter, Dorothy Ziemer, Marge, and I were on our way to Gulberg.

"I didn't have time to tell you earlier, but today we have a special guest artist at the club, a woman named Vera Chatterjee. She's British and married to an Indian prince who became a doctor. He's now disabled. She supports them with her magnificent artwork," Marge said as we drove.

"I'm looking forward to seeing her collages again," Sheila said. "I didn't order any the first time I saw them, but now I've located a reliable picture framer who can do them justice."

The American Women's Club luncheon was held at a spacious bungalow in Gulberg, the wealthy section of Lahore just past the racecourse. Although I expected only Americans at the club, there were British, European, and several Pakistani women, too.

The artist displayed her work in a room off the entry, and we were drawn to the motion and color in the figures of Indian dancers, drummers, and a caparisoned elephant. The dancers were cut from the suede side of leather and then dressed in silk or cotton costumes, wonderfully detailed with turbans and tiny jewels to complete each figure. They were exquisite.

I loved the artwork and knew they would be perfect to add color to our white walls. I ordered two, the bareback dancer and the seated drummer boy.

"They'll be ready in time for the December luncheon. I can deliver them to you then," Mrs. Chatterjee said. "It's too much bother to post them and deal with customs and taxes." The tall, willowy artist wore a *sari* and spoke with a British accent. "I'd love to make another trip to Lahore. My father was stationed here during the time of the British Raj, so I lived here for many years."

Lunch was served, and we conversed about our spouses, their jobs, and our children. I mentioned I hadn't finished my studies at the University of Nevada but planned to return when my sons were older.

A stout, *sari*-clad Pakistani woman startled me with her observation. "We go to college for an education so we don't have to work. You American women go to school so you can work."

We discussed how a man would be proud of a wife with a good education. But a Pakistani husband would not encourage her to work outside the home. A working wife might suggest that her husband could not provide for her properly. Many of my American friends dreamed of and pursued their own career in the evolving feminism of the times. Any man they'd consider marrying would have to allow her to become successful without his ego being bruised or their relationship jeopardized. Pakistani women weren't expected to use their talents to work or support the family. Education gave the women a higher status, but its purpose was not for earning a living.

I enjoyed the luncheon and especially the artist. The women were interesting, but I didn't want to spend very many afternoons playing bridge. Now that I had an *ayah*, I wanted to explore Lahore when I wasn't with my sons.

◇◇◇◇◇

JIM SURPRISED ME ONE DAY when he appeared at home in the middle of the afternoon. The animated look on his face told me that something unusual had happened.

"I have the president of the Guy F. Atkinson Company, Mr. George Atkinson, and his wife outside in my truck. There was a riot at the airport. The car I sent for Mr. Atkinson couldn't get through the mob there to meet the president of Germany, who arrived at the same time. The front entrance was jammed with traffic. So I put them in the pickup and left the airport by the back gates. As we drove through the streets, people cheered and yelled, thinking he was the president of Germany." Jim laughed at the American being mistaken for Germany's president.

The Mangla Dam project, a favorite of the main office executives, attracted specialists of all kinds to consult and solve the problems as they arose. The company's president and a son of Mr. Guy, the CEO, wanted to check the progress firsthand.

I stepped outside to meet them. George Atkinson was a tall man with a ruddy complexion and streaks of gray in his dark hair. Mildred smiled. She seemed calm and unfazed by their unexpected transportation and rerouting to WAPDA Flats. They were relieved to have their luggage arrive with them.

Alam's radar, always working, showed up as I was meeting the Atkinsons. He and Afsar carried the luggage up the stairs to the apartment above ours. Jim decided the apartment would be safer than taking them to a hotel. I went ahead to show them the way and to be sure the apartment was ready.

"This is fine." Mrs. Atkinson looked around. "How do you like Lahore?"

"I'm still finding my way around, learning where to shop, but it's a fascinating city, full of colleges and lovely architecture. I'm eager to explore more. How was your trip?"

"Long, but we didn't expect the problem at the airport. Jim was smart to take us out the back way."

George nodded his agreement.

I was leaving when I realized they could be hungry. "Would you like something to eat? You could join us for dinner."

"No, thank you so much. We ate on the airplane not long ago and don't need a thing," Mildred replied.

I knew they were probably ready to sleep more than anything.

The sun was low in the sky, the *muzzeim* was calling the faithful to prayer, and dusk was descending as I prepared dinner for my family. All of a sudden, the lights and the electric stove went off. I realized the Atkinson's power was off, too. I searched our cabinets for candles and found several tall ones. The only thing I could find to hold candles was my empty Coke bottles. I inserted the candles in the necks of two bottles and found a package of matches. I packed a few tea bags, a gin bottle full of boiled water, some fruit, and part of a loaf of bread for their breakfast. I added a few chocolate chip cookies I'd made the day before. I'd heard that the Atkinsons were strict Methodists and abstained from drinking alcohol. I'd have to explain the gin bottle. The stairwell still had some light from the setting sun as I made my way up the stairs.

George opened the door.

"I brought you some candles and a few things for breakfast in case you need them. The gin bottle is really boiled water for drinking and brushing your teeth so you don't get sick."

"How thoughtful of you. Thank you," George said.

They were delighted at the candles and makings for a simple breakfast. For a man who now headed the Guy F. Atkinson Company, he was easy to talk to and had a kind manner. I liked them both, and I was relieved they'd avoided any hostile demonstrations that had become so common.

◇◇◇◇◇

EACH MONDAY MORNING, I SENT a grocery list with Jim to forward to the American commissary at Baral Colony. Our orders were sent to us on the supply truck driven by Rashid that made three trips a week between Lahore and Mangla. Although I didn't know the whole process until later, an employee had to select the items on our list, take them to the checkout counter, and itemize each imported item for our bill. That would be almost everything since all our food items were imported and taxed by the Pakistan government.

The accounting of our grocery order was a chore for someone. We were allowed one bottle of spirits or hard liquor per week, two bottles of wine, and a case of beer per family. Liquor wasn't readily available in a Muslim country, and with all our recent guests, this was an important part of our order. When a week and then ten days passed after I'd sent my list with Jim and no groceries arrived, I was running low on food. Months later I learned of the food shortages at Baral Colony due to shipping delays and suspected hoarding by some residents.

Alam told me he went to the meat market early most mornings and brought fresh meat for his wife. He said he'd be happy to bring meat for us. Shopping was part of the *bearer's* job since we didn't have a cook. I gave him twenty rupees, the equivalent of five dollars. We discussed what was available, and he had some suggestions. I asked for undercut, the tenderloin cut of beef we knew better as filet mignon, and some stew meat. The weather had cooled enough so I could braise the stew meat long enough for it to be tender. I remembered seeing shrimp at Tollinton's Market that first day. Alam said fish and shrimp arrived on the overnight train from Karachi and was iced, so I requested two pounds.

Alam returned with an amazing amount of meat for the money. I had him chop up some of the stew meat for coarse hamburger and froze part of it. Pakistani beef was not slaughtered until years of pulling a cart or plow. Most cuts of beef were very muscular and tough so it had to be braised. The delicious slow-cooked curries were probably created to tenderize the old animals. Now with my homemade bread, shrimp for a special dinner, tenderloin steak, and stew meat, I wasn't worried if our commissary order took longer to reach us. Alam also brought the vegetables I'd requested— potatoes, carrots and onions. I planned our dinners around the bounty Alam had brought from the bazaar.

The dairy delivered the water buffalo milk three times a week. I followed the doctor's instructions, boiled it for the required twenty minutes, and let it cool. Then I strained the milk through a square of nylon stocking and added a little condensed milk for flavor. Then I stored it in glass bottles I'd bought in the bazaar and stored it in the refrigerator. Fortunately, the boys accepted the water buffalo milk as readily as they drank cow's milk at home. I was relieved they were again drinking the milk that they needed for the nutrients it provided.

Khan Explains *Purdah*

In 1947, British rule in India ended. The subcontinent was divided into two independent countries, the Dominion of Pakistan, and the Union of India, which remained part of the British Commonwealth of Nations. The large center section of the subcontinent of India, which the majority of people who were Hindu populated, retained the name of India. The new Dominion of Pakistan was comprised of West and East Pakistan, separated by over eight hundred miles of India. Although both portions of the new geographically divided country had people of the Muslim religion, their origins were different, with Bengali people the majority in the eastern section. Punjabi, Sind, and Kashmiri people of Caucasian and Aryan extraction comprised the western portion.

At the time of the partition, Muslims who owned lands in the geographic area of India had been given land of similar size and value in Pakistan, and Hindus from Pakistan received comparable land in India. The reassigned lands were not always equal, and few felt they had received an equitable exchange. More than twelve million people were relocated in a mass confusion of moving people. Exact numbers were impossible to determine, but close to one million people were killed in what was called ethnic cleansing in later decades. Each sect fought the other. Rapes of women and massive pillaging and chaos made the partition a bloody terror for many people.

When we arrived in Pakistan, I wasn't aware that the country was only fifteen years old, a new nation still trying to live up to the dominion status of an independent nation. We heard from older Pakistanis the horrors that occurred, but now a guarded peace reigned between the neighboring countries.

The stereotypical dark-haired, brown-skinned Indian was not the only kind of people I saw as I walked along the Mall or in the bazaars of Lahore. Over the centuries, trade routes that crossed the subcontinent had brought people from many areas to settle in the fertile plains. I also saw people with fair hair and blue eyes. Although the majority of people were dark-haired with skin tones ranging from pale tan to dark brown, the vast variety of people interested me. Nearly all men had mustaches; some had a mustache and beard. Occasionally, redheaded people appeared in the crowds. The red hair, I learned, was the outward sign that the person had made a *Haj* (pilgrimage) to Mecca. Occasionally, Oriental heritage showed in the rounder faces and slanted eyes, probably people who had come from China through Nepal and the northern mountains.

Along streets like the Mall, at hotels, or the places where Western businessmen mixed with Pakistanis, men usually adopted a Western-style suit or wore a shirt, tie, and slacks in hot weather. Men who dressed in the Western fashion usually spoke English. The comfortable, baggy pants that looked like a wide W when stretched out to dry on a line, called *shalwar*, were the everyday cool drawstring pants. These pants were worn with a very long shirt with a placket of buttons almost to the waist called a *kameez*. White was the color worn by all the *bearers* or men with higher job status. *Homals* or *malis* (gardeners) with lower-status jobs might wear gray outfits cut exactly the same, though of material that was more coarse. Other workers who did heavy labor or of even lesser means preferred the *dhoti* (ankle-length cloth tied at the waist). Sometimes, the *dhoti* tail was tied between the legs and tied depending on the type of work being done.

Women in public covered themselves from head to toe with a *burqua* (a long, black garment with a sheer panel covering the face). Another style, less frequently seen, was a long, white *burqua* with a mesh insert of about four inches, an oval, so her eyes, nose, and mouth could be seen a little and allow the woman to breathe. These garments showed little of the woman but her hands and sandaled feet. Women in school or business were getting away from the custom of keeping their faces covered, but not all.

At hotels or restaurants where women might not wear a *burqua*, I noticed the styles of clothing women wore beneath the *burqua*. I found the women's *shalwar kameez*, a long, tuniclike dress (the *kameez*) worn over voluminous pants (*shalwar*) gathered at the waist, often with embroidery on the neck and sleeves was quite attractive. The outfit was completed with a matching scarf or *dupatta* that covered their long, black hair. Young girls ran by, their scarf draped across the front of their neck with the tails flying behind them, a flirty style that covered their body from head to foot. These *shalwar kameez* outfits were popular with students and often made of bright-colored, shiny fabrics. Women who worked wore the same style made of cotton or more practical fabrics. Pakistani women also wore the *sari*, a lovely six-yard length of fabric wrapped around the waist and tucked into a slip or drawstring to secure it. The remaining fabric was draped over the left shoulder. A matching blouse was always worn with the *sari* with a hint of bare midriff showing. The end of the *sari* could also be used to cover the head or pulled across the woman's face for modesty. Women appeared at dressy occasions wearing lovely silk *saris*.

I was curious to see the women behind the *burqua*. I smiled and waved when I saw girls riding on the back seat of a horse-drawn *tonga*. Several times, bold young women would pull back the sheer black veil of their *burqua*, show their face, and laugh at their brazen behavior. I took this as a sign of friendship and waved back with a smile. I was eager to make friends in my new home.

◇◇◇◇◇

MY DAYS QUICKLY FILLED WITH baking bread, shopping for vegetables, writing letters home to our families, and learning about this strange new culture. I found myself alternately fascinated and puzzled by the customs. The one thing I was most curious about remained unexplained by the Faroukis or other Pakistanis we met socially. The custom of covering the women with a *burqua* baffled me. Why could only her father, brothers, and spouse see a woman's face after puberty? How could she have any kind of social life from behind the shroud she was required to wear all the time? How did women go to school or ask questions from behind this veil, or could they take it off in class? Few explanations had satisfied my primary question. Why?

American women in our host country were encouraged to dress modestly. I never went out to shop in sleeveless or low-cut dresses. Jim told me about one American woman who had attracted attention to herself in a negative way.

"One American woman who lives in Lahore goes to the bazaars with pink rollers in her hair. The Pakistanis think all American women go out with their hair rolled up. But the day she showed up in shorts and a halter top, she caused a near riot." From his expression, he didn't find it amusing.

"I wouldn't want to create such a bad impression, Jim, and you know I don't go out without doing my hair."

He smiled, remembering the times he waited while I combed my hair. "Just wanted to pass it along. Anti-American sentiment is prevalent, and with so many colleges here in Lahore, the younger men are sometimes radical in their opinions."

◇◇◇◇◇

ONE DAY WHILE I WATCHED the boys get acquainted with other children at the playground, I saw Claire Keller, whom I'd met last week. She looked lovely in a bright green dress that showed off her stately figure. She joined me to watch the boys. Her *bearer*, Khan, appeared and took her parcels to their apartment. As we chatted, I mentioned the girls who showed their faces from the back seat of the *tonga* as we drove behind them. I told her of my curiosity about the practice of covering the faces of women.

Khan reappeared to ask Claire a question. She'd listened to me as I tried to understand the practice of *purdah*. Claire turned to Khan.

"I think Khan might be able to explain it to you better than I can," Claire said, introducing me to her *bearer*.

He greeted me with the traditional *salaam* with hands to his forehead, lips, and chest.

"Khan, can you explain to Mrs. Aylworth about *purdah*? Tell her the story you told me, *shukreah*, please," Clair asked.

"Yes, *memsahib*." He nodded.

Khan leaned against a tree beside where we sat watching the children and began his story. "Maybe Khan has a nice she, but not so pretty she. Maybe she has bad eye. Maybe buck teeth. [Khan's remaining teeth were quite bucked.] Maybe have pockmarked face. By and by, she go down street. Men look at my she. Say, 'Oh, look, Khan's she not pretty she

... have buck teeth or pockmarked face. Ha ha. Khan's she homely she.' They make fun Khan's she. Or maybe Khan's she pretty she. She go down street. Other man look Khan's she and say, 'I like Khan's she. She pretty she. I like take Khan's she for my she.' By and by, Khan and she in house in middle of night and 'Rap rap rap.'" Khan demonstrates by rapping on the bench. "Khan hear noise. Go outside to see what make noise. Man on roof shoot Khan. Bang! Khan finished."

With this description of his hypothetical murder, Khan threw his arms wide and his head back and to one side, shut his eyes, and looked solemn. "By and by, police come. Ask questions. But man who shot Khan run away. Police not know who shot Khan.

"By and by, maybe three months go by. Man come to my parents, say, 'I like this she. I take her for my wife.' My parents not know this man same man that finished Khan." Again, he threw his arms out and resumed the deathlike pose. "They say, 'Yes, marry this man.' So man get my she, and Khan finished. But if she wear *burqua*, other man not know if she pretty, she homely, she young, or she old. Then he not finish Khan to get Khan's pretty she." Khan stopped to let the impact of his story settle.

Khan went on. "My first she, very pretty she. My uncle say, 'Don't take that she for wife. She too pretty. Be bad she.' I not listen to my uncle. I like that she so I marry she. We live in Karachi. I make good money. Bring all money to she. She spend my money. We have two bungalows and twelve nice, fat chickens. Very nice to live in Karachi. But one night, Khan come home. She not home. By and by, she come. Khan say, 'Where do you go?' She say, 'Oh, business in Karachi.' Many nights, Khan come home. She come home midnight. One night, she go out. Khan follow. She get on bus. Khan get on back of bus." Khan indicated by compressing his body to about half his standing height. "Scoot down and hide so she not see Khan. Bus go downtown Karachi. She get off bus. Khan get off bus and follow. As my she walk down street, throw back *burqua*. She have eyes all painted, lips painted, fingernails painted. She get in rickshaw. Khan lose she. Khan go home. By and by, she come home.

"'Where you been?' Khan say. 'Oh, business in Karachi.' Khan say, 'Here, you take two bungalows, take twelve fat chickens, take all my clothes, but get out.' Cost Khan four rupees to get papers for divorce. By and by, Khan go visit uncle in Rawalpindi. Tell uncle about bad she. Uncle say, 'You want this little girl, my niece, for your wife?' Khan say,

'Yes, I like your girl for my wife.' Khan go back to Karachi and work. After two years, come back, get uncle's daughter, and marry she. This one very good she. Wear *burqua*. Have two fine children, one boy three years, one girl two years old. This she good wife for Khan."

When Khan finished his story, Claire and I laughed in appreciation of his explanation of *purdah*.

Claire and her husband, also named Jim, had no children. She told me of the activities she had found to keep busy in Lahore—bridge, dinners, the American Women's Club, and the French lessons she was starting in January. I wanted to take lessons, too, and I knew that French would be useful on our trip home through Europe.

"Before I can plan anything, I need to be sure the *ayah* I just hired is able to take care of the boys," I told her. "Then I'd love to take French lessons with you."

"Great. We can share a taxi to Mrs. Martin's home. That's where she teaches. The lessons start in January."

"Jim is opposed to having servants, but he finally agreed to an *ayah*. So far, she's on a trial basis."

"Even with two of us, servants are necessary here in this heat," Claire said. "If the *ayah* you have doesn't work out, you will soon have *ayahs* knocking at your door. The word of mouth advertises very rapidly. The servants have already noticed you and your sons as newcomers."

Thanksgiving Gift Turkeys

THE TUESDAY BEFORE THANKSGIVING, JIM looked up from his work and saw Rashid, the supply truck driver, enter the Lahore office. Rashid drove a large flatbed truck each Monday, Wednesday, and Friday from Lahore to the project 135 miles north, loaded with materials for Mangla Dam. He returned to Lahore on Tuesday, Thursday, and Saturday. The driver and his assistant shuttled the items Jim purchased locally as well as those that arrived by air from the States. On the return trip to Lahore, the truck was often empty except for our commissary order.

"*Sahib*, we have a gift for you and Ziemer *sahib*. Mohammed Jamil in Rawalpindi sent them with us for your holiday for give thanks. He knew Americans like to eat turkeys on your special celebration. He sent two, one for Ziemer *sahib* and one for you."

"Fine. Thank you, Rashid. Just put them on the counter." Jim didn't look up from his paperwork.

The sky had darkened as evening decended. Jim wanted to finish and go home.

"They are now standing in front of the counter, *sahib*. Where do you wish me to put them?"

With that statement, Jim realized that the turkeys were alive. He walked

85

to the front of the office and peered over the counter. Two gray and black turkeys stood there, huddled in fear.

"Well, Rashid, let's put them in the cab of the pickup," Jim said.

As they loaded the turkeys, Ghulam, John Ziemer's driver, shook his head and turned to Jim. "*Sahib*, male bird not look good. Head down, weak, not going to live long. Better hit him in head tonight."

When Jim arrived home, he took Alam aside. "Until we can decide what to do with these turkeys, let's put them in one of the vacant servants' quarters for tonight."

Alam and Jim disappeared around the building with the birds, a pan for water, and a box of cereal for their dinner.

The following morning, Jim arranged to board the turkeys at the race-track with a veterinarian, Dr. Fazel-al-Din. The charge for their board was one rupee per bird per day.

Jim came in and told me, "We have a fine turkey for Thanksgiving dinner, a gift from a vendor near Rawalpindi. He sent two on the truck, one for Ziemers and one for us. The only problem is they're alive, so I boarded them at the racetrack with their vet."

Live birds were something I hadn't even considered as something to serve for Thanksgiving dinner. We'd been invited to the Baxters, a British family who lived in the flat next door, who were planning a potluck dinner for residents of WAPDA Flats. What would we do with a whole turkey with just the four of us? We'd have turkey leftovers forever. I'd think about it later.

We'd forgotten about the turkeys for the next few days. The Lahore office had a telegram from the main office that the company's new pilot, Ken Benesh, was flying to Karachi on a commercial carrier to take delivery of the company's new corporate airplane. The message said he'd meet the manufacturer's representative in Karachi. When he'd checked out the new airplane, he'd be arriving in Lahore any day with the new acquisition. This plane would save the executives many hours on the road to attend meetings with the Water and Power Authority of West Pakistan in Lahore or Karachi. Old-timers seemed amazed that the old-fashioned, fiscally conservative company would spend money on a private jet. The powers-that-be decided the time element and the early completion bonus were incentive enough to invest in the corporate aircraft.

The time it would save would more than offset the expense.

Ken's reputation preceded him to Lahore. Jim told me Ken was a military pilot and earned a reputation for his expert flying under battle conditions. Ken was one of the last planes out of Manila when the Japanese invaded the Philippines. Ken had landed and rescued American nurses who'd been imprisoned during the siege. He sounded like a hero from the stories we'd heard. I hoped I'd have a chance to meet him.

Jim came home a few nights after receiving the telegram with another man. I wiped my hands on a dishtowel and came into the living room to meet him.

"This is Ken Benesh," Jim said. "Have we got enough for one more for dinner?"

The pilot had a boyish grin, bright blue eyes with a twinkle of mischief, and a warm manner.

"Of course we do." I'd sent Alam to the market the day before where he'd bought local meat. "My last commissary order hasn't arrived, or we might have pork chops or chicken. We're having local stew meat tonight."

"Sounds good to me," Ken said with a smile. "Who are these guys?"

Mark and Kevin came in to meet Ken, who offered his hand in a grown-up fashion. Within minutes, they took him to see their toys, like he was their new playmate. Ken had three children of his own, so Kevin's eagerness to play or our loquacious Mark didn't bother him.

"My wife Lovelle and our three children should be here sometime next week," Ken said. "She wanted to spend a little time in Hawaii before the children had to start school."

Mangla International School had opened on schedule in early November.

"Did I hear that your wife was also a pilot?" Jim asked.

"Yes, Lovelle was in the WACs during the war and ferried planes all over the country," Ken said. "We met at the Houston base when I came home."

"We heard about your flight out of Manila at the end of the war," Jim said. "That sounded like a hair-raising mission."

Ken was modest. "Those nurses were so starved that they weighed next to nothing. It was easy to carry them to the airplane, toss one in, and go after another." Ken's self-effacing manner endeared him to us right away.

By the end of the evening, Ken felt like an old friend.

The next day, Ken took us out to the airport to see the company plane, a brand-new, dazzling white Aero Commander. A Pakistani crew was polishing the plane. One eager fellow started to wipe the windshield with a cloth he'd been using on the body of the plane.

"No, no, no!" Ken shouted.

That was the only time I had ever heard Ken raise his voice.

He rushed over to the aircraft, shouting and waving his arms. "The windshield is fiberglass. If there's a speck of dirt on the rag, it'll scratch the soft plastic," he said to the worker who spoke English.

The crew continued polishing the plane under Ken's watchful eye. Ken had a special cloth for the windshield so his visibility wouldn't be compromised.

Ken remained in Lahore for several days. Early Thanksgiving morning, he stopped by to pick up Jim and John Ziemer. They left for the airport, and after seeing how Ken scrutinized the Pakistani workers, I assumed Jim and John had offered to help him clean the airplane more to Ken's liking than the local crew.

I kept busy that day preparing food for the community potluck dinner that afternoon. I hadn't thought much about our British neighbors hosting Thanksgiving. Perhaps they'd forgiven the Americans for the revolution two centuries ago. Perhaps they were as relieved as we were over the resolution of the Cuban Missile Crisis. This Thanksgiving, we really had something to be grateful for that warranted a celebration.

Jim, John, and Ken returned in the early afternoon. They were all smiles, like they'd been up to some mischief. John waved as he climbed the stairs to his apartment to get Dorothy. Ken teased Mark and Kevin while I put finishing touches on the food I was taking to the potluck. Ken and Jim helped me carry the food next door.

"Welcome. Come on in. So glad you could come," Mrs. Baxter greeted us.

We introduced Ken and joined the neighbors already gathered. Mrs. Baxter had one room set up with toys for the children where they would eat. I looked in often and saw that my boys were happy to be playing with the other children.

We met several other neighbors I'd seen but not talked to. One was a woman named Helen Bentley, an American from Massachusetts. She mentioned that she rode horseback. I listened as she spoke to a couple next to us.

"I exercise a jumper for a British friend who has no time for his horse," she said.

"I rode horseback all the time on our ranch in Nevada," I said. "I'd love to ride."

"You could join the Rangers. They have army horses that are mustered out of the service when they're eight years old. The Rangers teach equestrian lessons three days a week at the Army Cantonment's practice ring. There's a small fee, but it isn't expensive," she said.

A little later, I spoke with Claire Keller, whom I had enjoyed talking to at the playground. I liked Claire and her sense of humor. She had flaming red hair and wore an electric blue dress that brought out her ivory skin and blue eyes. The Kellers were from Michigan, and he worked for Harza Engineering, one of the consultants in the Mangla Dam project consortium.

Later that night, Jim told me they had not just cleaned the airplane. They had flown the Aero Commander around Lahore and a little north so Ken could get a feel for the terrain and weather.

"It's a great little plane, and Ken is a swell pilot," Jim said. "He flew us up to Nowshera, the home base for the Pakistan Army Tank Corps. Ken had heard us talking in the office about that oversized flatbed car. The Pakistan army has only one oversized car big enough to transport the screw for the tunnel-boring machine, but they couldn't find it. Each division I contacted thought another one had the car. I kept meeting with dead ends, but we found it today." Jim grinned. He was elated.

The tunnel-boring machine was essentially a large screw that would bore thirty-six-foot-diameter tunnels to bring the water to the powerhouse. This specialized machine was essential in the sequence of events necessry for the critical schedule to be completed for early diversion of the river on schedule. Jim had told me of his frustration looking for the missing railcar. He was sure the car was at Wah army base just north of the job site, but he'd been too busy to drive there to look for it.

"I was convinced after looking at all the army logs that it must be at one of the army bases, and that's right where we found it, but not at Wah, but at Nowshera!" Jim grinned.

"Wouldn't any railcar work?" I asked.

"No, the boring shaft of the Mole is so big that it wouldn't fit in regular flatcars. I measured them myself to be sure. Now, I need to get the army to move that car to Karachi so the boring shaft can be hauled eight hundred miles to the job."

It didn't sound like an easy thing to accomplish, but nothing on the project had been easy.

As we put the boys to bed and turned off the lights, we talked about the neighbors we were getting acquainted with in our new home. After just five weeks, so much had changed in our lives. Shopping to find ordinary consumer goods was challenging and at times frustrating. The compensating factor for me was that Lahore was a vibrant city, full of energy and excitement against a backdrop of intrigue and stories.

◇◇◇◇◇

CHRISTMAS WAS JUST FOUR WEEKS away. I hoped to find some decorations and toys for our sons. It was also my birthday, but I didn't expect much since Christmas for the boys was my priority.

Early the next Sunday morning, our doorbell rang. I opened the door to find a Pakistani man who wore a Western-style suit and a solemn expression.

"Good morning, Memsahib. I am Doctor Fazel-al-Din, the veterinarian. It is my sad duty to inform you that, in spite of my best ministrations of antibiotic therapy, the male bird has met with an untimely demise. If you would, please step outside and have a look. I have the remains in my car so you can see he is finished."

Identify a dead turkey? I was dumfounded. I really hadn't seen the turkey the night they brought it in because it was dark. How would I recognize it? The doctor noted my hesitation, and Alam arrived at that moment.

"Or, if you prefer, you could send your servant out to see the bird," Dr. Fazel-al-Din said.

That sounded like a much better idea, so I sent Alam outside with the doctor. He could view the corpse. At first I didn't understand why, but I learned he felt he had to show us the corpse to assure us that the doctor hadn't cooked the turkey for himself.

When Alam returned, he nodded his head. "Is finished, *memsahib*."

That was the end of one gift bird.

Alam Cooks a Turkey

THE SECOND EDITION OF THE *Baral Town Crier*, the American colony's weekly newsletter arrived in mid-November. Baral Colony was growing fast with new families arriving at the rate of three families per day since early October. The paper printed the newcomer's names and addresses on the front page of each edition. Atkinson was a family-owned company and understood that a man with his wife to go home to each evening would be happier and more productive. As soon as each house was completed, a family was cleared to travel to Pakistan.

The long separation was the most difficult part of the decision to accept the job. Most families flew from Karachi to Rawalpindi's small airport, though some were routed through Lahore. Dorothy and I kept busy greeting friends from previous jobs as well as those newly hired for the Mangla project. The two vacant apartments at WAPDA Flats provided additional quarters when needed for these travelers. Dorothy and I often made impromptu potluck dinners and invited people to join us, knowing how tired they were. We got news from home in return, sometimes even a recent newspaper or magazine.

The *Baral Town Crier* had listings for clubs of all kinds that were forming. I was envious of the activities the people at Baral had available all within the town. One article in large bold type caught my attention:

91

EXAMINATIONS, VACCINATIONS, AND IMMUNIZATIONS OF PERSONAL SERVANTS

Baral Colony medical records indicate that a number of servants now employed by personnel residing in Baral Colony have not been physically examined and have not received the required vaccinations and immunizations. In order to provide a sound basis for a healthy community, all personnel are required to have their personal servants examined and immunized immediately.

We discussed the article with the Ziemers. Alam and Afsar had been working for the company for several months, but the *ayah* had been with us for only a week. We decided we should send all three to Dr. Selzer for the exams right away. John Ziemer verified that the company would pay for their exams, just as they did at Baral Colony for their servants. Dorothy telephoned Dr. Selzer for an appointment.

The next morning, I watched Alam, Afsar, and Miriam leave for the appointment. Dr. Selzer telephoned Dorothy before they returned with the results. Alam and Afsar each received a clean bill of health. The *ayah*, however, had chronic amoebic dysentery. Dr. Selzer said the *ayah*'s condition made her unsuitable to care for children or to prepare food. My heart sank at the possibility the woman may have spread disease to my children.

I called her in and explained the company's rules. "Here's your pay through the rest of the week, but we cannot employ you with the condition the doctor found. He said you have amoebic dysentery. He said it isn't safe for you to work with children."

"No, is not possible, *memsahib*," she said. "I not sick. Never be sick." She argued with me, fingering the bills I handed her.

Alam overheard our conversation and explained to her in Urdu. I heard him explain with a few English words sprinkled in, like "company" and "regulation." She nodded and accepted Alam's explanation. She gathered her *sari* and left, not even saying good-bye to the boys.

I was relieved to have a reason to fire her. I knew her nosy personality and phobias would annoy me more as time went by. The thought had crossed my mind that I'd need to find a replacement in time, so this medical issue precipitated my decision. She was not an easy personality to get along with, unlike Alam, who went about his work with quiet competence.

Alam had previously worked for a British family. He spoke English quite well and could interpret for the other servants or people who came to the door. He was well trained in unobtrusive, silent service, speaking only when spoken to and not volunteering his opinions. I appreciated his demeanor and dignified bearing. He was easy to have around, and he always appeared at just the moment when he was needed. I called it his radar. The *ayah*, on the other hand, had filled the room with her presence and endless questions, not many related to her job. When she was in the room, I could not write letters, read, or do anything but listen to her.

Although the *ayah* had given me a brief glimpse of life with someone to care for the boys, I was relieved to terminate her before the two-week trial was over. Once again, I found myself with no babysitter.

With her gone, we settled into a routine of going to the playground in the early mornings while it was cool and my bread was rising. If I had shopping to do, I took the boys with me in a taxi. A round trip to the Mall cost less than two dollars in American money. Sooner or later, I hoped we'd find another *ayah*. Next time, the medical exam would be first.

Alam and I discussed the babysitting problem. I couldn't let the boys play on the slide or swings without supervision. Cars frequently whipped around the building, so they couldn't even cross the driveway without an adult.

"*Memsahib*, you like *ayah*? Or maybe young man be okay to watch boys?" Alam asked.

I thought about that for a moment. Why not?

"If he likes children, that might be okay, Alam," I answered.

Dorothy came in the next day, bursting with news. George Archibald, the general manager of the Mangla project, had stopped in Lahore and then flown on to meetings in Karachi. Dorothy met him on his stop at the Lahore office. He told her we could use his Mercury sedan and his driver, Bashir, while he was away. We were delighted to have a car and driver for two days.

"Let's do some shopping. Do you think we should pick up that turkey and have it for dinner the day George returns from Karachi?"

"Great idea," I said.

This was a perfect opportunity to cook the second gift bird. Christmas was still a few weeks away when we might want a turkey. But at one rupee per day for the board bill, it was becoming too expensive a gift to keep the bird much longer.

We took Mark and Kevin with us that morning in the comfort of the spacious American sedan. Dorothy knew of a dressmaker on a side street off the Mall. While the tailor measured Dorothy, the boys and I walked around, looking into the nearby store windows. Shopkeepers displayed merchandise outside to attract customers.

"Ah, fine *babas, memsahib*," one merchant called as I looked at his display of block print tablecloths.

"This paisley pattern is lovely, and unlike anything I'd seen," I said, holding the most vibrant, crisp pattern up for closer inspection.

"We make with special process, first one color, hand-stamped. Then next color. Very best cotton is from Madras cotton, the finest." He held up a bolt of fabric, then another.

The selection was amazing and tempting, as Margaret Platt had written in her letter. I restrained myself from buying dress fabric until my sewing machine arrived, but I couldn't resist a colorful block print tablecloth. It was washable and compatible with the colors in our apartment. The shopkeeper took my rupees and put his palms together as we left his shop.

Dorothy finished her discussion with the tailor who wore a *karakul* hat of unborn lamb's wool. Dorothy selected a shirtdress from an ancient pattern book in his shop. The tailor measured the fabric she'd bought in Hong Kong and nodded. It was enough. We left with an appointment for a fitting next week. I decided I'd bring a dress I liked on our next visit. He assured me that he could copy it. We were both happy she had found a tailor to make women's clothes. A new dress should be ready after only one or two fittings. The cost of the tailor was more than the *dherzie* who came to the house, but he could fit women't clothing, and a dress was still a bargain.

Next, we stopped at the shoemaker's shop where the boys were measured for oxfords. The shoemaker measured their feet several times, jotting down the measurements on a notepad. The shoes would take at least two fittings, so it would be Christmas or maybe New Year's when they would be ready. Their shoes were already looking scuffed and felt tight. Although I had bought new shoes in larger sizes, we had no news of when our shipment, including those shoes, would arrive. They needed the shoemaker's shoes and soon.

When we pulled in to WAPDA Flats, Dorothy asked, "Why don't the boys stay with me while you take Bashir and Alam to pick up the turkey? There won't be room for all of us in the car."

"That's fine with me if you don't mind," I said.

Alam held the back door for me and explained our errand to Bashir as he climbed into the front seat. Bashir and Alam were silent during the short trip to the racetrack. Alam probably told him the turkey we were going to get was alive. I wondered how much Dr. Fazel-al-Din would charge for his ministrations and antibiotic therapy for the deceased male bird. We also owed nearly two week's board bill for the remaining bird. At the racecourse, Bashir parked behind the stables next to a building with Dr. Fazel-al-Din's name above the door.

We found the doctor inside, now dressed in a work outfit of khaki pants and shirt. He greeted me, and we settled the bill for twenty rupees. Then he led us to the stable. Here, our turkey lived in relative luxury, deep in straw and clucking happily. Alam picked it up and held the turkey, who protested loudly, in the front seat between his knees.

Bashir failed to hide his disdain at conveying this lowly creature in the big boss' car. Mr. Archibald was the *pukah sahib* (most important man) on the Mangla Dam project. Bashir enjoyed the status of being Mr. Archibald's personal driver. He grumbled softly in Urdu. To avoid having anyone see his unorthodox front seat passenger, Bashir drove to the side gate of WAPDA Flats, used most often by merchants and servants. Dorothy came around the building as we parked.

"That looks like a fine bird. I'll make the stuffing, and if you have some fresh rolls and some vegetables, we'll have a good dinner." Dorothy's brow wrinkled as she approached the problem. "I can cook it, but we may need some help to get it ready for the oven." Dorothy was trying to avoid mentioning the murder that was a necessary step before cooking the bird. "How much did the vet charge?" She changed the subject.

"I ransomed it from a luxury stall for twenty rupees," I told her. "Dorothy, I grew up on a ranch in Nevada and watched our hired man kill chickens all the time." Memories of my childhood came to mind of the ranch where a block of wood, a hatchet, and flying feathers were part of the process of preparing a chicken for Sunday dinner.

"I'll tell Alam how to do it."

I remembered how the hired man chopped off the head, hung the chickens by their feet to bleed, and finally gutted and plucked them. When he finished, my mother handed me a pair of tweezers to help her remove the pinfeathers. Most of our laying hens ended up cut and frozen in the big chest freezer in the fall.

Alam stood holding the bird. Bashir produced a large rag and dusted the front seat. He used a whisk broom to remove any telltale feathers left by the bird in the few blocks the turkey had been in the car.

I ignored Bashir's fussing and turned to Alam. "Do you know how to kill a turkey?"

I wasn't sure where Alam would find the necessary axe, but I imagined there would be a suitable tool in the servant's quarters. They probably butchered chickens all the time. Alam was a man. Surely he would know what to do.

"Yes, *memsahib*, I know." He dismissed my concern, acting insulted that I, a woman at least ten years younger than he, should offer any instructions.

Alam had a fair knowledge of English for everyday things, but I was never quite sure how much he understood directions in English. I wanted him to know one important step to getting the feathers off. I remembered my mother carrying buckets full of hot water to the chicken yard.

"Alam, after you kill it, if you dip it in hot water, the feathers will come off easier." I gestured the up-and-down motion of dunking the turkey in hot water.

"Yes, *memsahib*, I know. Is no problem."

"Good. If you kill and clean it, we'll cook it for Mr. Archibald's dinner tomorrow night."

Bashir's eyebrows raised when I mentioned this bird was for his boss' dinner. Maybe now he'd forgive me for bringing the turkey home in the car. Alam nodded and looked like he understood.

I collected the boys from Dorothy and left on another errand while I had Bashir and the car. Bashir had forgiven me, and he took us to the shopping area where I wanted to look for holiday decorations.

When we returned about an hour later, I opened the door, and the most horrible odor greeted me. It was a hot day, and clouds of steam poured from the kitchen. Alam and Afsar were scrubbing the entry floor, squatting on their haunches, oblivious to the obnoxious odor spilling from the kitchen. The large oval, stainless steel roasting pan straddled two front burners of the stove. Both burners were turned on high, the electric coils glowing a bright red. The roaster pan top didn't fit on the pan's bottom because of the clumps of wet black and gray feathers protruding between the top and bottom. I grabbed two potholders and lifted the top. In the boiling water sat the turkey with feathers and entrails all still intact. Even the feet stuck out over the edge of the pan. Only the head was missing. The pungent odor of wet feathers nearly knocked me over.

"Alam, *firsh sofacarow* (first clean it)!" I gestured with a knife to cut the stomach and then pantomimed removing the entrails. "After that, we cook it."

I rushed around, turning on the ceiling fans, trying to get the horrible smell of steamed feathers and cooked entrails out of the apartment.

"We weren't going to cook it until tomorrow." I looked at what appeared to be a well-done turkey drumstick.

Alam bristled at what he perceived to be my criticism. He didn't see anything wrong with what he'd done. I'd wanted to cook the turkey, didn't I? He drew himself up to his full height, which was a few inches shorter than me. He spoke in Urdu to Afsar. They took a butcher knife and spread newspapers on the kitchen floor. They were prepared to remove the entrails as I'd demonstrated.

"No, Alam, not here. Outside."

I opened the kitchen door to the hallway, shooing them and the offensive-smelling bird out of sight and smelling range. Bashir hovered in the hallway. He was wide-eyed as they carried the carcass of his recent passenger outside.

The doorbell rang, and I opened the door. Dorothy Ziemer stood there, wrinkling her nose. She saw the stricken look on my face. I couldn't get a word out of my mouth, I was so flustered.

"What happened? Are the boys all right?" She sniffed again. "What is that awful smell?"

I pointed to the now-empty pan of boiling water with feathers still clinging to the edges. She looked and held her nose as she helped me open windows, trying to get fresh air inside to dissipate the offensive odor. We sprayed deodorizer and even some of my perfume in the air. The tenacious odor clung to the steam and permeated the apartment.

Alam returned to show us the bird, now naked and done to a turn. Without its entrails and feathers, it looked almost edible, but an unappetizing odor still emanated from the bird.

"You look, *memsahib*. Is clean now." Alam looked hopefully at me.

"Thank you, Alam, but we have to throw it out." I sent him out again with the turkey, hoping that was the end of our second gift bird.

"I have some hamburger in the freezer," Dorothy said. "Guess we'll make meatloaf for dinner tomorrow night. George won't mind."

Once past the horror, we began to laugh about the turkey episode. "I am so relieved nothing was wrong with the boys," Dorothy said. "The look on your face really scared me."

The next day, Alam asked for an hour off to do some errands. He returned carrying a live turkey. It squirmed in his arms, and he set it down in the entry hall.

"You check up, *memsahib*. Feel how fat. Is good turkey for dinner. Is okay?" He gave the bird a gentle squeeze, urging me to feel how fat it was. I praised his choice, and I was touched at his gesture, but I wasn't sure I could deal with another live bird. The odor of those wet feathers remained fresh in my mind.

Alam had paid thirty rupees for the replacement turkey, one quarter of his monthly salary. He had nobly tried to make restitution in the way he felt best, but we knew what a hardship that expense would be to his wife and three children. Over his protestations, we reimbursed him.

Sherif, Our New Bearer

CLAIRE WAS RIGHT. THE DOORBELL began to ring right after breakfast the next morning. The *malis* (gardeners) appeared with bunches of flowers to sell, cut from the beds around our building. The *chowkidar* (watchman) was ordered to keep the gates closed until visitors were identified and approved. Delivery trucks were allowed if the resident gave him instructions that someone was expected and so were visitors or those who were known to the watchman. I arranged with the watchman to expect the buffalo milk deliveryman. The dairy would deliver milk in bottles every other day. Since the milk was not pasteurized, I had to boil the milk and skim it as Dr. Selzer had instructed. It seemed like a lot of work to do, but the boy's ready acceptance of the water buffalo milk made the pasteurizing process worth the effort. Another man appeared with fresh eggs in his large apron. He carried it carefully, opening it to show me his precious eggs, some white and some brown. I brought a bowl from the kitchen, and he selected a dozen for me. The egg seller provided a convenience I appreciated.

Alam arrived early one morning at the end of November with a young man.

"This is Sherif, *memsahib*. He want to be *bearer* for *memsahib*." Alam introduced the shy boy standing beside him.

Sherif had a slight build and light tan skin. Like Alam, he had wavy hair, hazel eyes, and a neat mustache. He spoke very little English, but he was clean and seemed eager to learn. His face broke into smile the minute he saw the boys.

"I train him. Make good *bearer, memsahib,*" Alam said. "He very much like children."

That was obvious to me as I watched them laugh and interact. The language barrier seemed less important. I hadn't considered hiring a young man to care for children, but Sherif took a liking to Mark and Kevin, and they liked him right away. Perhaps a male would have more respect from Mark, who ignored the *ayah.* They loved to play on the slide, and the dangerous gap worried me. First, however, we had to have Dr. Selzer give him the required medical tests. Alam gave him directions to Dr. Selzer's office. Later that day, Dr. Selzer called Dorothy to report Sherif had a clean bill of health.

Sherif became our *bearer* and child attendant. I wasn't sure what to call a male who served as an *ayah.* Sherif saw to it that the boys enjoyed having fun, yet he had a good instinct for danger. I liked the young man, and I told Alam that we would give Sherif a two-week trial.

Now Sherif needed uniforms. Alam reminded me of the *dherzie* (tailor) who worked for ten rupees a day, a little over two dollars. A few days later, the tailor arrived carrying his portable sewing machine. He bowed as he greeted me and selected a place to work on the front terrace. First, he spread a large, white cloth and placed his hand-cranked sewing machine on it. He was ready to work. He measured Sherif and then cut the fabric he'd spread on the cloth. By the end of the first day, he had sewed a shirt and started a pair of pants. Sherif needed three sets of uniforms to allow for washing. The *dherzie* also made new uniforms for Alam and Afsar. I was impressed at how quickly and accurately he cut on the fabric without a pattern. As he sewed, his toes held the fabric being fed into the back of the machine while his hands pulled and coaxed the garment into the final shape. His hand-cranked machine was in the middle of the circle made by his arms and legs.

As he was finishing the uniforms, I showed the tailor one of Mark's shirts that I'd like copied. He studied it for a few minutes. The shirt had short sleeves but was the same cut as men's long shirts. Within an hour, he copied it, adding a little room for growth. At the end of the week, for about fourteen dollars in American money, plus the cost of the cloth, we had three new uniforms for Sherif and three new shirts for Mark. I was impressed with the speed and focus of his efforts. After the first day, I almost forgot he was there, he was so quiet and unobtrusive.

On each trip to the bazaars, I looked for plastic pants for Kevin but there were none to be found. I wrote to Jim's mother, Grace Aylworth, and asked her to buy some and slip them inside pages of a woman's magazine. Jim's mother was a wonderful correspondent who answered my frequent aerograms right away. Her letters contained endless questions about the boys and the way we were. I told Grace that the plastic pants could be shipped flat in a magazine marked "reading material." The 300 percent import duty on a two-dollar pair of plastic pants seemed excessive, and they were a necessity. Weeks later, a bundle of magazines arrived with two new pairs of plastic pants tucked inside the *Ladies Home Journal*. I was pleased to have more changes for Kevin.

Each day, I hoped for mail from my mother. Only one brief note arrived the week after we did. I knew Mother was busy with her beauty shop, my teenage sisters, and the two rental cabins. We were so far from home, and I wanted some contact with her. I hadn't written to either her or Jim's parents about the possibility of our evacuation. I didn't want to worry our families.

◇◇◇◇◇

ONE EVENING, JIM PULLED INTO the yard while the children were still playing. Kevin ran for Jim. Mark turned to look just as another toddler threw a handful of sand directly into Mark's ear. Mark screamed. I tried to clean it out, but he cried louder. This was not something I should try to do myself, and I was afraid. Jim agreed, so we put the boys in the pickup and hurried to Dr. Selzer's office. The doctor lavaged the sand from Mark's ear, gently squeezing warm water from a syringe into his ear. Grains of sand flowed with the water into a basin he'd placed beneath Mark's head.

When he finished taking care of Mark's ear and my son's tears stopped, Dr. Selzer had other news for us. "Yesterday, I was called to the dairy with the water buffalo to treat one of the boys who milks the cows. He has typhus, and I had to quarantine the dairy. Their milk is no longer safe to drink." Dr. Selzer looked sad at his news. "Even with the pasteurizing process, it is too dangerous for you to drink."

"Let me take a look at Mark's eyes." The doctor lifted Mark to the examination table and looked at Mark's red eyes. "He has trachoma. I'll give you ointment for his eyes. Lay a thin line in the lower lid of each eye twice a day, and gently smooth it around both eyes. Trachoma is prevalent here. He may have rubbed his eyes with his hands, causing the bacteria to enter."

As we drove home, it occurred to me that we might not have known about the typhus outbreak at the dairy if Mark hadn't had the accident with the sand in his ear. Would the doctor have notified his patients? Even though we had all had typhus immunizations and I had boiled the milk as he'd instructed, could we have contracted typhus if we had continued to use the milk?

I sent an order to the American commissary, adding powdered milk, canned evaporated milk, and cocoa. By mixing them as Dorothy did, I hoped it would taste enough like cow's milk for the boys to drink it. The buffalo milk had been wonderful for a short time.

The instructions for the eye ointment said to put a small amount inside the lower eyelid and rub it gently to spread to around in the eye. Mark laid his head in my lap and relaxed as I put the ointment is as directed and gently massaged his eyelid.

◇◇◇◇◇

As the days passed, I saw a wonderful bond developing between Sherif, Mark, and Kevin

"Alam, how did you find Sherif? How did you know he would like to take care of my boys?" I felt this was a rare coincidence that such a likable young man appeared just when we needed him.

"Is my cousin-brother, *memsahib*. His mother and my father are brother and sister, so he's my cousin-brother. Good Kashmiri boy. Big family. All very much love children."

"Could you interpret so I can show him how to make bread?"

Bread making had become a time-consuming job, and I could use some help. Sherif was eager to learn any skills that would help elevate him to a *bearer*'s position in the future. The pay scale for a *bearer* was higher and even more for a cook. Many cooks/*bearers* served both functions in smaller households like ours.

"No problem, *memsahib*. You show and tell him how much to put in," Alam said.

The next day, I showed Sherif, with Alam interpreting, how to test the water temperature, dissolve the yeast, and then add the flour, milk, and a little sugar and salt. He repeated each ingredient and amount. I showed him how to let it rise with a cloth over it for an hour or so. We came back to find the dough had risen to a mound above the bowl. Then I showed him how to punch it down, fold it over, cover it again with the cloth, and wait another hour. After the next rising, we formed the dough into two loaves and put it in the greased pans. When it rose again, I told Sherif that our bread was ready to bake. He nodded and slid the pans into the preheated oven.

When the bread came out of the oven, Sherif beamed with a sense of accomplishment. We had made bread, and it was delicious. Sherif had a high degree of intelligence, but sadly, he had never gone to school or learned to read and write.

Jim's story that night was not as positive as the progress I had made with Sherif. He poured a drink and sat down to relax before dinner. The boys had been fed some time before and were in their pajamas when he got home. Two dinners as well as two breakfasts were necessary in our family with Jim's long hours.

"Ken, John, and I got chewed out for the ride in the company plane on Thanksgiving," he said. "I'm sure it was because we rode in the plane before George Archibald. However, he told Ken that it was because company life insurance covered all three of us. He told Ken that he was flying a payload with four death benefits due if we'd crashed. And that would have made the company's insurance rates go up. The thing that saved us from serious trouble was that we found the missing oversized flatcar at Nowshera. Now we have a way to move the Mole from Karachi to the job site."

Lahore, the Pearl of the Punjab

LAHORE, THE PROVINCIAL CAPITAL OF West Pakistan, is a favorite city of the Punjab. People speak "Lahore" with the lilt and slight roll of the tongue, like a wealthy prince of India might speak the name of his favorite courtesan. Her popularity and desirability are verified by the variety of powers who have captured and occupied her in this favored location along the path from the Khyber Pass to Delhi and Kashmir.

"Labokla," one of many names found for Lahore in history, was mentioned by Ptolomey in his writings as an important ancient city between the Indus River and Kashmir. Lahore's Golden Era blossomed under the Moguls with their lovely turreted architecture. Beginning with Akbar who laid out the Lahore Fort, the grand mosque raised by Aurangzeb, and Shah Jahan who built the Taj Mahal and the exquisite Shalimar Gardens. Many favored this city on the banks of the Ravi River. The Moguls reign ended when the Sikh despoiler, Ranjit Singh arrived and stabled his horses in the lovely Badshahi Mosque. The seventy years of Sikh reign ended with the British Raj who also used buildings like Anarkali's Tomb for storage, and kept ammunition in the lovely Victorian railway station. Lahore's history showed it was a magnet for invaders of all kinds.

On Sunday morning, Jim decided it was time for us to see some of

Lahore. "Let's go see the Shalimar Gardens. I know you'll like it, and it's a world-famous *serai* built by Shah Jahan, the same Mogul ruler who built the Taj Mahal."

He didn't need to convince me, I was ready to see something outside the compound.

We walked through the gates of the Shalimar Gardens, tall enough to accommodate the elephants with their *howdahs* used for travel by the Moguls, and found ourselves inside the walled garden. The long canals within carried water to fountains that were everywhere, too many to count. The highest level had four pavilions, a large pool, and decorated open platforms of lacy cut marble.

"Musicians and dancers often appear here for concerts," Jim said.

I could see what a beautiful background this would be, and the water would carry the sound of the music. We followed the pathways along the long, narrow waterways.

"The higher levels spill to the lower ones. The Mogul king who built the canal system to provide water for the gardens also built the Jahengir's Palace and the smaller one to Shah Jahan," Jim said. "We'll look at that another day. It's in town."

We had driven a few miles outside of Lahore to the Shalimar Gardens.

"The waterways are all laid out north-south or east-west. Flowering, aromatic plants were in the upper levels, and the lower level was all fruit trees. Too bad they've not been kept up." Jim pointed to the lower level where men squatted to repair the bricks that were damaged in the pathways. I could imagine the beautifully dressed Indian princesses lounging by the cool waterways, picking fruit off the trees of the gardens planted there for their enjoyment.

On the way home, we stopped at the zoo to show the boys something more in their realm of interest, animals. The zoo was small but had a number of animals they liked, monkeys, a tiger, and an elephant ride for half a rupee each.

"Let's ride the elephant," Mark said.

"That sounds like fun," I said.

Jim bought our tickets, and watched as we climbed to the platform and stepped over to sit on the *howdah*. Jim waved at the boys as we lumbered around the zoo's trail, swaying back and forth on the tall elephant.

Later, as we walked past the tiger's cage, the gold and black cat lolled in the sun with his back to the visitors. We watched as two young men tried to get his attention, but he wouldn't look at them. One man tossed his cigarette through the wire, where it landed on the tiger's back. The cat leaped up, shook off the offending spark, and hissed at the man. I clenched my fists, wanting to tell him that was not an acceptable way to treat any animal. Jim held me back.

That afternoon, I took the boys out to the playground. Jim had left to meet an airplane with a shipment that needed to go to the job tomorrow, but he assured me this was a short afternoon's work. I was always happy to see my neighbor, Marge. She always had news of what was going on, and without a telephone, I learned of many things in the complex. Today she told me of a wedding planned at WAPDA Flats this evening.

"The Warren's cook have a son who's going to be married. The wedding will be on the far side of our building in the parking area. The parents invited all the Americans."

This was a rare opportunity to see a traditional Muslim wedding, and I was eager to go. I could hardly wait to tell Jim about the wedding. When Jim arrived home, I served our dinner while telling him about the event.

"I'm really tired tonight and have to meet an early shipment in the morning. You go ahead and enjoy the wedding. I'll take care of Mark and Kevin," he said.

"If you're sure you don't mind. The celebration is just across the yard, so I won't be far if you need me." I kissed them all good-bye and hurried out the door.

Jim hadn't been alone with his sons in a long time, so an evening together might be good.

As I crossed the courtyard, the beat of drums and music drew me to the large *shamiana* (tent) on the far side of the compound. The music was lively and happy in a slightly minor key with a flute, drums, and some strings, probably a sitar. The groom arrived on the shoulders of several friends. He wore a white *salwar kameez* outfit and looked radiant. His face was partly covered by the sparkling head covering made of tinsel, mirrored coins, and spangles called a *sehra*. A large Urdu-lettered breastplate covered his chest. His glittering *sehra* reflected the lighted candles and torches carried by his parade of male attendants. He smiled and waved at the crowd.

The women took me into a second *shamiana* where the bride prepared for the ceremony. She wore a red *sari* embroidered in gold, heavy makeup, and her nails and lips were colored dark red. Gold bracelets adorned her arms, and gold earrings and necklaces peeked under her veil-covered, long, black hair. She smiled shyly. I asked an *ayah* I recognized to tell her I wished her happiness. She smiled and squeezed my hand as she thanked me.

All activity revolved around her and a mirror positioned on a table. Two chairs faced the table, and she sat in one, checking out the angle of her reflection in the mirror. The chair next to her would be for the groom to sit by her side. Her veil and his headdress would be removed, and they would see each other's reflection in the mirror. Since this was an arranged marriage, this would be the first time either had seen the face of the other, unless they had grown up together and played as children before puberty when she wore the veil and kept *purdah*.

The music and dancing continued long into the night with women gathered in the tent, the men dancing with each other in rhythmic movements. Faces of the people shone with laughter and happiness as they clapped and sang along with the musicians. The women's ululating, a high-pitched call that sounded like "ki-ki-ki-ki," showed the joy they felt for the couple.

The evening grew colder, and I reluctantly left the music to go tuck my sons into bed. The vividness of the music, the smells of the delicious, aromatic foods prepared lovingly by the groom's father and his family, and the shy smile of the bride floated through my dreams that night.

◇◇◇◇◇

WITHIN THE FIRST FEW WEEKS, the children's shoes were showing signs of wear due to the ankle-deep sand in the playground. The local shoe stores had many styles, but none was in narrow sizes we needed. Jim told me about a shoemaker on the Mall just across from his office. Like the local tailors, they could copy the American shoes that fit Mark and Kevin's narrow feet. Several fittings would be necessary to complete a new pair of shoes. The items I had packed in Nevada in early October would not reach us until January. I remembered the new shoes whose soles I scuffed on the sidewalk before I packed them, which would be the right size for now if only we had them. Meanwhile, we had to make due, and I decided to take them with me to see the shoemaker.

One day in November, after firing the *ayah*, I took the boys shopping with me. We rode into town with Jim and then walked along the tree-lined divided boulevard, the Mall, a modern street far different from the bazaars and shops of the Old City or Anarkali Bazaar. I bought a brass vase, some colorful placemats, and coasters and searched for new socks for the boys.

As I was crossing the Mall to return to Jim's office with the boys and my bulky packages, I looked to the left for oncoming traffic. I barely had time to grab Mark's arm and pull him back to the safety of the sidewalk as a speeding taxi flew past. I should have looked to the right to check for oncoming cars since Pakistan's traffic used the British system. Relief that both boys were fine replaced my fear of the speeding taxi; embarrassment at my mistake followed my confusion.

Just then, young Majid, the boy Jim had introduced to me to on our first day, appeared. Jim considered him to be a pest. The child couldn't have been more than ten years old with huge dark eyes that peered at me beneath his shock of raven hair. He shook his head in concern and walked up to help me like a long lost friend.

His eyes fixed on my face with a serious expression. "I carry your packages, *memsahib*! Too much for you to carry. Is too much traffic. Too many cars. Let me help you." His wide brown eyes flashed as he spoke, lecturing me on the dangers of Lahore traffic. Majid looked like countless other Pakistani boys but had a personality uniquely his own.

He noticed my plight and immediately took over to help me. "*Memsahib*, I help you cross Mall street. Very busy." Majid assumed a protective attitude and opened his arms to relieve me of my bulky packages.

I saw his willingness to help and surrendered my purchases into his outstretched arm. He smelled faintly of charcoal and spices I recognized from the bazaar's open food stalls.

"You wait, *memsahib*." He stepped into the Mall and, in a perfect imitation of a policeman's posture, held up one hand.

Traffic coming from the right screeched to a halt. I held Mark's hand and balanced Kevin on my hip as we crossed to the middle of the road.

"You wait," he said again.

He repeated the process of stopping the traffic approaching on the left and ushered us across the other two lanes of traffic. His serious expression convinced the drivers to do his bidding without question, fearlessly halting cars while shepherding us across the wide, divided boulevard.

We walked along the sidewalk. My shoes tapped a staccato on the pavement while his bare feet padded softly in rhythm.

"You American?" he pronounced it as many Pakistanis did. Amer-ee-can.

"Yes," I answered.

"*Sahib* work dam?"

"Yes."

"You have two *babas*?"

"Yes, two boys. Mark and Kevin." I nodded to each boy.

"Ah, *bahut acha* (very good)." His expressive face ruptured into a broad grin.

I had already noticed that male children were much preferred.

When we reached the office, I retrieved my packages from Majid. I gave him a half rupee for his help. Lahore was full of beggars, but in my eyes, Majid was not a beggar, but an entrepreneur. He observed, found opportunities, and lived by his wits. When an American lady he recognized appeared, he asked if she needed a taxi and got one for her. He might get a small tip from the driver and certainly from the lady. He knew which women drove a car and would watch the car so it wouldn't be broken into or stolen. He didn't ask directly for money but found a service he could render and accepted *baksheesh* (a tip) for his services. Majid exemplified the independent spirit of one who has learned to fend for himself.

"*Memsahib*, I come to your house to clean *baba*'s shoes." His eye for detail noticed the scuffed shoes Mark wore and lack of white polish on Kevin's baby high-top shoes.

The driver had opened the car door and heard Majid's offer.

"Thank you, Majid. I'm sure our *homal* can take care of them when we get home."

"You like very much Pakistan, *memsahib*. Majid, your servant, always help." He feigned dusting the car seat with his long rectangle of cloth that served as a scarf, sweatband, or package wrap as the need arose. "Thank you for *baksheesh*." He clutched the half rupee coin I gave him. "God give you long life. I, Majid, only can buy *chapatti* for my father, my mother, and all brothers and sisters. Father blind. Cannot work. Mother cannot talk or hear. I take care of them."

The enormity of his situation seemed unbelievable, but how could anyone make up such a tragic story? No wonder he worked so hard to buy *chapattis* (flatbread) for his family. Later, ladies from our apartment complex confirmed his situation was true when they paid a visit to his parents' home.

Jim came out of his office. Majid disappeared. I imagined an American boy his age clad in baseball cap and tossing a ball around, not hustling to find food money for his family.

"I see Majid found you," Jim said.

"Yes, I was glad he did. He came along, carried my packages, and helped us cross the Mall. I appreciated his help." I defended the boy.

"And how much did you appreciate him? In money, I mean?" Jim asked.

"I only gave him ten cents, a half rupee," I answered.

"From now on, pretend each rupee is a dollar, and tip accordingly. He would have been overpaid with half that amount," Jim said. "Americans are notorious for paying too much for goods and services. The company policy is to try to keep in line with the regular prices the people of Pakistan can afford, or inflation will make their lives out of control when we leave."

Jim's explanation was as logical as why American teenagers weren't allowed to babysit and take a job from a local resident. Unemployment was very high.

I wasn't sure I agreed a few *annas* would make much difference to the economy, so I nodded my agreement but inwardly questioned this philosophy. Jim thought of Majid as a pest and called him Lahore's little hustler, but I was pleased when I saw him. I liked the way he found a way to help instead of asking for charity. When he recognized me, he always hurried to offer assistance. A smile of greeting was always ready. He had an uncanny way of finding me, no matter where I shopped.

THE FOLLOWING SUNDAY, THE DOORBELL rang. Alam had the day off so Jim answered the door. Our first few weeks had been so busy that I was pleased that Jim took an entire day off. I hoped it wasn't someone selling something.

At our door was Freddie, the Anglo Pakistani clerk who worked in Jim's office. He brought his fiancée, Florence, to meet us. The young lady hung back as I invited them inside. Away from the office, Freddie became much more sociable and talkative.

"This is Florence, my fiancé. We've just attended church where they've posted our bans," he announced.

"How wonderful. I'm pleased to meet you, Florence. Please come in." I said.

I was happy for them. As practicing Christians in a Muslim country, that made them a very small minority. They planned their wedding for early next year.

Florence radiated her pleasure as Freddie told us of their plans. She wore a Western-style tailored suit and spoke perfect English. Her British accent and mannerisms convinced me I was talking to someone from England. Florence spoke quite formally and deferred to Freddie, the only hint of subservience that might have shown her Pakistani heritage. She and Freddie, as did most Anglo Indians, tried to separate themselves from their Indian heritage and cultivate the tastes, habits, and preferences that that they felt their English parents and grandparents would have approved. Their Anglophile tendencies were passed on in the way they raised their children.

When I offered refreshments, they accepted a cup of tea and cookies. By their birth to a mixed family, Pakistanis or British did not readily accept Anglo Indians. The Anglo Indians tended to marry up and hoped for lighter and lighter children to erase the Indian appearance in their prodigy. It was a sad social situation for those of mixed race in the early sixties before widespread intermarriage was common. Pakistan was Muslim, so being Christian also put them in a minority of religion as well.

"Have you seen Bhowani Junction?" Florence asked.

"No, I haven't had the chance to go to a movie here," I said. "It stars Stuart Granger and Ava Gardener, so it should be a good."

"It is quite a popular movie. You know it was filmed in Lahore, don't you?" she asked.

"No, I wasn't aware of that."

"Even though they call the town Bhowani Junction, it is really Lahore in the book."

"That must have been exciting. Did you see them filming?"

"Oh, yes, and some of my friends and family had bit parts and made extra money. There is quite a growing film industry in Pakistan now and has been in India for some time. Most of the people around the railroad community are quite keen on it."

In the movie, Ava Gardner portrayed an Anglo Indian woman whose family worked for the railroad. Both Florence's and Freddie's fathers were railroad employees, and the film focused on the Anglo-Indian segment of society. They openly discussed the discrimination of the Anglo Pakistanis by both the Muslim and Christian communities.

We enjoyed their visit, and I learned more about a subject I hadn't even suspected might be a problem in Pakistan. The intermarriage of Pakistanis and British might not be as shocking to the world in the early sixties as the mixture of the American Negro and the whites in America, but their social situations were very similar. My heart went out to this couple and their tenuous social status. They departed with the promise of an invitation to their wedding.

Within twenty minutes, the doorbell rang again. So much for a quiet Sunday! Would the *mali* be back with flowers to sell on a Sunday? I hoped not.

Jim answered the door to find Jamal Farouki, the consultant from his office, smiling with his effusive charm.

"I've brought Najma to meet you," Jamal said, introducing his wife.

Jamal looked like a Pakistani version of our popular movie actor, Errol Flynn, tall and imperious. His wife Najma wore a silk *sari* and was comfortable without the Muslim headdress or *burqua* to covering her. She spoke English very well with a slight British accent. I knew they were Muslim, and I was thinking about what to offer them for refreshment. I knew there were strict dietary laws banning pork and alcoholic beverages.

Jim brought them into the living room and took over as a gracious host. "Would you care for a drink, Jamal?"

"Yes, please. Scotch and soda would be fine."

His answer solved that problem. Najma asked for a Coke. I served some cheese and crackers. Jim later told me that Jamal even carried a letter from his doctor advising that he was exempt from the Muslim alcohol prohibition due to health reasons.

"Jamal, tell Irene about your family history." Jim handed Jamal the scotch.

Jamal settled back on the sofa, took a sip, and began his story. "My family descended from the Mogul rulers of India. We have traced our family history back to the fourteen hundreds." Then he told us of the land exchange his family received during the partition of India and Pakistan. "The land we had in India had good crops, and water was plentiful not far east of the border, in Gujarat Province. The land we got in exchange in Pakistan is dry and too far from water supply, and it provides little for our sustenance. The land has saline saturation problems from poor farming methods. It will take a lot of money to remove the salt and make it productive land again."

Perhaps the drought his land suffered was less painful when watered by the soothing liquid of a drink. Jamal and Najma's situation explained the plight of many Indians diminished by the politics of partition.

They were educated, socially prominent people struggling to maintain their status, but with their land exchanged for a less productive land in Pakistan, Jamal's financial situation was not as strong as it might have been. Someone who owned a lot of productive land would probably not have been interested in taking a job with Mangla Dam Contractors, where long hours and hard work were the order of the day.

Jamal's family ancestry made him the first Pakistani-offered membership in the exclusive Punjab Club in Lahore. Social clubs like the Punjab Club in Lahore and the Lantern Club in Jhelum were gathering places for the British and their guests so they could enjoy cocktails and dinners in congenial quarters. The British knew their time of rule in the subcontinent was ending and promoted high-placed Pakistanis in positions of social prominence in hopes of having leaders emerge. Men of Jamal's status were expected to step up and run the country when the British relinquished control. Jamal was a valuable employee because of his family and social connections. His ability to speak Urdu and several other dialects made him a valuable interpreter of business and customs for the Americans. And at the Punjab Club, business was often transacted during social events.

Najma and I talked and were soon laughing together. She was down-to-earth. She had a good sense of humor, and she was wonderful to tell me about the local customs. I'd been in Pakistan just long enough to want to know more of the culture. Like most women, we were soon talking about our hair while Jim and Jamal talked business.

When Jim refilled the drinks, he asked me to slice some of the salami I'd brought from the States. I did and added that to the plate of cheese and crackers. Jamal and Najma loved this Italian deli treat I'd brought. Before long, I'd refilled the tray again. I was sure there were pork products in this salami and raised an eyebrow to ask Jim. He shook his head that it didn't matter, and our guests continued talking and enjoying the salami.

"I can't find a good hairdresser I can trust to do a perm," Najma said. "My sister and I used to do each other's hair with the home perm rods, but she moved to Karachi."

"My mom was a beauty operator. I watched her roll the perm rods into her customer's hair all my life."

In my mind, I pictured my mother's hands folding a thin tissue paper over the ends of the customer's wet hair, smoothing it around the plastic rods to the scalp, securing it with the rubber band, and then sectioning another grid of hair until pink, blue, and gray rods covered the whole head. It didn't look difficult, and Mom had enlisted me to roll her hair a few times, which turned out fine.

"If we can read the directions, we can do it ourselves!"

We laughed at our resourcefulness and made a date the following week. We would try the home permanent.

"Shall we go to for dinner next Saturday night?" Jamal asked as they departed. "You haven't had a chance to see the excellent belly dancer who is playing at Falletti's. She's quite good at the Egyptian style of dancing."

We joined Najma and Jamal the following Saturday night for dinner. Now that I understood his position on the Muslim dietary rules, I enjoyed their company without worrying about offending their religion if I ate or drank forbidden Muslim foods in their presence. They explained the culture to me from their viewpoint. Just as some of our Christian friends interpreted their church's doctrines differently, so was Jamal with the Muslim dietary laws.

"I really like my perm," Najma said as we finished dinner. "Thanks for doing it for me."

"It was fun to get together. I'm glad it turned out well. My mom would be proud that I remembered what she taught me."

Najma and I got along well, and she talked more when it was just the two of us. I felt I could ask her anything about the customs and receive good advice.

Dinner in the dining room was much more relaxing with friends to laugh with than my first night. The food was good, and the service was as attentive as I remembered. The *bearers* chased the bold birds away from the breadbasket, cleared the food, and responded to a slight gesture. I was learning subtle hand and eye movements so I didn't have to interrupt a conversation to ask for something.

The cabaret opened just as we finished dinner. Music spilled from the darkened room of the popular nightspot. We were drawn to the dim lighting and music. The host seated us at a table right on the edge of the dance floor. The band changed music from cha-cha to the Twist and then to a samba rhythm, making me long to dance. Jim was not a dancer, so I sat and watched the couples swaying to the rhythm of the music. My foot tapped along to the beat.

The bandleader was the same young man I'd heard singing that first night. He sang several familiar songs and again sang "She's My Kind of Girl". He looked our way as he sang, making me feel flattered but also a bit uncomfortable. Jim hardly noticed as he and Jamal talked business.

"That's Charlie, the bandleader. Wait until you hear his drum solo." Najma noticed me watching him .

After a few more dance numbers, the bandleader took over the drums and did an amazing drum solo as couples left the dance floor, unable to keep up with the speed of his beat.

He took a bow and then announced the main attraction. "Ladies and gentlemen, the lady you've all been waiting for. Mumtaz."

The belly dancer moved from the darkened perimeter, flirting with the spotlight as she showed an arm, then a leg, and a hint of her whole body as she danced to the center of the floor.

One musician played the drums, and another played a mandolin. I heard the high notes of the flute. The dark-haired woman stepped around the floor, her anklets chiming *chink-chink chink-chink* as her fluid arms and hands writhed around her shoulders and hips. Her hips traced circles, right and then left. Her finger cymbals clinked in rhythm with the anklets while arabesques of shadows played around the room as the lights followed her. The spotlight followed her gyrating hips and shoulders, casting her shadow along the walls as her bare feet slapped the floor. Anklets chinked slowly and then faster with the music. During the finale of her dance, she writhed on the floor, bending back from the knees and sinuously moving her flexible abdominal muscles. The crowd applauded, wanting more. She rose gracefully, gyrating around the tables and accepting the bills the men tucked into her low hip belt as she left the stage.

"Some of the belly dancing mimics the movements of labor," Najma said.

"She is amazing," Jamal said. "Not often do we have such a talented belly dancer, especially the Egyptian style."He applauded enthusiastically and tipped the dancer.

Najma agreed with him and applauded. Najma and I enjoyed her artistry as much as the men enjoyed the glimpse of flesh. The play of lights and shadows added an air of mystery and special artistry to her performance.

A Pakistani man in a Western suit stopped to greet Jim and Jamal.

"Rahman, I want you to meet my wife Irene. I believe you know Najma and Jamal Farouki," Jim said.

"Ah, Jim, I am so happy to meet your lovely wife. Hello, Najma, This is Zeva." He introduced a Pakistani lady in a Western-style dress that was just above her knees.

She was the first Pakistani woman I'd seen who wore clothes that looked like American fashion magazine's latest mod styles. She looked lovely and smiled at me as she welcomed me to Lahore. When the music started again, Rahman and Zeva did an impressive cha-cha.

"Ramon's wife keeps *purdah*," Jamal said. "So his girlfriend lives in an apartment in another section of Lahore."

Muslims were technically allowed to take as many as four wives, but due to the cost of supporting multiple wives and the religious requirement that each be treated equally, few men chose to practice polygamy.

After Rahman left, a man who resembled Omar Sharif, a handsome man, stopped at our table to greet Jim. His tailored suit, cut in the latest Italian style, fit him to perfection. He smiled and shook hands with Jim and Jamal and greeted Najma. Then his eyes locked on mine, and he raised one eyebrow. He had a smile on his lips as he waited for Jim to introduce us. Jim noticed his pause and looked in my direction.

"This is Mohamed Javed Khan," Jim said.

"Welcome to Pakistan. I am pleased to meet you," Javed said, his dark eyes flashing.

The man exuded confidence as he puffed on a cigarette. He had a roguish look and accepted a drink when Jim offered one. He spoke business with Jim and Jamal and appeared well acquainted with details of parts for the dam.

When the band changed to a popular American twist song, he asked Jim, "May I have the honor of this dance with your wife?" He looked at Jim, then cast a smile in my direction.

They could talk business some other time. I was delighted to be asked to dance. In the five years since high school graduation, I had little opportunity to do so.

"Go ahead, you like to dance, and Javed is a good dancer," Jim said.

Javed led me into the midst of the dancers. I followed his lead and danced the Twist. The music and this handsome partner made me feel carefree. The band changed tempo, and Javed showed me the basic cha-cha steps that weren't hard to learn. Then the band played a jitterbug. Javed and I twirled around the floor. The spotlight followed our every move. He held me close but discreetly when the band played a slower dance. The band took a break, and he walked me back to the table. Only then did I notice the jagged scar on his left cheek beneath his eye.

"Thank you." His dark, smoldering eyes lingered as Jim continued his conversation and then looked up to notice I had returned. "I enjoyed dancing with your lovely wife." Javed passed my hand back to Jim's, and he departed as quickly as he had appeared.

The waiter appeared with a fresh round of drinks. "Javed *sahib* ordered for you." The waiter served our table a round of cocktails.

I sipped the drink and thought of this new acquaintance, Javed. He was a wonderful dancer, and I had such fun dancing with him. He was gracious to order drinks for us as he left. I wondered why he hadn't stayed and joined us. Where was his wife? Did he come here alone, or was she in *purdah*, too?

Jamal must have sensed my curiosity and told us about Javed. "Javed is from one of our wealthiest families He married a British lady who prefers the coolness of England to the heat of the Punjab. She spends most of the year in England and brings their two children home only for the cooler season."

"How did he get that scar?" I asked.

"A motorcycle accident. Javed likes fast cars, fast motorcycles, and the *shikar*."

"What is the *shikar*?" I wanted to know more.

"The hunt, madam," Jamal replied. "It is a time-honored sport for men to hunt the wild animals like boars, who roam the borders between here and India. In the days of my grandfather, the *shikar* would bring out many men on elephants caparisoned with beautiful silk and linen drapes, drivers to chase the game, and keepers for the animals. Some used falcons who were trained to retrieve the game birds. Others liked shooting with dogs to flush out the birds. The most exotic were the tiger hunts using elephants to roust the animals from the bush. Those hunts took two or three days, sometimes longer. The sport was a sign of wealth and power, and few remain who have the means to continue the *shikar*."

"What do they do with the wild boars they shoot?" I remembered that Muslims don't eat pork.

"Some hunters sell them across the border in India to Christian butchers or give the boar to Christian servants who eat pork. One favorite hunting ground is near Amritsar in India, about seventeen miles east of Lahore, along what is now the border. Sometimes they cross the border without knowing it. The metalsmiths of Pakistan still make the best rings in the world for the peregrine falcon used to hunt birds and retrieve them. Those rings are sought from all over the world and are much in demand." Jamal knew my love of the whole story and all the details.

We returned home that night with my feet still feeling the rhythm of the cha-cha. The dance was infectious. I loved to dance, and Javed was a superb dancer. Jim was pleased someone wanted to dance with me since he wouldn't. Finding good dance music and an excellent partner was a pleasant surprise.

Pakistan isn't so bad after all. This could be fun.

The Pakistanis liked to dance and enjoy life just as Americans did. Pakistani people had the same needs and desires as we did—food, clothing, shelter, and the desire for a better life for their children than they had. People were different, but we were alike in these basic human desires.

I was beginning to enjoy Lahore, even with the difficulties. I had never before lived without a car, radio, or telephone, and that was the hardest part. But perhaps other things could compensate.

Polo Game and Mr. Guy
Comes to Dinner

As THE WEEKS PASSED, THE produce man at Tollinton's Market recognized me and smiled when he saw me looking over his vegetables and fruit. The taxi from WAPDA Flats to the market was about a dollar. I had learned that Americans paid more than the British, and negotiating was expected for every purchase. The merchants respected the British more than Americans. Or perhaps the older merchants were more accustomed to British. We looked alike, so the accent was the main giveaway.

"How much are you asking?" I drew out the "a" as I'd heard my English stepfather say.

He grew up in the Manchester area, so he had the Midlands speech patterns. I could speak with his voice echoing in my mind when I remembered to use it. I began to enjoy bargaining, making shopping into a game.

The Punjab heat had changed to pleasant, warm days in November. Now in December, Punjab temperatures dropped, and the weather turned cold. The *chowkidar* wore a vest over his *shalwar kameez*, as did the servants, and wrapped a blanket over his shoulders. He hurried to hail a taxi for Helen and me as we left for the polo field. I shivered through the sweater I wore over my blouse, wishing I had my jacket that was still somewhere in transit on the high seas.

Helen Bently and I were on our way to see a polo game, my first.

"Have you ever watched a polo match?" Helen asked as our taxi sped along Racecourse Road.

"No, but I love anything to do with horses, so I'm eager to see a polo game. I grew up in Nevada where rodeos are the cowboy's idea of competition. Bronc and bull riding, calf roping, and bull dogging are their sports. We always had horses on our ranch. We used Western saddles, but I did ride a few times with an English saddle."

"Polo is an ancient sport," Helen said. "It started in Mongolia and moved to Persia where the royals took a liking to it. The game began when they tossed the skull of a sheep or goat and scores of riders chased it. The sport became popular and more organized, especially after it spread to India brought here by the Moguls. The British found it an exciting sport and added rules and time limits. Their primary concern was not to kill the poor horses with running beyond their endurance."

We got out and paid the taxi driver at the Army's Cantonment field. Helen led me to the bleachers flanking the field. We found seats, and she greeted three men wearing Pakistan army uniforms. When we were seated, I had a chance to look at the horses. More than a dozen gathered at each end of the field. I watched as the riders checked their cinches, mounted their horses, and swung their mallets to warm up. Each rider wore a helmet, high boots, and jodhpurs. The smell of linseed oil from their saddles wafted to my nostrils as they jogged by. Their bridles jingled. The warm, pungent smell of horses brought back memories of our ranch in Nevada and reminded me of home.

"The British made rules about how many players and set time limits to each *chukkar*. Each rider has four horses so none or the horses are overworked." Helen pointed out the man who timed the games.

We watched riders prepare the polo ponies, as they pranced and preened, preparing for the game. One horse squealed and stomped when another got too close, his ears laid back in warning. The horses strained at the reins as they sidestepped onto the field.

Helen pointed to a black horse with a white blaze on its face. "That's Sheik Abdul's mare. He had her sent from Arabia. Later, he'll breed her to improve his stable."

Helen knew the animals and their owners. I watched the mare as she wheeled to follow the ball with no visible commands from the rider. The mare appeared to have a natural love of the game and the competition.

"He brought the horse from Arabia?" I was surprised. After the poverty I'd seen, I hadn't considered there were wealthy people in Pakistan, too.

"If they have money, they prefer the bloodlines of Arabian horses," she said. "The Arab has the most endurance as well as the preferred confirmation of equine beauty."

The soldier spoke up as he noted that I was seeing my first polo game. "The Moguls rode the small, sturdy ponies from Central Asia. The word 'polo' probably came from the Balti language of Northern Pakistan and Baltistan. They called the ball a '*pholo*,' so they take credit for creating the game." The soldier smiled, enjoying my interest. "Polo is also popular in India. The Urdu name for the game is *buzkashi*."

The horses galloped by right in front of us. Each rider swung a mallet, trying to hit the ball to the goal at the end of the field. The horses wheeled and turned gracefully and made lightning-quick sprints in pursuit of the ball. We watched one team score a goal and then chase the ball to the other end of the field. At the whistle, the players reined in their mounts and walked to the ends of the field.

"That's the end of the first *chukka*," Helen said.

"How many *chukkas* do they play?"

"They play four seven and a half minute *chukkas*, which is as long as any horse should run at a full gallop." Helen turned to chat with a uniformed army officer. "Next week, I start riding his horse again. He has a jumper he never has time to ride. I love the horse, so I ride him two or three times a week."

"I'd love to ride again," I said. "I grew up with horses on our ranch, but it has been a few years since I've had the opportunity with the boys."

The game was fast, horses turning and changing direction in the blink of an eye, the mallet swinging a ball I often couldn't see in the forest of equine legs. The teams changed ends of the field with each *chukka*. The horses wheeled and turned with lightning speed, and I noticed the men all swung their mallets with their right hands. Another *chukka* ended, and the riders exchanged their sweaty mounts for fresh ones.

The sun hung low on the horizon, and the chill of late afternoon made us shiver. Helen wanted to see the Arabian mare up close, and so did I, so we walked over to see the polo ponies. The smell of sweaty horses and hay hung in the air. When the mare reached out, looking for a treat, I stroked her neck and ears. We left as the sun hung low in the western sky and found a passing taxi to take us back to the apartment complex.

"Come in for a drink," Helen said when we returned to WAPDA Flats. "I'll give you the contact information for the Rangers." I followed her upstairs to her flat across the courtyard from ours.

"The Rangers' horses are stabled at the Army Cantonment and meet the class at the training ring. I usually join them with my friend's jumper," she said. "I believe they charge sixty rupees a month for three days a week for lessons and riding."

I could hardly wait to tell Jim. Sixty rupees a month was only twelve dollars in American money. I took the Rangers' information Helen wrote down for me. I could hardly wait to ride again.

I hurried across the courtyard to our flat and dashed up the steps to find Dorothy Ziemer coming down the stairs. She looked serious, even a little worried.

"Did you get my note?" she asked.

"No, I just got home," I said.

She hurried to explain what I'd missed. "Mr. Guy and Rachel Atkinson are in town. This is the only night they will be here, so I invited them for dinner at seven. They want to meet you and Jim, too."

Dorothy paused, seeing the impact her news had on me. Mr. Guy, the founder and patriarch of Jim's company, was coming to dinner tonight. I gasped. I probably smelled like a stable since I couldn't resist petting the horses. I needed to warm up and take a shower.

"Do you have any bread? Rolls? How about some of your chocolate chip cookies?" Dorothy asked.

We had often improvised dinners often when visitors arrived to stay at WAPDA Flats. Impromptu guests were becoming more frequent, but Mr. Guy? What would I possibly talk to the chairman of the board about? I was twenty-two years old, and Mr. Guy, as all the men affectionately called him, was in his eighties, old enough to be my grandfather. Everyone admired this man who had taken his small construction company to one of the largest and most respected in the industry. Mangla Dam would be the jewel in their crown of impressive dam jobs when it was completed. Neither his age nor world events could keep this legendary man from inspecting the

Pakistan project himself. He was probably only interested in the dam. The men could do the talking and tell him about the project.

What could I possibly have to say? I relaxed a little and focused on our immediate problem, food.

"Yes, I made bread and cookies this morning," I answered.

Dorothy sighed, relieved at what I had to contribute. "Good. I have chicken cooking. My cupboard was getting low, and my commissary order hasn't arrived yet."

We checked our pantry to see what I had to add. "Here's a jar of pickles, a can of smoked oysters, and canned green beans. Will that help?"

"Yes, we'll have an appetizer plate with drinks, and I'll use the green beans. I have potatoes, but your bread is wonderful. I'll take your Jell-O salad and cookies. We'll have plenty."

As she and Alam left with the rest of tonight's dinner, she called back, "Jim will be here at seven."

At least he'd be home early if he knew we were having dinner with the big boss.

Alam gathered up the food, and he was leaving with Dorothy when I remembered that Sherif needed instructions and Alam was the interpreter for me.

"Alam, please tell Sherif I need him to watch the boys tonight. There's plenty of food for the boys and him, too. Please ask him to change the boys into their pajamas."

I took a quick shower and dressed, and I was ready when Jim arrived home. Sherif was doing fine with the boys, following my instructions. I was a little nervous as I waited for Jim to shower and dress.

Mr. Guy may be old, but he has children and grandchildren. I decided he might not be that hard to talk to. I would ask him questions about himself or his family. I could listen and let him and his wife do the talking if the men ran out of conversation about the project.

We walked upstairs to the Ziemer's apartment at seven o'clock. Any apprehension I'd had about meeting two elderly people disappeared with their warmth and friendliness. Mr. Guy was an imposing man, well over six foot tall with sparkling blue eyes, large working man's hands, and a shock of white hair. Rachel was petite and lively, even after the long trip from Mangla. She was a former schoolteacher and talked a mile a minute about the traffic and sights they had seen along the Grand Trunk Road. They had traveled to many countries, so they had many stories to tell. Dorothy and John had spent some time assigned to the Ambuclau Dam in the Philippines. Mr. Guy had made the trip to see that job, too, located high in the mountains above Manila, where the Ziemers had lived during that remote project.

"Whenever anyone asked me if they could bring anything, I always asked for potatoes." Dorothy laughed. "We got tired of rice with every meal."

Tonight, she served mashed potatoes with the chicken.

"What do you think is the biggest problem in Pakistan?" Rachel asked.

"Education for all the children," I answered without hesitation. "Only those with enough money for tuition can afford to send their children to learn basic reading and writing. For example, Alam's pay is one hundred and twenty rupees a month. He has three young children. School costs thirty rupees a month for each child. They wouldn't have enough for food and other necessities if they sent even one of the children to school. Girls aren't taught to read and write since their purpose in life is to marry and have children."

"Don't the people see that as a problem?' Mr. Guy asked.

"The sad thing is that it suits the wealthy Pakistanis to keep people uneducated. They need servants to do the work in their homes and fields. Keeping an uneducated class of people is by design, not accident. Educated women don't use their learning to work and contribute. The culture frowns on it so they don't compete for jobs with men."

"Why, what a shame, and such a waste of a woman's education," Rachel said.

"Yes, and to waste the talents of half the population who might otherwise contribute to society and to the family's income." Women in America were just beginning to campaign for equality in the workplace.

"Aren't the Muslims very religious people?" Rachel asked. "I've heard their Koran has the same ideas of right and wrong as our Ten Commandments."

"They pray five times a day. I can hear the call to prayer from the corner mosque. I can hear them chanting the prayers in unison." I said. "Some things may be the same, but our heritage is based on the Judaic-Christian ethics. I'm not sure if Muslims have the same rules."

"The Koran may have the same moral laws as our Ten Commandments, but I'd say most Pakistanis have an elastic conscience," Jim said. "'Don't steal' is a part of the Koran, but in reality, stealing is a sin only if you get caught. At least that's what we've seen. Anything of value that's not locked up disappears. We have to be sure the railroad sends all our shipments on express trains to reduce pilferage."

Mr. Guy's eyebrows rose at Jim's statement.

Rachel's face showed surprise. "Do most of the women you've met wear a veil?"

"Many do, but Lahore is a college town and more progressive. Many wealthy families now allow education for girls. Sometimes, girls go without the veil over their faces but always wear a *dupatta*, or scarf, to cover their hair and show their modesty," I said. "When the women keep strict *purdah*, it becomes a gauze curtain standing in the way of any social interchange since they cannot come to public events even with their husbands."

I told them about Mr. Khan's gracious welcome dinner and the way his wife's absence kept interaction between Pakistanis and Americans difficult. The cultural differences created a barrier. Even though men might invite Americans to their homes or a restaurant, the absence of their women in *purdah* made social interchange as we knew it unrealistic.

After Mr. Guy had enjoyed his cocktail and the appetizers Dorothy had conjured from our joint pantries, we sat down to dinner. Alam was at his best, displaying the same ceremony and style that befitted the *pukka sahib* (big boss) when Mr. Archibald was our dinner guest.

Alam held each chair and seated the three women. Before I could reach for my napkin, Alam fanned it with a flourish and placed it on my lap. My freshly baked bread was on the table with the butter dish beside it. Alam disappeared into the kitchen and returned with the platter of chicken. He approached Rachel from the right, holding the spoon and serving fork in one hand and, with great dexterity, using the serving pieces like tongs to place the piece of chicken she indicated precisely on her plate. Next, he served Dorothy and me. He repeated serving of the men also in age order, first Mr. Guy, John, and then Jim. Afsar waited near the kitchen door with the potatoes, which Alam served in the same manner. He returned the bowl of potatoes to Afsar, who handed him the green beans. Alam served the vegetables in the same order with dignity and grace. Then he disappeared into the hallway, listening and waiting, unobtrusively ready in case we needed something.

Mr. Guy digested my comments with a nod. Then he complimented Dorothy and me on the dinner. He was happy with our everyday fare, so I needn't have worried about entertaining the boss. If we had a week to prepare, I doubt we could have pleased this gentle, kind man more. Conversation flowed easily, and we laughed a lot.

"How was the progress on the job, sir?" John asked.

"It's coming along ahead of schedule, just like we planned. I'm sure the TBM will help us drive those tunnels more rapidly than we could do on previous jobs. That should put us in a good position for the early completion."

So Mr. Guy had been out in the excavation area to check on the job's progress.

"The training program has been very successful," Mr. Guy said. "When we hired some of these men, they had never seen equipment like we have. Some of them have been trained, and they are now ready to drive the big rigs. There's a huge unemployed population in this country but few skilled workers. We're going to change that by creating some crackerjack specialists who can tear apart an engine and put it back together as good as mechanics in the States."

"We have heard good things about the training school," John said. "Even with the time and cost of educating a crew, we will still save more money than bringing in all skilled workers from the States."

I knew the men liked having Mr. Guy visit. They were honored that the president of the company was interested enough to make the long trip to check on the job at his age. They worried about him and tried to be protective. Rumor had it that he liked to inspect everything he could. His age made little difference.

"The town is wonderful," I said. "We had a chance to see it in October."

"Yes, we stayed in a house, and it had all the comforts of a home in America," Rachel said. "We had a tour of the hospital, which is first rate."

"How did you like it, sir?" Jim asked.

"Well, when we laid out the plans for the town, the engineers asked me what kind of hospital I wanted. I thought about it. Then I decided we didn't quite need a Cadillac hospital. But we needed better than a Chevrolet hospital, so I told them to build me a Buick hospital. And the Buick hospital seems to be just right." Mr. Guy grinned.

We laughed at his comparison of hospitals to automobiles.

As we finished each course, Alam took the plate from the guest's left side and disappeared into the kitchen. Next, he brought the plate of cookies I'd baked and one with slices of apple and cheese. Alam offered coffee or tea. We relaxed and talked about their travel plans.

My fears of spending an evening with Mr. Guy vanished as we enjoyed visiting with him and Rachel. We finally said good night and returned to our apartment. Once we were alone, Jim was eager to tell me what had happened at his office that afternoon.

"I looked up to find them coming into the office earlier than we expected," Jim said. "They asked where the restrooms were, so I showed them the way through the car dealership. Rachel came back and sat in the office. After some time passed, and Mr. Guy hadn't returned, I went back to the men's room to see if he had a problem. I was standing outside the men's room, listening for any signs that he might be ill and need help. Suddenly the door opened.

"'Is everything alright, sir?' I asked, not wanting to embarrass him.

"'Well, I did have a little problem,' Mr. Guy admitted.

"'Is there anything I can do to help?'

"'I dropped the key in the toilet.'

"'Why didn't you call me? I'd have gotten it out for you.'

"'I dropped it, and I got it out by myself.' And that was the end of the discussion."

Mr. Guy had displayed one of the qualities that endeared him to the men who worked for him. His reputation for never asking anyone to do something that he wouldn't do himself gained the admiration of his employees.

"Ever since I came to work for Atkinson, I heard the old-timers tell each other, 'Do or die for Mr. Guy.'" Jim said, awe apparent in his voice. "Today I saw why."

Christmas Surprises

"HURRY, MOM, LET'S GO TO the party." Mark was getting into the spirit of Christmas with our talk of Santa, which he knew meant gifts.

The cards I'd sent to our parents and friends stretched the imagination to call them Christmas cards, but they were the best I could find in a Muslim country. The moonlight picture of camels in the mountains with a star in the sky was the closest to the season that I found. I helped each boy add a scribble with crayon beside their name before mailing the holiday greetings to our families.

Our neighbors, the Baxters, again hosted a potluck Christmas party, as they had done for Thanksgiving. The Baxter's flat glittered with festive Christmas decorations they'd brought from England. Mrs. Baxter had asked me if Alam could work for her that night to assist her cook and *bearer*. I had seen Alam and Usef smoking by the gate on their breaks so I knew they were friends, and I was pleased for this evening's work so Alam had the opportunity to earn extra money for his family.

"Merry Christmas. How good to see you. Mark and Kevin, would you like to join the children in Eugene's room?" Kevin and Eugene were the same age and had become friends. "The *ayah* will watch the children."

Mark and Kevin saw the familiar faces their playmates and hardly noticed when we left them to join the adults.

Alam took the dish I'd brought. Usef, the Baxter's *bearer*, and Alam bustled around, bringing trays of food and glasses. I looked around the room at the international group of people who lived in our apartment complex, Europeans, Mexican, Pakistani, and a few American families. I'd become acquainted with a few, but many were new to me. The men worked for companies who were associated either with Mangla Dam or some aspect of the Indus Basin project. The women I'd met had children, and we gathered at the playground area.

Jim and I were listening to a man explain Pakistan's agricultural problems. Alam walked by with a tray of appetizers, offering them to us and the woman seated beside me.

She spoke softly to Alam, "Could you bring me a scotch and water, please?"

"Yes, *memsahib*." Alam mixed her drink at the sideboard and brought her drink on his tray.

She thanked him, took a sip, and coughed. Her face contorted.

Alam must have made the drink too strong. Though the color looked right.

Jim's thoughts were the same as mine. "Let me take that one. Why don't you make her a new one, Alam?"

Jim tasted the drink and coughed. He screwed up his face, too. "Alam, what's in this drink?" Jim went to the sideboard with Alam and watched as Alam explained how he made the drink.

"*Sahib*, I make same as your drink. I pour scotch to here." He pointed to an imaginary line about a third of the way up the glass. "Then put ice and water."

We watched him demonstrate, pouring the scotch and then filling the glass from the bottle of Beefeater's gin. Jim and I looked at each other. Alam had assumed that the gin bottle contained boiled water. Alam didn't realize the Baxter's Beefeater's bottle contained gin, not water. Gin with scotch made a terrible drink. We apologized to the woman and our hosts for his mistake and explained why Alam had been confused.

Helen Bennett came over to talk, and I told her I'd sent my request to ride with the Rangers.

"I filled out the application and sent it to the address you gave me," I said. "But I haven't heard anything."

She nodded and patted my hand. "Remember, nothing happens fast here, only in their own time. Be patient."

I'd hoped to receive an acceptance by now. I had no choice but to take her advice. Everything happened in Pakistani time. This was one of the frustrations I was learning to live with in Pakistan.

⬫⬫⬫⬫⬫

THE HOLIDAY SEASON BROUGHT A flurry of social gatherings. I liked life in Lahore more as time went by. French classes started in early January, along with nursery school for Mark. I had hopes that the Rangers would accept me and I could ride horseback.

A steady stream of travelers came through Lahore to Mangla, often bringing newspapers or current magazines from the States. Some travelers were persuaded to hand-carry items to people at Baral Colony. One stranger stopped by our apartment one day and thrust a package of fruitcake sent by Jim's Uncle Frank via Mr. Doyle's underground.

"You should see the stack of packages he's got in his office, and he talks everyone he can into bringing something to the folks in Baral Colony."

We had invitations to several holiday parties, so I made my first appointment at a beauty shop. Women from WAPDA Flats recommended the owner as a professional stylist. She was reasonable, and her shop was just down Edgerton Road next to a tea shop. After that amazing hairdo I'd had in Hong Kong, I wanted a professional hairstyle to look good for the holidays.

Alam delivered my note requesting an appointment. He returned with the owner's reply for an appointment on the day I'd requested and a time that was perfect.

A few days later, the svelte, exotic-looking Pakistani woman greeted me and showed me to her chair. She arranged a neck roll, then a towel, and a cape.

"I don't want a haircut. Just a style and some curls. We're going to a party," I said.

"As you wish, *memsahib*." She smiled and took me to the shampoo bowl.

She washed my hair in water that alternated between being too hot or too cold. She tried to adjust the temperature, but the plumbing didn't cooperate. When the shampoo was finished, she wrapped a towel around my hair, disappeared behind a curtain into the backroom, and left me for about five minutes. The shop was cold, and I was shivering with my wet hair. When she returned, she towel-dried my hair, added setting lotion, and set it in rollers.

She led me to the dryer, which I hoped would warm me. The first blasts of air from the machine were cold but gradually warmed and warmed and warmed so much that I felt like my head was burning. I called to her, and she adjusted some knobs. Now, cold air blew on my wet hair. This process of too hot and then too cold went on for what seemed like a very long time. I was weary at the constant changes in temperature and asked if she could move me to another dryer. This was their only hair dryer.

When she took my hair out of the rollers, my hair was still damp. As she combed my locks into place, I lost any hope of the curls I'd hoped for. My hair was straight and limp by the time she finished. My professional hairstyle was disappointing.

After that experience, I washed my own hair and dried it in the sun of our balcony. My electric dryer with the hose and hood to fit over my curling rollers was another thing I missed.

The American Consulate children's Christmas party was two days before Christmas. That afternoon, the sun streamed down after the nippy morning mist burned off. I dressed Mark and Kevin in their best outfits, and I was proud of how handsome they looked. Mark had a white shirt and clip-on tie and a jacket and dress pants that were beginning to show what my friends would have called "high water," shorter than the length most guys preferred. Mark wasn't fussy about his pants, but he did object to wearing his dressy shoes. They were getting tight. The shoemaker had promised the new shoes before New Year's, but they weren't ready on our last visit. Kevin looked adorable in his red jodhpur pants and matching corduroy jacket with a collar I'd been able to turn up, hiding his measles spots as we left Hong Kong.

Jim was at work, so the boys and I hurried to the front gate to find a taxi. The *chowkidar* smiled his approval at my handsome sons and hailed a passing taxi for us. He had become a protective older male who tended the gate near the playground, and he kept an eye on the children who might want to explore beyond the gates. I couldn't speak much to him but smiled.

He smiled back. "*Acha*."

The taxi dropped us at the front gate of the impressive American Consulate compound with an American flag flying from a tall pole in the front. Two gates opened into a horseshoe-shaped driveway flanked by expansive lawns, flowerbeds, and manicured shrubs where families with children had gathered. Tables were set up outside the mansion with refreshments. I'd hoped to see the inside of the consulate, but even in the cooling weather, the party was set up outside. This was the event for which we American women had wrapped gifts weeks ago. I knew the children would like the toys I'd seen as we wrapped.

Everyone was focused on the animals on the lawn. I looked around, and I was drawn to the variety of animals, almost like a small circus had been transported to the consulate's lawn. A bear *walla* (handler) showed a scruffy-looking bear with a collar and chain around his neck anchored to a ring in the ground. The bear's coat was matted and coarse, but he rolled over, danced, and sat at the handler's command. The bear seemed docile enough, and the gray around his muzzle indicated he was old. I kept my sons out of his reach just to be safe. We walked a little farther to see what else was here.

The monkey *walla* displayed his charges, two wrinkle-faced capuchin monkeys who were dressed in red jackets and pillbox hats, each tethered by a leash. They chattered, climbed the handler's arm, and did somersaults. A tightrope gave the monkeys a chance to demonstrate their balancing skill to the delight of the children.

A snake charmer sat on the ground with two covered baskets in front of him. The handler removed the cover from one basket and blew on a flute-like instrument. Slowly, a hooded king cobra rose from the basket, higher and higher, with its hood expanding around its head. As the handler moved the instrument, the snake's writhing body swayed in motion with the flute. At one point, the cobra slithered away from the handler, moving through the grass with graceful twists. I gasped and pulled the boys further away. The snake charmer took the cover from the second basket, releasing a long, furry brown animal I'd never seen before.

"It's a mongoose," I heard someone exclaim.

The freed animal moved with amazing speed, pounced on the cobra, and picked it up in his mouth. At the *walla*'s command, the mongoose carried the cobra to the basket and dropped it inside. The handler covered the basket with the fitted top, securing the snake inside. I hoped the snake was safely contained with so many children around. I carried Kevin and held Mark's hand firmly in my own. I moved the boys away.

Next, we watched a *walla* who showed a parrot and cockatiel on a perch. The parrot talked and strutted for the children while the cockatiel squawked along with him.

The highlight of the party was Santa Claus, who rode through the front gate on a camel, her baby trotting beside. Santa looked as authentic with a white beard, red suit, and ample padding. He signaled the camel to kneel and then dismounted. The children's excitement grew as Santa distributed treats to each child from his red sack. The boys were thrilled to see the camels, and the appearance of Santa reassured them that Christmas was coming, even in Pakistan.

Bearers offered cookies, candies, tea, and punch. The compound was filled with more Americans than I'd seen in one place in Lahore since our arrival. Jim Roberts, one of Jim's professors from the University of Nevada, introduced me to his wife and children. I recognized a few women who had been at the gift wrapping coffee in November. A choir from a Christian church sang carols, and I sang along to the familiar hymns. Each child who attended that day carried home a new Stateside Christmas toy, courtesy of the American consul general, distributed by the volunteers, the consul staff, and Santa.

Jim came home that night to find two happy, excited boys. Right behind him was Ken, who was carrying a box on his shoulder.

"Hi, Ken. What have you got there?" I saw another box in the hallway.

"I was in the commissary this morning and saw your order. The manager checked it out for me, and I brought it with me since I had to make a quick run to Lahore." Ken's grin spread over his face as I gave him a hug.

"I didn't think I'd see these things until next week. Thank you so much, Ken."

He made one more trip back to the car to bring in another box of groceries. What a thoughtful friend he was to think of us and bring our commissary orders on the airplane.

He stayed for chocolate chip cookies. We enjoyed this modest, self-effacing man.

"Mr. Guy came out to the airport and asked me to take him up for a ride. He can tell terrain and he knows what kind of rocks he's looking at from a distance. He spotted something he wanted to see up close. He thought it might be the kind of rock they needed for the dam." Ken stopped to sip his coffee.

"What did you do?" I asked.

"We landed on a dirt road, and I never saw so many men show up out of nowhere," Ken said. "One man appeared with a car and drove us to the rocks Mr. Guy wanted to see. Then the villager drove us back to the airplane, and I flew Mr. Guy back to Mangla."

We had heard that Ken had a special ability to judge terrain and land an aircraft in places that weren't paved landing strips, a skill he'd learned during the war,

"Can you stay for dinner, Ken. We've got plenty?"

He had become a frequent, and welcome guest. When he had once heard me fretting about the delays in my commissary order, he often picked them up and delivered them to us.

"Not tonight. Thanks anyway. I've got to get back." He waved good-bye and left as quickly as he had come.

Mark tugged on Jim's pants, eager to tell him about the Christmas party. "Dad, you should have seen the bear. The snake got away. Then the animal caught him and brought him back." Mark stopped for a breath.

"Just animals? No Santa Claus?"

"Then Santa came on a camel. He didn't have a sleigh." Mark told Jim the whole story.

"Baby camel, too," Kevin said. "And a big bear."

"Wow! What else did you see?" Jim laughed at their story.

"Monkey with a red jacket like mine." Kevin jumped up and down.

"So who did the tricks, the monkey or you?" Jim asked Kevin with a serious look on his face.

"The monkey." Kevin laughed.

We'd never seen a Christmas party quite like this one. I liked the Middle Eastern touch with Santa arriving on a camel for our first Christmas in Pakistan. The best gift of all was Ken, our special Santa, who arrived in an Aero Commander and delivered my grocery order in record time.

◇◇◇◇◇

SEARCHING THE BAZAARS FOR DECORATIONS and suitable toys for our two sons was disappointing. Christmas decorations were rare in a Muslim country. I bought a few sparkling tinsel decorations called *sehra,* used in weddings as a headpiece for the groom. Three *sehras* added sparkle and color with the tinsel glued all over it. We bought a fragrant cedar tree for about ten dollars American that stood in the corner of the living room.

We found a string of expensive colored lights in one shop that were 220 volts. They would work in Lahore, but since they wouldn't work at Baral Colony, where homes were built with 110-volt power, we decided against them. We strung popcorn, construction paper chains the boys made, and red tissue paper poinsettias I made with instructions Jim's mother had sent. The gardeners brought flowers to the door two or three times a week, so I bought their bouquets of roses, chrysanthemums, marigolds, and zinnias, which brightened our home. We were ready to celebrate Christmas for the first time in a Muslim country far from home. Almost.

Finding gifts for the boys was more difficult than I'd imagined. The toys we found were made in China with parts I was afraid would be in Kevin's mouth, so I rejected those. Jim and I attended the Better Homes Show in Lahore, an annual event where artwork and furniture of all kinds were displayed. We bought a child-sized rattan table with matching barrel-shaped chairs. The set would fit in the boy's bedroom and give them a place to color, draw, or play with blocks rather than sitting on the cold terrazzo floors. After searching one bazaar after another and in despair that we'd never find a really exciting present, we found an oversized tricycle for Mark with a drive chain like a real bicycle. The same store had a red car with pedals for Kevin.

The tricycle is enormous for a four year old. How could he reach the high pedals?

"He'll grow into it," Jim said.

Late Christmas Eve after the boys fell asleep, Jim and I moved the tricycle and car from the basement storage room and partially hid them behind the tree. We put the smaller wrapped toys under the branches and went to bed, leaving a plate of cookies on the coffee table for Santa.

Christmas morning dawned clear and cold. The *muzzeim's* call to prayer awakened us as usual at dawn. Today, we heard no sounds of prisoners' chains dragging on Jail Road. I wondered why. Jim, who was usually gone by this time, drew his arms around me and gave me a big hug.

"Happy birthday." He gave me a birthday kiss.

Today was my twenty-third birthday. We looked forward to a quiet day at home. I thought Mangla Dam's offices were closed because of Christmas, but Jim reminded me the day before that the founder of Pakistan, Jinnah, had been born on December 25th. Today was a national holiday and Jim didn't have to work with all the businesses closed to honor Jinnah.

We were ready to rouse the boys when they burst into our room. Both were excited and wanted us to see what was under the tree. Before we could get coffee or put on our clothes, the doorbell rang. We weren't expecting anyone, and I wasn't ready for guests so early on a holiday morning. I hurried to find my bathrobe.

"*Asalaam alekum, sahib,*" I heard from the front hallway.

Jim's muffled voice came to me in the bedroom, where I combed my hair and scrambled into my clothes instead of my bathrobe. Who would be coming to call so early on Christmas Day? To my surprise, Jim was showing three gentlemen into the living room.

"Ah, *memsahib*, allow me to weesh you Happy Christmas." The gentleman who spoke was a stranger to me.

I looked at Jim, who introduced the first man, his brother-in-law, and his uncle. They were merchants who produced some of the furniture for the homes at Baral Colony. They brought a huge basket full of oranges as a Christmas gift.

They sat on the sofa, apparently settling in for a long visit. I was baffled at what to do with unexpected guests on Christmas morning. The doorbell rang again. Two men appeared, bearing a bag with a bottle of something, probably liquor, sticking out of the top of the package. They joined the first three, and the five of them filled our living room's seating capacity.

Mark and Kevin climbed into their chairs at the dining room table, ready for their breakfast. I put out their food, mindful of the guests and wondering if I had enough bread to make more French toast for so many people. I'd partially prepared our breakfast the night before but didn't have enough to offer them. Muslims were hospitable people, always offering food and tea to visitors as they arrived. I didn't want to be rude to business associates of Jim's, but I was bewildered.

At that moment, Alam and Sherif arrived, letting themselves in through the door from the entry hall to the kitchen. Alam assessed the situation and glanced at me with a puzzled look on his face.

"Would you like coffee? Or tea?" I asked.

"Tea, please," they each said, directing their choice to Alam, who disappeared into the kitchen.

The doorbell rang again. This time, the building manger stood there, looking for his Christmas *baksheesh*. Jim spoke to him in the hall where he also met the gardener, who also came to collect his Christmas tip. Alam seemed to take a very long time to prepare the tea.

After running out of polite conversation, the three gentlemen who had first arrived finished their tea and repeated their "Happy Christmas" greetings as they departed. Another group of four well-dressed men arrived just after the first three left. They wished us a "Happy Christmas" and handed us packages of fruitcake, more oranges, and a paisley patterned scarf.

"For *sahib*'s wife," one said with a smile as he presented it to me.

"Thank you. It's lovely." I held up the silver and black silk scarf.

We repeated the offer of tea, and by the time the next visitors arrived, I decided to cut the fruitcake and offer that as well. Alam moved at a snail pace serving them tea, and made the day seem longer than any I could remember. Why couldn't he move a little faster or keep a pot of water boiling on the stove for tea?

The boys finished breakfast and wanted to try out their tricycle and toy car. With all these strangers in our living room, I felt torn between seeing my son's delight at their gifts or playing the role of hostess to this sudden stream of guests. I asked Sherif to take the boys outside to play, hoping to join them soon. I found my shoes, but I had no time to put them on when the doorbell rang and more visitors arrived. They all seemed eager to experience our Christmas Day celebration with us, but I found myself resenting them at a time that was a traditional, intimate family day. Then I realized that they weren't aware that our Christmas was first a religious holiday and an occasion for a gift exchange between close friends and family.

More gardeners came with a few more flowers with their palms extended for their Christmas *baksheesh*. The building manager returned to speak with Jim. I went to the door to discuss a concern with him.

"The children cannot get to the swings and playground without crossing the driveway. Would it be possible to block this section of the driveway just from the side gate to the front gate so they can cross safely?" I asked.

"Oh, no, *memsahib*. How could we do that and not allow the cars?" He shrugged.

"Why can't we make it safer for the children? If you moved the large planter boxes with the palm trees to the driveway, two here and two at the front corner, cars could drive around the back to reach the front gate or use the side gate by our apartment. Why don't you ask the WAPDA office if that is possible?"

Maybe he'd ask his boss for permission.

"Yes, *memsahib*," he said so Jim would give him his Christmas *baksheesh*.

I had a feeling he had no intention of doing anything about the dangerous situation at the playground.

There was no gracious way to stop the visitors, so we continued to receive them and the gifts. Jim became more uncomfortable as he saw the quantity of oranges, fruit, lovely brass vases, carved *sheesham* wood boxes, and another scarf for me. He was torn because the company policy was never to accept gifts or favors. How could he refuse a Christmas gift, especially when hand-delivered to our home on Christmas Day?

When a few visitors learned it was also my birthday, they congratulated me and spent more time lingering. Alam often disappeared into the kitchen, and he was even slower serving our guests when a few guests requested an alcoholic drink.

By late afternoon, twenty-seven uninvited and unexpected visitors had come to our home, most bringing gifts. As he cleaned up the cups and glasses, Alam was slamming doors, banging trays of glasses, and rattling teacups as he put them away. His usually congenial attitude soured with a look of annoyance as the last guests departed. I looked at him, trying to decide how to ask him what was wrong. He told me before I had a chance to phrase my question.

"My service is to American and British, *memsahib*. My service not to Pakistanis," he declared with emphatic disdain for his countrymen.

For all his extra work with so many guests, we gave him a generous Christmas bonus and two large baskets of oranges. He didn't refuse them. I hoped his family enjoyed some of the unexpected bounty of our Christmas.

When I went out to the playground to get the boys, several small Pakistani children were peeking around the back corner of the building, watching Mark try out his new tricycle and Kevin's attempts to push his feet in a circle so his car would move. I thought about suggesting they share their toys or take turns with the other children. As if reading my mind, Alam appeared beside me. How had he read my thoughts?

"No, *memsahib*, not good to give children what they can never have. Ame-ree-can only can buy these toys for children. Our *babas* happy with Pakistani toys."

My first impulse was to point out the importance of teaching my children to share. Alam's boundaries for his own children were established, and I had to respect them.

Finally, as the sun set over the western horizon, our family was alone at the end of a long and bewildering Christmas Day. Even when our families at home had invited guests for a holiday, we never had a crowd like the unexpected one that arrived today. I realized the Pakistani idea of our Christmas and the close family celebration we were accustomed to was far different. They could not be expected to know our traditions, and we had no telephone so a person could call to ask if it were convenient to stop by. The number of people who had come to call was overwhelming and touching at the same time.

Only when we were alone did our thoughts turn to our families, Jim's parents, Grace and Am Aylworth, and my mother and sisters. We found the boys' gifts that Grace and Am had sent under the tree. We watched them open the books sent by Grace with plastic pants for Kevin hidden within the pages of first- and second-grade readers.

The lack of mail from my mother or my sisters worried me. Today, I felt so far from home. I'd written everyone about the 300 percent import duty and discouraged gifts other than books or educational materials. I knew Mom was busy with her big house, her beauty shop, and two rental cottages. But I couldn't believe my mother had not sent me a birthday card or Christmas cards for her only grandsons. If we were in the States or had a telephone, Mom would have called. She was probably all wrapped up in her new husband, Frank.

New Year's 1962

JIM WAS OFF WORK THE day after Christmas. Mark and Kevin were excited with their new toys, modest by American standards, but they delighted in each discovery. I'd saved some Matchbox toy trucks I'd bought in Hong Kong, the books from Grace, and a few local toys. The table and chairs we'd bought were perfect in their room.

The box of books Jim's mother sent also contained a surprise for my Pakistani friend who wanted to read several books that were banned in Pakistan. I'd written in early November asking Grace to send *Tropic of Cancer*, *Lady Chatterley's Lover*, and *Lolita*. Tucked in the box, hidden beneath the reading primers and children's books, were the banned volumes. Our subterfuge worked to smuggle in suspect books as well as plastic pants.

Mark's tricycle was huge for a four-year-old and had chain drive, the kind found on a regular two-wheel bicycle, but it didn't have a chain guard. Kevin's toy car was a little difficult for him to pedal, but he tried hard to keep up with his brother. We laughed when he deserted his car, ran after Mark, and climbed on the small platform on the back of Mark's tricycle. He could ride with his brother by holding onto Mark's shoulders.

Mark's pants had caught in the chain's teeth that first day, and they were torn. I was more concerned about Mark's fingers than the pants, and

140

I showed Sherif the problem. I told him to watch closely to be sure Mark didn't try to extract the pants by himself. Sherif understood more than he spoke, and our gestures worked to communicate. We solved the problem by securing Mark's pants snugly against his leg with rubber bands. This kept the fabric out of the exposed chain. He was soon riding with wild abandon around the front driveway.

The year's end brought a flurry of social gatherings. I was enjoying life in Lahore. We had Mark's pre-school and my French lessons lined up for January, and some interesting friends. Sherif was a big help, and the *dhobi* was reliable and pleasant.

The Trade Travel Club Annual Ball was held at the Ambassador Hotel that last week of 1962. The Ziemers joined us, and the dinner was elegant. The music was good, and Jim tried a couple of slow dances. We enjoyed the evening but missed the livelier scene at the Falletti's. There was no band at Falletti's until after New Year's Eve. Their popular leader, Chuck, and his group were summoned to Karachi to fill in when a touring American band's drummer became ill. Chuck's personality as a master of ceremonies, as well as his singing and his drum solos, had given him a widespread reputation.

Jerome Fernandez, the Pan American Airlines office manager in Lahore, and his wife Sheila hosted a dinner party for twelve of us the same week. Jerome and Sheila were from Goa, the Portuguese colony on the West Coast of India. Sheila was a beautiful, gracious hostess. We enjoyed the warmth of their hospitality but shivered as we huddled around their small fireplace. Their home was one of the sprawling bungalows I'd admired. The large rooms and high ceilings had no central heating and relied on fireplaces that barely warmed the chill. The delicious food became cold in minutes. We loved their company and hospitality, but I was happy to claim my sweater and shawl as we said our good-byes.

After that evening I realized how fortunate we were that WAPDA Flats had a thermostat to control the temperature, a luxury by local standards. Our apartment was comfortable and in a convenient location. The only thing I would change was that kitchen.

Jim and I had received an invitation to the gala New Year's Eve dinner and dance at Mangla. The American colony was celebrating the success of the Honeymoon Express' great year-end effort. Starting in October, three families per day had been arriving at Baral from the States. In a Herculean effort, management decided to move seven families per day between

December 22 and December 24 so the women and children could be reunited with the men. This would be a joyful time, but as much as we wanted to be a part of the Baral community, the long drive discouraged us. Our household shipment should arrive soon, and we would need to travel that long road to Mangla once it arrived. We decided against the party so far away, and accepted Jamal's invitation to the Punjab Club.

We enjoyed Najma and Jamal, and the Punjab Club, an institution in Lahore, sounded elegant. The four of us were regulars at Falletti's on Saturday nights where I had the bonus of Javed as a dance partner. We danced well together, both of us enjoying the music as people watched us whirl around the floor. Jim talked business with Jamal as they sipped their drinks, happy to see me enjoying something I loved.

New Year's Eve, we met Jamal and Najma at the Punjab Club. Najma looked lovely in a turquoise blue *sari* that set off her bronze skin and shiny black hair. I'd taken the afternoon to wind my hair in curls and wore my black cocktail dress and pearls. Jim and Jamal looked elegant in their suits. People came by to greet Jamal and Najma, who introduced us to a number of new people.

Jamal showed us around the club. Stereotypical British gentlemen smoked cigars or pipes with gold chains adorning their waistcoat, and some even sported a waxed handlebar mustache, a popular style. This bastion of conservative British manners was a typical gentleman's social club. We strolled through large rooms furnished with leather sofas and chairs, heavy mahogany furniture, and Oriental rugs. Huge brass pots held palms, a reminder that we were in the Punjab, not in England. We walked by one paneled room where the aroma of fine cigar smoke wafted past the palm trees into the hallway. The whiff of bay rum pipe tobacco permeated the club. My mind had wandered, remembering those holiday dinners at home and the aroma of a similar pipe tobacco my British stepfather favored in his pipe. He would have been right at home here.

A small combo played music with a few couples dancing sedately around the floor. Then the band played Irish and English folk tunes, some Broadway musicals, and dance music. People picked up on the tempo, but the people were a little older than the Falletti's crowd.

Appetizers and cocktails went on for some time. A buffet table set up in the entry had a floral arrangement of marigolds and other fall flowers. As I surveyed the appetizers, an Englishman who had quite a few cocktails commented on the contents of each item. He pointed to the marigolds.

"These are edible, you know." He selected a flower from the center of the arrangement. "Ah." He popped the flower in his mouth and chewed it.

The astonished server frowned at his action. Jamal later heard he had been banned from the Punjab Club for his behavior that night, considered unfitting for a gentleman.

Dinner was served later than usual so the guests could ring in the New Year at midnight. We followed Jamal and Najma to the dining room. A large ebony table with columns of candles marching down the center, the crystal stemware gleaming in the soft light, gave the room an ethereal atmosphere. The silverware fanned out on either side of the plates, looking elegant enough for a photograph in a gourmet magazine. The place setting had several forks, knives, spoons, and more across the top of the dinner plate.

"I think you'll enjoy the other couples we invited to join us tonight. They all grew up in India, and their fathers worked for the British before the partition," Najma said.

"Ah, there they are. Jim and Irene, I'd like you to meet Lloyd Wilkinson and his wife Daphne." Jim shook hands with the men. "This is Robert and Helen Hamilton. Lloyd and Robert both work as consultants on the Indus Basin project."

When introductions were finished, we found our seats at the dinner table. The men soon found many aspects of the project to talk about. The women discussed schools they were considering for their children who were approaching high school age. Both couples had teenage children and discussed the merits of sending the children to private boarding schools in Europe. Jamal and Najma's daughter was in her early teens.

"Najma, is Shaheen going to wear the veil?" Daphne asked Najma.

"No, Jamal and I discussed it, and as a birthday gift, we gave her the right to choose. She'll be going to college in Lahore, and many of the girls aren't wearing the *burqua* to school."

"Very sensible for this generation," Helen said.

During a lull in the conversation, Jim made a statement that he'd mentioned to me before. "When I see men saluting British officers or the British flag, I think, if Pakistanis had a vote today, most people would choose to be back under British rule."

"Not sure I'd agree with you, Jim," Mr. Wilkinson said. "Mohammed Ali Jinnah and the Muslim League led what they believed the majority of people wanted, a separate Muslim country for Pakistan."

"Lloyd, I agree with you. The Muslims wanted independence, but even Nehru was reluctant to endorse Viceroy Mountbatten's cockamamie idea of dividing the country with only two month's notice," Robert said. "It took them years to straighten things out when they divided the country. For example, the railway equipment. How do you divide railcars? By the number of miles they travel? Divide the cars proportionately by population? It was a bloody mess."

"They only had two months to divide India?" I asked.

All this had happened in 1947 when I was a child starting school. Our news in American covered little of the earth-shaking event on this side of the world.

"Yes, Lord Mountbatten was sent to India early in 1947 with orders to let India become independent. He made the announcement in June. People heard about it from their radios and word of mouth. No one was prepared, and Mountbatten feared riots and fighting. Moving twelve million people caused problems that weren't resolved for years. Reports estimated that a million people died in the fighting that accompanied partition," Lloyd said.

"I remember being terrified when we had to move from India to Pakistan," Jamal said. "I was a teenager and didn't want to leave my friends, and many of them were Hindus. We all got along fine, each respecting the other's religion and customs in our village."

We had heard the replacement land Jamal's family received in exchange for their fertile land in India was poor and unable to sustain productive agriculture. His family suffered a great diminution of income.

"The problem was that three old men made the decision for so many millions of people. Jinnah was sick, Mountbatten had a military career and would go back to England, and Jawaharal Nehru was pushed to decide on the partition right away instead of trying to keep the peace. Gandhi pleaded for nonviolence and fasted to try to make the people see the futility of killing their neighbors. He was nearly successful, but a religious fanatic assassinated him less than a year after the partition," Robert said.

"Sad. Then Jinnah died of cancer half a year after the partition. He got his dying wish," Jamal spoke the words sadly. "Pakistanis still honor and revere him for creating the Muslim League and pushing through the separate Muslim country."

"Why was it so important to have a Muslim country if the different religions got along?" All that trouble for dividing a country that had existed for centuries baffled me.

"The Muslim League wanted to assure the Muslims their way of life," Helen said.

"So they divided the country in just two months? How did they decide where to divide the two countries?"

"They brought a retired judge, Sir Cyril Radcliffe, from England," Lloyd said. "He'd never been to India and knew nothing about the geography or infrastructure, but Nehru and Jinnah approved. Mountbatten locked him away in an isolated location so no one could influence him."

"I remember we were so worried when the new border was disclosed," Najma said. "We hoped that Amritsar would be in Pakistan, but the Sikhs wanted the city with the Golden Temple to be in India, so the new border was drawn between Amritsar and Lahore, the sister cities that attracted artists and writers."

"The Punjab was divided, but the eastern Pakistani border with India caused riots in Calcutta that went on for months," Jamal said.

"Yes," Robert said, "Radcliffe didn't realize the new borders separated the jute fields from the factories that processed it, or that the cotton mills were now in a different country from the cotton fields. The man had never been to India or knew the terrain he was dividing. Businesses wanted to carry on as usual, but chaos ensued. It took a long time to straighten out."

"Perhaps if Nehru and Mrs. Mountbatten had a hand in it, things might have been smoother." Daphne smirked.

The others chuckled at the inside joke.

I looked surprised, but Najma shrugged and said softly, "They both had affairs, none too discreetly."

"What happened to the princes? I heard there were hundreds of little kingdoms within the borders of India, all owned and ruled by the prince who owned the land," Jim asked.

"Most were absorbed, but a few larger and more influential ones were allowed to remain. A few still exist," Robert said. "The viceroy collected taxes more easily from the wealthy ones, and it was to his advantage to let them be."

The dinner had many courses. The conversation with the people who knew so much about the political history of the country gave me an insight into what had happened to create this country where we lived. I hadn't realized that Pakistan had existed only during the past fifteen years. No wonder it felt like India.

We lingered over each course, served in silence by the table *bearers*. They made an art of presenting food in an unobtrusive manner. Whatever we might need, a hand would reach out and provide it. As each course was finished, an arm from an unseen body floated from the darkness behind us into the circle of candlelight, quickly whisking away plates and utensils. Each course had a different wine, and most servings were small enough to enjoy a taste of many dishes.

At midnight, the band played "Auld Lang Syne." Jim and I swayed around the floor as we rang in the new year of 1963 with a kiss.

The evening drew to a close, and we said good night.

"This was a different New Year, wasn't it?" Jim asked.

I looked around at the Punjab Club and felt the importance of British tradition in their long rule in India. We were learning about the problems brought on by the partition of Pakistan, so recently cleaved from ancient India. In the two months I'd been here, I felt like I had learned much, but there was more I wanted to know. Our friends had mentioned that the Punjab Club had hosted Sir Cyril Radcliffe, the English judge who came to Lahore and stayed at Falletti's Hotel when he needed a break during those months preparing for the partition. Perhaps he found solace among his fellow British expatriates as he struggled with his assignment to create the new country's borders. The Punjab Club had been a gathering place for British administrators when India employed a large bureaucracy of the British East India Company to run the country, the brightest crown jewel of the British Empire. We felt the dignity of the era clinging to the men who walked these halls. Their anguish over losing India left generations of civil servants' ghosts languishing in its polished, once-vibrant bastion of British dominion in the sub-continent.

French Lessons and Taxi Adventures

ONE CHILLY MORNING IN JANUARY, Claire and I started French lessons held at the home of Mrs. Etienne Martin. We'd found a taxi that took us to Mrs. Martin's apartment, part of a large home on the outskirts Gulberg, Lahore's popular residential neighborhood for foreigners. A thin coating of frost left a white glaze on the lawns. We climbed the steps to Mrs. Martin's apartment and rang the bell.

"*Bonjour, madams.*" Mrs. Martin smiled and opened the door to welcome us. "Come. Sit down, and we will get acquainted."

Mrs Martin was dressed in a fashionable skirt and blouse with a silk scarf tied at her neck. I caught a whiff of perfume, a mixture of roses and spices. Mrs. Martin was from Paris, and her American husband had whisked her away to Lahore. We took our seats around her dining room table covered with a lace trimmed linen tablecloth

"First, we will learn some vocabulary words and conjugate our first verb, to be."Mrs. Martin's hair was swept up in a chic chignon, and she proceeded like a stern teacher.

Mrs. Martin gave us the words, and we repeated them and wrote the vocabulary words and verb conjugations in French. The hour passed quickly.

"See you on Friday." She waved as we left. The class would meet on Tuesday and Friday mornings. Claire and I found a taxi for the return trip to WAPDA Flats. We chatted along the way about the class. When we got out of the vehicle, Claire turned to pay the driver while I tried to brush something sticky from the back of my legs.

Claire took one look and said, "You're going to need some polish remover to get that off. It looks like grease."

The taxi's last passenger must have had an engine in the backseat, and my precious nylons had broad grease stripes across the back. Nail polish remover didn't work, and I lost one pair of precious nylon stockings.

The next week, the *chowkidar* flagged down a taxi passing by. Claire gave him the address in Gulberg. We had driven less than a mile along Racecourse Road when he pulled off the pavement and stopped in the dirt at the side of the road.

"Petrol finished." He drummed his fingers on the steering wheel.

Claire and I were perplexed. We had been going along smoothly. No sputtering engine indicated the gas running out. He shrugged his shoulders and sat there, waiting for us to get out. We looked at each other and got out.

"Do we pay him anything?" I asked Claire.

"No, we didn't get where we're going. We don't owe him anything. Let's see if we can find another taxi."

We scanned the traffic along Racecourse Road, hoping for a taxi to appear. As we walked a little ways past his car, the driver started his engine, made a quick U-turn, and headed back toward town. We looked at each other, perplexed at his actions and annoyed to be dumped after a few blocks. How would we get to class on time?

As we paced back and forth, another taxi came along. We flagged him down and made it to the class with no more wasted time. Once the experience was over, Claire and I laughed. We couldn't figure out why he didn't want to take us to our destination.

Mrs. Moran laughed when we told her of our taxi driver's actions. "You never know what these taxi drivers will do. I've had some unbelievable things happen."

The hour ended as I was finding the words intriguing as well as listening to her accent. I loved the sound of the words. How wonderful to find a French class in Pakistan, of all places. In high school, when I had studied Spanish, I'd had a difficult time choosing between the two languages. Now my problem would be to keep the Urdu words I heard spoken by the servants separated from the French I was trying to learn.

Another day on the way to our class, Claire glanced into the backseat of the taxi that stopped for us. She backed out and sent him on his way with a few words in Urdu.

"What's wrong?" I hadn't seen inside as Claire had.

"He's been carrying goats. The taxi reeked of straw and manure." We learned to look before entering a taxi to see what surprises previous passengers might have left.

One day later in spring when the weather warmed, we were about halfway between Mrs. Martin's home and WAPDA Flats when the driver braked and slowed the car. He pulled the taxi off the road, the thumping noise giving the telltale sound of a flat tire. He got out and looked at the tire. He shrugged his shoulders, sat down, and lit a cigarette.

"What's he going to do? Can't he change the tire?" I asked Claire.

She was proficient in Urdu and turned to question the driver. "He says he doesn't have a spare tire."

"We'd better look for another taxi, don't you think?"

"Yes, but he said his cousin will be coming by soon, and if we wait, he can take us home."

We discussed the chances of his cousin coming along before we baked in the heat of the midday sun.

"Let's find another taxi," I said.

Clair agreed. We stood by the road, watching for taxis. The heat was becoming more intense as the midday sun beat down on us.

A *tonga* driver going the other way saw us waving and turned around to pick us up. The *tonga* was better than waiting for a cousin who might never show up. We got into the *tonga* and watched the homes along Gulberg Road pass by at a more sedate pace than they had from a taxi, to the tune of the clip-clop of the horse's hooves. At least we were shaded and moving in the right direction.

By far the most hair-raising taxi ride was the day we were returning to WAPDA Flats from the Mall. We'd given the driver our address when we got in, but he turned to ask us the address again a few blocks from our building.

"WAPDA Flats. Corner Racecourse Road? Is corner Jail Road, too?"

"Yes, that's it," I replied.

He tried to slow down, but his brakes didn't respond. He tried the emergency brake, and our speed decreased, but we were not sure that the driver would be able to stop. He turned the key, shutting off the engine, and then opened the driver's door and put out his foot. From my seat right behind him, I saw him extend his leg, press his heel on the pavement, and push as hard as he could. He steered with one hand, held onto the door with the other, and leaned into his extended foot, his body now half outside the vehicle. He continued to push his weight on his foot as the taxi slowed. It slowed a little more and then bounced off the pavement to the dirt walking path. The taxi shuddered to a stop right in front of WAPDA Flats.

Claire and I breathed again, almost in unison. We were shaken but relieved to be home. I wondered what remained of the driver's shoe. We left him a good tip and added another incredible taxi story to our growing list.

A Second Christmas in January

THE NEW YEAR OF 1963 began with a chill in the air and frost covering the stubble of grass at WAPDA Flats. I shivered as I took Mark by taxi to the private nursery school in Gulberg. Jim agreed with me that the preschool experience with social interaction would be good to prepare him for kindergarten next September. The nursery school teacher accepted Mark, and we enrolled him with a tuition of twenty dollars a month. I'd have to take him and pick him up by taxi.

Jim's mom, Grace, a first-grade teacher, felt he was progressing fine with reading picture books to Kevin, doing simple arithmetic, and spelling the words I taught him. However, we worried about the pidgin English and syntax he was copying from Sherif and the servants. Sherif was learning English with Alam's help. Mark also picked up some of the Urdu words he heard and mixed them with English. One day when I gave Mark cough medicine, he held up his hand and said, "*bas, bas,*" shaking his head. My son was telling me to stop in Urdu.

I also heard him say, "Is I am do it." And another time, he said, "Is I am helping." We encouraged the boys to say *shukreah* (thank you) or to agree with the speaker with *acha* (okay or yes). When Jim or I heard him speaking with his sentences reversed, we'd correct him, and Mark would

151

correct himself. Sherif's English was still limited. He didn't notice mistakes as we did and probably wouldn't have corrected Mark.

Starting the second week of January, Sherif came to work at seven thirty to care for Kevin, and I left with Mark before eight to take him to nursery school by taxi. I returned to pick him up when school was over at eleven. Taxi fare for the two round trips was about fifteen rupees a day with tips, about three dollars per day. A car would have been a great convenience, but the *chowkidar* hailed taxis for me each morning.

Mark came home happy the first day but reluctant to give many details. By listening and asking subtle questions, I learned they made paper hats, modeled clay, and colored. The teacher showed them pictures to identify. Mark said that was easy.

"Do you go outside to play?"

"Yes, we play outside. They have rabbits, and we fed them," Mark said. "After that, we get juice, grapes, and crackers." Snacks seemed a popular part of the program for Mark.

By now, Sherif was reliable at preparing boy's lunches. With Alam's help in translating, I showed him how to mix the bread that I baked three days a week and instructed him when to punch the dough down. He didn't need to write things down, but he remembered the amounts of ingredients. Before long, I could leave after starting the bread and depend on him to keep an eye on the rising process while he watched Kevin. That left me free to do other things.

One day, I went to the picture framer Mrs. Baxter had recommended to pick up my collages I had taken to him in December. The man's frames were exquisite, wide contoured frames covered in jute, gold gilt trim, and glass to protect the delicate dancing figure. They turned out better than I expected, and I could hardly wait to hang the pictures. As soon as I arrived home, I found nails and a hammer. The collages of Indian dancers added beauty and texture to our wide expanses of white walls. We could use some more decorative items, so I began to look for interesting things to buy and take home with us. Four months had passed, and still our shipment hadn't arrived.

Jim received a notice that our shipment of household goods had arrived at the job and was stored in the warehouse. I was eager to go to Baral to replenish my clothing and reclaim other useful things I had packed last September in Reno. The Friday after the news that our shipment was here,

Jim took the day off, and we drove north. Again, Jim had parts to deliver to the job.

"Jim, the Christmas tree may not survive the heat on the balcony. Why don't we take it to Dora? She'll find a place for it in her yard."

Jim loaded our live cedar Christmas tree in the pickup.

Traffic on the Grand Trunk Road wasn't as bad in winter with the crops harvested. I remembered how we crept along behind slow-moving vehicles on our first trip. Camel caravans, herds of flat-tailed sheep, and brightly painted trucks still competed for space on the two-lane road. I felt more comfortable watching for opportunities to pass. This trip, I was prepared with snacks and a bottle of boiled water.

At the huge warehouse at Mangla, a man led us down the aisles to the wooden crate that contained our shipment. As they pried it open, I recognized the boxes I had packed last September. Jim saw my sewing machine, a handsome old Singer in an oak cabinet, wrapped in blankets next to Kevin's crib.

"I thought you weren't going to bring any furniture?" Jim looked puzzled.

The company didn't want people to bring heavy furniture so they provided furnished houses.

"Jim, do you remember when I bought this? You were in college, and I only paid twenty dollars. I thought a treadle machine would be a good idea so the power wouldn't be a problem. One small cabinet and the crib don't weigh that much."

Jim shrugged. "You're right." Jim spoke the sweetest words that a husband can say.

We sorted through household items in the boxes, repacking our 110-volt appliances, like my mixer and iron, knowing they couldn't be used in Lahore without transformers. With all the baking I did, the mixer would be the most useful item in the shipment, but not with 110-volt power. I found my measuring cups and spoons and put them in the truck, though I had managed without them for months. We found our coats, pants, and sweaters from South Dakota's winters. The boy's new shoes, with the soles I'd scuffed to make them look used, were a welcome sight. Wooden Play-School toys were a treasure. *Today felt more like Christmas than December 25 had been.*

My record player was 110-volt, but I put it in the truck, along with my small collection of 78 RPM records. We would get a converter, and I would once again have the music I missed more than anything. We loaded our treasures in the pickup and drove up the hill to the town.

Ray and Dora Haugen were pleased when we brought them our Christmas tree. Their yard was already the most beautiful on their block. Dora insisted we stay for lunch. I talked to her while Ray and Jim caught up on the news about the job.

"The ManDamCo Club restaurant and bar will be open in April. You'll have to come back then and try it," Ray said.

"They're hiring two French chefs, so the food should be wonderful," Dora said.

After lunch, the Haugens gave us a walking tour of the new town center. The stores and post office lined up along the main road with a few small business spaces still vacant.

"Let's check the commissary," Dora said. "We heard they were supposed to get cottage cheese soon. Let's see if it came in. I'd love some cottage cheese."

"So would I," I said as we headed for the commissary.

We walked up and down the aisles that looked like a modern market in the States but lacked most dairy products. Frozen milk wasn't something I'd want to try, but cheese was now a regular item. There wasn't any cottage cheese, but I selected many items I could use to add variety to our meals.

As we left the commissary, Dora introduced us to Reverend Paul Pulliam as he walked by. He and Jim shook hands, and we saw why this man had such appeal. We had heard of the new minister who had lived in Pakistan for many years, married another missionary's daughter, and exuded charisma. The community leaders who emerged in the early days of Baral Colony heard of this outstanding man and recruited him from Gordon College in Rawalpindi as the pastor of their community protestant church.

"Did you take the money to the *tonga* man yet?" Dora asked him.

We had heard about the story of how Paul was on the way from Rawalpindi to interview at Mangla when he came upon a seriously injured man whose *tonga* and horse had been in an accident,.The horse had to be destroyed. The man's arm had a compound fracture, and Paul took him to the nearest hospital in the company car. When the Americans at Mangla heard of the poor man's loss of his livelihood, they took up a collection and had enough money to replace his *tonga* and horse as well as give him money for medical bills. We had sent our contributions from Lahore.

"Yes, a group of the ladies accompanied me when I took it to his village. The generosity of the Americans overwhelmed the fellow. I think it was an interesting encounter from both perspectives." Paul chuckled.

"How so?" Jim asked.

"Well, the American women were shocked when they discovered that the man had two wives. The Pakistani women were astonished at the miniskirts worn by the American women and kept fingering the silk stockings, not knowing what these women's legs had over them."

We all laughed at his description of the visit. We said good-bye and decided to drive back to Lahore the same day.

The pickup was loaded with the possessions we chose to take home, the boxes of food items from the commissary, and a few equipment parts to return to Lahore. With a fresh supply of warm clothing and new shoes for the boys, I felt like we had made a bountiful trip.

"Let's take a few minutes to see how the job is progressing." Jim turned toward the machinery working around the old Mangla Fort.

He drove up the road to a spot where we could see the progress. We marveled at how much earth had been moved and watched the fleet of trucks busy hauling the excavated materials. I asked Jim about the name of the project, Mangla.

"Jim, do you know how they named it Mangla?"

"After the fort, I guess," Jim said.

"How did the fort get the name of Mangla?" I persisted.

"I'm not sure anyone knows exactly where the name came from," Jim said.

"Remember that book you gave me published by WAPDA? The book told the story of a famous female goddess known as Mangla Devi. She lived near the fort, and local worshippers came to her. Their hearts were heavy with worries and bursting with wishes. The story said that the ritual was for people to first take a dip in the Jhelum River, right where the river made a big curve."

"Isn't it too cold to swim in the river, Mom?" Mark asked.

"Yes, it would be cold now. In summer, it would be refreshing."

Mark agreed, nodding his head. "What happened after they swam?"

"They asked the goddess for favors or to grant their heart's desire. Her name came to mean 'one who answers your fondest wishes.' She was known to be very generous." I tried to remember all the details of Mangla Devi' s story. "In Punjabi, *mang* means 'ask,' and *lai* means 'have it.' So she granted the wishes of all who came to ask."

"I like Mangla Devi," Mark said.

"Me, too." Kevin echoed.

"I hadn't heard that one." Jim wasn't much for religion, but he liked action stories.

"Well, if Mangla Devi is still around and listens to wishes, we should wish for the early diversion of the river and to complete the project early. And we have to hope she grants our wish," I said. "How could it hurt?"

Jim laughed. I chuckled at finding something he hadn't read since he was a voracious reader. I knew not everyone agreed that this was a proper explanation of the word Mangla, but without an authentic etymological explanation, it was an interesting one. I chose to believe it was true since no one could tell us where the name Mangla came from. It might be true. Wasn't India originally the land of mystics and magic?

◇◇◇◇◇

WHEN WE ARRIVED HOME, I had shocking news in the first mail in months from my mother. She had sold the big house with two rental cottages in Reno. Frank, her husband, persuaded her to sell and move my sisters and her to Florida. How much farther from Nevada could they have gone? I was devastated that she sold the house that I still considered our family home. Florida? What was she thinking? Mother hated the heat and the humidity. My sisters' father must be furious to have his daughters so far away from Reno.

I was relieved to hear from her, but her news brought fresh concerns. Was Frank making any money? Without an income to support them, the proceeds from the sale of her house wouldn't last long.

Gone was my mental picture of the home where I had spent my high school years. I loved walking home with my books cradled in my arms, my footsteps crunching the deep red, yellow, and golden leaves that fell from the canopy of mature trees in front of the stately homes along our street. Many like ours had become guesthouses where paying guests filled the unused bedrooms. My favorite room was the dining room where we enjoyed holiday dinners with the table laden with Mom's favorite dishes.

On that table, I had helped my sisters with their homework projects. I had cut fabric for a new skirt or dress on the dining room table. The telephone was at one end of the room, and I spent hours talking to friends, tethered to the wall outlet late into the evening. What happened to that big mahogany table, the heart of our family?

I looked down the length of my own dining room table in Lahore, halfway around the world. Wherever we lived, this was where my family gathered for food and conversation. Most afternoons, the table also served as my desk. That tradition of our family home would always be with me, no matter where I lived.

A much different letter arrived from Jim's Uncle Frank, his mother's oldest brother who was a retired pharmacist. His pharmacist's group was planning a tour of the Orient. He was considering coming to Lahore to visit us when the rest of the group returned to California. The timing was perfect. Jim was scheduled to take a week's vacation in May. A visit from a family member was wonderful news, especially Frank, who had been a frequent visitor in our home when Jim first worked for Atkinson and we'd lived in South San Francisco. He planned to spend a few days in Hong Kong and asked what he could bring us.

∞∞∞∞

IN THE DAYS FOLLOWING OUR trip to Baral Colony, Kevin discovered that the knobs of my record player were a great new toy. He twisted them off and found places to hide them. He giggled in great delight. We found a transformer to change the 220-volt power plugs to 110 volt so I could play my records. When I wanted to to turn on the record player, I couldn't find the knobs. My mischievous toddler thought it was great fun to hide them from Mom. I found one in his mouth and another under his pillow. I lectured Kevin to leave Mom's record player alone. He agreed, and a few minutes later, he twisted the knobs off again and scurried away with his prize.

I caught him by the arm and gave him a swat on his bottom, well padded with a thick cloth diaper.

"No," I told him for emphasis.

Alam walked by just as I swatted Kevin. The look on his face showed

complete shock. I had struck a male child. How could a mere woman challenge the superiority of a male and chastise him? Never mind that a jolt of
electricity could have hurt my child or he could have swallowed the knobs.
Even as a mother, I had no right to chastise the superior male, my errant
son. Unfortunately, Alam saw my transgression, and I felt the backlash.

Alam came and went that day, making a point to avoid looking at me.
He did the minimum of chores. Three days passed before he spoke to me
again. Those three days taught me the backlash of the male-dominated
society. I decided that, in the future, I would chastise my sons in private
rather than risk offending Alam's Muslim view of a women's place in the
world.

My status as mother was beneath a male child in this society, and punishment for a wrongdoing not something a lowly female was allowed to do.

16

Anarkali Bazaar During Ramadan

THE PALMS OF SHERIF'S HANDS were covered in red, like mercurochrome. Did he have some kind of skin disease? I'd mixed the day's bread early that morning, and I wasn't sure he should touch it. I had to leave soon and depended on him to punch the bread down in an hour or so. I wasn't sure what to do until Alam appeared. He spoke to Sherif in Urdu and then turned to me.

"*Memsahib*, Sherif's friend get married last night. At weddings, people paint their hands red with henna dye for good luck and happy marriage."

I looked more closely at Sherif's hands. Intricate patterns covered his palms, the back of his hands, and up his forearms, like miniature paintings.

"How do they make such pretty designs? I thought henna was a powder?"

Alam looked at the patterns. "Is good artist. Mix henna with oil. Make paste. Then artist use small brush. Copy Persian script or story for wish of happiness for couple getting married."

We all laughed at my mistake as I learned another Pakistani custom. I was still reluctant to have him handling the bread dough or kneading it with henna, so I gave him other chores and handled the bread dough myself.

159

"Don't ask the servants to do anything very strenuous, especially if it is hot or late in the day. Ramadan begins next week, and devout Muslims fast from before sunrise until the sun sets," Jim told me at breakfast. "They don't even drink water, so they may become very weak and even dehydrated. None of them can be expected to do a normal day's work during Ramadan."

Devout Muslims observed Ramadan as a time for spiritual reflection, prayers, and charity. They rise early, eat their first meal before the sun is up, and then fast all day until the sun sets. Ramadan follows the lunar calendar, so the celebration is sometimes in the hot weather months, a difficult time for people to maintain their strength for such long periods of abstaining from water, food, or sex. After sunset, they break the fast by first eating three dates, performing the *Maghib* prayer and sitting down to *Ifter*, the main evening meal. The Night of Destiny, celebrated on the twenty-seventh day of Ramadan, is celebrated as the first time Mohamed was given the Quran by the Archangel Gabriel.

At the end of the thirty days of fasting, people watch for the *Hillal* moon, a tiny thumbnail sliver in the sky that signifies the end of the fast. When the crescent moon appeared, fasting ended, and the celebration of Eid began. First was the "Sweet Eid" when people indulged in dried fruits, candy, and baked goods. Next came the "Meat Eid" when they roasted chickens, goats, and beef, the best they could afford. Families bought new clothes, traveled to their home villages to celebrate with their relatives when possible, and exchanged gifts with each other.

I heeded Jim's advice and tried not to give Alam, Afsar, or Sherif any more chores than necessary. I felt sorry for them when I saw them moving so slowly in the late afternoon. I also tried to send them on an errand away from the dining room when we had lunch. I didn't want to torture them with serving or smelling our midday meal.

◇◇◇◇◇

JIM'S NEW ALARM CLOCK WE'D bought wasn't working. We had found it a week before Ramadan began, deep inside Anarkali Bazaar in the walled Old City of Lahore. The clock shop nestled among stores that sold all kinds of merchandise. The bazaar was amazing, looking like a movie set with the cast of characters in exotic robes and dress that represented different areas of the Punjab, all drawn to this historic marketplace. As we explored, Jim had told me how the section of the Old City of Lahore was named Anarkali Bazaar.

"The Mogul's possessiveness of their women made even a glance at another man a crime," Jim told me. "The story was that a beautiful young girl named Anarkali, or Pomegranate Blossom, looked at a young man, Salim, the son of her intended husband, Akbar. He saw them gaze at one another in the mirror. Akbar was furious and had her buried alive upright, enclosed in a tomb of stone and mortar. Later when the son she smiled at, Salim, later called Emperor Jahangir, came to power, he built the unique, octagonal-shaped structure over the original tomb where she was buried alive. People named it Anarkali's tomb."

I shuddered at the fate of that poor girl. *She was a victim of the male superiority prevalent in this country.*

"The clock isn't working, and I'll need it in the morning," Jim said one day during Ramadan. "We have an important shipment arriving tomorrow on the early flight, and I need to meet it at five in the morning. I might miss the flight without an alarm clock. Could you exchange it for me?"

"No problem. I'll be glad to go this afternoon," I said.

"John said you could have his car and driver. Ghulam will wait for you and bring you home," Jim said.

It was always easier to have a car than to hunt for a taxi, and during Ramadan, who knew how many taxi drivers would take the afternoon off and not return to work?

The entrance to the Anarkali Bazaar angled off the Mall just past the traffic island with the cannon, Zam Zama, a symbol of the unity cast from the weapons of the tribes who melted down their guns after peace was restored. The cannon sat on the island in the road's fork, marking the gate to the Old City. Although Pakistan was separated from India by partition in 1947, serious talk of a Muslim nation had begun in the late 1800s under the foresighted Mogul ruler, Akbar. The cannon, placed near the gates of the Old City, was a reminder to many people daily. The founders who cast the heavy artillery piece also chose Lahore as the provincial capital, which it has remained.

I smiled, remembering the opening scene of Rudyard Kipling's *Kim*. This was the spot where the boy met his *chela* (mentor) and his adventures begin. As I turned into Anarkali Bazaar, I thought of Pomegranate Blossom and how that lady's story added to the texture of Lahore.

Through the centuries, Lahore had been known by many names, like El
Ahwar, Lahanur, and Loharkotta. As names evolved, some evidence shows
that, by the sixth century, Labokla was the name of the walled city on the
banks of the Ravi River. The Ravi, one of the tributaries of the Indus, is
born high in the Himalayas and flows through the Punjab, watering the
fertile land, "the breadbasket" of the subcontinent. In the site known now as
Lahore, romantics still say, "If you haven't seen Lahore, you haven't lived."
Such is the reputation of this cultured city of universities, mosques, and
memorials to Mogul, Sikh, and Hindu leaders. Artists, poets, musicians,
and philosophers have historically been drawn to Lahore and its companion
city, Amritsar, seventeen miles to the east. Artists and writers still flourish in
its academic and cultural climate.

Anarkali Bazaar's shops lined the ancient alleys that doglegged through
the Old City to the Kashmiri Serai. Here, all kinds of camels, horses, and
cattle could be sold or traded. The businesses lining its meandering path
had colorful awnings shading the open stalls from the heat. Alleyways with
no signs or markings led to businesses secreted in the labyrinth of ancient
buildings. Shopkeepers loudly hawked their wares inviting every passerby
to come inside and "just have a look." Tea stalls, interspersed with fabric,
hardware, and jewelry shops, all emitted scents from incense to dust and
exotic, pungent spices. Tea runners sat idly in front of the tea stalls with no
customers this day.

Today, the charcoal fires were cold. No aromas of cooking meats
or vegetables permeated the air, for it was Ramadan. No food would be
cooked until the sun set in the western sky. Ghulam dropped me at the Mall
entrance to the bazaar. We agreed to meet in an hour. The Ford sedan was
too large for the narrow streets. He drove off in search of a parking place.
I hoped the shopkeeper would be willing to exchange Jim's alarm clock. If
he refused, I would buy a new one. I was surprised Jim didn't hear the pris-
oner's chains or the *muzzim's* call to prayer. They awoke me each morning
at dawn. Some days I was able to go back to sleep, but usually I got up to
start the baking and chores early before the heat.

I enjoyed looking at the shops as I walked further into the bazaar and
away from the more familiar area of the Mall. I bought some buttons and
ribbon, handing the storekeeper a five-rupee note, about one American
dollar. He counted my change in Urdu, fumbled under the counter, and
handed my purchases to me in a small paper. I looked at it as I walked along.

It was a sheet of binder paper with chemistry problems written on it, folded in half, and glued on the edges to make a small paper bag. Inside were my buttons and ribbon. Typically, nothing that could possibly be reused was wasted. Paper was scarce in a country with few forests.

Several shops displayed decorative brassware and candlesticks. Another had carved wooden boxes. I could use some of them to decorate our apartment.

"Come inside, *memsahib*. Very nice workmanship. Made in Kashmir. I give it special price to you."

The next shopkeeper smiled and pretended to dust off a chair for me. "Only just come sit here, madam. My best prices for you only. What do you like?"

To show any interest in an item, the shopkeeper erupted into hyped salesmanship and a quick rush of bargaining. I passed several shops, unwilling to play the bargaining game.

Then a shop displaying wood carvings of animals and a glittering array of etched brassware caught my eye. I walked up the two sloping wooden steps to the shop. Shops were elevated to keep their floors dry during the monsoon rains. I held a carved brass vase etched with intricate floral patterns. The base had an interesting pedestal and was an exquisite classical shape.

"*Kitna rupeah* (How much)?"

"For you, I make special price, *memsahib*. Twelve rupees."

I put the vase back and started to walk away.

"Wait, *memsahib*. For only ten rupees, you can have it."

"Five rupees." I got into the negotiation game.

"*Memsahib*, fine workmanship in this beautiful vase." His eyes never left mine.

"Nine rupees."

Again, I turned to leave. "Six rupees." I shrugged.

"Oh, *memsahib*, Allah grant you long life. Give to me eight rupees only, and this beautiful vase is yours. And I also give you incense." He sweetened the deal with the incense.

Now I was having fun with his game. "Seven rupees."

"*Memsahib*, my children are hungry. Seven and a half, and it is yours."

To save face for coming down in price, he had to indicate extraordinary need, his hungry children. He smiled when I nodded to cinch the deal. He wrapped the vase in a length of fabric and tied it with string. He took my money with a nod of *saalam* and a bow.

The surging flow of people parted to make room for me in the current of humanity going in the same direction. Few women seemed to be out, even in *burquas*, and it was getting later in the afternoon. Most of the men were clad in the white or gray *shalwar kameez*, the traditional dress. Very few were in suits or Western clothes, and everyone looked alike. I followed a tide of shiny black hair with a few hennaed reds mixed in. I walked on, looking for the shop where we bought the clock. It was farther than I remembered. I felt eyes staring at my tall frame, blonde hair, and pale skin. People hurried along on their way home. I felt jostled, and the press of bodies was closer than I liked. The smell of sweat and so many bodies made me wonder if they had abstained from bathing for Ramadan, too. I had twenty-five minutes to find the shop, make the exchange, and meet Ghulam at five o'clock.

Around the next turn, I found the shop. The owner, a tall, gray-haired man, offered me a chair. His silver *karaku*l hat was of finest lamb's wool. He looked like a prosperous businessman. Checking the alarm clock, he confirmed it didn't work. He handed me a new one after checking to be sure the replacement clock worked. He apologized for my trouble. I felt relieved at how accommodating he was and how easy the exchange had been. Now I was eager to go home.

Daylight faded to a growing dusk as I left the clock shop. Little light shone on the narrow streets with two- and three-story buildings casting long shadows. I joined the moving throng and felt a hand squeeze my right buttock. I glanced around and saw only Pakistani men. I seemed to be the only American or European. I could see no other women. The hand that touched me could have been anyone in such a crowd. The next curve had long, winding alleys leading deeper into the bazaar to areas where I had never been. The growing darkness made the alleyways more frightening than they looked in daylight.

Just then, a hand groped my left breast, squeezing and lingering as it passed over my body. I set my face in a blank expression, trying to quell the fear that rose inside me. The bazaar's convoluted pathways and hidden alleys were a mysterious maze. I needed to get back to the Mall with darkness fast approaching. No one would hear me call for help over the noises in the bazaar. Who could be touching me? I'd hit him with my purse if I only knew which man he was. Just a few hundred feet straight ahead was safety and the Mall, but also more dark doorways. I wanted to run, but in the press of the crowd, there was no way to move faster. I straightened up to my full height of five-foot-nine and walked with as much confidence as I could muster. I kept my face composed so I didn't show the fear that made my knees weak and a quiver go through my body. When I glanced to the left, I felt a hand touch my right breast.

Did the same man keep touching me, enjoying himself at my expense? Who was it? Fear gripped me as I shivered in the growing chill. I held my head high, pretending not to notice the violating touch.

I clutched my packages to my chest to serve as a shield. I moved closer to the middle of the alleyway where the danger of bumping oncoming traffic seemed less intimidating than the groping of whoever was in the crowd matching my pace and moving in the same direction. Another hand brushed against my hip, lingering and giving my bottom a squeeze. I concentrated on my breathing with long, slow, deep breaths.

"Keep calm," I told myself.

"*Memsahib*, here!" Ghulam was waving and working his way toward me through the mass of people.

I was relieved to see him. He scooped my parcels into his arm and draped his other arm over my shoulders, forming a protective shield. In a short block, we were back at the Mall and the waiting car.

I had no idea if someone was following me or if more than one man took the chance to touch an uncovered and unprotected woman walking alone as darkness fell. That it happened in the bazaar named for Anakarli, who had the misfortune to look at a man other than her betrothed in the mirror, gave me an eerie chill.

I sank into the back seat, relieved to be in the safety and security of the car as darkness descended. The distant cry of the *muzzeim* called the faithful to prayer as another day's long fast for the observation of Ramadan ended.

Never again would I go to Anarkali Bazaar alone and late in the afternoon.

Encounter with the Motorcycle

THE AFTERNOON SUN PIERCED MY EYES AS I walked out from the shade of the apartment breezeway and scanned the playground, looking for Mark and Kevin across the driveway. I squinted and blinked my eyes, adjusting to the glare of the late afternoon sun. The oppressive heat slowed my movements as I stepped off the curb into the driveway. The boys were pushing their trucks and bulldozers in the sandbox where several other children played while their *ayahs* and Sherif watched nearby.

"Mark. Kevin. Time for dinner," I called to get their attention.

When Mark heard me, he stood, brushed off his pants, took Kevin's arm, and started toward me. Sherif bent to pick up their trucks. I heard the roar of a motorcycle engine revving up to a loud crescendo. The gleam of steel leaned into the curve of the apartment building as it came into view from my left, roaring toward us at a terrifying speed.

"Stop! Stay there!" I shouted to my sons.

Could they hear me above the noise? The driver was about to cut between me and my sons, who were walking straight toward the motorcycle and me.

"Stop! Don't move!" I yelled, louder this time.

Totally oblivious to the children playing so close by, the cyclist roared

166

his powerful machine between us. Behind me, the staccato of small feet running echoed in the passageway. A blur of red hair with small arms and legs churned past me, hurrying to reach the sandbox and my sons, his new friends. The new Irish boy from the flat next door bolted out from the passageway into the roadway, and with a sickening thud, the motorcycle and child collided. I stared in disbelief. The child lay very still, stunned, as I started toward him. His mother appeared, matching my steps as we raced toward the still child. He stirred, then let out a wail of fear at the blood he saw on his body. Right behind the mother, a redheaded man bent and scooped up his son.

I turned to the silent Pakistani motorcyclist watching the distraught family. I wanted to slap him or shake him to make him realize how reckless he was.

"Can't you see there are children playing here? You were going too fast right next to the playground."

I could feel the eyes of other parents and servants watching me as I strode to the shiny vehicle, reached for the ignition, and turned off the motor. As the machine belched into silence, I put the keys in my pocket.

I hurried across the driveway to my sons, hugged them, and led them away from the injured child and his parents. Sherif took their hands and took them inside. A small group of neighbors had gathered with suggestions for the newly arrived parents of where to take the child for medical care. Even when the boy's sobs had subsided, fear still filled his eyes.

The police arrived, and the motorcyclist asked them to order me to give him back his key. I refused. He wheeled his vehicle to the parking area at the rear of the complex. The building manager, who had joined the police, asked me to return the key.

"When the building management acknowledges the danger to the children with traffic between the building the playground, I will return the key," I said. "Not before."

Such behavior was unheard of for a woman in a Muslim country. Taking away the man's transportation was not my place, but I was adamant and turned my fury at the motorcyclist into trying to eliminate this danger to our children. Several times in the past, I had asked that the driveway be blocked so children could reach the playground without crossing through traffic. My requests had been ignored. This unfortunate accident was an opportunity to leverage a positive change.

With the building manager's attention now focused on the present accident, I pointed to the large containers with palms that flanked each apartment entrance. "They would work well as traffic blockades. This accident could have been prevented if they had blocked the road as I'd suggested before." I spoke with as calm a voice as I could muster. I was shaking with fury and fright for the injured child.

The child's father joined the group and listened to my ideas. I handed him the motorcycle key. I knew a man would have more authority than I would, especially since his son was the one who had been injured. I explained to him my previous requests and my idea of using the potted palms to block the driveway. He nodded agreement with me as he accepted the key.

The police and building manager walked a short distance away, discussing our demands and gesturing. They called the *chowkidar* to bring the *mali*. He listened to them and nodded his head as they gestured some directions.

The next day, large palm containers, two at each end of the playground, stood in the roadway and created a barrier to through traffic. The children now had a safe path to the playground. The little boy's injuries were superficial, and he had no broken bones. With bandages on his arms and head, he was back playing with Mark and Kevin a few days later.

The owner of the motorcycle rang my doorbell the next morning. He mumbled some words about the "sad accident." I took him across the hall to Mr. Laurie, the boy's father, who listened to the man's apology and handed him his key.

Movies and the Bollywood Invasion

"LET'S GO SEE A MOVIE," Claire said after we'd studied our French verbs for almost an hour.

The musical she suggested was playing in a theater near downtown Lahore. I hadn't seen a movie in six months, and I was eager for some diversion. The taxi dropped us at the theater. We bought our tickets and stepped into the cool theater.

"We need to sit in the *purdah* section," Claire whispered.

This was new to me. The *purdah* section in a theater? The usher took us up a flight of stairs, drew back a heavy velvet curtain, and showed us to our seats. We were in the balcony and hovered above the gallery of seats below. We looked ahead at the screen, but short walls that separated our section from those on either side and prevented anyone from seeing us. One couple shared the partitioned section two rows in front of us. The man's arm was draped around the *sari*-clad woman's shoulders. Her *dupatta* shielded her face from those on either side, and we couldn't see her face from behind, so they were obscured from anyone's view.

The movie started, and the American musical captured me and transported us back to the United States with the costumes and singing. The man in front of us kissed his lady friend a few times during the movie, and we heard giggles from the partitions to our right and left.

◇◇◇◇◇

THE MAIL BROUGHT A NOTE from Dora at Baral Colony. She and two other women were planning to visit Lahore for some shopping. They also had tickets to a special showing of a panoramic movie called *America*, which we'd heard would be showing soon. Dorothy Ziemer had a similar note from Norma. Dorothy and I decided we'd like to see the same film that would be shown in a large tent near Faltetti's next week. We decided to ask the ladies to stay with us.

"Two of them can stay with me if you can take one," Dorothy said.

"Dora is like another grandmother to my boys. They'd love to see her," I said.

We wrote back with our invitations. We'd also go shopping to show them around Lahore.

My family liked the bread and rolls I baked, but we also loved the sourdough French bread we enjoyed in the San Francisco Bay Area. Making bread was time-consuming, but it was a better solution than the poor local offerings. I looked through the cookbook Grace sent for Christmas. I found a recipe that described how to make sourdough bread. Our guests who were coming next week might like it, too. They'd all lived in the Bay Area.

The process required taking water from a boiled potato and allowing it to sour at room temperature to make the starter. I did as the recipe called for and then added the yeast to the rancid-smelling liquid from the boiled potato. The addition of flour helped diminish the pungent starter, but it didn't smell appetizing. I hoped this experiment was worth a few cups of flour to see if it worked. When the right number of days had passed, I added the noxious-smelling starter to my bread dough along with some apprehension. It would either be a flop or a favorite, I decided.

Late that afternoon, I took the loaves of bread from the oven just as the doorbell rang. There was Ken with a large grocery order he'd brought from Mangla.

"Ken, you are really an angel!" I hugged him and took a sack of groceries from his arm.

"What do I smell?" Ken's nose sniffed the air. He smiled in anticipation.

"I've just made my first batch of sourdough bread. It's an experiment, and I'm not sure it will be any good. Do you want to be my tester?"

"Sourdough bread is my favorite. I'd love to try it," he said eagerly.

"Come on in. We'll cut some for you. Would you like some butter or a sandwich?"

"No, just the bread. Could I have a little mustard on it?" Ken asked shyly.

"Of course." I cut the bread and watched him coat it with a thin layer of mustard.

"This is delicious! I'm amazed you made real sourdough bread. How did you do it?"

I explained the process, and he shook his head. "You do more cooking here than anyone I ever knew in the States, other than maybe a ranch cook."

"Can you stay for dinner? Jim should be home soon," I said.

We enjoyed Ken's company, and dinner was the least I could offer for his thoughtfulness in bringing my groceries in the company airplane every chance he had.

"No, I just wanted to drop off your groceries. I'm flying back to Mangla this evening, or I'd stay to enjoy more of that bread."

"Here, take another slice. One for the road!" I handed Ken a second slice of bread on a napkin. He tucked it in his pocket and waved good-bye.

Dora, Norma, and Vivian arrived a few days later. Norma had a balloon-skirted dress that gathered at the bottom. She'd bought or had it made in Hong Kong but didn't try it on, and she found it was too long. I looked at the voluminous skirt and could see it would need to be taken apart and shortened from the waist, a time-consuming job.

Dorothy and I took them to the women's tailor as our first stop. The tailor quoted her a sizable fee but promised it by the next day, so she was happy. Then we took them to the Old City bazaar with all the fancy fabric shops and watched the three women indulge in some serious retail therapy they'd missed the last few months at Baral Colony.

We had dinner at our home the night they arrived, with Dorothy contributing several dishes to the meal. Dorothy and I had become a good team with spontaneous meals for our many surprise guests. Company was fun, and we each kept a well-stocked pantry. The women looked around our living room, and admired the Indian collages I'd bought that hung on our wall.

"These are wonderful. Where did you find them?" Vi was intrigued.

I told her the story of Vera Chatterjee and her artwork. They took down Mrs. Chatterjee's address in New Delhi.

"I wonder if she'd come to Baral and show her work," Dora said. "I'd buy some, and I'm sure many of the women would, too."

They decided to invite her to one of the luncheons.

We caught up on news of the progress at Mangla Dam and were glad to hear the dental issues were resolved when a new dentist was hired. Norma filled us in on the job news.

"They had some problems with the Mole, and the first tunnel took fifty-one days to dig. They've modified the cutting blades, reinforced the ribs so they shore up the top of the tunnels as they go, and lined them with steel. They hope to dig the next tunnels much faster."

Norma's husband was one of the consultants brought in to expedite problems. After dinner, Norma took me aside to speak to me alone.

"I feel terrible that we got your house at Baral."

Norma was sweet to feel she should apologize. We were settled and enjoying Lahore, so I wasn't worried about the house at Baral. We had no idea if or when that transfer might occur.

"Norma, don't even think about it. They'll have a house for us if we do get transferred!"

At this point, we were settled in Lahore and liked it just fine. An empty house didn't make sense.

We all lined up on the day of the panoramic show. The production was amazing, showing landmarks in our country: the Empire State Building, Niagara Falls, the U.S. Capitol, and the Mall in Washington DC. It panned across the country to the Grand Canyon and ended at the Golden Gate Bridge in San Francisco. We stood in the tent, holding on to the rails so we could turn our heads and follow the images that the cameras showed all around the tent. The scenes showed our beautiful country in rich color portrayed with patriotic and symphonic music to accompany the exquisite photography. By the end, when the California coast and San Francisco's cable cars took the viewers on rides down the hillsides, tears streamed down my face. I felt the pride and reverence for the majesty of our country.

Perhaps it felt even more precious when we viewed it from half a world away, but waves of homesickness washed over me. We still had nearly two years on our contract before we'd see our beloved homeland again, and I was overwhelmed with emotion.

We were grateful for the women's company to share the beautiful film, a group of Americans all full of nostalgia for our country. After a few drinks and dinner with laughter and more stories, I felt better, but the cloak of nostalgia hung over me for some days after they departed.

◇◇◇◇◇

THE FOLLOWING WEEK, TRUCKS AND swarms of people filled the central court-yard of WAPDA Flats. Pakistan's flourishing movie industry was shooting a romantic film, and the company took over WAPDA Flats where our court-yard was the setting of the film. Workers bustled around the compound, laying long, snakelike cables along the stairwells from the front terrace through the breezeway beside our front door, and past the playground to bring power from the poles behind the complex. Other crewmembers posi-tioned the large cameras and platform in the driveway. The director con-sulted with the actors, a handsome, tall Pakistani in an open-necked shirt, and the star, a dark-haired woman in a deep red *sari*. Makeup men hovered over her while attendants scurried to do the bidding of the directors.

We watched the children carefully with all the electrical cables and so many people in the yard. Jim warned me to lock the doors each time we came in or out. The transient workers had a reputation for stealing anything that wasn't under lock and key.

When the filming began, I found a perfect vantage point on our terrace near the front corner of the living room. Here I could sit and read between the action scenes as they filmed from my balcony seat. The director shouted to the star several times, then showed her how he wanted her to run up the seven steps, stop, and turn with her arm up toward the sky. She was animated, her makeup and expressions were colorful, and she threw herself into the role with emotion. The high heels she wore caught on the bottom of her long *sari*. After several takes, the director had her clutch the *sari* and lift the skirt as she ran up the steps. Her long, red-painted fingernails accented her delicate hands as she gestured. I aimed our movie camera at her as their cameras rolled, hoping to capture a part of the drama she por-trayed so well.

Later when they took a break, I put the movie camera on the hall credenza and locked the door as I went outside to call in the boys for lunch. Sherif usually went in and out through the kitchen door that opened onto the breezeway. He went ahead, carrying the boy's toy trucks while I chatted with Marge for a few minutes.

When I opened the front door of our apartment, the first thing I saw was the hall credenza with nothing on it. The movie camera was gone. We were outside for only a few minutes, but it had disappeared from where I'd left it on the credenza. The front door required a key to open. *Perhaps the kitchen door was easier for someone to pick the lock, enter, and sneak out.*

But Sherif remembered closing and locking it with his key. Our movie camera had disappeared, along with some precious memories of our boys and the movies of our early explorations of Lahore and the trips to Baral Colony. I felt violated and angry that this technical film crew had swarmed all over the courtyard, made noise and chaos for days, and then stolen my movie camera. The next day, we learned that several wallets and cameras belonging to other residents were also missing. Management had assured us that the movie company people were trustworthy.

We felt betrayed that people we treated as guests would return our hospitality in this manner.

Riding with the Rangers

MY FINGERS TREMBLED AS I opened the envelope with a return address from the West Pakistan Rangers. Weeks had passed since I sent my application. I hoped I'd been accepted. The letter of acceptance gave directions to the army's riding arena and the times to meet on Tuesday, Thursday, and Saturday afternoons. The enclosed statement for sixty rupees would be my fee for one month, about twelve dollars in American money, and a one-time fee of fifty rupees, or about ten dollars, to join. I was elated after waiting so long for their reply. I could hardly wait to ride again. Even hard-working *tonga* horses caught my eye as they passed. I'd loved horses for as long as I could remember.

Helen had told me about the Rangers, a mounted military unit created in 1948 after the partition of India and Pakistan, to replace the British border guards. They had been called the Home Guards and now were known as the West Pakistan Rangers. Their duties included patrolling the borders in the desert areas where they used horses or camels.

"The horses are mustered out of the Rangers when they reach the age of eight years old," Helen had told me. "Most of the riders are teenage Pakistani girls from wealthy families. Their private school curriculum includes riding lessons. Should the young lady find herself invited to a country estate for the weekend while visiting in England, riding provides her with a useful social skill expected in upper-class British families."

At Helen's suggestion, I bought a pith helmet to keep the sun off my face. I'd had a pair of khaki jodhpur pants made by the women's tailor and returned to the shoemaker several times for fittings of the low riding boots that turned out to be quite comfortable.

The next Tuesday afternoon, I left Mark and Kevin with Sherif. They were still sleeping since I needed to leave during their naps. Wearing my new jodhpur pants, a cotton shirt, and my riding boots, I walked through the entrance gate, hoping for a taxi. The *chowkidar* smiled as he hurried to hail one for me. I felt like all I needed was a whip and I could pass as a circus ringmaster in these pants. I'd never worn anything fancier than new Levi's jeans to ride a horse.

I gave the driver the address of the Cantonment field on the outskirts of the Gulberg's sprawling bungalows with bougainvillea-covered walls and guarded gates. Soon we were driving through open fields, modest homes, and over the canal to an oval practice ring enclosed by a white fence.

The taxi pulled off the pavement with a bump and came to a stop. As I got out and paid the driver, a remuda of horses arrived, two by two, with a *syce* (groom) mounted on one of each pair and leading the second horse on his right. The column stopped in the sparse shade of the scraggy trees where the girls leaned on the fence chatting in Urdu. The *syces* dismounted and tied the horses to the fence. The girls asked the *syces* questions in Urdu. From their tone, I guessed they were requesting the horse they wanted to ride.

The uniformed soldier in charge rode up at the end of the column on a beautiful white stallion. He was a handsome man in his khaki uniform with a bandolier across his chest, a turban fanned in the Pathan style, and an air of absolute authority. His trimmed mustache and raven hair framed his bronze face. He followed the others, turned his mount in a circle, and approached the girls at a fast trot. He stopped the horse, kicked him lightly in the ribs, and pulled on the reins at the same time. The stallion reared on his hind legs with his mane and tail fanning with the speed of the movement. He held the pose for a moment, a perfect equine statue, and then dropped gracefully, stamping his hooves with impatience.

"*Acha.*" I smiled at him, pleased at his display of horsemanship.

The soldier called the girls' names, then motioned to the *syce* to bring the horse he chose. He went through the group, matching the girls with the horses. Even without speaking Urdu, I could tell some of the girls were asking him for their favorite mounts. I heard one of them call him Corporal Akbar. Army ranks puzzled me, and I never knew which were superior to the others, but his orders and the speed with which the *syces* and girls responded left no doubt that he was the boss, regardless of his rank. Finally, he turned to me.

"This horse, you ride." He pointed to a solid bay gelding.

It was the last horse I would have chosen, but the only remaining horses were two pony-sized mares. At least the horse was tall enough for my long legs. I approached the bay from the left and checked the length of the stirrups. They were too short for me. Before I could adjust them, the *syce* took the buckle from my hands. I had learned to saddle and bridle my horse when I was very young and preferred to check my own equipment. Would the *syce* be offended if I checked the cinch? I'd seen horses hold their breath when the saddle was cinched, and an unsuspecting rider could find himself on the ground with the saddle under the horse's belly. I really wanted to check that cinch, but the *syce* was impatient for me to mount. He held his hands cupped expectantly.

I had always put my foot into the stirrup and mounted on my own, but not wanting to offend the *syce*, I stepped into his palms and felt his upward lift as I swung my right leg over and settled into the saddle. His watchful eye followed my every movement.

"*Acha?*" He adjusted the length of the stirrup's strap to the length I'd indicated. He moved to the other side and adjusted the right stirrup to match. That was better.

"*Acha.*" I tested the length and nodded.

His features relaxed, and he patted the horse. The cinch felt secure, and the saddle stayed in place as I tested my weight in the stirrups. The mounted group filed into the oval enclosure with the soldier on the white stallion leading. Some of the horses pranced and showed their eagerness. The heavy-footed bay responded little to my kicks, and his speed didn't improve, but continued in his one speed, slow. We walked our mounts counterclockwise around the ring. My mount's tail swished flies. He ambled along behind the other horses.

"Reverse. Trot," the commander called.

The horses turned all at once, and to my surprise, even the bay gelding reversed with little direction from me. The *syces* spoke Urdu to the horses, but they understood English commands in the ring. Reining this big lug of a horse to get him to change direction was like driving a Mack truck with no power steering.

"Reverse. Canter," the commander called.

The horses reversed and cantered. My mount tried to pass off his trot as a canter. I kicked and swatted him, and he finally broke into a halfhearted canter, but no energy or speed was forthcoming. He still lagged behind the others.

The soldier in charge directed one girl to lead the horses in a formation with half the horses cantering clockwise and the others counterclockwise. At diagonal points on opposite ends of the ring, the leaders cantered toward each other, passing alternately in the center of the ring in a thread-the-needle formation. When our turn came to go, my steed took that moment to lift his tail, taking ample time to relieve himself, and slowed to a near stop. This delay made us too late to keep up with the formation. I kicked him, encouraged him with my hand across his withers, and clucked in his ear. Nothing I did made him move any faster. I felt embarrassed at my horse's lack of decorum, but I didn't know what I could do with his lethargy. The girls looked at me with disdain for breaking the formation. The leader commanded the riders to circle the horses around the ring again, and this time I was able to keep the horse moving without such a delay.

When the drill formations were completed to the soldier's satisfaction, he led us out of the ring for a cross-country ride. At the intersection of Canal Road, the soldier raised his arm to stop the traffic until we'd all crossed. We rode two abreast along the canal at a trot, my horse's gait jarring me with each step.

Clusters of mud houses bordered the pathway on the left along the banks of the canal on our right. The mud houses had low-walled enclosures around them where goats and chickens shared the space with small children. A thin woman, wearing a flowered *shalwar kameez*, watched us from her doorway. Her long scarf, a *dupatta*, was draped around her head, but she made no effort to cover her face. She touched her lips and then her chest and swept her hand toward the ground in a *salaam* of greeting to our passing group. The baby she picked up wore only a long shirt. His bare bottom was visible beneath the hem when she swung him to her hip. I could see callouses on the baby's bottom from scooting on the hard-packed earth. As soon as the last horse passed, she hurried to check for droppings.

We rode several miles along the canal where *dhobis* stood in the water beating the clothing on the rocks at the water's edge. They soaped and rinsed the clothing in the canal and then dipped the garments in a bucket of bluing solution. Articles of clothing draped over each bush and rock as they dried in the sun. They paused in their work to wave at our passing group.

We reached a large field where few weeds grew in the hard-packed dirt. Each girl took off to ride her horse as she liked, some trotting and some just doing figure eights or cantering in small circles. A few let the horses run, enjoying the freedom of a gallop across the sand. I coaxed the old bay into a halfhearted canter. I enjoyed the freedom of riding in the open, but I wished I had a more enthusiastic horse. When the commander decided it was time to return, he whistled, gathered the group into formation, two abreast, for the ride back to the cantonment. After the effort expended during his brief canter, my horse had no interest in moving very quickly. I kept nudging him to keep up with the other horses.

The sun was sinking low in the sky when we returned along the canal. The reflection of the trees mirrored on the water cast a golden glow on the darkened canal's water, and the trees shadows lengthened as we returned to the cantonment.

The next day, my thighs were sore, but I had loved the group and being around the horses. I looked forward to the next time. As the weeks went by, the soldier gave me better mounts. After trying several horses, I'd decided I liked a blaze-faced sorrel mare. She stepped smartly in the ring, kept up with the other horses, and she was responsive to my commands. I was learning the drills and found it gratifying when I rode a more agile mount. Corporal Akbar became more congenial, even smiling and joking with the girls and me as we rode in the field.

Each evening when we returned, the women waited along the canals, watching for the chance to scoop up any dung from the horses. They patted it on the walls, and when dry, they added it to their cooking fires. One evening, small boys ran along beside the horses until the corporal shouted a sharp command. They dropped back and respected his authority.

The days lengthened as the spring time approached, but the sun was still low when we returned each afternoon. The rhythm of the horses' hooves gave the sinking sun a retreat cadence as it dipped low in the western sky. The blue-gray haze of cooking fires made the colors blend and shimmer in a kaleidoscopic of muted, hazy colors against the sky as evening descended on the Punjab at the buffalo dung hour.

The Lahore Horse Show

RAMADAN AND THE EID-AL-FATR CELEBRATIONS ended at the end of February. As the religious rigors of daily fasting ended, Lahore came to life with anticipation of the tenth annual horse and cattle show. The second week of March kicked off the season's busiest social week. Men traveled to Lahore from all districts of the country with their prize specimens of horses and cattle to display and sell at the prestigious show. Local newspapers called the show "The Pride of the Punjab." Excitement was palpable in the air, and in conversations I heard at the Mall, in the bazaars, and at Falletti's Hotel. People looked forward to the event with excitement.

We bought season tickets, hoping Jim could also attend some of the events that stretched over a five-day period. I loved horses, so rodeos or any kind of horse show was a magnet to me. The year before, we watched the news coverage of Jacqueline Kennedy and her sister when they attended the Lahore Horse Show on their tour in India and Pakistan. At the conclusion of that year's show, President Ayub Khan had presented Mrs. Kennedy with a magnificent Arabian horse, a black stallion with a white diamond marking on his forehead named Sadar.

George Archibald and his wife Adeline planned to see the horse show and were hosting a dinner party at the Punjab Club that Saturday night to which we and the Ziemers were invited. We were also invited to a wedding at one o'clock the same Saturday afternoon. *No problem. We'll make it to both events that day.*

A few days before the big weekend, Jim told me that one of the new employees, Bob and Mary Jean, had tickets to the horse show but couldn't find hotel reservation in Lahore. Jim asked if they could stay with us for two nights. They had a toddler who was Kevin's age. That was more than I'd expected, but we could manage. I started planning extra food. I'd send Alam to the bazaar early Friday morning to buy fresh meat for dinner.

Opening day of the horse show was Wednesday, and I took Mark with me. We found our seats and looked around at the crowd as we waited for the opening ceremonies to begin. The red sandstone stadium was filled. A sea of people in the white clothing was broken by splashes of red, orange, blue, and purple colors of the women's new outfits from the recent Eid celebrations. The green and white flag of Pakistan with the single star and crescent moon of Islam fluttered above the stadium. The sun glistened on the instruments of the band, ready to herald the appearance of the president to begin the festivities.

The trumpets sounded as the president of Pakistan, Field Marshall Mohammed Ayub Khan, arrived and spoke to the audience in Urdu and English, welcoming everyone to this event. He spoke with humor and dignity in his opening remarks. President Ayub Khan had spoken at a Lahore Women's Club event. I remembered how he towered over most other men. He had shown his sense of humor with the women that day as he fielded questions about topics that women posed to him. Ayub Khan was a Pathan from the Northwest Frontier Province who came to power by a bloodless coup when he ousted President Mirza in 1958. He continued to rule the country under martial law.

The president finished his opening remarks, and a military group marched to a British military tattoo to the music of the drums and a bagpipe, filling the stadium with their colorful uniforms and sounds. There were tent pegging contests, camel races, and a parade of sleek animals for sale. The crowd loved the whirling dervishes who danced in colorful red, gold, and green costumes, their flying feet showing beneath their harem pants. The music grew faster and faster with their feet and whirling noise-makers keeping every eye on their movements. Their dance was a religious ritual as well as entertaining.

Then came my favorite events, the equestrians. Rows of horses showed their precise formation. Then the horses passed each other and whirled in turns at the precise moment they were trained to do, finishing in neat rows that looked like toy horses from our vantage point high in the stands. Dancing horses performed with amazing agility. Their hooves beat in time as if they floated on springs while a drummer accompanied them. The horsemanship displayed by the riders was a thing of beauty to watch. Those cloaked in long-robed garments reminded me of the Arabic origins of the horses imported to Pakistan. Then to my surprise, dancing camels with rubbery strides and graceful, high-stepping showmanship performed to the delight of the crowd. These gangly-looking animals showed an agility I didn't know was possible.

Mark enjoyed the show but tired before the finale. We caught a taxi outside the grandstands and were soon home where I laid him down for a nap before dinner. I was delighted at the pageantry of the spectacular show. Mark's attention had never lagged.

On Thursday, I hurried through my chores, making extra bread to be sure I'd have enough for company, and had Sherif boil extra water for cooking and drinking. I gave Alam the money and told him what kinds of meat to buy so I'd have enough for our houseguests.

Bob and Mary Jean arrived on Friday afternoon. Their son Timmy was Kevin's age. Soon the two toddlers were playing together and copying each other's antics. Bob and Mary Jean were both tall, handsome people. Mary Jean had long, blonde hair and a soft-spoken, reserved manner. Both were still culture shocked by what they'd found in Pakistan, but they were trying to be good sports and adapt. She told me how helpful her neighbors had been, making her feel right at home.

I had dinner prepared, knowing they would be tired from the journey. We had drinks and got acquainted over dinner while we discussed our plans for the weekend.

On Saturday morning, I made breakfast and hurried to get ready. We had the wedding at midday. Our guests were leaving for the horse show. We gave them several suggestions but felt they would enjoy Falletti's Hotel or the Ambassador Hotel. We were planning to attend the Archibald's dinner.

The wedding was a coworker of Jim's from the Karachi office. His fiancée worked in Lahore, so they planned to be married here. Then they planned to go to Srinagar in Kashmir for their honeymoon. The lake and beautiful mountains sounded to me like Lake Tahoe, beautiful, high pine forests and clean air. Their week would be spent on a rented houseboat complete with servants to cook and cater to their every whim. We heard rave reviews from other Americans who had gone to Srinigar on vacation. I had dreams that we could someday also visit this mountain Shangri-La.

The civil ceremony, performed by a local minister, brought tears to my eyes, as always happened to me at weddings. The happy couple hosted a small reception, then caught the plane to India and their honeymoon.

We returned in late afternoon, checked on the boys, and showed Sherif the dinner I'd planned for them. We changed clothes and left Sherif with instructions for the evening. Our houseguests hadn't yet returned from the horse show.

We met the Ziemers as they came downstairs. John decided all four of us should go in his company sedan. Jim had a Pakistani driver's license so John gave his driver, Ghulam, the night off. Dorothy and I laughed at how quickly the events of the weekend had changed, now different from when we had first arrived. We felt isolated. This week, we were in the thick of activity, a welcome change from reading in the newsletter about the activities at Baral Colony that we sometimes envied.

We arrived at the Punjab Club where George Archibald and his wife Adeline were already there along with the Thorpes and Ken. Jamal and Najma arrived and were introduced to Lloyd and Virginia Thorpe. When I saw Ken, I realized the Archibalds had flown to Lahore with him, saving those long hours on the road. Virginia and Lloyd had rented a car from the company's car pool.

We enjoyed a more light and lively evening than on New Year's Eve when the conversation had been political but informative. We laughed and joked all evening over stories of the culture clashes between our Americans and the Pakistanis, and there were many examples.

George Archibald related management's side of the Baral Colony's American resident's gripes posed in a recent meeting. He said everyone wanted to bring over his own personal vehicles. Some could afford the 300 percent import duty and wanted the freedom of their own vehicle. George was more concerned with all the repair problems that would take the men away from the job they were being paid to make their priority. The program put in place for residents to rent a car and driver also avoided a rigid Pakistani law that allowed the police to take the driver from any accident, even minor, directly to jail. They stayed in jail until proven innocent, no matter how long it took. This dangerous repercussion of private ownership of motor vehicles was of even greater concern than the cost of repairs. We understood, although I still felt the loss of my independence. I had sold our station wagon when we left the States. It was one adjustment that made sense under the circumstances.

"Are you planning to buy some towel bars in Lahore, George?" Lloyd Thorpe asked with a sly wink to the rest of us.

George roared and told how one woman arrived, looked around the newly completed house, noticed there was no towel rack in the kitchen, and took the next plane home. The story was not funny at the time.

The washhouses were another problem George heard more about than he wanted.

"Why can't these women get their laundry done in the two hours twice a week we give them? There are more catfights about 'Her clothes were left in the washer' and 'Why can't they be here to take their clothes out of the dryer?'" George shook his head in disgust.

Most men didn't want to deal with details, especially George, who had a complicated dam to build.

Ken sat listening to the stories, taking it all in.

"Are you staying at WAPDA Flats tonight?" I asked.

"No, I got my favorite room at Falletti's. I always ask for the room Rudyard Kipling stayed in when he was in Lahore."

"That must be an elegant room." I was intrigued. Rudyard Kipling's room!

"No, it's one of their smaller rooms, but it has bookshelves and quaint furniture that's supposed to be the same that Kipling liked when he stayed there. It has an ambience I like, and it's in a quiet wing of the hotel."

How could he sleep knowing that a writer like Rudyard Kipling may have written some of his famous stories right in that room? I wondered if I'd have been able to sleep in such a wealth of memories.

The evening ended with more stories, most of them about our adjustment to the culture of our host country. Language was always an obstacle, but so was religion. Often things happened that made Americans feel like we'd stepped back in a time warp of several decades.

We thanked the Faroukis and the Archibalds as we left to go home. It had been a long day, and the activity was catching up with me. Our friends always reminded me that I was the youngest in the group and should still be ready to party. Jamal and Najma said good night as we left the club. They turned a different direction in the parking lot.

Only after they departed did we realize our transportation dilemma. The Thorpes had let their car and driver off for the evening so he wouldn't be tired for drive back to Mangla early the next day. John Ziemer's Ford sedan was the only vehicle we had. George, John, and Jim had a short executive conference and made a decision. Like stacking wood, the nine of us managed to find seats in our only vehicle. Luckily, sedans in the 1960s had wide bench seats, and we took advantage of every inch. Jim drove, Adeline sat in the middle, and George Archibald put me on his lap in the front seat. The Ziemers, Lloyd and Virginia Thorpe, and Ken all managed to squeeze into the backseat with the two women perched on their husband's laps.

Falletti's Hotel was only a few miles from the Punjab Club where we would drop off our passengers. Surely nine of us could make it that far in the now low-riding sedan.

George had relaxed and enjoyed the evening of multiple courses and different wines with each course, as well as the formal British service. He was in fine spirits as we settled in for the drive across Lahore. By the time we'd driven a short distance, I felt George rolling down the window beside us.

"Isn't it hot in here?" George's head turned to consult his friends in the backseat. Without waiting for an answer, he lowered the right front window.

A few blocks further, he asked his entourage again, "Are you too cold back there?" He promptly rolled the window back up.

As George controlled the temperature and our fresh air supply, we chuckled and then guffawed. Then gales of laughter came from the rear seat passengers. I squealed and acted insulted when he brushed my leg each time as he rolled the window up and down. This was the response he wanted. Our serious boss showed the slapstick side of his sense of humor.

We arrived at the hotel, and I unfolded myself from the packed car into the cool air. George turned to assist Adeline from the car. For a *pukah sahib* (big boss), George Archibald was a regular guy, though he appeared quite old in my eyes, probably in his early seventies. We had heard of his retirement to an idyllic home on a lake in Minnesota that he and Adeline were enjoying before Mangla.

When the company won the bid for Mangla Dam, he was persuaded to return to long days and hard work. No one but George could manage the operation of such a widely diverse workforce of men. He had the right amount of forcefulness and yet weighed the human side, making him ideal as one of the three managers of the project. He, Errol Platt, and Joe McNabb were different personalities but were effective co-managers. Joe handled the construction, Errol dealt with the business operation, and George supervised the imports, exports, and customs and coordinated with the Pakistani government.

The next morning came too soon. The *muezzin* called the faithful to prayer at dawn. I dressed and prepared breakfast for our houseguests. Bob and Mary Jean had enjoyed their dinner at the International Hotel after taking in the horse show. Today, they planned to do some sightseeing in Lahore and invited us to join them for lunch before they left to return to Baral Colony. As tired as we were from the week's activities, we agreed to meet them at Falletti's Hotel for lunch.

Bob told us of his initiation in labor negotiations as we looked at the [NOT involved in labor negotiations] menus. He, Mary Jean, and Timmy had arrived just a few weeks before. Bob's ankle was in a cast, and he was walking with the aid of crutches. His injury was new enough that he was still in pain. He told us of his first day on the job. [Mgr negotiators: Joe McNab, Errol Platt, Tom Jackson]

"Errol Platt told me to be ready to negotiate as we drove down the hill [& George W Douglas] where we met an angry mob of Pakistanis. They were yelling and shouting their demands. The interpreters told us what they wanted. Errol listened and turned to consult me," Bob said. "I wasn't familiar with the labor contract, but Errol kept pointing to me as the authority. I nodded and agreed with him. My ankle hurt so bad, and I couldn't walk very far even with crutches. How could we get out of this mess, I wondered." [This was Tom Jackson's ankle]

Like many newcomers, Bob wondered what kind of place he brought his family to and how he was supposed to negotiate when he couldn't speak the language.

After that tense confrontation, Bob explained that Errol led the group of Americans back to the offices where they made their plans to placate the workers' representatives. Without realizing it, Bob's presence made enough difference to settle the dispute.

Just as the Americans at Mangla had their grievances, the labor force had a riot at Thill Colony, the labor camp for Pakistani employees. Their complaint had to do with the workers wanting to cook their own Pakistani food rather than eat in the mess hall where management provided free food.

Management had decided men could not work long hours on the job without adequate food. They expected the Pakistanis to work the same hours as the Americans did, eight- to ten-hour shifts, unheard of for most of them. With the extreme heat, most workers took a long break after their midday meal for a siesta, a three-hour break, during the hottest part of the day. Americans plowed right through the day with no more than an hour for lunch.

The workers wanted to allow each man to cook his midday meal over open fires. Management rejected this idea for many reasons, including the scarcity of firewood. The inefficiency of each one cooking was considered time wasted. Management did, however, agree to serve traditional Pakistani food and hired Pakistani cooks for the free food for all workers.

Americans didn't observe the religious rituals practiced by either Hindu or Muslim workers. The Pakistanis cooks were required to bathe and say prayers, and Pakistanis would eat only food prepared by members of the same caste, a holdover from the Indian caste system still observed. No food could be prepared in pots or with utensils used in preparing pork, so if pork were served, separate kitchens would have to cook their meals.

Mary Jean and Bob decided to try Pakistani food. I wasn't terribly hungry, so I decided I'd try their selections, too. The food was very spicy, so I ate a token amount of each dish using *chapatis* (the staple flatbread) to dilute the heat of the spices. The curry brought tears to my eyes, and I stopped after one bite. *Pikoras* (thin potatoes crusted with spices and flour) also burst with spicy flavor. Chicken *tikka* (chicken crusted with spices and barbecued to a crisp skin) also burned my mouth. Water only intensified the heat of the spices, so I nibbled on the rice and *chapatis*.

We finished lunch and said good-bye to Bob and Mary Jean, wishing them a safe trip to Baral Colony. They'd been easy houseguests with their own plans that didn't interfere with ours.

At home later that afternoon, I began to have sharp pains in the upper part of my abdomen. I didn't feel well and spent the rest of the afternoon fighting the ravages of the spicy foods. I was glad Jim was home to care for the boys. We'd given Sherif the rest of Sunday off since he'd worked longer hours with our guests. Jim preferred no servants in the house on Sunday, his only day off.

By the next day, I knew I had a problem with the pains in my stomach. Jim took me to Dr. Selzer, who ran some tests. I had amoebic dysentery. He said my liver was still okay and then gave me a prescription and some difficult instructions.

"It is best you stay in bed for the next two weeks. The low dose of arsenic in the medication will kill the amoebic dysentery, but it could cause heart damage if you do any exercise or exertion."

How was I going to care for the boys and cook if I stayed in bed? I was sick but also tired after the busy weekend. I had no choice but to comply. I hated to miss riding or my French class. We had bought some John Master's books so I spent my time in bed reading *The Night Runners of Bengal* and learning about the events leading up to the Sepoy Rebellion of the mid-1850s against the British. Another Masters book, *The Deceivers*, told of the brutal "thugees" who had terrorized travelers during the past century in India. The books kept me entertained without a radio, and I felt I was learning more about this intriguing country. By the time I'd read several books, I was feeling much better. I had more to do than stay in bed.

◇◇◇◇◇

WE HAD ANOTHER LETTER FROM Jim's Uncle Frank. He'd be here in early May and wanted to know if we wanted anything from Hong Kong that he could bring. Jim and I agreed we could afford a new movie camera to replace the one that had been stolen. Frank's offer and stop in Hong Kong was the perfect time to replace it. I wrote him at once with our request.

◇◇◇◇◇

A FEW WEEKS AFTER THE activities of horse show week, a group of Americans from Lahore planned a trip to Mangla to see the project. Jim and I were asked to accompany the group. Dorothy Ziemer invited Mark and Kevin to stay with them for the one night. Sherif would be there to care for them during the two days we'd be away.

We met the group on the bus for the trip to Baral Colony. WAPDA Flats neighbors, couples I'd seen at the American Consulate Christmas party or the Women's Club, and a few new faces were aboard, all in fine spirits. We laughed and enjoyed the hair-raising traffic along the Grand Trunk Road. I felt more secure in a bus than Jim's smaller pickup truck.

We arrived at Baral Colony in time for a catered lunch at the new ManDamCo Club. The club had been designed like an elegant supper club in the States. After lunch, we were issued the required hard hats, and boarded the bus again for the tour of the project. The bus bounced along the seventeen miles to Jari Dam, following a water truck that sprayed the dusty road. The guide who joined us at Baral Colony told us more about the scope of the project.

"When completed and the reservoir is full, the space off to your left will be one hundred square-mile reservoir, Mangla Lake. We're approaching the beginnings of Jari Dam, which will require seventeen million cubic yards of excavation and forty-three million cubic yards of embankment. The Jari Dam has its own aggregate plant to manufacture the right sizes of rock needed as well as a repair yard to service the equipment working here."

He told us that the ridges between Jari and Mangla Dams had to be made higher to hold the amount of water the lake would contain, so they were building a large barrage, the Sukian Dike. That structure would be one hundred and forty feet high and over sixteen thousand feet in length when finished, and contain over 12 million cubic yards of fill for the embankment. The sheer quantities of earth to be moved impressed the visitors. Jim had told me these statistics before, but seeing the landscape made it so much more real than the quantities of earth that were just numbers to me.

We returned to the site of Mangla Dam and drove across the Jhelum River on the bridge built by the American contractor to use for the heavy equipment rather than the older bridge used by local traffic. The heavy equipment, when loaded with material, carried far more weight than the existing bridge could have supported.

The bus stopped where excavation was in progress for the main dam and the spillway. George Archibald met our group on the hill. The old fort at Mangla peeked over his shoulder across the river. When completed, this three-tiered spillway where we stood would have over a million yards of concrete, like three large washbowls, to handle the huge volume of water expected during the monsoons.

George had the bearing of a proud and ferocious lion as he addressed us. People quieted down the moment he started to speak, and he held their attention. Set up between him and the excavation site were large charts with cutaway diagrams of the dam. He explained how the earth dam would hold back such a huge quantity of water. That was something I'd often wondered.

"First, we have to excavate all the earth from the core of the dam site down to bedrock. Then we'll fill the trench, this wide arc you see here, with an impervious clay core. Next, we'll compact the earth as we place it on top of the clay core. Then we'll compact and add various sizes of gravel to the engineers' specifications and finish with larger rocks called rip-rap." George used his cutaway illustrations to explain as he talked. "When completed, the dam will require 85 million cubic yards of material. The spillway and other structures will take over a million cubic yards of concrete. That's what this large batch plant is doing, making the right size gravel and rock for this project, and Jari Dam has it's own smaller one. This is the largest concrete batch plant I've ever seen."

I was duly impressed with our general manager and his articulate explanation. I learned more about how a well-designed earth dam could be strong enough to hold the enormous weight of the water behind it. The most impressive dam I'd ever seen was Hoover Dam, a thick wedge of concrete in the red rock canyons south of Las Vegas. Lake Mead stretched for miles behind it.

On the way back, many of the visitors told us they were so happy to have had a chance to see Baral Colony, undoubtedly the most elegant construction camp ever built overseas for construction families.

One woman thanked us as she left the bus, "I feel like I've been to America for the weekend, and it was wonderful. We didn't even need to spend the airfare."

Captain Akbar's White Stallion

THE REMUDA OF HORSES STOOD in the scant shade of spindly trees, switching their tails to ward off the ever-present flies. Each *syce* (groom) held the reins of two horses and ran a hand over their charges as they stamped in the powdery Punjab dust. The flies buzzed from one horse to another, lazily circling the swishing tails of the horses.

The man in charge was Corporal Akbar, mounted on the beautiful white stallion. He pranced up to the small group of girls waiting for him. He wore his authority like he did his Ranger's uniform. Today, he glanced around at the girls, saw me, and spoke to one of the *syces*.

As I waited in the hot sun, my mind went back to the five-gaited horse I'd ridden in Pennsylvania, remembering the floating feeling of his feather light gait. My thoughts were interrupted when I realized the white stallion had stopped and stood snorting in front of me. I looked up to see the corporal looking down at me. Was it Corporal Akbar? I could never remember army ranks. His fiery eyes were like liquid quicksilver boring into me. I met his eyes and held them, refusing to be intimidated. The last three months of riding sessions, he had graduated me from that heavy-footed brown gelding to a sorrel mare who responded with spirit and kept pace with the other horses. *Don't give me that stupid gelding again.*

If he wanted to humiliate or subjugate me by giving me the worst horse to ride, he'd certainly succeeded. Riding that clunker of a horse had been a test, and a miserable experience.

The stallion reared partway, arching his neck.

"*Acha! Bahut acha*, Captain," I said in my halting Urdu.

The horse far exceeded very good, but with my limited knowledge of the language, no other superlatives were ready on my tongue.

The corporal, whom I'd just given a field promotion to captain, dismounted. He looked at me with an almost lecherous smirk on his bronzed face.

He handed me the reins of the white stallion. "You, this horse ride." He took the sorrel mare's reins from the *syce*.

I could hardly believe my good fortune. Did he think this spirited horse would intimidate me? I accepted the reins and the leg up offered by the *syce*, who hurried to adjust the stirrups for me.

Captain Akbar mounted the sorrel mare I'd expected would be my mount today. Riding the sorrel mare, the leader signaled the group into the practice ring. I followed on the white stallion who responded to the slightest movement of my hand or shift in my weight. The figure eights and thread-the-needle formations, torturously executed by the clunky brown gelding that first day, were like a waltz performed by the delicate feet of the fine-tuned animal under me today. What joy!

After we'd done all the patterns of the drills, he turned to me, bowed slightly forward in his saddle, and gestured for me to lead half of the riders. I started forward on one side of the ring with him leading the other half of the riders. I nudged the stallion, and the corporal moved the sorrel mare in beside me. Our mounts pranced across the arena as gracefully as a pair of dancers.

When Captain Akbar finished the drills to his satisfaction, he led us down Canal Road. Even the horses seemed to enjoy the freedom of riding through the small clusters of mud houses and seeing the familiar people who greeted us. Young boys splashed in the canal. A few *dhobis* were finishing their day's laundry, folding and stacking the garments.

When we reached the open field, the stallion snorted, and his feet beat a staccato rhythm, telegraphing me insistently of his eagerness to run. Two of the girls took off, running their mounts across the sand. Two others started after them, the horses enjoying the freedom of movement as they were born to do. I wanted to run as much as the stallion did and could contain him no longer. I let the reins slacken, and he felt my agreement. I leaned forward and nudged him with my heels. Within a few strides, we were racing across the sand at a flat-out gallop. The wind blew my hair straight behind me. Strands whipped my face as we turned. The horse loved to run, and I felt like I was flying on a white cloud.

We circled the large open field, and I turned him in wide, running sweeping figure eights and leaned my weight to signal him which way to turn. At my slightest command, he changed leads as readily as he did in the ring. At the far end of the field was a small embankment. I let him find his own way, ready for the jump I knew was coming. At the top, he leaped forward in a high arc. I looked down to see a white-clad man, his eyes wide with surprise at the sight of a horse vaulting over his head. I saw him pulling at his voluminous trousers as I glanced back at his startled face. The stallion had cleared him easily, but the frightened man's face still was frozen in surprise as we thundered across the sand. I let him run, slowly pulling him to a canter. He snorted, shaking his head, not wanting to slacken his pace. This horse was born to run.

Captain Akbar whipped the bay mare to her fastest speed and caught up with us. "*Bas* (stop)!"

Breathless from the exhilaration of the ride, I pulled the stallion to a stop. My sweat-stained shirt clung to my breasts as I turned to face Captain Akbar. He wheeled the mare to a stop in front of us. Anger flashed from his eyes that rested a few moments too long on my chest and clinging blouse. His look also showed surprise and admiration.

He mustered as much English as he could to admonish me in a loud voice. "You walk, yes. You trot, yes. You canter, yes. You gallop, no!"

"Yes, Captain." I tried to look demure and repentant.

If I had sinned or broken some rules I didn't know about, I really didn't care. My spirit still flew across the sand with the excitement of the most amazing horse I'd ever ridden. I just wanted to shout and laugh from the sheer delight of it. I tried biting my cheeks to keep them from breaking into a smile. Two of the girls riding by on their mounts smiled and gave me a thumbs-up behind the captain's back.

I turned the stallion back toward Canal Road, knowing moments like this were rare and could not last. The captain reined in his mount beside me and signaled the others to follow. He smiled often as he kept the sorrel mare beside the stallion, his leg nudging mine, as we led the group along the canal. The trees cast ethereal shadows on our path. Our horses walked close beside each other, matching stride for stride in perfect synchronization all the way back to the cantonment.

Life and Death in Baral Colony

MILESTONES OF LIFE OCCURRED IN the American town. The first wedding took place on February 3, 1963, when Cecile Cole, a first-grade teacher at Mangla International School, and Earnest Woods of the Baral City administrative offices, were married at a ceremony at the home of the school superintendent, Herb and Jeannette Armstrong. Reverend Paul Pulliam officiated. The first birth of an American child was in March 1963, just a week after the hospital opened. Tahlia Marie Barton was born to Mr. and Mrs. John Barton. Over the six years, more than one hundred babies were born in the Mangla hospital, Mr. Guy's "Buick" hospital.

One Pakistani worker died during the fall of 1962 in a construction accident, the first fatality on the Mangla Dam project. Management tightened the already strict safety procedures to prevent additional accidents. The safety record for such a large project was exemplary.

One Sunday morning in April 1963, the first death of an American, a child of only three years old, shocked the close-knit community of Americans. The child awoke before his parents and older brother and found his family's anti-malaria pills that we'd all been given and recommended to take as a malaria prevention. The parents found the child and rushed him to the hospital, but he had consumed a lethal dose of anti-malaria pills. He died in the distraught parents' arms.

After the shock, denial, and grief of the child's death, the parents decided they wanted to take him home to America for burial. They could not bury their child and leave him half a world away from America. Pakistani law and custom required burial of a body within twenty-four hours. The grieving parents told the company their desire to take their child home for burial. Moving a body out of Pakistan was rarely done, and the red tape required for airline transportation posed enormous obstacles. The parents relied on the company, their expertise, and knowledge of Pakistan's import and export regulations. Jim and John Ziemer were familiar with getting materials and equipment for the job through Pakistani customs and immigration, as was the staff in the Karachi office. Transporting a corpse was something no one had ever dealt with.

John Ziemer took the call from the management at Baral. "John, we need your help and Jim's with a problem. We have a deceased American child, and the parents want to take him home. Can you arrange it?"

"Jim, we have a problem," John said. Lahore was the closest airport to the job and would be the first stop on the family's way home. "How do we ship a body to the United States?"

Jim, stunned, called the airline representative to see what they required.

"First, the body has to be embalmed to transport it on a commercial airplane," the airline representative told him. "I'd suggest you call the University Medical Center or Presbyterian Hospital to see if they can embalm it. Sorry, I mean, him."

The Presbyterian Hospital in Lahore had the facilities, as did a teaching college with a medical program. Neither one was used to doing this procedure except on rare occasions, but agreed to do it on one condition. The parents could not open the coffin or look at the child after the embalming was done. The technicians couldn't guarantee their chemicals would make him look as lifelike as funeral homes in American could, but they could satisfy the airline's requirement.

Jim called the airline back, and they agreed to transport the casket in the cargo bay of the airplane with the parents aboard as passengers. They had one more regulation to tell Jim about.

"Even with the embalming, the body has to leave the country within seventy-two hours of the death."

The parents agreed, and the body was taken to the designated facility and prepared on day two. The hours passed, and the deadline was getting closer. Jim and John remained while the body was embalmed, and they had it ready with all the necessary exit documents.

Just before the deadline, a flight was available. The body, in a truck with Jim, John, and two men to help, met the aircraft at the far end of the airstrip, away from view of the terminal, and loaded the coffin into the cargo bay.

The airplane taxied to the main gate where passengers, including the parents and older child, boarded the aircraft. Only the parents and airline crew knew that a body was aboard. Superstition would have prevented other passengers from taking the flight. Jim watched the flight depart for Karachi. If the connecting flight was on time, the documents they carried would allow them out of the country with the secret cargo, barely within the seventy-two-hour deadline.

Jim came home early that day and told me the story after he'd seen the family off. He was visibly upset and shaking from the ordeal. I couldn't imagine how terrible the parents must have felt, going home under such devastating circumstances.

We unlocked the metal cabinet in the pantry and took out the bottle of anti-malaria pills. We had taken them on occasion. We weren't exposed to mosquitoes that carried malaria in Lahore, and it seemed unnecessary to take them. I tasted our pills, candy-coated, something that could attract a child. My youngest sister, Alice, had nearly died at age three when she took an overdose of baby aspirin, which Mother had unfortunately called her "candy." Our all-night vigil to see if she would live was the most tragic memory of my childhood.

We threw away our anti-malaria pills. We didn't want to risk having them in our home.

◇◇◇◇◇

INTERNATIONAL NEWS TOLD OF THE scandal in the British Parliament when Joseph Profumo, a member of that august body, was discovered having an affair with Christine Keeler, an infamous prostitute who was also seeing a Russian spy at the same time. Our own Profumo scandal, as the guys liked to call it, was discovered when one of the British consultants on the management team at Baral Colony was discovered to be having an affair with another British employee's wife. In a town as small as Baral Colony, management had no choice but to terminate both employees. Within days, both couples were sent home to England. This was not nearly as profound a life event as the others, but it created a few days of shocking scandal to give Baral Colony a tasty tidbit of gossip and comic relief.

Rumors of other dalliances flew around from time to time. One woman went to George Archibald with the suspicion that one of her neighbors was involved with one of her servants. George called in the husband to squelch this rumor.

The husband listened and shook his head. "I don't believe it. But if that woman can tell me which *bearer* it is, I'll fire him."

The men laughed at the tales of idle tongues.

◇◇◇◇◇

LIFE IN LAHORE WAS OFTEN like juggling one crisis or event after the other, and things always happened when I least expected. The second week of April, the Mangla International School's concert choir, a group of forty American teenagers, was invited to Lahore to perform two concerts. Their music teacher, Mary Pearson, started the group in November. In five months since school started, they were now performing goodwill tours in Pakistan. They had recently performed in Rawalpindi, and word spread. They were now scheduled for concerts at two colleges in Lahore. The group needed housing for the overnight trip. Dorothy and I asked other residents of WAPDA Flats if they could host some of the young people. The response was wonderful. Dorothy and I took three, using the living room couch for one girl, and the vacant apartments could sleep five in each one. Within a few days of our request, our neighbors offered their guest rooms to the choir members. We did separate the boys and girls, as we knew their parents would have wanted.

Three girls stayed with us, and I felt like I was back at a high school slumber party. We laughed, played my records, and danced late into the evening. They were fun to have around.

Mrs. Pearson's choir sang with spirit and exuberance to the Pakistani audiences. Their enthusiasm and genuine love of singing brought goodwill from the Americans to people in our host country and gave the Pakistanis a good impression of our American teenagers. The audiences and local newspapers praised their musicianship and their skilled director. The choir became wonderful ambassadors for the Mangla Dam Contractors and the Americans.

Baral Colony now had a nickname, "The Home of the Choir."

The Urologist, the Tailor, and Our New Cook

DR. SELZER THOUGHT I HAD suffered a gall bladder attack, but he was also concerned about my kidney. The X-ray he took showed that my kidney was not in the correct position but appeared to have dropped. A dye injection X-ray study would give a more accurate diagnosis. The machine needed wasn't available in Lahore, but our American hospital at Baral had the equipment to do the test. We sent Dr. Selzer's request to the doctors at Baral Colony. They replied that they would be happy to see me. I was relieved to have another option, and we decided to do that test before considering any treatment or surgery. I was more confident in the opinions of our American doctors.

Dr. Selzer wanted me to see a Pakistani urologist, and arranged the visit for May second at three o'clock. I'd recovered from the dysentery in the weeks following the horse show and felt better much better. I respected Dr. Selzer, so I agreed to go for a consultation.

◇◇◇◇◇

WITH THE CONTINUAL STREAM OF visitors we had, I could see why most women had a cook. My life revolved around that beast of a kitchen with inadequate counters, no cabinets or storage drawers, and the most primitive stove, sink, and refrigerator I'd ever seen. The trips for fresh fruits and produce consumed much of my time or Alam's when he was available. Our orders from the commissary often took a week or longer. The frequent guests exhausted our supply of food. Jim reluctantly acknowledged that cooking was a far bigger undertaking than it was at home.

The medical issues had slowed me down, and I was delighted when I heard the news that our British neighbors planned to return to England. Their cook, Hassan, knew how to make bread, cakes, and cookies, and he had the reputation as a very good cook. He was looking for another job. Hassan's work for the British made his salary expectations reasonable. They didn't pay as much as Americans did. I talked to him, and in a few days Hassan would come to work for us for one hundred and thirty-five rupees, about twenty-eight dollars per month. I was elated, and Jim accepted the news without much more than a brief grumble about money.

Hassan had a cheerful personality and always had a cookie or fruit treat ready for the boys when they wandered into the kitchen. He knew to season foods for Americans and surprised us the first night with "potato crisps," potatoes he sliced as thin as a potato chip, cooked them in oil, and drained for delicious chips. The lamb he cooked convinced us that we had a winner. I was glad that my family ate lamb, perhaps it was goat, because either one was more tender than the old beef that was slaughtered when its working years were over.

Now we had Sherif to help with the boys and Hassan to cook and shop. Alam and Afsar still came daily to push the dust, make the beds, and serve food when we had guests. Sherif was taking on more responsibilities as time went on. The *dhobi* came twice a week, leaving all the clothes and linens clean, folded, and ironed, socks and underwear included. Sherif was great to take the boys to the playground, but he did not read or write, so I read to them and found coloring projects and other games to keep them occupied inside during the heat of the day. My days were full, but the heavy burden of shopping and cooking was well under control with Hassan. Jim might appear with unexpected dinner guests, and I could enjoy the company more without having to do all the cooking. Neither of us realized how much entertaining we'd be doing with his job in Lahore.

Hassan and Sherif needed uniforms, which we had to provide. Alam and Afsar's uniforms were wearing out. Nazir, the *dherzie*, sent word through Alam that he'd be coming in two days. I made a trip to the bazaar and bought fabric so we were ready when he arrived.

Nazir spread his heavy cloth on the terrazzo floor and placed his hand-cranked sewing machine in front of him. He measured the white fabric I'd bought for the uniforms, four yards for the shirts that reached the knees and four yards for the pants.

"*Acha*," he said.

I had bought enough. Sherif wanted American-style trousers with a zipper. Hassan preferred the traditional *shalwar kameez* baggy pants that looked like a large W when hung on the line to dry. A drawstring through the wide top created a waistline when tied and hung loosely to the tapered band at the ankle. Nazir measured each man, made notes on his cloth, and cut the new fabric without a pattern. Then he sat cross-legged in front of his machine and picked up the cut pieces of fabric.

I watched him place the fabric in his machine, using his feet to hold the cut pieces together between his toes as well as his fingers as he fed the cut pieces into the machine. Then, with a quick turn of his hand, he set the wheel of the machine whirling as a line of stitches appeared, straight and perfect. The fabric flew through the presser foot. The first day, Nazir made a complete two-piece uniform for Sherif and pants for Hassan. Each day, he completed two or three garments, all custom fitted to each man.

By the end of the week, he had made uniforms all around and sewed two pair of short pants and short-sleeved shirts for Mark and Kevin, copying their American garments. I asked if he could shorten two skirts for me, and he agreed since precise fitting wasn't involved. His fee was seven rupees per day, about one and a half American dollars, and he produced a good day's work.

When Nazir stood up for a break, I was surprised that he could walk without stiffness after sitting cross-legged for so long.

◇◇◇◇◇

JIM HAD A WEEK'S VACATION, which the company urged him to take as soon as possible. He'd now been here for a year. We considered and then rejected traveling to Europe or Beirut due to the expense of airfare for the four of us. Even if we traveled before Kevin's second birthday, while he still flew for 10 percent, it was costly. Jim's Uncle Frank planned to arrive about the same time as Jim planned to take the days off, so he would go with us. Frank wanted to see the job, so while we were at Baral Colony, the American doctors could evaluate me. Jim's love of history and reading made it important for him to see the Khyber Pass and the areas of Pakistan north of Lahore.

"Let's see as much of Pakistan and the Kashmir area while we're here, and maybe see India, too, while we're this far around the world."

That sounded sensible to me, and I agreed.

On Saturday night, we discussed our plans with Jamal and Najma over dinner at Faletti's. Jamal listened to Jim's tentative plan, and told him some other areas we hadn't considered, like the Swat Valley and a resort in the mountains bordering Kashmir.

"I've heard from some of the men at the job that there are guns made in the mountains near Peshawar," Jim said. "Why would they make guns so far from populated areas?"

"You've heard of the Pathan tribes, right?" Jamal's interest in history and Muslim culture made him a treasure trove of knowledge.

"Yes, of course." Jim sipped his scotch and listened.

"Pathans live by the code they call *Pathanwali*, the way of the Pathans." Jamal signaled the *bearer* for another scotch. "The code of honor requires them to give food and shelter to any man who asks for it, even an enemy, until he can be brought to justice. They have an exaggerated opinion of their own honor, and revenge is mandatory. *Badal*, the taking of revenge, may be carried on for generations. So the tribes are in a state of continual warfare against each other, the government, and anyone who offends them."

"What do they fight over?" I was curious now.

"The same things men all over the world fight over, land, money, and love." Jamal laughed at the simplicity of the problem.

"And they need guns for that?"

We were puzzled by these mysterious people.

"Where there is a need, there is profit." Jamal lit his cigarette and sipped his drink.

"Jamal, tell him about the gun factory," Najma said.

"There was a man named Sher Din Shahabudin who decided to make a superior gun for a reasonable price to sell to his tribes. He put a lot of his money into buying steel from Bombay, which he had shipped to Kohat where he lived. Then he brought workers skilled in finely calibrated medical instruments from Sialkot to work the metal."

"We bought medical instruments from a factory in Sialkot, but Dr. Frewing asked that the next order be European or American made. We'e supposed to buy locally if they're available, as you know." Jim said.

Jamal nodded. "When Sher Din had the materials and specialists, he built a factory and began making guns. He was successful for quite a few years."

"When did he build this factory?" I asked.

"Early in the century before the First World War, as I remember," Jamal said. "Then Sher Din Shahabudin died. His five sons ran the factory for a few years, but they fought and split up. One kept making guns near Kohat, one moved into Quetta, and another moved closer to Peshawar. The other two lost interest in the gun business."

"Do they still sell guns?" Jim asked.

"The last I heard, some of the brothers do. They may be dead now, but some of their children may have carried on the gun making. Their family knows how."

Jamal told us that travel permits were necessary to travel into Swat Valley. Jamal would help Jim do the necessary paperwork for the permits.

We heard the band begin to play as we finished dinner. The cabaret host had saved our favorite table, and Chuck, the bandleader, waved as we entered. People soon packed the cabaret, and dancers filled the dance floor.

Jim and Jamal were still discussing possible places to visit when Javed appeared at our table. I was happy to see him. We hadn't been to Falletti's for a few weeks.

"Good evening, Jamal, Jim. Najma, you look lovely as always. And Irene, how nice to see you again. Jim, may I have the honor of a dance with your wife?"

"Of course. She loves to dance." Jim smiled his consent and returned to the discussion.

"I've missed seeing you," Javed said. "How have you been?"

"Fine, just busy with so many guests, and we made a trip to Mangla Dam project again with a group of Americans from here," I said.

"Were they impressed with the dam?"

"Yes, but more impressed with the town. It is amazing."

"Would you like to go with me on a *shikar*?" Javed changed the subject suddenly.

"What is a *shikar*?" I'd heard the word but didn't remember the meaning.

"It's a hunt. We go late at night in jeeps these days, not elephants. It's fun."

I was speechless and didn't quite know how to respond. I'd love the adventure and wondered how we'd fit in with his group of friends. Did he plan to invite Jim, too?

The music changed to a faster dance, and we didn't talk more. We danced the cha-cha, the Twist, and then the swing as the band segued between the various rhythms. He showed me the rumba, and I was getting the steps when the band took a break. I was breathless when he returned me to our table. I was happy to see my favorite dance partner. I didn't answer him about the *shikar*.

◇◇◇◇◇

FRANK'S LETTER MAILED FROM HONG KONG arrived the following week. He would arrive in Lahore in a few days, on May second at eleven thirty in the morning. We could pick him up, and still keep the appointment with the urologist.

Frank waved as he walked toward us across the tarmac and found the gate where we'd arrived eight months ago. He held up his hand when I started to hug him.

"Don't get too close," he said. "I picked up a cold in Hong Kong and can't seem to shake it. Goodness, look at these boys. They've grown."

He shook Jim's hand and shifted his camera and courier bag to reach his handkerchief. Frank was now in his mid-seventies and beginning to slow down.

"How was your tour?" Jim asked as we waited for Frank's luggage.

"Wonderful. We saw so much. Part of the group went on to Australia, but I was this close that I decided to fly the rest of the way around the world and see you." He smiled, looking at Jim's tan. "It looks like the climate suits you, Jim."

"Yes, you know I've always liked hot weather."

"Well, I'm glad you do. The humidity got to me," Frank said. "I've never liked heat the way you do, Jim. I'm tired of restaurant food. That's for sure." Frank smiled as he directed that remark to me. Frank always complimented my cooking when he'd been our dinner guest.

He looked around at our home when we got to WAPDA Flats. "This is not bad for a foreign assignment, Jim. I'm glad I could stop and see how you kids are doing."

We introduced him to Sherif and Hassan, who made a simple but tasty lunch. Frank was ready to rest, so we left him to unpack as we hurried to the urologist's office. Jim drove to a business section of Lahore with offices on the second floor and shops on the street level. We climbed the steps and found the doctor's office.

"I'm Dr. Yusef. This way, please."

The doctor showed me to his examination room and handed me a gown. "Please put this on."

The room had a paper sheet over the examination table, an aging porcelain sink with a chipped rim, and a table with an assortment of stainless steel instruments standing in a cylindrical holder. The worn linoleum and scratched paint didn't look like the doctor was very prosperous.

He returned, examined me, and looked at the X-rays Dr. Selzer had sent to him. "Your right kidney is turned and quite a bit lower than your left one. See on the X-rays where it is?" He pointed to a shadow on the film he'd held in front of a lighted viewing screen. "The best treatment would be to tie the kidney to your ribs. That would require surgery, but we could secure it in the proper position."

I caught my breath. My biggest fear about coming to Pakistan was having to undergo any surgery or hospitalization. With the increased heat these last few weeks, I knew the risk of infection would be greater than in the cooler months. My symptoms had started with the dysentery and stomach pains Dr. Selzer thought was a gall bladder attack. Now this doctor wanted to operate on my kidney. I remembered my mother having surgery for a "dropped right kidney" when I was seven years old, so perhaps it was an inherited condition.

"Is there anything that might help without resorting to surgery?" I asked.

"You must gain some weight. You are quite thin. Additional fat in the body cavity would give your kidneys more padding to keep it in the proper place," he said. "You must not ride horseback anymore. That causes too much bouncing and stress on the kidney."

Give up riding with the Rangers! I'd finally been given good horses to
ride and loved riding. I wasn't sure that would hurt my body. I'd ridden
since I was a child.

"Another thing," the doctor said, "you American women must keep
cleaner like our Pakistani women do."

This statement shocked me more than his idea that I quit riding. Had
he never smelled the odors wafting from the women's bodies beneath the
burquas in the bazaars?

"What do you mean? I shower every day, sometimes twice." I was
insulted.

"Yes, but you don't shave your pubic area daily like our women do. That
helps prevent bladder and kidney infections."

I didn't see how that could possibly cause infections. This man had
his opinions, which were far different from any doctor I'd ever had or any
women I knew. Shave daily? He had to be kidding. All women I knew hated
the aftereffects of the shaving required as the prerequisite to delivering a
baby.

Marge stopped me in the driveway when we returned to WAPDA Flats.
She had been diagnosed with hepatitis last November. The doctor said her
kitchen was full of bacteria from her cook's negligent cleaning methods. She
was recovered now.

She asked how I was, and I told her about the urologist. Then she
gave me some shocking news. "We just learned that Dr. Selzer doesn't have
a medical license. He went to medical school in Germany before World
War Two and fled to escape the Nazi regime before he completed his final
exams."

I was shocked and didn't know what to believe. How many Americans like us and other foreigners in Lahore depended on his treatment? His
calm manner and compassion made him a fine physician, even if he wasn't
licensed. Where would we find another physician to care for our family? I
did not intend to have the surgery Dr. Yusef suggested. I certainly didn't
agree with his ideas of hygiene. I would place my faith in the doctors at
Baral Colony.

Life in Lahore was interesting, and even with the challenges, I'd adapted,
adjusted, and found our lives enjoyable. But I'd learned that finding good
doctors, hospitals, and schools wasn't easy. Mark would start kindergarten
in September, in just a few months. Jim and I could adapt wherever we

lived, but I had to consider the boys and their needs. When I weighed all the issues, I knew the transfer to Baral Colony would be better for our family.

Frank had spent the afternoon taking a nap and unpacking. We offered him his favorite drink, a gin and tonic, and sat in the living room to catch up on his trip. From the French doors in the living room, Frank noticed Nazir sewing on the balcony. He was fascinated at the speed with which Nazir turned the sewing machine and the way he used both his hands and feet to work. He saw the garments Nazir produced in a short time. Frank was impressed with the skill Nazir demonstrated in cutting the fabric without a pattern.

Over dinner that night, we told Frank of our plans to visit northwest Pakistan and the Khyber Pass, Swat, an independent sheikdom north of Peshawar. Then we planned to go to Kashmir in the mountains of Azad Kashmir, a place called Murree. The British spent summers in its higher elevation for relief from the heat of the Punjab.

Frank was eager to see the dam project that had brought us to Pakistan. This would work out well. Jim could show him the project while I had the dye injection X-rays and saw the doctor. I hoped that surgery wouldn't be necessary. Then we would be on our way for a much-needed vacation for Jim.

We left Lahore on May eleventh. Frank had shaken his cold, the boys were clad in new outfits, and we were excited to be on our way. We had reservations on the inaugural flight of Pakistan International Airlines first scheduled flight from Lahore to Mangla. The airline added this short 135-mile route to their itinerary due to the growing population of Americans at Mangla who wanted to travel. Now, instead of a four-hour road trip, the flight took thirty-five minutes and cost sixty rupees, or about twelve dollars, each way. The company had completed the airstrip to the Pakistani government's requirements. Mangla airport was now open for commercial flights.

We had reserved a rental car and requested Bashir as our driver. We met him when he had driven our women friends to Lahore in February. He was clean and spoke good English besides being a good driver.

Our short flight landed, and Bashir was waiting. We loaded our luggage into the car, and they dropped me off at the hospital. Jim took his uncle and the boys, all wearing the mandatory hard hats, in a borrowed a jeep for a tour of the job.

The X-ray technicians were fun, joking with me to relieve my anxiety over the procedure. They put in the IV, injected the dye, and then pushed a button that raised the table. This brought me to an upright position in front of the X-ray machine for different views of my kidney. An American doctor came in during the dye test, consulted with the technicians, and returned when the procedure was completed.

He looked at the pictures and said, "Your kidney is a bit low, but with your height and lean body type, it's not out of the range of normal. You have no reason to worry about the position. Surgery to tie a kidney to the ribs has not been done in many years. It's now considered an antiquated procedure by our standards."

I was jubilant with relief. My mother's surgery had been in 1947. Now just sixteen years later, that was considered antiquated. With the doctor's reassurance, we collected Bashir, Uncle Frank, and our two sons and set off on our trip. We loaded our suitcases, one packed with chocolate chip cookies, graham crackers, apples, and bananas for the boy's snacks. Jim and his uncle sat in the backseat with Mark so Jim could visit with his uncle. Kevin sat in my lap in the front next to Bashir. I was becoming accustomed to being the copilot.

We were on our way to see the Khyber Pass, the narrow passage that funneled travelers since Alexander the Great from the Silk Road through the mountains that separated the subcontinent of India from Asia.

Northwest Frontier Odyssey

WE LEFT BARAL COLONY AND turned north at Dina on the Grand Trunk Road. Jim's plan was to follow the GT Road to its termination at the western end of the Khyber Pass. He'd made reservations at the Dean Hotel in Peshawar for tonight.

The country looked like the fields of grain we'd passed on our previous trips from Lahore, the vast breadbasket of the Punjab that was dotted with water buffalo grazing and oxen walking in endless circles to turn the water-wheels for irrigation. Farmers wielded tools that looked like holdovers from the Middle Ages and caught Frank's attention.

"Look at that scythe." He watched a man who looked like he could have stepped out of the Bible harvesting grain with the long-handled tool.

The variety of vehicles, herds of sheep and goats, camel caravans, and oxcarts, all sharing the same highway, astonished Frank as it had us. Now we accepted the potpourri of chaotic traffic as normal.

"Let's drive a few miles north of Rawalpindi and see where they're building the new capital, Islamabad," Jim said to Bashir.

Rawalpindi had been the capital of West Pakistan since the partition from India. The new town had been surveyed and laid out in a wide plain that narrowed as we drove north to become a V-shaped slice between the

Hindu Kush Mountains to our west and the Himalayas to the east. We drove around the embryonic city that looked like one more construction site to me. Although many people considered Lahore's central location a better choice for the capital of West Pakistan, some in government protested the city's proximity to the Indian border, making it a security risk. The choice of Islamabad for the new capital in this northern location dismayed those who favored Karachi or Lahore as the capital. Lahore remained the provincial capital of West Pakistan and was the favorite city of many with its colleges, museums, and fine examples of Mogul architecture.

The only building completed in Islamabad was a mosque with minarets on each of the four corners. The impressive structure covered the length of a football field. We got out and walked around. The size of the mosque reminded me of a story about how one Mogul determined the size of a building. I told the boys the story I'd read.

"Genghis Khan had a son named Ogedai, who lived on a flat plain north of those mountains." I pointed to the western hills. "Ogedai wanted to build his palace in the city he called Karakoram. He couldn't decide how big to build it, so Ogedai called for his best archer. He told the archer to shoot an arrow that way." I pointed at the long wall of the mosque. The boys looked at the longest wall of the mosque. "Ogedai told him to shoot an arrow the other way to decide how wide it should be. Ogedai built his palace almost as big as this mosque."

"How could he shoot an arrow so far?" Mark looked at the width of the mosque.

"I could shoot that much." Kevin spread his arms wide and shot a pretend arrow.

They teased each other and ran along the nearly completed building.

"Wow, that's big." Mark picked up a rock.

"Many people will live here and come to pray. It's like a church," I said.

"This mosque could accommodate a whole town," Frank said.

We turned back to Rawalpindi with its established shopping areas and well-worn streets. The bazaars teemed with people as they did in Lahore. I didn't feel the same vitality and energy we felt in Lahore's bazaars. Perhaps the presence of the colleges and so many young people gave Lahore that vibrancy.

We stopped at the Fleishman's Hotel, which we knew served American-

style food. The lobby showed signs of former grandeur with shabby upholstered furniture and worn carpeting. The lunch break gave us a chance
to stretch our legs and wash the dust from the construction site from our
hands. The boys were soon chasing each other around the potted palms in
the lobby until Jim herded them into the car.

"Let's make a stop at Taxila and check it out," Jim told Bashir.

A short drive from Rawalpindi was the ancient town of Taxila, where
archeologists had discovered ruins of a sophisticated ancient civilization.
The museum displayed artifacts that had been excavated. These unearthed
treasures, some little more than shards, gave clues about the ancient people
who had once inhabited the Indus River Valley. Taxila, along with Harappa
and Mohenjo Daro, gave archeologists evidence of a civilization had flourished for six hundred years during what they called it the Goldilocks
period. The area experienced a perfect climate, not too wet and not too
dry. According to the archeologist's studies of the river and flood deposits,
civilization began to grow about forty-five hundred years ago. The climatic
conditions at that time provided a perfect balance of rain and temperatures
that were ideal for intensive agriculture, which sustained the people with
ample food and produced a surplus for lucrative trade. When the climate
changed, monsoons leached the soil, and the water supply wasn't as depend-
able. The change in climate contributed to the abandonment of the Indus
River cities.

We surveyed the articles on display and tried to imagine what the
people would have been like and how much different thay might have been.
The broken pottery was not terribly interesting to me, but Frank found
it intriguing. I was more interested to learn that they found evidence of
some common written words that tied the Indus civilizations to those of
Greek and Roman words. Those words that were left behind were confirming evidence that the trade routes had come this far to the East. The words
for horse, mother, and father has similar root sounds as did the Hindi or
similar Urdu language.

We finished touring the museum, and Bashir turned the car west
toward Peshawar.

"How far is Peshawar?" I asked.

"Two hours, *memsahib*," he replied.

We drove across the Indus River at the confluence of the Kabul River
which had joined the Indus from the east from the Hindu Kush Mountains.

"This is new bridge," Bashir said. "Attock Fort there." He pointed above us to the impressive mass of the fort that strategically controlled this passageway.

"Now we're in the Northwest Frontier Province," Jim said.

The name made me think of the Old West in America.

"People thought the Indus River should be the border of Pakistan at the partition time," Bashir said. "This beginning of no man's land. No law. No government can control. No one want to fight tribal men. Tribes no want to be Pakistani or Indian. Want to be only tribe."

"Why did they want this to be the border?" I asked.

"Desert from Indus River to mountains too hot. No crops grow. People live in mountains. Far from towns. Women never come out of house. Keep inside. Tribal people very strict in mountains."

"What tribes are there in the mountains?" I asked.

"Different tribes, Pathans, Afridis, and Yusafazai. All live in mountains long time," he said with a tone of respect in his voice. "They guard Khyber Pass and all mountain roads. No man, no camel pass without give money, *baksheesh*, to Khyberi tribesmen.Other tribes live in south, like Waziri and Masud tribes."

"Then why is the Northwest Frontier Province part of Pakistan?" I was puzzled.

"British soldier make border line many years ago, through tribal villages. No one change it." Bashir shrugged.

Frank was an avid reader of history and had served as a young man in Europe during World War I. He had some contributions to the conversation I hadn't heard about.

"Back in the eighteen hundreds, India's elite army was known as the Queen's Army. One of their officers, a fellow named Durand, was assigned to this area during the British Raj. The British didn't want to control Afghanistan, but the Indus River as a border would have left too much land to the tribes. Durrand took a map and pen and drew a line from north to south through the mountains on the map between Afghanistan and India, which is now Pakistan. The Durand Line is still the border."

"*Sahib* know. Is true," Bashir said, agreeing with Frank.

By late afternoon, we reached Peshawar, a sprawling town in a valley of green trees surrounded by mountains. This was the last outpost of civilization in the Northwest Frontier Province.

"Yusafazi tribes came from Afghanistan maybe four hundred or five hundred years ago and stayed in Peshawar. All Pathans, mountain tribes."

"I read that their rulers liked to spend time in Peshawar." Frank said.

Bashir drove us through the town and stopped at the *Kissa kha'hannie* Bazaar, the famous Storyteller's Bazaar. We walked through the market where artisans showed their wares. Silversmiths displayed polished candelabra, mirrors, vases, and platters. Brassware plates, often filigreed with intricate cuts as well as coasters and trays, gleamed with polish. Merchants showed stacks of fabrics, a variety of cottons, silks, and embroidered pieces. We could smell the spices at the open-air food stalls, busy with shoppers. Some offered water pipes for smoking hashish and lovely carved wooden boxes. I agreed that Peshawar felt a lot like the old frontier towns of the American West, but with a decidedly Eastern flavor.

A little further, a barber was the cutting a man's hair as he sat chatting with a friend.

"Best coppersmiths live here in Peshawar." Bashir pointed to some lovely work as we walked.

Beyond the copper shop was a courtyard where we saw delicate, slim, young boys with eyes rimmed with kohl like a girl. They were practicing dance steps.

"Dancing boys," Bashir said casually, looking toward the fabric stores ahead.

Men with water pipes sat, cross-legged and relaxed, offering a puff of the pipe to anyone with the money to try it. Jim looked at the water pipe, checked several others the man had for sale, and decided to buy one as a souvenir.

Old men squatted before the shops, watching the crowd, chewing betel nut, and spitting the red juice on the streets. An old man had a tablet in front of him. He listened to the words spoken by the man crouched in front of him and then wrote them on the paper before him.

The artisans sat working on their products, stopping to wait on a customer when one showed an interest. We walked to the end of the bazaar where a meat market with a few goat carcasses hung. The shopkeepers didn't seem as eager to make a sale as those I'd met in Lahore, but it was late, and soon this bazaar would be deserted.

As we walked back to the car, I saw exotic-looking people, travelers, I guessed, from all over the northern areas. The ones without beards with round faces came from China or Tibet, and the hawk-faced, lean men with their blankets not quite covering their bandoliers were the Pathan tribesmen, somber and wary. Peshawar was the crossroads all travelers had to pass to get to India. One group of very tall men walked by, also covered by their bandoliers and a self-confident step.

"Afridi men," Bashir said softly as they passed.

The Pathan's clothing we saw the most consisted of long, cotton turbans wrapped around the head, sandals on the feet, the long *shalwar* shirt, baggy *kameez* pantaloons like I'd seen in Lahore, but in a dusty tan color; and a cotton cloth tied around the waist. One shop had cone-shaped frames with notes tucked into the corner.

"What are these for, Bashir?" I asked.

He picked up the cone and put it on his head to show me. "Pathan man first put cone and then wrap cloth for turban."

"Oh." I had wondered how they shaped their turbans so well.

"Bashir, they all wear the same kind of clothes but in a tan color. Don't they like white?"

"*Memsahib*, white or bright colors too easy to see in dust of mountains. Dye cloth with oil of dwarf palm tree. Make color called *khaki* also used by army. Very popular now."

"That's right," Frank said. "Those British soldiers in white pants and red jackets made easy targets, so they adopted the *khaki* uniforms for their own protection in these hills."

We checked into our hotel for the night. Jim told Bashir we wouldn't need him any more tonight but we'd like to leave at seven thirty the next morning. That sounded early to me, but Jim had planned a full day for tomorrow.

We settled into two adjacent rooms with clean, fairly modern furniture and good beds. We had not seen any other restaurants that would serve American food, so the hotel dining room appeared to be our only choice. After Frank's illness and my recent problems, we didn't dare try the local food, enticing as the aroma was coming from the charcoal braziers where meats and vegetables cooked in a cloud of spices.

Dinner wouldn't be served until seven thirty that night. The boys were getting hungry, so I gave them a snack after we checked into our hotel. We waited in the lobby for the restaurant to open where Frank bought us a cocktail. The lounge and reception area was one large room, and the few people who came through looked either foreign or American.

Three American men struck up a conversation with Jim. When they heard Jim worked on Mangla Dam, they were interested. Soon they were discussing the project, and we learned they were in the American military stationed at the Peshawar air base. We had heard of the air base where Gary Francis Powers was rumored to have taken off before being shot down in the Soviet Union in his U-2 airplane in 1961. The flight and his capture in Russia had made the headlines two years before.

"You come on out and visit the air base. You're Americans and welcome at the base. We've got good hamburgers, and you can eat at the cafeteria."

We had no idea that we'd be welcome at the base, and we were pleased at their invitation. We thanked them, and decided to visit the base the next day.

25

Landi Kotal,
the Smuggler's Village

THE NEXT MORNING BASHIR ARRIVED just as we finished breakfast. I wondered where he had spent the night. Part of the rental charges we paid for the Ford sedan was given to the driver for his own expenses. We assumed he found quarters in the hotel or nearby. I noticed he wore a Band-Aid over his right thumb where a small cut had been the day before.

Frank and Jim studied the map. The skies were overcast with ominous dark patches where storm clouds gathered. They decided to take the road through the Khyber Pass to the border of Afghanistan, a distance of about twenty-six miles. We drove westward, still on the Grand Trunk Road, for several miles until we reached a guard shack and gate at the Fort Jamrud end of the pass. The somber armed guard stepped out of a tiny building that barely offered him shelter. He stopped us and spoke to Bashir.

"Forty rupees *baksheesh, sahib,*" Bashir interpreted for us.

The Khyberi tribesmen extracted their tribute for our passage as we entered the Khyber Pass. The two-lane asphalt road began to wind upward in a serpentine climb through the hills and turned in curves and switchbacks between jagged, barren mountains. A second parallel road was traveled by few strings of mules, bullocks, and straggly ponies that leaned into the

218

climb on a dirt road. Calling it the Khyber Pass brought a crossing over a high mountain to my mind, but this ancient roadway followed the path of an ancient riverbed, now dry or a trickle at the most. The road meandered between the mountains and got narrower or narrower, making me wonder if the camels with wide loads of cotton I'd seen on the roads could wedge themselves through these small spaces. Ancient explorers as well as modern-day travelers found this the best route through the inhospitable mountains. Each twist and turn gave a view of canyons and chasms carved by centuries of streams as they cascaded down the rocky hillsides. This was the same road taken by Alexander the Great, Huns and Afghans, Genghis Khan, and the Moguls as they journeyed on their way to seek the riches of India. At each turn, we could look between the mountains to the vertical fissures in the rocky piles that made up these hills.

"One sniper could pick off an entire army division from one of these peaks," Frank said.

"Yes, *sahib*, has happened long time ago," Bashir said.

"What happened?"

"Army want to catch one man who shoot many soldiers. They offer one thousand rupees reward for him, but no one can find him in these high mountains." Bashir pointed to a peak in front of us. "Two weeks, he shoot soldiers, officers. Never miss."

"How did they catch him?" Jim was intrigued.

"Young man come. Say he can find man who shoot. No one believe him. Milk face. Shy boy-man with Khyber militia. Not even shave yet."

So an adolescent boy thought he could catch a man who had eluded all the others. "What happened?" I was interested in Bashir's story.

"Boy start early in morning. All quiet. Then soldiers hear one shot fired. Body of old man roll down hillside. Soldiers pick up body. Sniper finished."

"Did they pay him the reward?" Frank asked.

"Oh, yes, Army pay Yakub Khan one thousand rupees. Then soldiers learn Yakub find old man because he knows ways of old sniper. No problem. Sniper was his father."

We sat in stunned silence after Bashir's story.

Bashir drove slowly on the switchback curves. I held Kevin firmly on my lap. Jim and Frank took photos from the side windows when an opportunity arose. Mark stood in the middle of the backseat, watching for trucks, which had become a favorite game for Mark. He'd call out "circus truck" when he saw a multicolored truck patterned with garish designs, and Kevin would echo his cry.

The air smelled of dust and rain, heavy and damp. Each mountain crest had a fort or lookout with silhouettes of men and their rifles outlined against the skyline. Turbaned men's eyes peered from each vantage point, sharpshooters whose legacy was to protect this ancient caravan route. Every mile of the road was under surveillance by a hidden sentry.

Traffic crawled with heavily laden trucks laboring up the steep slopes and then accelerating on the downhill grades. We followed a truck with a canvas cover for many miles. We reached a posted sign that said "It Is Absolutely Forbidden to Cross This Border into Afghan Territory."

The truck driver stopped and got out with his assistant. They unloaded dozens of cardboard boxes, stacking them at the side of the road just past the sign. Most of the boxes were a similar size and shape. We wondered what the mysterious cargo could be.

"Pull over to the side of the road, please, Bashir." Jim was intrigued to watch this transfer of goods.

Curious, we watched the men unloading. What was in the boxes? Was this merchandise they were leaving at the border? Why didn't they go over the border and deliver the goods?

When they finished unloading the truck, they climbed back in, turned the vehicle around, and drove back toward Peshawar. Bashir explained the problem when he saw how puzzled we were.

"Pakistani truck not licensed to drive in Afghanistan, and driver not have visa to cross border. Soon Afghan truck pick up shipment." He made the whole operation sound like a normal way of delivering merchandise between countries.

We looked westward toward Afghanistan with flat, dry sand and clumps of gray-green grass. We could see no sign of humanity in the barren landscape ahead. The arid desert reminded us of our home state of Nevada.

Then in the distance, dust swirls appeared on the horizon. A covered truck, traveling fast, came into view from Afghanistan. When the truck reached the border, the driver turned the truck around, backed up close to the stack of boxes, and loaded them on his truck. The men got in and drove off the way they had come.

Bashir turned the car around since we couldn't cross the border either. We turned back toward Peshawar as the rains started. Before long, the sky opened up and the rain began. Soon the rain turned into a deluge. Water ran across the pavement. Bashir turned the windshield wipers on, but visibility was marginal. The rain continued for a few miles, then slowed to a drizzle.

Jim and Frank were disappointed they couldn't take photographs.

"Ahead is Landi Kotal, famous shopping village." Bashir gestured to the tented city to the right of the road ahead.

He slowed the car, and we had a view of the village below the level of the roadway that I hadn't noticed on the trip westward. Tent-like sheets of fabric held up with tall tent pegs covered the town. The rooflike covering made it nearly invisible from the road. My neighbors in Lahore had told me about Landi Kotal. I had to see it.

"You can get anything from anywhere in the world in the village at Landi Kotal in the Khyber Pass," they told me, "even nylon stockings from the States and beautiful silks from China."

Their excitement when they told me about Landi Kotal told me this was a place we should see. The women had called it a smuggler's lair where traders from Turkey, China, and gypsies from all over came with goods of mysterious origin to sell.

"Let's have a look." I turned to ask Jim.

Jim wasn't interested. He didn't like rain or cold and didn't want to get wet. Neither did his Uncle Frank, but I didn't want to miss this fabled spot.

"Go if you'd like," Jim said. "I'll stay in the car with the boys so they don't get muddy."

He and Frank sat comfortably unmoving in the car. I got out before they could change their minds.

"*Memsahib* cannot go alone here." Bashir didn't leave any room to argue.

He looked around and walked up to a turbaned tribesman with a blanket partially covering the bandolier slung over his shoulder. The man leaned against a post beside the packed earthen steps that led to the lower level of the bazaar. Bashir spoke a few words to him, and without hesitation, the man handed Bashir his umbrella. We walked a little further with Bashir holding the borrowed umbrella over my head.

"We go down here, *memsahib*." Bashir turned toward the steps cut into the hillside and offered his arm to me.

I took his offer of assistance, and we descended the long flight of irregular dirt steps and arrived on the main street of Landi Kotal. Gray blankets and sheets of canvas supported by tent pegs covered the streets in a patchwork of camouflage, protecting people beneath it from the sun as well as the rain. A haze of smoke from cooking fires hung over the buildings in a cloud that smelled of spices and charcoal. We walked under the cover, protected from the drizzle, along the packed earth streets. Men lounged against the wall, watching us. Their piercing gaze roamed up and down my body. I felt like they were undressing me with their eyes. Bashir kept my arm linked in his as we passed the onlookers.

At the far end of the street, camels grazed in a makeshift corral, part of a camel caravan. Horses tethered in the next corral had a sign in Urdu script, probably offering them for sale. Goats bleated from pens nearby. Their odor mixed with that of the camels and horses.

Shops of all kinds lined the labyrinth of pathways. One shop had pots and pans. Another had ropes, hardware, and *charpoys*, lightweight beds made of rope crisscrossed on a wooden frame. The next street had shops with windows that displayed watches and glittering gold jewelry. I saw fine porcelain figurines, delicate and exquisite, interspersed with the fine chinaware. This shopkeeper gestured for me to come in and examine when he saw my glance at his merchandise.

A horse-drawn covered wagon passed on a cross street. A trio of small hands clutched the tailgate. Dark-eyed children peered around a curtain across the wagon's rear opening. Were these the gypsies? If so, these may be the ones whom I had heard brought merchandise from all over Asia to this infamous marketplace.

We turned down another street where beautiful fabrics filled the shop windows. We went inside where I could examine the material. I touched one that had a lovely pattern on a silky fabric. As I considered the choices, I heard Bashir conversing with the owner and the word *baksheesh*. So Bashir was negotiating his percentage of anything I bought, if I understood their nods of agreement. I was a little annoyed, but I was becoming used to the custom. Bashir had commandeered an umbrella to keep me dry, so I couldn't begrudge him a little extra cash that was expected when they brought a customer.

I didn't find what I wanted. The term "art silk" from China was rayon, not real silk in spite of the elegant name. Bashir saw a cigarette lighter in the shop next door, and he was waiting for his change from his purchase. I decided to go on to the store just across the street.

Bashir stopped me as I stepped into the roadway, his expression serious.

"Please, *memsahib*, you cannot go alone here. These men are Pathans, not safe for woman alone."

I accepted his admonishment and knew he was right. I waited for him to finish his purchase, and we went across to the other shop. I found two fabrics that were exactly what I'd hoped to find, exquisite and the right price. With these fabrics, I would have two new dresses I could wear with our blossoming social life.

"*Kitna rupeah* (How much)?"

I wanted Bashir to know I understood some Urdu. I had hopes he would help me negotiate the price as well as get his *baksheesh* he'd already discussed with the second shopkeeper. With Bashir translating, I bought the fabric and watched as the merchant cut it. I noticed he added a few extra inches, making a generous cut. He gave me a big, toothless smile as I paid him the rupees we'd agreed on. Bashir waited to carry my package. I turned away as he collected my package and discreetly collected his *baksheesh*.

Next, I saw a store with socks for the boys and bought several pair for them and Jim. They were better quality than I'd found in Lahore.

Bashir and I hadn't been gone very long, but I decided we should get back. I didn't want to leave my family waiting long. We made our way back, passing men carrying bandoliers and rifles slung over their shoulders. They looked at me with unabashed curiosity, watching my every step as we ascended the earth steps to street level. These weren't the friendly shopkeepers we knew and enjoyed in Lahore. They looked desperate and poor, and I heard an angry undercurrent in the words I heard them speak.

Bashir returned the man's umbrella along with a few coins I gave him for a tip. The man bowed in a *salaam*, touching his hands to his forehead, his lips, and his heart as he called "*Shukreah*."

He had thanked me. I smiled as I got in the car. The man turned and looked at me with the most unexpected blue eyes.

"Jim, did you see that man's eyes? They were as blue as mine," I said.

"Alexander is rumored to have left some of his men behind when he retreated back to Macedonia in 326 BC. These people could be his descendants," Jim replied.

Our next stop was the American air base at Peshawar. Jim showed our ID cards, his employment with Mangla Dam Contractors, and Frank's passport. The guard looked over our documents, then smiled and welcomed us to the base. He indicated a building where the cafeteria and restroom facilities for visitors were located. We drove around the buildings, construction equipment, and machinery. The sturdy wood construction of the barracks, the metal hangars, and neat, clean lines were far different from the mud hut villages and crude construction we had seen in Peshawar.

Frank and Jim were intrigued. The airstrip took up quite a large area against the hills to the north of the buildings. Activity revolved around this area.

"There isn't anything here that they'd need cranes that size to move," Jim noted.

After four years in the naval construction battalion and part-time jobs with a local contractor in Reno during college vacations, Jim had considerable knowledge of construction even before he'd joined the Atkinson Company four years earlier. Jim knew equipment and what each was used for.

"There's more here than we can see," Jim said.

"What do you think?" Frank asked.

"Well, if Gary Francis Powers did take off from this base in a U-2 surveillance aircraft, where are the airplanes? And what are they lifting that is heavy enough for those cranes? A smaller one would do fine for the equipment we can see."

We ended our drive around the base, looking at the neat, military facility. Uniformed men waved as they recognized fellow Americans. Jim directed Bashir to stop at the cafeteria building. More smiling airmen welcomed us as we joined the line with our trays and ordered hamburgers, French fries, and shakes. We relished the taste of American food and exchanged small talk with the guys who joined us, curious to see what we were doing visiting this remote base.

Waziristan, Home of
Handmade Guns

WE LEFT THE AIR BASE, and Jim surprised Bashir with our next destination.

"Turn south here, Bashir. I'd like to go to Kohat and see the guns they make in that area." Jim casually settled back in the seat. I noticed the shocked look on Bashir's face.

Oh, *sahib*, not good for Amer-ee-cans go to Kohat. Long way. Many tribes there."

Going to Kohat was a surprise to me. I wasn't sure why Jim wanted to go thirty miles in this remote area. The mountainous area between West Pakistan and Afghanistan was bleak and barren, and there was nothing worth seeing.

"I've heard they make guns there. Isn't that right?" Jim asked.

"Yes, *sahib*, they do. Not safe. Many tribes. Not good to take *memsahib* and *babas* to mountains. Tribes not like strangers."

"If they want to sell guns, they must expect visitors." Jim wasn't to be dissuaded.

Bashir reluctantly turned the car south into Wazeristan Province. The first few miles, he drove slowly, as if hoping Jim would change his mind and return to Peshawar. Jim and I had explored remote places and visited ghost

225

towns in Nevada, so the remoteness didn't worry me. But Bashir's uneasiness made me wary of what we were doing in this frontier area.

To distract Bashir and calm the tension in the car, I asked him the names of several things in Urdu. Yesterday, I'd asked him the Urdu names of different things I'd seen. Today, I asked him numbers, and he taught me to count.

"*Ek, do, teen, char, ponch*," he said. "Is one, two three, four, five."

I repeated the words, and wrote them in the small notebook I carried in my purse with the translations beside them.

Bashir was pleased that I wanted to learn, and graciously told me the words I asked.

The road, though paved, became more potholed and bumpy as we went. Few signs of villages were visible from the road, but some dirt roads wandered into the mountains, the kind Jim would have taken just to see where they went in Nevada. I hoped he wouldn't ask to drive on the unpaved trails I saw. Few cars passed us, and the trucks that passed looked ancient and in poor repair. *I'd hate to have car problems in this area.*

"This looks like the same kind of terrain as Afghanistan, at least the part we saw from the Khyber Pass," I said. "The people don't look the same as in Lahore."

We passed a gathering of hawk-faced, tall men talking beside one truck at the junction of a side road that disappeared into the mountains. They followed us with their eyes, stone-faced and solemn.

"What tribes are there in the mountains?" I asked.

"Many different tribes. Waziri and Yusafazi. And best fighters are Afridis. All part of Pathans."

"What do the men do for work?" I saw few goats and little grass to graze on with the scabbed land covered more with rocks and sand than soil.

"No man. No camel pass without give money, *baksheesh*, for safe journey to tribes," Bashir said with reverence. "Some Waziri men fix engines. Mechanics. Work in Punjab. Repair trucks."

We drove nearly thirty miles, the road becoming worse as we drove south. By the time we reached Kohat. The landscape showed more promise of green and a few trees. The mountains above Kohat had another pass into Afghanistan, though not as traveled as the Khyber Pass. Jim and Bashir got out and inquired about where to buy guns. Jim had been told that the men of the mountain tribes made excellent guns. Rumor had it that they could copy any gun they saw and produce a working copy with their machining skill. None of the people Bashir asked in Kohat could direct us to anyone who sold guns. There was no store or factory. Only through knowing a gunsmith could someone buy a gun.

We turned around and started back toward Peshawar. Bashir saw Jim's disappointment.

"We try Darra. North. Almost back to Peshawar," Bashir said.

At Darra, Bashir made another inquiry with much Urdu back and forth. The man's hand gestures gave him directions to a man who made guns. We drove us to the house of a stone-faced man. Bashir spoke in Urdu, pointing toward Jim and the car.

The turbaned man with a long, untrimmed beard and mustache walked over to the car to greet Jim, and Bashir introduced them. As they shook hands, Frank joined them. The man offered his hand to Frank, and a look of respect came over his face, probably at Frank's age and gray hair. Frank smiled but stayed in the background, watching the transaction. I waited in the car with the boys where I could watch. Bashir translated Jim's desire to buy a gun. The solemn man was eager to do business and went back to his house, a mud and stone façade that was partly built into the hillside.

The tribesman returned with two weapons. He took Jim to the end of the road and set up a target about fifty feet away. He loaded the gun and handed it to Jim to test the weapon. Jim turned to the target, aimed, and fired. He couldn't see where the bullet hit, but the target was untouched. The man loaded the second gun, and Jim shot several rounds with that one. Again, the target was intact. After trying two other guns the man brought, Jim debated buying one that was beautifully crafted and had hit the target.

I'd sat in the car through the first trials. I would have liked to try the gun myself. I'd grown up with a BB gun and had shot a .22 caliber a few times. Jim said I was a good shot, and I could usually hit a target. I got out since we needed to stretch our legs before the drive back. I walked around the car where we could see better. Then we stood by the car with Kevin in my arms and held Mark by the hand so he'd stay close to me. I wore a sweater over my bare shoulders, and my dress was well below the knee, modest by American standards. But by Pakistani standards, I was far from covered. My face showed as well as my hair. My lower legs and ankles were also visible.

I heard the cry of an infant and looked toward the gunmaker's house.

A few *charpoys* were around the front of the house's packed earth front yard. A woman came out of the house and reached beneath the *charpoy*, where a bundle was tied beneath the crossed rope bed. The cries came from beneath the charpoy where her baby lay. A blanket over the *charpoy's* ropes provided shade, and he was elevated off the ground. She untied the ends of the scarf that supported the baby and put him over her shoulder. She walked toward us when I noticed a group of villagers who had appeared from other houses. They gathered around and stared at me. The women's faces were hidden behind their scarves. They talked to each other, pointing and gesturing at my sons and me. Mark's blond hair fascinated them, and one woman came forward, gesturing and smiling at his hair. Apparently, they had never seen blond hair like Mark's. One young boy came up to Mark and stared. He spoke a few words, and soon others joined him.

I smiled. "*A salaam alekum.*"

The words I heard them speaking didn't sound like the Urdu I heard in Lahore. They were talking about us, and I felt on display and uncomfortable.

"*Baba?*" I asked the woman with the infant, knowing the word for baby must be right.

She nodded and looked at my sons for the first time. Her eyes lingered on Mark's hair. Bashir walked quickly to the car and indicated with a gesture that I should get back inside. I followed his directions without hesitation, welcoming the security and privacy of the car. Jim and Frank came a few moments later and got into the car, and we left Darra.

"What about the gun you wanted to buy?" I thought of the long afternoon in the middle of nowhere searching for guns. I had no idea why he needed another gun when he seldom used the hunting guns we'd left stored in the States.

"The last one shot straight and was well made. His price was fair, but I wasn't sure how I'd deal with the red tape it takes. Foreigners aren't allowed to own guns in Pakistan," Jim said.

I was relieved. Why had we gone on this wild goose chase in the first place?

"The gun maker offered us tea," Jim said as a peace offering. He knew I liked meeting the people. "I didn't think you would want any tea made here."

"How right you are." I hadn't seen any running water, electrical lines, or even firewood. Not only would it be difficult work for our hosts to make a cup of tea, but I didn't want to risk more dysentery.

Our last night in Peshawar, we sat in the hotel lobby having a cocktail with Frank while we waited for the dining rooms to open. Several air force men gathered in the lobby. They recognized us as Americans, and we were soon talking with them. When Jim told them we'd driven to Kohat and Darra, they were shocked. Their reaction gave me the feeling that we'd done something foolish and dangerous. I was relieved that we had returned unscathed.

Kevin and Mark ran around the room, full of energy from the long day in the car.

"Let me take those boys out to run around," the redheaded American offered. "I have little brothers at home, and I miss them."

He grinned as his dimples showed in his ruddy cheeks. His friend, a crew cut young man with freckles and sandy hair, brought a tennis ball out of his jacket pocket and began bouncing it.

"Do you guys like to play catch?"

"Are you sure it isn't too much trouble?" I asked.

"These youngsters need to work off some energy," the redhead said.

He took them by the hand. As they went outside, I watched through the window as the boys followed him, walking on the curb and then jumping over the narrow flowerbeds. Kevin ran over to the deepest puddle and walked through it, splashing his shoes. The other boy tossed the ball back and forth with Mark. By the time the dining room opened, both boys were laughing and happy with their newfound friends.

"So, you work at the dam?" a dark-haired airman asked Jim.

"Yes, I will before too long, but for now, I do the buying of local materials in Lahore," Jim said.

"Are there any single ladies at the American town?" he asked. "It's pretty impossible to find a date in this country with all the women hidden behind their veil and fathers with guns."

"Well, some of the nurses and teachers are single," Jim told him. "There are quite a few high school-aged girls, too, but they may be a little young. I can sympathize with you."

We exchanged addresses with the airmen and promised to get them an invitation to visit with our friends at Mangla.

As time went by, many airmen from the Peshawar base found a warm welcome and American hospitality at Baral Colony. Mangla Dam workers visited Peshawar air base and received the same friendly welcome as we had. Over the six years the American contractor worked on the Mangla Dam, several marriages resulted from the friendship between Mangla's young women and Peshawar's airmen. They loved their visits to Baral Colony where they could get a taste of cold beer and unveiled women to talk to so far from home.

The Valley of Swat

THE NEXT MORNING, WE FOLLOWED the Grand Trunk Road a few miles eastward and then turned north, following the map. We reached the Kabul River where the road dropped sharply down an embankment and stopped at the edge of the riverbank. The map indicated the road had a bridge,

There, crossing the small river, were a couple of dozen tires lashed together in a makeshift floating bridge. Boards laid across the tires gave the vehicle's tires a flat surface. I looked at the makeshift bridge in disbelief. Were we really going to drive across the flimsy-looking structure? Would it hold the weight of the car and our family? Bashir got out of the car and surveyed the road ahead.

Armed guards stepped out of the guard shack beside the entrance to the bridge. After examining our identification papers, and collecting *baksheesh* for the toll, they waved us on. The camera was on my lap, partially covered by the folds of my full-skirted dress.

"You can't take pictures of bridges. It's against the law," Jim told me.

"I know," I said.

When we were in the middle of the stream, creeping along at about two miles per hour, I raised the camera and aimed it over Bashir's shoulder toward the opposite bank. I didn't plan to blow up the bridge. I just wanted to see if a picture of this unbelievable floating bridge would turn out. Later when the film was developed, I found my forbidden photo would be of little value for espionage. I had snapped a picture of the back of Bashir's head and the car's hood. Who would believe that we crossed a river on a bridge on rubber tires and planks anyway?

We climbed the hill on the opposite bank of the river, now on the way to Saidu Sherif in the Valley of Swat. The landscape changed to green rolling hills dotted with orchards in their finest spring blossoms. We climbed a grade into the Malakand Mountains where a road branched to the left and to the right. We took the right fork and continued toward Saidu Sherif. At a cut in the hillside, we were surprised to see a tall stone monument, an obelisque dedicated to an early British Army soldier, John Nicholson. We stopped and read the brass plate on the base.

"He was one of the British soldiers I read about," Frank said. "He, Neville Chamberlin, and John Abbott were famous for their escapades in the Queen's Army. Chamberlain served in Kohat, as I remember, and Abbot was in this area, too."

We drove through a beautiful green valley to the town of Saidu Sherif to the rest house where we had reservations for the night. The Valley of Swat blanketed in rolling hills of emerald green with an azure sky above was a welcome bit of beauty after the stark landscape and serious demeanor of the Northwest Frontier Province and the people who lived on the borders. Always wary of strangers and the possibility of invasion, the people of the Khyber Pass and the Wazeristan Provinces lived on the brink of danger.

The Valley of Swat was an independent sheikdom within the borders of Pakistan, wedged in between Pakistan, Afghanistan, Chitral to the north, and Hazara. The people we saw looked prosperous, taller, and leaner than those in the southern regions. The sultan of Swat had ruled this indepen-dent sheikdom. When the sultan died, his son, the Wali of Swat, inher-ited the land and buildings that had belonged to his father. Most people were tenant farmers but enjoyed the free schools and health care that the benevolent family rulers had traditionally given the people. The aura of peace and lush orchards gave us a feeling we hadn't experienced anywhere else in Pakistan. On the horizon, the silhouette of the mountains formed an impressive backdrop to the idyllic scenery around us.

The rest house was located at the crest of a hill and sprawled along the crest overlooking the verdant valley. The present Wali of Swat owned the hotel. We walked around the well-tended grounds, enjoyed the gardens and orchards, and watched the sun sink over the jagged edges of the mountains to the west. In recent years, various consultants had advised management that, to attract American tourists, they must provide Western-style food for their guests. The valley was enjoying an upsurge in tourism. Many Americans now at Baral were eager to see this region that reminded many of the Alps in Switzerland.

The next morning, we ordered breakfast in the dining room. The full English breakfast was designed to make foreign travelers happy. The scrambled eggs looked fine, light, and steaming. The toast, marmalade, and butter were all familiar. The only thing I questioned was the cylindrical, sliced meat in a pale whitish gravy nestled on my plate beside the scrambled eggs. It felt spongy when I prodded it with the tines of the fork.

I asked the waiter, "What kind of animal does this come from?" I was trying to be delicate.

"Sheep, *memsahib*," he answered.

"Do people in Swat use all parts of the sheep?" I asked.

"Yes, *memsahib*," he replied.

"Is this from a male sheep?" I pointed to the quarter dollar-sized slices of meat.

"Yes, *memsahib*, is male sheep."

He looked a bit sheepish and walked to the next table to dust off some crumbs. I decided eggs and toast were sufficient for breakfast.

After breakfast, Jim wanted to hike up the mountain to see a statue of Buddha that had been in Saidu Sherif for centuries. How a Buddha statue came to a Muslim country probably had an explanation from millennium of explorers who traipsed through this valley to join the Silk Road. The restaurant host offered to serve as our guide. Frank decided to stay and read and offered to keep an eye on Mark and Kevin. The three of them were settled around the fire, the boys assembling blocks and checking out other contents of the lobby's toy box as well as playing with some of their own trucks I'd brought.

Jim and I followed the guide, a man who wore *karakul* hat in a soft gray that matched his beard. He set off on the hill above the rest house. Soon the path disappeared into weeds, taller as we went, and damp from the heavy morning dew and fog. We walked along following the guide, past a fork in the trail and higher up the hill. We stepped over a couple of small streams, the water crystal clear. The skies soon opened up, and the rain began, slowly at first. Then heavier rain was upon us. I held my sweater above my head, but it was no substitute for an umbrella.

"How much farther to the Buddha statue?" Jim asked the guide.

He spoke in rapid Urdu, gesturing around the bend of the hill and indicating with his gestures of the terrain.

Jim turned to me. "What do you think he's saying?"

"He said it's two more hills past this one and higher up the mountain," I said. "It sounds pretty far."

Reluctantly, we turned back and found Frank and the boys, warm and dry by the fire. We changed into dry clothing and rejoined them in the lobby. Bashir had arrived while we were exploring. Frank looked at his swollen thumb and pointed out the red streaks coming from under Bashir's bandage.

"We need to get him medical attention," Frank said.

Jim and I agreed. We inquired at the desk where to find a doctor. Frank knew what antibiotics he needed, but his years as a pharmacist made him defer to a doctor's orders.

We packed and checked out. Jim and Frank loaded the luggage. We followed the directions across the Swat Valley, winding through the orchards and rolling hills until we came to the clinic.

The sight of a family of Americans and Bashir arriving at the Swat hospital was probably not an everyday occurance. The line of people waiting for treatment was about forty feet long. As we took our place in line, the people, one by one, stepped aside and pushed us to the front of the line.

When we protested, several said, "*Shukreah* (please)" and stood aside, insisting we go to the front of the line. We were guests in their country, and they would consider it poor manners to allow a guest to wait. Their gestures all showed the same insistence on treating us as honored guests. They smiled their satisfaction when we progressed in the line. Within a few minutes, the nurse saw us.

She put us in a room. "Wait right here. The doctor is coming."

The doctor greeted us and welcomed us to Swat with formality. Then he looked at Bashir's hand. "Yes, he's got a nasty infection. It's good you brought him in."

The doctor cleaned and bandaged the wound with an ointment and gave him antibiotic pills for the infection. Within a short time, we were on our way again. We offered payment, but they waved us away. The people of Swat enjoyed the largess of the Wali of Swat, who provided medical care for the people. The medical care was free, even to foreign visitors.

Murree, the Kashmir Hill Station

WE LEFT THE VALLEY OF Swat with visions of this magical green Shangri-La etched in our minds. People of Swat appeared to enjoy a far better life than those who belonged to the warrior tribes in the wild Northwest Frontier Province. Survival in those barren hills must have taken all their energy. This tiny sheikdom, cloistered from the world, provided its people with education, medical care, and a productive, fruit-growing valley. We would never forget the hospitality the people showed to us.

We drove south and crossed the Kabul River on the boards laid over a floating roadbed of lashed-together tires. Again, I prayed this makeshift structure would support the weight of our car. Armed guards scowled at us, foreigners who might bring strange ways to their secluded lives.

Back on the Grand Trunk Road, we retraced our route to Rawalpindi and then turned north into the mountains on the road to Kashmir. The resort hill station of Murree was our destination for the night. We had to travel only about twenty-five miles from the valley, but each curve of the winding road angled upward. Soon, we were far above the valley floor with views at each gap in the trees. We were in the foothills of the Himalayas. Above the lower hills, we could see the lofty snow-covered peaks east of us.

We stopped by the road while Bashir let the car's engine cool. A stream ran down the mountain and provided a natural drinking fountain of clear, snow-melted water. We were thirsty, yet I was reluctant to drink it. Bashir had no hesitation.

"Water in nature purifies itself by running through earth and rocks. Within a short distance, the earth's natural filter makes it safe to drink," Frank said.

So with our usual precaution of drinking only boiled water cast aside, we quenched our thirst in the convenient roadside waterfall. The mountains and pine trees at this elevation reminded me of the mountains near Reno and the Mount Rose Highway we took to Lake Tahoe for summer picnics. It was almost like stepping back in time but on the other side of the world.

The British had built Murree as what they called a "hill station," an escape from the Punjab heat. Located nearly seven thousand feet above sea level, the hills around Murree were dotted with summer cottages, rest houses, and resorts that featured a variety of sports activities for families. We saw attendants rolling large, water-filled barrels over the packed earth tennis courts and noticed horseshoe pits as we arrived at the Cecil Hotel. We had learned of this resort through some of Jim's British coworkers, and Jamal had recommended we try it.

We were early in the season, so the summer tourists hadn't yet arrived. As the late afternoon sun dipped behind the pines, the temperature dropped. We shivered in our summer clothing as we checked into the hotel.

The impressive two-story hotel of gray stone blocks sat nestled into the pine-covered hills. Its exquisite woodwork trim showed the talent of local carpenters. The lobby displayed the grandeur of an English country home with heavy mahogany furniture, red-hued carpeting, and tapestries of the hunt. After we checked in, the desk clerk summoned a team of *bearers* to carry our luggage up the hill to the annex, a wooden building behind the main structure where our rooms were located. The *bearers* of our luggage also were blue-eyed, fair-skinned men who carried our bags up the path balanced on their heads. We passed the tennis courts and horseshoe pits and read signs for walking trails named for British counties.

After inspecting our rooms and unpacking clothing for tonight, we returned to the main building. The aroma of meat and spices cooking led the way to the dining room off the lobby. A few other guests were grouped around an enormous lobby fireplace capable of holding a huge log. Tonight, it had only two small logs that produced little heat. Jim looked around for more wood but found only a few more twigs and small logs stacked in the woodbox.

Frank was soon engaged in conversation with a man he introduced to us as Lawrence Edgerton. He smiled, his white teeth flashing beneath his handlebar mustache. His wife, Daphne, had red hair and fair skin, and both greeted us with warmth that belied the stereotypical British reserve.

"Hello. Good fire you've got there," Mr. Edgerton said, as he gestured toward the fireplace.

"Well, I'd like to see it about four times that size." Jim smiled. "We hadn't planned on the cold."

"Yes, it's chilly for May. Usually, the weather is beastly hot by the end of April. Daphne always likes to get up to the hill station early in the season to organize the bridge groups and tennis tournaments. What brings you colonists to this part of the world?" Mr. Edgerton asked with a twinkle in his blue eyes.

"Jim does the purchasing for Mangla Dam," Frank told him. "Have you heard of it?"

"We've heard of little else in 'Pindi these last few months. Good show these Americans have going there. Never saw a rail line built so fast. They put a wonderful town in place with all the conveniences. Great job. I hear they'll have their own airstrip soon." Mr. Edgerton's tone showed respect for the American endeavors. He referred to Rawalpindi as 'Pindi, as the locals did.

"The airstrip was completed a week ago. We flew from Lahore on Pakistan International Airline's first flight last Saturday," Jim told him, a note of pride in his voice.

"Jolly good!" Our new acquaintance was impressed with the former colonists.

"We've been to visit friends at Baral Colony. That has to be the finest company town ever built for an offshore job," Mr. Edgerton said.

"The company wanted families to be happy. You know what they say, 'If Mama's happy, everyone's happy,'" Frank quoted an unknown source.

Two other couples joined our group. They were all interested in hearing about Mangla Dam. After dinner, they had more questions and insisted we join them for brandy. The discussion came to the disputed territory of Azad Kashmir. Mark and Kevin were exploring the nooks and artifacts in the lobby and marching up and down the staircase.

"Strange that Kashmir became part of India when the people are eighty percent Muslim," Jim stated.

"You know the story of how that happened?" Mr. Edgerton lit a cigar, sipped his brandy, and proceeded to explain. "The day of the partition was August 14, 1947, at midnight. The ruler of Kashmir was Hari Singh, one of the princes the Indians left to run his kingdom of the Vale of Kashmir. He fled to Jammu, leaving his troops to fight against the Indians. The Pakistani strategy for taking Kashmir was to attack from the north rather than fight the Indians on the narrow road from Delhi to Srinigar. The Pathan tribesmen, mercenaries who made up a large part of Pakistan's army, had positioned themselves at the bridge over the Jhelum River at the town of Muzaffarabad. Their commander gave the order to cross the bridge and take Srinigar from the north." He sipped his brandy.

"That sounds like a good plan." Jim listened attentively.

"The new Pakistani army's mercenaries included some Pathan tribesmen. The unspoken understanding was that, with the low pay, they could loot the shops when the town was taken. The leader of the army called ahead and found the power lines were cut, and he knew he had a clear path to Srinigar. Kashmir would belong to Pakistan. The commander looked around for his troops, and the tribesmen were nowhere to be found. They were looting and pillaging the village shops, raping the women, and taking their spoils in the village."

"How terrible," I said.

"That's war, and a part of the victory." Uncle Frank shook his head in disgust.

"So what happened?" Jim was eager for Mr. Edgerton to continue.

"It took them two days to round up the Pathans. When they approached Srinigar, the Indian troops were already in possession."

"It's still a sore subject, and Pakistan should have had Kashmir with a majority of Muslims," Jim said. "Now I can understand why they're bitter and probably a little chagrined."

We said good night to the Edgerton's. It was getting late, and the boys were ready for bed.

When we returned to our room, I was looking forward to a hot bath. Only cold water came from the taps where Jim had found hot water before dinner. We called the front desk and were told the water was heated only at certain hours. It was now too late. We added more thin summer clothes and all the blankets we could find. There was no central heating either, so going to bed early to keep warm was the only sensible thing to do. The British idea of a posh resort and ours were two very different concepts. Without hot water and central heat, we felt we were roughing it in this lovely spot. *At least we're camping indoors.*

The next morning, Bashir greeted us outside the lobby. He had no jacket or extra clothing, and he was shivering in his thin white shirt. He had stayed in the quarters reserved for drivers and servants at the hotel. None of us had warm clothing, and ready-made clothing wasn't available. Our plan had been to stay another day, but since we weren't prepared, we decided to return to Baral Colony. We could visit our friends and see what treasures the commissary had to offer. I wondered as we left Murree if the Edgertons were out playing tennis to get the season started. People were tossing horseshoes and playing tennis on the dirt courts, all wearing jackets.

We wound back down the steep mountain with a view of the Punjab below at each switchback. The green belt of spring crops bordered the Indus River as it tumbled down the mountains to the west. The Jhelum River joined the Indus farther south of where Mangla Dam was under construction. Grids of dark green outlined the canal system installed so long ago by the British, interspersed with the shades of green of winter wheat crops. Behind us, the runoff of streams flowed to the fertile Indus Valley and on to the Sea of Arabia. This was a close-up look at the vast amount of water that flowed from the tallest mountains on earth to the valley below, a blessing and a curse if not contained. The dam would provide the reservoir to distribute the water as needed instead of floods and droughts.

We drove down the mountain to the Indus Valley below, the air warming as we descended. The British had chosen a beautiful, secluded spot for a hill station that was a great escape from the heat of the valley stretched before us.

The Snake in the Dynamite Shack

THE DRIVE BACK TO BARAL Colony felt faster than when we drove north last week. Now we warmed ourselves in the sunshine and familiarity of the English language spoken at Baral Colony. Jim stopped at the company's new warehouse, a gargantuan building that covered about three acres and contained all the supplies and parts for the job. The mandate from management was to have parts on hand for any repairs necessary. This avoided costly delays waiting for a part to ship from the States.

Jim brought Burt Andrews out to the car and introduced him to his Uncle Frank. They exchanged pleasantries with Burt, one of the company's old-timers. Burt took pride in the organization of the warehouse. He knew what materials were on hand and could locate anything in short order. The card system of inventory, laboriously kept by hand, identified and located every part and bit of material or equipment, its replacement parts, and the site where it was stored.

"Jim, you're not going to believe this," Burt said. "The other day, one of the Pakistanis, Ahmed, came to me and said there was water in the dynamite shack. I knew we had a problem."

Jim looked at Burt, waiting to hear what happened.

"You know we put the dynamite storage shack in a remote area, far from traffic or work in progress. Ahmed and I drove back to the shack to inspect the dynamite." Burt wiped his suntanned brow with his handkerchief. Burt was known for his colorful language and capacity to enjoy food and drinks.

We nodded, waiting to see what happened.

"I stepped into the shack where it was dark, but I could see the black liquid glistening on the tamped earth of the shed. I pried open a case of dynamite. My hand was wet, and it wasn't water. It was nitro." Burt spouted a few of his more explicit epithets. "I stepped back toward the door, wiping the stuff off my hand.

"'Sahib, sanp!' Ahmed croaked, pointing to the snake under my boot. I could see the whites of his eyes glowing in the dark of the shack. I looked down to see a pit viper twitching under my foot. The snake's head was pinned under the toe of my boot. It was mad and trying to get away.

"I told Ahmed 'Go outside and find a stick.' After what seemed like twenty-four hours later, while I stood with my boot on the snake, he returned. He said, 'Sahib, no stick.' That was not too surprising since wood was scarce and anything that could be used in a cooking fire would be picked up and taken home by anyone passing by." Burt explained this for Frank's benefit. "I ordered him to go knock a board off one of those boxes of dynamite. He moved in slow motion while I watched the snake continue to writhe. That snake was looking for the best place to bite me."

Burt wiped his brow again. "The Pakistani raised the stick to strike the snake. A ray of sunlight shone on the chemical-laden puddles on either side of the snake. I knew one spark could set off the dynamite and blow the shack and us sky high. 'Stop. Don't strike it. Squish it,' I said. I gestured a gentle pushing motion toward the ground. Nodding, he placed the stick a few inches behind my boot, pushed into the snake's body, and held it there until it stopped moving."

We breathed a sigh of relief that Burt hadn't been bitten. "Ahmed asked what I was going to do with the bad dynamite. I took a crew and moved the dynamite to a remote spot upstream on the Jhelum River, well removed from the dam work in progress. We used a dynamite cap and a three hundred-foot line and blew up the leaking dynamite. We made the Jhelum River a new channel about fifteen feet wide."

Jim laughed, and Uncle Frank shook his head in disbelief. I hadn't even thought of snakes in Lahore, except for the cobra and handler at the American Embassy party last Christmas. The handler with the help of the mongoose had that snake under close control.

"Are there many snakes here, Burt?" I asked.

"More than I've seen on any other job. Cobras and pit vipers are common, but the ones that are the most deadly are the kraits. They're small but even the baby kraits that are the size of your little finger have enough deadly poison to kill you in minutes. They come out at night and hang out around the bushes," Burt said. "With all the excavation we're doing, we're stirring up nests of snakes from here to Mirapur."

I shuddered at the thought of snakes.

"Guess you've been away for the past week, or you probably would have heard about Fuzzy," Burt continued.

"Fuzzy was here?" Jim looked surprised. "Fuzzy Casstevens is the company's tire expert, Frank. He can look at a tire and tell you where it was driven, what speed, and who drove it, according to his reputation." Jim chuckled.

"Well, he may not want to come back here again," Burt said. "Fuzzy was inspecting the tires of the biggest dump trucks to see why they were wearing out so fast. We had to pay twenty-five thousand dollars to ship new tires for one rig by air, and management wanted to know why. Fuzzy stepped inside a tire that was taller than he was. He looked down and saw a pit viper curled up inside the tire with him. The guys say, when he saw that snake, he set a new high jump and broad jump record."

We laughed, but to me, it wasn't funny. I'd hate to encounter one of those deadly snakes.

Jim and Burt disappeared into the warehouse and soon returned with an armload of sheets and bedding.

"We can stay in a vacant house. It's furnished. We just have to make the beds," Jim said.

This was great. We had hoped for the bachelor quarters since the town was now full of families who occupied nearly every house.

The next two days, we relaxed and enjoyed Baral Colony. We tried the swimming pools and dined in the restaurant that had just opened in April. We were amazed at the commissary. Frank was impressed at the marvelous facilities and the homes that were comparable to suburban developments in the United States.

On Saturday morning, we dropped off the key and borrowed linens at the warehouse on the way to the Mangla airstrip. We said good-bye to Bashir, thanked him, and handed him an envelope with his tip for the week. I was happy to see that his thumb had healed, and I wished him well. He had been an excellent driver and travel companion, even giving me a few Urdu lessons.

We were back in Lahore a week after we left. We had seen vastly different areas of this mosaic country. Hassan returned from his week's vacation the next morning. We told him about our trip to Peshawar. I spoke a few words that Bashir had taught me that I had written in my notebook.

Hassan looked puzzled. "Where you learn *Pushtu*?"

"The driver. Don't you understand it?"

I was crushed after all my efforts to learn and copy numbers, descriptions, and phrases in my notebook. That meant Bashir was probably a Pathan, too, though he never said he was. No wonder he knew so much about the tribes.

"No, *memsahib*. I no speak *Pushtu*. Only *Punjabi*," he said with pride. Then he smiled. His eyes lit up. "You go air base at Peshawar?"

"Yes, we did." I was not too surprised that he knew about it.

"Did you see airplane come out of mountain?" He gestured the mountain opening like a curtain and the airplane being wheeled out.

"No, we missed that," I said.

"People in Peshawar see airplane come out of mountain," he said.

So that was where the U-2 airplanes were hidden, in the mountains of the air base. Jim was right about the equipment being so large that something unseen was nearby that required those cranes.

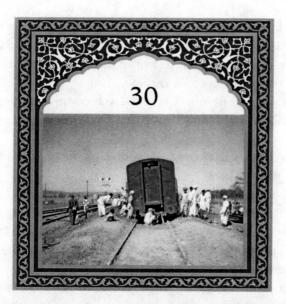

30

Kevin's First Stitches and Our Transfer to Baral

WE ARRIVED BACK IN LAHORE the day before Kevin's second birthday. I invited a few of the younger children for a party. I asked Hassan if he could bake a cake. He did a wonderful job. I realized how much time I had been spending in the kitchen. It was a simple cake and punch event in keeping with the age of the four guests we invited who were Kevin's age. They enjoyed playing in the living room and building a fort between the coffee table and the couch with cardboard boxes.

Uncle Frank's day of departure arrived. The three weeks had flown by with the trip north and showing him around Lahore. Frank had enjoyed seeing Pakistan and spending time with our family. We had put the new movie camera he brought us from Hong Kong to good use. We hugged him farewell at the airport and promised to write.

◇◇◇◇◇

KEVIN WAS PLAYING WITH A neighbor's child who accidentally hit him in the forehead with a sharp toy. Claire was catching me up on the French lessons in our living room when it happened. No one saw exactly what he hit Kevin with, but the blood was flowing from a deep gouge in the middle of his forehead when Sherif brought him in crying. I pressed a towel to the wound to compress the cut. It looked deep, and it was just above his eyebrow toward the center of his forehead.

"He needs to see a doctor," Claire said, echoing my thoughts.

Where should I take him? I knew that Dr. Selzer might decline to do stitches.

As I pondered, Claire came up with a solution. "The Presbyterian Hospital has good doctors."

"Great. Let's go."

I told Sherif where we were going and asked him to stay with Mark until I returned. The *chowkidar* was nowhere to be found, so Claire flagged down a taxi just outside the front gate while I held Kevin. She opened the door and backed out just as quickly.

"This one has been hauling goats." She closed the door and dismissed the driver.

Another taxi made a U-turn when he saw her waving hand and came to the gate. Claire inspected it quickly and passed approval. The driver even spoke English. Claire gave him directions to the hospital with an added "*Jeldy chelo* (Go fast)!" I pressed the towel against Kevin's head.

"*Baba* hurt?" The driver's face clouded with concern. Pakistanis adored their children, and he saw my look of fear for my son.

"Yes, cut," I told him.

The driver took off in a squeal of tires and sped around slower traffic with skill, taking either side of the road that was available. Although we were going fast, I didn't feel any danger due to his skill in handling his vehicle. He arrived at the hospital and hurried to open the door for me.

The hospital floors were shined to a high polish, and a faint odor of disinfectant was a reassuring smell. Within a few minutes, a white-coated doctor came to the examination room and looked at Kevin.

"I'll need to take him to surgery to sew that cut," he said. "It's quite deep. Just wait right here. It won't take long." Then he smiled and put out his hand to Kevin. "Would you like to come with me?"

Kevin took the doctor's hand and walked beside him like they were going out to play. He had no fear of the hospital. I felt a pang of guilt knowing he was going to experience some pain for the first time in his life.

I was torn, wanting to go with him to comfort him. Claire laid a restraining hand on my arm. I stayed in my chair.

Several minutes went by as Claire sat beside me being quietly support-ive. Then I heard Kevin scream. He screamed again. I wanted to run and find him, but I wasn't sure into which room they had taken him. My heart raced, and I felt panic rising inside me when I noticed the screaming had stopped. A soft sob replaced it. A few more minutes passed. Then Kevin and the doctor walked back, hand in hand. The doctor handed him to me. A few tears stained his cheeks, but he wasn't upset now that his ordeal was over. He was very brave for a two-year-old having his first stitches.

I held Kevin and reassured him all the way home in the taxi. We turned into the driveway and saw Mark playing with Carl and some bigger boys.

"Put me down, Mom." Kevin tried to wriggle free to join them.

I noticed Jim's pickup truck was parked in the driveway. It wasn't even five o'clock yet.

"Sherif, don't let Kevin go up the slide. Watch him, please."

"*Acha.*" Sherif held out his arms to Kevin while I went to see why Jim was home so early.

Jim met me at the front door. He had a smile on his face with little twitches in the corners of his mouth. I told him about Kevin's stitches, and his smile faded.

"Where did you take him?"

"Presbyterian Hospital. The doctor was wonderful. But he's already got a little lump on his bottom from the shot they gave him. It must have been penicillin or maybe a tetanus shot."

We walked to the playground so Jim could see Kevin.

"Hi, Dad. Kevin got a bad cut and had to have stitches," Mark told Jim.

"Let's see your bandage," Jim said.

Neither of our boys had previously had any injuries to require stitches. I was glad it wasn't worse or closer to his eye.

Kevin held up his arms for Jim to pick him up.

"He'll be okay." Jim looked at Kevin's bandaged forehead. "You're tough, aren't you?"

"Yes," Kevin said, sniffing back a tear.

Jim took me aside and looked serious. "I came home early today to tell you some news. We've been transferred to Mangla. They want me there by next week."

31

My Visit to the *Purdah* Quarters

WE'D KNOWN ALL ALONG OUR assignment in Lahore was temporary, yet the sudden news of our transfer to Mangla was a surprise. After dinner, Jim and I discussed the details of the move.

"Kevin's stitches need to be taken out in a few days." I knew that could also be done at the American Hospital at Baral Colony.

Kevin's right buttock had a large swollen lump in the middle where they'd given him a shot. The pain went down his leg. He cried and couldn't bear weight on that leg. I had to carry him, or if Sherif were around, he carried Kevin everywhere for several days. I wanted to talk to the doctor about what caused this severe reaction. I suspected he was allergic to penicillin.

"I need to pay my fees to the Rangers, say good-bye to Mrs. Moran, and pay her for the French lessons," I said.

I was reluctant to leave Lahore. I was enjoying life here in this vibrant city that now felt familiar. Claire and I had shared some of the best laughs of all time. Who could be better at finding the right taxis than Claire? She was an amazing and delightful friend.

"They were going to tell us next week, but they want me there by July 4," Jim said.

That would have given us just two day's notice.

"Dorothy persuaded John to tell us earlier so they could have a dinner party for us Saturday night."

Dorothy was the other good friend I would miss. How could I do without her living nearby? She was a pro at improvising and found humor in our foibles. What a treasure she'd been to me.

"Don't forget. We promised Rahman we'd meet his wife on Sunday," I said.

Rahman had invited us many times before, and we had accepted an invitation to meet his wife who kept strict *purdah*. I didn't want to miss that opportunity for anything. An invitation from a Pakistani was a sincere desire to entertain, not the "We'll have to get together sometime" we Americans were prone to say. Pakistanis were the most hospitable people I'd ever met. Making guests comfortable and offering food and drink is a religious duty as well as a great pleasure. Jim's long hours hadn't yet allowed Rahman the pleasure he insisted would be his when we could be his guests.

We accepted the Ziemer's Saturday night invitation and planned to visit Rahman in his home. This was the first time I'd had the chance to visit women in the *purdah* quarters. I had visions of secluded chambers with guards to prevent men from entering.

Jim planned to leave early Monday morning, and I'd follow two days later with the boys so I could say good-bye to take care of details before departing. Packing our clothing and few possessions wouldn't take long. We'd leave the furnishings and dishes in the flat. The house at Baral Colony would be furnished with the similar items. Jim arranged the truck to pick up my sewing machine in its oak cabinet and a few boxes that would go ahead on Monday's run to Baral Colany.

On Saturday night, the Ziemers invited Jerome and Sheila Fernandez as well as Jamal and Najma, who had become our close friends. Dorothy's dinner was a poignant one as we said our goodbyes to the Fernandez'.

We walked downstairs with Jamal and Najma. Jamal turned to Jim, "Let's go to Falletti's for a farewell drink for all the good times we've had. We won't stay late. Just a brandy."

Jim agreed, to my surprise, and we drove to Falletti's. The walnut-faced *bearer* I'd seen so often looked like a statue, so elegant in his belted tunic and spotless turban. All the times I'd seen him, I'd never had a camera to take his photo. How sad. His face was a classic portrait I'd never forget.

Jamal found us a table just as the belly dancer's act was ready to begin. Charlie, the bandleader, announced her with his velvet smooth voice. We watched as we sipped our drink. Her clinking anklets and coins on her belt chimed in rhythm to the slap of her bare feet and gyrating hips. When she finished, Rahman and Zeva came out to do the first dance when they spotted us from across the room.

"Jim, Irene, how nice to see you," Rahman said. Zeva was smiling at his side. "Are you planning to come tomorrow?"

"Yes, of course," Jim answered.

"I'd like you to meet us at the Railroad Club in the Cantonment about four o'clock if that's okay with you." Rahman observed Muslim laws and served no alcohol in his home, but he wanted to meet us where the men could enjoy a drink before dinner.

I noticed Zeva and Rahman made a handsome couple when they returned to the dance floor. She wore Western miniskirts, showing her bronzed legs. Her long raven hair fanned behind her when they turned. She embraced the look of mod young American women seen in fashion magazines I wasn't bold enough to wear myself. I thought she exhibited amazing self-confidence. Zeva and her sister were the only Muslim women we ever saw drink alcohol in public or smoke, although perhaps others did as well in the privacy of their homes. Perhaps Rahman's position as a national cricket star and her place as his public partner accounted for that.

Rahman had traveled the world as one of Pakistan's star cricket players. His success in sports and business showed in his confident manner and sophisticated ability to talk about any subject comfortably in English or Urdu. He was handsome and friendly, so I was looking forward to meeting his wife and the children he'd proudly told us about.

Rahman was one of the few Pakistanis we met who took advantage of the Koran's permission for a man to take multiple wives. The Muslim religion was specific that a man could take as many as four wives if he were financially able to take care of them, and the holy book also stated that he had to treat each one equally. Rahman made no secret that he had a wife who kept strictly to the modest practice of covering herself when in public. No man outside her family was allowed to see her face. Everyone seemed to know that Rahman had a house in one part of Lahore for Zeva. The custom was to bring the second wife into the family home where all would live together. Rahman was wealthy enough to keep Zeva in a separate home.

Rahman's plan, as he explained it, was that, once we met his wife and she had accepted us, he could then sneak her out of the house without his parents' knowledge and bring her to our home. To allow a man other than her father, brother, or husband to see her face would be a great show of friendship to Jim and me. Then we could have the opportunity to entertain them in return if his plan worked. He had explained how the marriage had been arranged when we first met him.

"I had the choice of Sameea or her younger sister Norjahan when our parents arranged our marriage." As a dutiful son and follower of customs of Muslim families, he chose Sameea, the older sister. "My brother Ahmed married Norjahan, so we are one big happy family."

Apparently, jealousy doesn't enter into arranged marriages. We said good-bye to Rahman and stayed for a little longer, enjoying Najma and Jamal. I watched the dancers, hoping to see Javed tonight so I could say good-bye to him. This was one of the few nights Javed didn't appear.

◇◇◇◇◇

WE ARRIVED AT THE RAILROAD Club the next day and found Rahman there with two other men from the nearby town of Sargota. One of the men was English, and the other was Hungarian. Rahman's brother, Ahmed, arrived, and introductions were made all around.

"How is the irrigation in Sargota doing?" Rahman asked the Englishman as he offered him cigarette.

"Slow, and the heat isn't helping." He lit his cigarette.

The Hungarian also lit up a cigarette. I hoped the ceiling fans moving the heavy air would dissipate the smoke.

"The canal system served well for many years," he said. "But the reservoir Mangla Dam will provide will give the farmers a steady supply of water during the growing season. We are eager to see the job." He directed his remark to Jim.

"I'll be working at Mangla soon," Jim said. "I can take you around when you come to visit."

"Don't tell me you are moving? So soon?" Rahman was crestfallen.

Jim told me that his company provided materials needed during construction of the town and that Rahman was reliable.

As the sun sank lower in the sky, we all followed Rahman to a residential neighborhood nearby. The *bearer* opened the door and bowed in the traditional greeting. I looked around the living room where photos of Rahman's cricket days hung on one wall. A table held trophies and a photo album with more cricket pictures. We sat on Western-style furniture lined up around the walls like a furniture store. I had the feeling that the plastic wrap had been removed in our honor. This room didn't feel like it was used often. A photo of President Ayub Khan hung on one wall, and prayer rugs lay side by side on top of the larger Oriental carpet. Next to the living room, I could see a large dining room with the table set for dinner.

As the men's conversation turned to business, Rahman's sister-in-law, Norjahan, came in to meet me. She wore a bright green *sari* and spoke fluent English. She smiled and invited me to join the women. I followed her through a curtained doorway in the hall to the separate quarters where the women were sequestered. Norjahan introduced me to Sameea, Rahman's wife. Sameea grasped my hand and smiled a warm greeting as she gestured for me to sit down. She wore kohl rimmed eyes and faint lipstick, but otherwise no makeup adorned this lovely, matronly looking woman. Her warmth and excitement at meeting me was overwhelming.

"*Shukreah* (please)." She gestured to a velvet-covered sofa where she sat next to me.

This room felt more lived in with Urdu newspapers and children's books, toys, and smells of incense and perfumes of the occupants. Sameea appeared older than I had expected, probably because she wore no makeup. She had a motherly, calm face, unlined and yet animated when she spoke to her children. She picked up her knitting needles and yarn. Her fingers moved over the fabric.

Sameea asked Norjahan for me to tell her about my home in America. I hesitated, wondering which one I should tell her about, the ranch where I grew up as a child, or the college apartment Jim and I lived in during his college days, or the little house we'd lived in while we waited to depart for Pakistan. I told her about my family, my two younger sisters, and my mom who could cut and style hair. She was pleased to hear about my mother, so I made the right choice. I told her about Nevada's heat and cold winters and the nearby desert.

"It sounds like Pakistan, with the Sind Desert to the south." Norjahan said, smiling.

"Yes, some parts of Nevada are, but at our home town of Reno, the

Truckee River runs through it and there are many trees, so the valley is quite green and lovely," I said.

With Norjahan interpreting, we exchanged information about how many children we had, their names, and ages. As if on cue, three black-haired, brown-eyed children appeared, shyly hiding their faces in the folds of their mother's *sari*. I smiled, and soon the little girl came to sit on my lap. The two boys, a little older, ran to their toy trucks and began pushing them around. The boys looked exactly like Rahman. Norjahan and Ahmed had two sons as well, so the boys all played together. Norjahan taught part time at Punjab University, so at home, she did not wear her head covered, as she did in the classroom.

"Do you cover yourself when you go to work or shopping?" I had to ask her.

"It is easier than the men staring at me," she said. "And my father still would not like to see me without a veil or a *dupatta*, though Ahmed is more liberal."

A traditional Muslim wife, Sameea had not learned English. Probably her education ended at about twelve years of age when puberty and her parents' adherence to Muslim law required her to wear the veil. I tried my limited Urdu vocabulary, but I feared I now mixed it with Pushtu words Bashir had taught me on our trip. She didn't mind my mistakes but nodded and praised my efforts at Urdu. Her warm smiles and interest in my dress, my earrings, and purse all brought compliments in Urdu, translated by the sister-in-law.

"Jersey?" I finally had to ask about the project she was working on.

Sweaters were referred to as jerseys in Pakistan. She showed me several others she had made for the boys. She picked up the yarn and needles again, and working at an astonishingly fast pace, her fingers flew, and the needles clicked. I had never seen anyone knit so fast.

"*Baba's?*" I wondered if the sweater would be for one of the babies.

She laughed. "No, Rahman's."

She held the partly completed garment for my inspection. I touched it and nodded my approval. Her knitting was beautifully done and with no dropped stitches. I envied her skill.

"*Bahut acha* (very good)" was the best I could do in Urdu, wishing I knew how to comment on her expert craftsmanship, which was an art.

"What do you do in Lahore for entertainment?" Norjahan asked.

"I've enjoyed riding horseback with the Rangers. And we cook a lot of dinners. Men from Jim's company men often come for dinner." They both listened intently.

"Aren't you afraid of the horses? That you could fall off?" Sameea asked through Norjahan.

"I learned to ride as a child, and have rarely fallen off a horse," I laughed.

One of the babies started to cry, and Sameea put down her knitting and picked him up. She put him on the nursery table and changed his diaper. I couldn't help but notice that the boy was circumcised, as was our custom with American baby boys. Perhaps this was a Muslim practice not related to economic position. I'd seen naked baby boys in the bazaar and when riding though the villages along the canal. Somehow I had thought that was related to being able to afford it or having medical care, but more likely, it was part of the culture.

Rahman's parents lived in one wing of the sprawling house, but we didn't see them. The brother, his wife, and the five children lived in one wing. The parents were older and loved the grandchildren but preferred their quieter quarters when guests arrived. Rahman's mother would not meet the guests since she kept strict *purdah.*

The women's days were spent with the children, doing their hair and nails, ordering meals, and supervising the preparation of each dish. Five times a day, prayers were offered to Allah, which the women observed for training of the children. The sister-in-law worked at the Punjab University as a teacher part time, so her sons stayed with their *ayah* and played with Sameea's and Rahman's children. When they went out, both wore head-to-foot *burqas* or black scarves with a sheer panel for visibility. Both women seemed happy with their cloistered life of being hidden from view. I wondered if I could accept this kind of isolation and not feel angry.

When we ran out of conversation, I went back to the dining room just as the men were sitting down for lunch. I found it easier to talk or listen to business talk than try to find more to say with the language barrier. I would need to learn more Urdu to have a friendship with Sameea. How would we handle conversations if the subject of Zeva, her husband's dance partner, arose? How much did she know about the other woman?

During the meal, the curtain opened and closed several times. I saw a flash of emerald green and cerise *saris* with veiled brown eyes peering out to watch us. Rahman's *bearer* served tray after tray of *samosas* (pastry filled with potatoes and spices), chicken *tikka* (Pakistani buffalo wings), *chapatis* (a delicious flatbread), and curried vegetables. It was prepared with American tastes in mind, and none of it was too spicy. Probably because it wasn't seasoned beyond my tolerance, I thought this was the best Pakistani meal I had eaten.

When it was time to depart, I slipped behind the curtain to say good-bye to the women and thank them for the wonderful dinner. Their warm *salaams* of good-bye made me sorry we would be leaving soon for Baral. Even with the language barrier, I felt their overtures of friendship were sincere. We had found more good friends just as we were leaving.

Life in the Golden Ghetto

NINE MONTHS HAD PASSED SINCE our first trip to Baral Colony, and we'd seen changes on each of our brief visits in January, March, and May. The graded dirt roads were now asphalt-paved streets, and the infant town became a community. Homes, apartments, and duplexes to house five hundred families were completed. Front yards, now carpeted with green grass and sapling trees added color. Flowers blooming in many yards showed the individuality of the occupants. The hospital, school, and shopping complex with commissary were all open and serving the hundreds of people now living at Baral Colony. Where we saw barren streets last October, people now walked on paved sidewalks. Vehicles passed without stirring the clouds of dust as we had seen on our first trip.

Across the river, millions of dollars of equipment moved earth at an astonishing rate against the majestic backdrop of the Himalayas. On a clear day, K2, the second-highest mountain in the world was visible over the foothills. The rail spur built by the company now delivered boxcars directly into the enormous warehouse, guarded with fencing and security patrols to protect the precious parts from burglary or vandalism. Mangla Dam crews worked around the clock under lights in a frantic rush to excavate and divert the river before the monsoons of late September 1965.

With seventeen months to go and the electric enthusiasm of the Americans, the goal of diversion and early completion moved according to the schedule. Management had every intention of achieving that ambitious goal.

Baral Colony sat on a 240-acre flat plateau in the shadow of the rocky mountains. The project was situated partially in Pakistan, and part was located in the disputed territory of Kashmir. A seven-foot-high brick wall topped by three strands of barbed wire strung on metal pipes angled outward enclosed the completed town. The wall provided security for the residents and a barrier to animals, camel caravans, as well as curious strangers and salesmen. The safety of the American and British families was of primary concern to the management. The wall also kept the Americans and British separated from the real Pakistan I had come to enjoy.

Jim had gone ahead early that Monday morning. I had finished our packing, paid the Rangers, and said good-bye to Claire and Dorothy.

"Promise you'll write," I said to Claire.

"Of course I will. We'll be knocking on your door at Baral when Jim has to make trips to check the powerhouse. So we'll see you before long."

We hugged, and I left my dear friend with a heavy heart. I knew that nothing lasts forever, but I had such a wonderful time with Claire that I hated to leave.

"You can stay with us anytime you want to come to visit in Lahore," Dorothy said. "You won't want to miss next year's horse show."

How right she was. I'd loved that event.

The company sent a sedan for the boys and me and a driver I'd never met before, Akbar. He was portlier than Bashir, but he smiled with easy acceptance of the boys and their questions. I settled in for the long drive, taking the right side of the backseat so I could watch for oncoming traffic. Midsummer heat had temperatures well over one hundred degrees for weeks, and my energy wilted at the oppressive heat and humidity.

Akbar stopped twice for the boys and me to walk around, and by midday, we turned off at Dina east toward the mountains. As we entered Baral Colony, I showed our police cards. The guard handed me an envelope. I recognized Jim's handwriting.

"Our house is at 114 Second Avenue. Go left at the Main Street to the school, turn right to the end, and then turn left at the last street. It's the fourth house on the left."

Akbar turned left on the Main Street. I looked to the left at G Street and saw our first assigned house with the pale blue walls just two houses off the main street. We passed the post office, the shops, the bowling alley, and commissary. The pool we had opened in April, and children were splashing and laughing while the mothers watched from the chaise lounges.

The town now had all the comforts of a country club in the middle of the Punjab. I could get used to this kind of life. The pool looked appealing, especially in today's heat. Two long blocks later was the school, also brick, with playground equipment visible in the yard. After two short blocks, the road ended. We turned left and saw the number 114 that Jim's note said was our house number.

This house was located far from the post office and market, but it would be close for Mark when he started kindergarten in two months. I wished we'd been assigned a house closer to the shopping areas. The town was now filled to capacity, and at least this was a house instead of an apartment, where there would be no other children and the boys would not find friends easily. I'd have to be happy with the house we were assigned.

Jim came out to meet us and gave me a hug. "Come on in and see your new house."

We followed him inside. The brand-new house was furnished in Danish modern furniture. Again, I could see the hand of a decorator had selected the gold rug and chairs, green sofa, and red lampshades. It was a bit colorful for my taste, but the hand-woven block print draperies coordinated the room with their classic designs copied from ancient Persian tiles. One end of the large living room served as a dining room, with teak table, buffet, and chairs in matching upholstery. The chairs had an unusual design with a heart-shaped seat and balanced on three legs. One leg supported the narrow front, and two legs supported the back of the chair.

As we unpacked, I put a basket of snacks and drinks on the table. Kevin tried to crawl up into the chair to reach a cookie. The chair tipped, landing on top of him. The three-legged design wouldn't support the weight of a toddler on one side. He cried in surprise and frustration. I picked him up and placed his bottom in the center of the seat. As long as he didn't move, he was fine. Jim picked Mark up, making sure he sat balanced in the chair. The chairs would be a challenge.

The master bedroom had a queen-sized bed, dresser, and nightstands of dark oak furniture with pale aqua walls. Again, the draperies coordinated with the room's colors. The spacious bedroom had room for my sewing machine cabinet and an adjoining bathroom. Twin beds, a dresser, and their own bathroom furnished the boys' room. Both rooms had large windows where the sun streamed in. The air-conditioners couldn't cool the rooms with the direct sun pouring in. I closed the drapes to give the cooler a chance. Jim rarely noticed the heat.

The modern kitchen had new appliances, a large refrigerator, a four-burner stove, and ample counter space was a pleasant upgrade from our kitchen in Lahore. Under the window was a space to put the boys' table and chairs we'd selected last Christmas. Jim had the rest of our household shipment delivered from the warehouse. I recognized boxes I'd packed ten months ago. I was pleased to get reacquainted with my mixer, iron, and toaster. Our 110-volt appliances would work at Baral. This kitchen had no curtains, but I could make some in no time.

"Best of all, the water supply from the higher mountains was purified and safe to drink. I think you won't miss boiling the water for twenty minutes," Jim said.

"What a great time saver that will be. And a relief to have good drinking water."

Knowing that minor hardware items were not likely to be found in the new homes, I'd packed a towel bar and extra light bulbs. I'd found some stores in Lahore where I could order any additional items I might need. I wouldn't be one of George Archibald's annoying women who complained for lack of a kitchen towel rack.

The yard had a few random tufts of grass, but it was flat and mostly dirt. It definitely needed some work. We needed bushes, more grass, and a fence or wall to keep the boys within the confines of the large yard. Shortly after we arrived, Kevin ran for the road. The deep drainage ditch was parallel to the road for water runoff during the monsoons . It was crossed by using a poured concrete section of sidewalk that joined the concrete sidewalk. Kevin kept running to the road to peer under that bridge. A concrete slab created two patios, one in the front and one behind the house. These paved areas provided a place for the boys to ride their tricycle and Kevin's tractor from our shipment.

The size and layout of the house made it convenient, and the furniture looked like something from a designer magazine. But it felt so far from Lahore and even from the stores in Baral Colony. I'd get used to it in time.

The kitchen was wonderful and had the same set of stainless steel pots and pans we'd had in Lahore.

"Do you think we'll be able to get a telephone?" I asked Jim.

I missed having a telephone. Most of our friends had television at home and were used to seeing news and shows. Jim didn't want one when he was in college, and he didn't think we needed one in South Dakota. I could do without television, and our little radio might only be able to receive Pakistani broadcasts in Urdu. I yearned for some outside contact. I could call my friends in Lahore or even splurge on a call home to my Mom. After all, we'd be saving money on servants. Jim had insisted we try life without help or at least fewer servants.

"Only superintendents or men with jobs requiring them to be on call have telephones, and then it was like pulling teeth to get so many approved by the government," Jim said.

So much for contact with the outside world.

The company pickup truck Jim had used in Lahore remained there for the man who replaced him. He had no vehicle assigned to him at Baral. A small jitney bus circled the town every twenty minutes, but I soon found I had no knack for figuring out its schedule. I missed it more than I rode it. It was four long blocks to the store, but the one hundred ten-degree heat was brutal in July. Kevin cried, and I had to carry him home if we walked. How I wished for a taxi or even a horse-drawn *tonga* to come rescue us.

Each morning, Jim walked four blocks to the shopping area, hoping one of his coworkers would stop and offer him a ride, which the company policy dictated. Usually, the men waved and kept on going. A few blocks from home, he would catch a jitney bus to the warehouse. After the freedom we had enjoyed in Lahore, this was a completely different world. Our neighbors either worked at the Jari Dam, seventeen miles away, or worked the swing shift with different hours.

"Jim, maybe we should buy a car," I said.

I had noticed several private cars parked in front of the homes I passed on the jitney bus. I had driven since I was a teenager and felt grounded without a vehicle and the independence it provided.

"We would have to pay three hundred percent import duty on a car." He reminded me of what I knew already. "Those who have bought cars from others find getting parts and reliable mechanics nearly impossible."

Jim was right. We had to forget having a car. I did notice a few women who had little motor scooters. I could get around with the two boys on that, and we could buy two scooters so Jim would have a way to work, too. We wouldn't dare drive them on roads outside the project with the terrifying traffic, but scooters would give us freedom. We had seen whole families, father, mother, and children, all clinging to motor scooters in Lahore.

"We don't need scooters either," Jim said. He refused to discuss it further.

Shopping at the commissary turned out to be a time-consuming chore. All imported items, which included most of the food sold there, had to be itemized, and the buyer charged the required import tax. When the line was long and the people ahead had a large order, the checkout process often took over an hour. Grocery delivery was available, but it often took hours to arrive. If I bought just a few things and needed those items for dinner, they might not arrive until late evening, so I usually took them with me. Mark was always willing to help, insisting on carrying a small package. The heat didn't bother Mark as much as it did Kevin. Mark was protective of his younger brother, and hated to hear him cry.

Our first Saturday, Jim came with us to shop at the commissary. We walked around the town, similar to many small towns, but everything was new. Our post office had mail from Jim's parents and his Great Aunt Isabel, our faithful correspondent. We stopped at the bowling alley for a hamburger and soda. The pool was crowded with teenagers and mothers with children sunbathing and splashing in the water. The pools and new sports courts were welcome additions to the town.

We stopped to check out our assigned washhouse on the way home. It was located the length of two football fields from our house and served about fifteen homes. Each corner had a similar concrete block facility, each equipped with two washers and two dryers. We read the schedule posted on the wall. My assigned times were from two to three thirty on Tuesday and Friday afternoons. Below the schedule was the large print sign:

NO SERVANTS ALLOWED TO ENTER THE WASHHOUSE OR USE THE MACHINES. NO EXCEPTIONS.

There were more conveniences at Baral Colony but also a lot more rules and regulations. How would I haul sheets and all our clothes back and forth? We should have bought a bigger wagon for the boys. Even with the variety of stores in Lahore, I had never seen a child's wagon like we could buy in the States. Consumer goods and ready-made clothing hadn't reached Pakistan in the early sixties. How I wished I could have brought our reliable *dhobi* from Lahore! He wouldn't even mind doing the laundry in the bathtub.

The following Tuesday, I had no choice but to do some laundry. I sorted the loads and walked to the washhouse about five hundred feet away. The perimeter wall that surrounded the town paralleled the road on my left for about three hundred feet, about halfway to the washhouse. I could hear the bleating of goats, the bells of the camels, and shouts of the camel *wallas* as they urged their charges along the hilly path. The wall had some small spaces forming a pattern between the bricks from about four to six feet high, making it possible to glimpse the tall camels as they passed by, snorting as they went. I started the first two loads of clothes and walked back to the house where the boys were napping. In July, the heat at this time of day was at its peak and brutally hot. By two thirty, I walked back to the washhouse with two more loads. The first hadn't quite finished, so I waited. They had taken thirty-five minutes. I started the next two loads, began the dryer with the first batches, and made another trip home for the final loads. Shortly after three, I was waiting for the machines to finish as the minutes ticked by slowly. I was aware it was now past my allocated time, and I was now using someone else's scheduled time. If someone appeared, I would have to apologize and get the clothes out of the machines. This was the horror of the washhouses Dora had told us about when they visited Lahore.

Why did management allocate exactly ninety minutes per family of four if the machines took one hundred and five minutes? No wonder there were disputes in the washhouses. Thankfully, no one came that day, and I got my mountain of clothing, sheets, and towels finished. Probably anyone assigned with this brutally hot time of day would defer washing if she could. If we lived closer, I'd consider using the machines in the cooler night hours.

WITHIN THE FIRST WEEK WE were at Baral, I hired and fired three *bearers*. The neighbor's *bearers* kept sending me men who wanted a job. I interviewed them and checked their folded reference letters and medical cards. This was a little more expedient than in Lahore since they knew they had to follow the company rules for employment. The first man was so obnoxious that I sent him off after five hours. He knew little and was too argumentative for me to even want in my house.

The second one spoke good English and Urdu and could read and write in both languages. Within the first day, it was easy to tell he had never worked in a house. When I asked him about it, he admitted his real plan was to get a job in the mechanical field as a truck driver. I sent him to the personnel office where they could help place him. As he was leaving, I asked him to carry a large basket of clothes to the washhouse. He cheerfully helped me with the note I'd written to the personnel office folded into his shirt pocket. He smiled and waved as he left.

The third one was an older man who spent a whole morning polishing brass coasters, lamps, and vases while paying no attention to the boys. I needed someone to help me keep Kevin out of the street more than to polish brass, so within a few days, I dismissed him, too.

My neighbor told me the servants were saying I had too many *bearers* in a week. Some said I had fired seven *bearers*. They thought I was too particular. Perhaps I was, but I knew how good servants could make life easier, and argumentative or obnoxious ones were an aggravation I didn't need in this brutal heat.

◇◇◇◇◇

THE BARAL COLONY WE MOVED into that July of 1963 had evolved into a community like many small towns in America. A Boy Scout troop had formed, and boys earned merit badges as their American counterparts in the States could do. Teenagers enjoyed Sunday school picnics, and classes of all kinds kept people busy. Bowling leagues and bridge games filled the off-duty hours of many people. We now could see the activities we had read about in the newsletter.

Few women worked outside the home in those days, but the need for teachers created jobs, as did a few of the company's secretarial positions that needed someone quickly. A few wives took those jobs for which no Pakistani was available or qualified.

The women of Baral Colony had noticed some needs and ways to help the women in the villages nearby. Women volunteered at the hospital, and one group taught typing to village girls by teaching them on donated or borrowed typewriters. They started a class and taught village girls to type.

"We'll teach you, and you can teach other girls." Their hope was that the girls would find a way to earn money and become independent.

When the American women visited the village of Dina, they learned that the women never had any prenatal care. The American women applied for a grant from the Red Cross, and with that grant providing funds, they established a free woman's clinic in Dina. Now pregnant mothers could have prenatal care and childbirth preparation classes. A doctor in Dina provided medical exams many had never had, and soon a midwife was added to the staff. When the clinic first opened, they saw 67 patients in the first five days with the line extending down the side street of Dina. It took the Americans over a year to receive the grant and get the clinic going, but the ready acceptance and reliance on the clinic showed how badly it was needed.

The beautiful embroidered items that local women made caught the attention of the Americans. The story behind the handiwork was a sad one. The items were made by women whose husbands had divorced them, often brutally cutting off the tips of their noses. The women felt disfigured and their natural instinct was to remain secluded in their homes. Two missionaries in Lahore , Elsa and Friedl Peters, of the Anglican Church of Pakistan, opened a shop where they employed the women to continue their work in the company of women who had suffered a similar fate. By working together, the women also had a support system of similarly battered sisters.

Jeannette Armstrong, the wife of the Mangla International School's Superintendent, Herb Armstrong, learned of these women through the missionaries. She and the Dostians, a group of women, arranged to rent a shop from the company which they staffed with volunteers and sold the hand embroidered work produced by the women in the Peter's shop. The TSA (Technical Services Association) shop remained open in Baral Colony where American women and visitors could buy the products created by these women. When the Americans left after six years, the women had earned a considerable amount of money in a country with family income that was among the lowest in the world. The shop allowed sixty more women to join the Peter's workforce to keep up with the demand.

The men also contributed when they saw a need they had the ability to remedy. A typhoon knocked out power over a wide area of the Punjab around the dam site, plunging the whole area in darkness. Management sent work crews to the downed power lines and repaired them before the government could respond. They had the men and equipment to make the repairs faster, so they did it voluntarily.

Stories of many kindnesses and help for the Pakistani people came of this interaction of Americans and Pakistanis during the years we occupied a place in that remote corner of the Punjab. These are a few that I learned about and admired when they came to my attention. As Reverend Pulliam said, "Ameericans are like military families. They know they won't be there very long, so do things right now."

What Kind of Monster Is That?

AFTER DISMISSING THE THIRD *BEARER* who had helped carry the laundry, I found myself alone on my assigned laundry day. After lunch, I put Mark and Kevin to bed for their naps. I sorted and stuffed the first two loads of laundry in pillowcases. I put one in Kevin's small wagon that barely held one bulging pillowcase. I tried balancing the other load on top, but as I pulled the wagon along the sidewalk, it jiggled, and the laundry fell off. Frustrated, I left the wagon and tossed the two pillowcases over my shoulders, which felt easier than carrying the weight of the laundry in front of me. I thought of balancing it on my head as I had seen the Pakistani women do.

I walked along the road near the perimeter brick wall and saw a flutter of movement in the tall grasses in the ditch to my left. I turned to see a grayish-brown reptile that looked like a huge lizard. It was over four feet long, had webbed feet, and jagged tufts behind its neck. It ran fast and disappeared under the concrete walkway I had to cross to reach the washhouse. I had never seen anything like that creature, and I was terrified. What was it? Would it bite? Would it attack? I peeked under the bridge, but now it wasn't there. I hurried into the washhouse, wary of finding the creature. After checking behind the machines and under the utility sink, I started two loads of clothes, one in each of the two machines. I checked my watch, and hurried home.

Thirty minutes later, I returned with two more loads of laundry. Again, I looked under the bridge before I walked over it to the washhouse. I decided those four loads of laundry were enough for today. I didn't want to encounter that ugly monster again. I felt vulnerable with my hands full of clothing, unable to protect myself if it attacked. I was shaking when I returned home with the completed laundry, carefully watching the ditches on either side of the road. When Jim came home, I was still shaking as I told him about the huge monster I'd seen.

After dinner, we walked two blocks to the home of Dawn and Otis Armstrong. Otis was the personnel manager who served as the mayor of the town and knew everyone. He would know who to call for an emergency. I felt the creature was an emergency.

The Armstrong's *bearer*, Azim, opened the door and invited us inside. He was a fair skinned, handsome Pakistani, slight of build with formal manners. We told him we needed to see Mr. Armstrong.

"*Memsahib*, good evening. *Sahib* is coming one minute. Come in, please. You want water? Drink?" he asked.

"Yes, please, Azim. Water would be good," I answered. It was still hot as the sun was descending in the sky.

"You need *bearer*?" Azim ushered us into the Armstrong's living room.

"I'm not sure, Azim. We were trying to get by without one, but I miss Sherif. He didn't want to leave Lahore, and neither did Hassan, our cook," I said.

Jim didn't want servants at all, but I could see there was a lot of work here, too. The laundry and shopping here were just a different kind of inconvenience.

"You know Usef work for Mrs. Baxter at WAPDA Flats?" he asked.

"Yes, we knew Usef well. Why?"

"He's working just there in English *sahib*'s house, British colony side. Ellis *sahib* go back to London. Soon Usef have no job. Is good cook-*bearer*," Azim said.

I had heard Mrs. Baxter praise Usef many times in Lahore, and I had noticed how attentive he was with her son, Keith, a toddler about Kevin's age. Mrs. Baxter had taught him to bake, and she had spoken highly of the young man. He was here at Baral Colony, and he needed a job. I needed someone who had experience so I didn't need to train him. Training took time and patience.

"Yes, Azim, I'd like to talk to him right away." Now I was pleased I hadn't settled for one of the incompetent *bearers* even if I had earned a reputation for being particular.

Otis appeared, shook Jim's hand, and hugged me. I told him about the lizard. The creature was fast and looked fearsome. I was afraid it might harm the boys if they were outside. I certainly didn't want to face that monster again.

Typical of Otis, he teased me at first. "What time did you see it? And what did you drink for lunch?" he asked with a twinkle in his eye.

Otis listened as I described the scaly creature and how fearsome it looked. Otis mustered a crew and searched the area around the washhouse. One resident had stacked wood along the wall behind his house. The crew found the giant monitor lizard hiding in the woodpile. The service crew said it was the largest monitor lizard they had ever seen, over five feet long, and was a mature female.

"The work crew killed it and took it outside the camp to bury it," Otis said. "The female can lay eggs that all develop into females if no male is around. They're nasty creatures from what the men told me. They feed on carrion, insects, rodents, and small animals. But one that big might even attack a small child, they tell me. It's a good thing we got it. I wonder if there are any more."

Our New Bearer and the Gauze Curtain

THE NEXT DAY, AZIM AND Usef appeared at my front door. I was pleased to see Azim had wasted no time in bringing Usef. The two men looked alike except Usef's shoulders were broader and he was more muscular than Azim.

"You two look like brothers," I said.

"Is my cousin-brother," Usef said.

That explained how the right person kept appearing as if by magic. Alam had brought Sherif, who was his cousin-brother, too.

Usef and Azim came inside where we discussed the timing of Usef's English employer. I didn't want to steal Mr. Ellis' servant, but neither did I want another family hiring him. Azim's recommendation had more credibility than the random fellows who had appeared in need of work. Azim's training compared with Alam's, who conducted himself like I imagined an English butler would, yet he could cook and clean, too.

"When Ellis *sahib* go back to England, I be happy work for *memsahib*." Usef decided.

Kevin walked in and recognized Usef. He ran into Usef's arms. He must have recognized Usef from Lahore. That was even better. I knew that, now, or within two weeks, we would have a *bearer* far more qualified than any we'd found so far in Baral. Yet to me, those two weeks seemed like forever with the brutal July heat of over one hundred degrees sapping my energy every day. As if they read my thoughts, the two men had a temporary solution to suggest.

Usef had a brief consultation with Azim in Urdu. "Is no problem, *memsahib*. I have good *homal*, cleaning man. Come for two weeks help you. We train him. Clean very good."

His disarming smile was reassuring. Azim nodded his agreement.

"Is good *homal*," Azim said.

"Fine. So Usef will bring the *homal* to help for two weeks and then come to work when Mr. Ellis returns to England at the end of August. Right, Azim? Usef?" I looked from one to the other.

They both agreed, and we shook hands. They bowed their way out the front door.

Usef returned the next morning with a boy named Khan. Usef gave Khan a quick course in housecleaning with rapid-fire Urdu instructions. Usef returned every day to check up on Khan's work. Usef also brought an older man and introduced me to Akbar.

"This Akbar, is good *mali*, *memsahib*." Usef nodded at the older man. "You share with Henderson *sahib*. Cost only forty rupees per month."

Although our skimpy yard hardly warranted a gardener, perhaps it would be worth eight dollars a month to chase away any snakes. Those skimpy bushes could hide the finger-sized kraits, the small snakes I'd heard were deadly poisonous. I had been afraid of letting the boys play outside since the monitor lizard scare. I'd heard that other women had their gardeners beat the bushes to chase away snakes before letting the children out to play. I needed him to do the same thing. I was impressed that Usef was looking after our house as if he were already on the payroll.

"Usef, tell Akbar I need him to help me carry the laundry to the wash-house on Tuesday and Friday afternoons. He can work short hours those days, but I need his help."

Akbar was agreeable to the laundry detail, though it was far from the division of labor in most Pakistani households. His willingness to help with laundry confirmed my decision to hire him. *Bearers* found they had to do more diverse duties if they wanted to work in Baral Colony than they would have done in Lahore. And the *mali* was agreeable to be my assistant *dhobi*.

Well, I was the laundress, but now I would have help carrying the clothes to the machines.

Meanwhile, Khan followed Usef's instructions diligently. I was satisfied with the temporary arrangement.

Jim came home for lunch most days and hurried back to work within the hour. When the boys laid down for their nap, I assembled my pen, address book, and stack of mail to answer on the dining room table. As the house quieted, I collected my thoughts to write our parents. I looked through the window to the patio where Khan was getting his shoes and preparing to leave for the afternoon rest period. I watched him put on his shoes outside the kitchen door. Then he took the garbage can, placed it in front of him, and sorted through the container. He removed a glass jar, some tin cans, and a few sheets of paper. He would sell the jar and cans for a few *annas*. Each rupee was worth about twenty-one cents in the United States. Sixteen *annas* made one rupee. An *anna* was further divided into *pice*, but inflation had made using the tiny *pice* coins rare. Khan gathered anything that could be reused or sold and tied the items in his scarf. He carried his salable items and the garbage as he continued to the utility building behind our house.

The buildings were rest houses for the servants in the afternoon, and each building served four houses. The bottom half of the walls was constructed of concrete blocks. Screens completed the sides, which kept out insects and allowed for ventilation. The rooms each had *charpoys* where servants could rest during the heat. They also had a toilet and a water faucet for the required ablutions before prayers. At prayer time, they lined up at the water faucet and washed their faces, hands, and feet before kneeling on their prayer rugs and facing Mecca to pray. Unlike in Lahore, we didn't have a loudspeaker calling them to pray, but most observed the same five times a day ritual as I had seen in Lahore.

When I told Jim I hired a part-time gardener for forty rupees a month, he laughed. "Well, perhaps I can borrow a truck on Sunday so we can buy some plants for the yard. He'll need something to tend."

By now, Jim was getting used to the idea of servants. He saw a definite need to improve our bleak landscaping. The company would provide materials for a fence, brick barbeque pit, and additional plants for the front yard. We would pay only for the labor to install it. We sketched our plans and waited for cooler weather to begin making our yard beautiful.

Our neighbors nearly all had servants, so that made the whole idea more acceptable to Jim. We heard that a few Americans refused to hire any Pakistani employees, fearful of theft or lack of privacy. One woman wanted to show the Pakistanis that American women were capable of doing their own work. Under normal conditions, I could, too, but not with heat sapping my energy.

◇◇◇◇◇

THE *BARAL TOWN CRIER*'S NEXT edition had an article telling us about the medical department's blood bank registry. We were so remote from any facilities with blood available that we would have our own living blood bank registry. Muslims did not believe in transfusions or having blood from a stranger given to a family member, so any local donors or blood banks were rare. The doctors were dedicated to maintaining the health of the population the best possible in a country with many diseases. People were asked to have their blood drawn and typed so we would have an emergency supply available through out own residents. After our blood was typed, our blood type was noted on the identity cards carried by all personnel. Jim's blood was a rare Type A negative, while mine was a common O positive type.

Jim came home one evening with an unusual invitation to dinner. "Haji Ali Khan is a prominent businessman in Jhelum. The work on Mangla Dam had made him even more prosperous than he was already. He insists I bring three of the men and their wives to dinner on the last Saturday night in July. Their wives aren't eager to come when they learned he has two wives. Maybe you could talk to them. It would be a great honor for him." Jim was being the diplomatic go-between for Mr. Khan.

I was eager for another opportunity to visit women behind the veil in their homes, so I urged the women to accept the invitation. They had not strayed far from the American colony. None of them had visited a home where the women were in *purdah*. They were curious but reluctant to go until I encouraged them to come with us. This would be a wonderful adventure.

The title Haji before the name of a Muslim is a title of respect that indicates he has made the pilgrimage to Mecca. This is a goal for every adult Muslim to accomplish once in his lifetime, though, in reality, only the wealthy can afford the time and expense of the trip.

On Saturday night, our group of eight Americans traveled twenty miles to Jhelum in two of the company's white Ford sedans, which announced to everyone who saw us that we were Mangla Dam Contractors Americans.

Jim knew his way around Jhelum and drove right to the office where our host waited. He showed us inside where folding chairs were set up between the desks. A card table covered with a pattered cloth held appetizers of chicken *tikka* (a spicy chicken wing dish) and *pikoras* (wafer-thin potato slices fried with spices and flour around the outside). Haji Ali served scotch, bourbon, vodka, and beer from a well-stocked bar as well as nonalcoholic fruit drinks and Cokes. The servants brought out tray after tray of delicious delicacies. The most delicious were the *shami kebobs* that looked like patties of ground beef. The meat was boiled until tender and then pounded between two stones until it became finer than any ground meat I'd ever seen. Spices were added, and they were seared on a charcoal fire to further flavor the dish. I complimented the host and asked if his servants did it all.

"No, certain dishes only my wife can prepare so well. Sameea cooked all day to make sure the food was just right," he said proudly.

Time passed quickly, and after so many appetizers, I wasn't hungry at all when our host announced that it was time to go to his house for dinner. The evening had not cooled much when we stepped outside of his office. There in the street were four *tongas* waiting to take us to Haji Ali's home. I selected the *tonga* with a palomino-colored mare. Here in the little town of Jhelum, late at night, I asked the driver if I could drive his horse. He was reluctant at first, but Haji Ali spoke to him and probably tipped him. He turned the reins over to me but sat beside me, watching closely to see if I knew how to handle a horse. We clomped along under a nearly full moon past quiet houses. The hooves of the horses clip-clopped in harmony with their harness bells and the squeak of the wheels in the quiet night.

The night air smelled of cooking fires, now burned down to embers on the sides of the road. Men sat or lay on *charpoys*, enjoying the sociability of the dying fires. Coals from their *hookah* pipes and the acrid smell of smoke swirled in the air.

Haji Ali called a greeting to the women of the house. We followed him into his large living room, which also served as a dining room. Chairs were arranged around the table, and the scent of spices and roasted lamb wafted through the room.

"When can we meet your wives?" I asked.

"Come with me." He gestured to me and the other women.

He was pleased to show off his wives and introduce them to Americans. We followed him through a curtained doorway to a large room that stretched across the back of the house. In the center of the room, five *charpoys* placed side by side held five black-haired children, sleeping, oblivious to the noise of the guest's voices.

"This is my first wife, Sameea." He brought a shy woman who wore a flowered yellow and purple *shalwar kameez* outfit to meet me.

She fumbled with her matching scarf, which covered the back part of her hair, and cast her eyes downward, as she smiled in greeting. She moved to his other side as another woman about the same height and age wearing a blue patterned outfit of a silky fabric stepped forward beside her husband.

The next introduction surprised me. "And this is my second wife, Sameea. Her three sons are just there." He pointed to the three younger boys sleeping closest to us. "The other boy and girl are from my first wife." He smiled at the peaceful scene of five children and their two mothers living in harmony together.

My mind was full of questions. How had both wives been named Sameea and not changed or used another name? *How confusing.*

"Haji Ali." I took him aside when the others returned to the dining room. "How can you tell which Sameea is which? Isn't it confusing with the same name for both?"

"At first, yes, but we are now quite accustomed to the similar names," he said.

"And how can you show which wife you might like?" My curiosity couldn't be contained. "And when you call Sameea, how do you know which one will answer?"

"Well, we have our little signals and private signs." He smiled. "So no one has her feelings hurt."

He was pleased with his diplomacy. I was more puzzled than ever. How would any wife I know share her husband's home and bed with another woman? And how could there be any secrets in a relatively small house where only a thin door gave his bedroom privacy from the large, open bedroom of the *purdah* quarters? What surprised me most about this kind of arrangement was the women's lack of anger or resentment. They had to accept this as part of the culture where male superiority was unquestioned. *How sad, and what a waste of intelligence and talent in the female half of the population.*

I joined the others now seated around the table where *pulao* (a rice and vegetable dish), lentil soup, and roasted lamb was served. More *shami kebobs* and *pikuras* were passed.

Our host joined the eight Americans at the table. I looked toward the doorway to see if the two Sameeas would be peeking through the curtain to watch as Rahman's wife and sister-in-law had done just a month ago in Lahore. The curtain fluttered, but I couldn't see them looking. Perhaps the late hour, five children who would be up early, and cooking this elaborate dinner for us made them retire early. By now, it was past ten o'clock.

"The lamb is delicious," one of the men told Haji Ali. "And so is the rice, *pulau*, and everything." They all complimented our host.

"How is the progress of the dam coming along?" Haji Ali asked.

The men gave him a broad, generic update. He asked questions about the Sukian Dike, which interested him most.

"If the company needs more help with excavation on the dike, I have many donkeys and boys to assist."

I watched the faces of the men, all who must have been accomplished poker players from the lack of expression in their faces. The contractor had the largest capacity and most efficient shovels and earthmoving equipment in the world working, so I doubted they would revert to the ancient methods our gracious host was offering.

"That is very kind of you," Jim answered. "I will make our supervisors aware of your workers."

The evening ended near midnight with a return trip in the *tongas* to our Ford sedans, left in the care of Haji Ali's *chowkidar*. On the way home, we chatted about the evening. Bill and his wife Jan were intrigued by the fact that he had two wives.

"Don't forget. Muslims can take as many as four wives according to the Koran," Jim told them. "In the years before Mohammed wrote those laws, Arab men could have a harem as large as he wanted. Mohammed limited the number and encouraged having only one wife since it would be hard to treat two wives equally and not hurt any feelings. In cases where the wife's sister or cousin isn't married, a wealthy man might take her as a second wife."

We chatted and laughed all the way back to Baral Colony. Traffic was light on the Grand Trunk Road. We turned off in a short distance at Dina, and soon the Mangla Fort was outlined in the moonlight against the Himalayan foothills. As we drove up the hill to Baral, the full moon shone on the Jhelum River. The project had brought many of us to this strange land and provided us with experiences we had never expected when we left home. Haji Ali had given us a wonderful evening of Pakistani food and a perplexing relationship puzzle to ponder.

Imagine. Two wives named Sameea. I chuckled to myself as we drifted off to sleep.

35

Surprise Visitors and Jim Saves
Mrs. Archibald

THE NEXT BARAL COLONY NEWSLETTER contained an announcement that
Jayne Coffey, a dancer who had operated a dance school in Washington,
would be teaching modern dance for adults in Baral. I signed up and joined
seven other women for her class held three mornings a week. We learned
basic ballet positions, and Jayne taught us several routines. She ordered
black dancer's tights, long-sleeved scoop-necked tops, and fishnet stockings as the basis for our costumes. Christmas was only a few months away,
and we practiced our dances, one to "Jingle Bells." The dances we learned
had eight counts to each sequence so they were easy to learn. We tapped a
teacher's domed metal bell placed on the floor. Jayne found candy-striped
fabric in the local bazaar, and we made oversized bows for our backsides.
We found a shoemaker in Rawalpindi who made us red high heels so our
shoes matched our striped bows. I had envied my friends who took ballet as
children, and now I was learning some basic steps. I often took Kevin with
me. He played with his toys, rested on a blanket on the floor, and kicked
his feet in time with the routines. Dance class was fun, and I loved learning
something new.

The adult singers group began rehearsals for the Christmas show. It didn't take much urging from my friends for me to join the group. I'd been singing in the church choir since I was seven years old. Singing the familiar carols made it feel like Christmas was coming soon.

Jim joined a recreational basketball team that played once a week. He was fast and enjoyed the exercise of the game. They played for two hours, and Jim loved the physical activity now that his job involved sitting at a desk. He missed the excitement of Lahore and running around town dealing with the various governmental agencies even though he said little.

"Adjust, adapt, and accept," I kept telling myself. Nothing lasts forever, especially with a construction company.

Reading our mail was a highlight of the day. Letters from home were our precious contact with our families. I wrote Jim's parents twice a week as well as letters to my mother and friends. Today's mail had a note from Adeline Archibald, the wife of, the general manager:

Could you please help me hostess the ladies' teas next week? We have two scheduled so we don't miss anyone. Since you lived in Lahore, I am sure you will know many people. Please let me know if you are available. Warmest wishes, Ad.

Adeline Archibald was one of the oldest women in the American colony, and I was one of the youngest. I liked her and knew the heat sapped her strength, as it did mine. She was about seventy years old. I knew she had some vision problems. We'd had such fun at the Punjab Club during the week of the horse show, and I was pleased she'd asked me. I sent a note saying that I'd be delighted to help.

The first day of the tea, I caught the elusive jitney bus wearing a dress made of the lovely silk fabric I'd bought at Landi Kotal. The bus had air-conditioning, but the driver chose not to run it this day. We jerked around corners to the far side of Baral, below the hospital. I was feeling the heat and asked him to turn on the air-conditioning. As he did so, a blast of hot air blew my skirt and hair. By the time the temperature began to drop, we arrived at the Archibald's home. I dabbed my forehead and straightened my skirt. Feeling a bit worse for the wear, I put on the name tag Adeline had waiting, along with a smile.

Adeline was happy to see me. She was uncomfortable entertaining large groups of people. With three men sharing the management responsibility, each spouse would usually do some entertaining. Margaret Platt was always hosting some event, and Adeline did the best she could, considering her age. Helen

McNabb was more involved in golf and those associated activities, so a tea wasn't her favorite function.

To my surprise, I did recognize many women whom I'd met on our trips or in Lahore. When one looked alone, I introduced her to others, mentioning their common interests. Dawn, Otis Armstrong's wife, was also helping to hostess. When she learned I would be coming the next day, she offered to pick me up with Otis' car and driver. The trip in an air-conditioned car was easier than taking the bus, and I arrived unwrinkled the following day.

George Archibald arrived as the last of the women were saying their goodbyes. Adeline looked tired and sank into a chair as the last guest left. I worried about this lady who looked frailer than the day before. George saw me and stopped to chat.

"How's everything?" George asked. "Do you miss Lahore?"

"I miss the people and horseback riding, but it is lovely here," I said. How could I tell him how much I missed the real Pakistan with its excitement? "Did you hear about the big monitor lizard I met on the way to the washhouse?"

George's eyes widened. "Yes, Otis told me about that. They are nasty creatures, but so are all the snakes. Is your house okay?"

"Yes, George, it's fine. Now if I could just get the washing machines to handle six loads in my ninety-minute time allowance, I'd be happy." I smiled.

George frowned. "Why can't you do that? Don't they all take thirty minutes?"

"No, George, their cycle is thirty-five minutes. Three loads take one hundred and five minutes, not the ninety minutes scheduled."

I laughed it off, but I could see George made a mental note on the washing machines. No detail escaped him.

"Did you have a towel bar in the kitchen?" He remembered the woman he'd told us about that night at the Punjab Club.

"Yes, I bought one before we left Lahore, and Jim screwed it into the cabinet."

"Good girl." He nodded his approval.

◇◇◇◇◇

THE DANCE LESSONS AND REHEARSALS for the Christmas show were fun. I was ready to leave for rehearsal one day when a black Mercedes stopped in front of the house. Much to my surprise, Javed, my dance partner from Lahore, and another man came to the door.

"Javed! Please come in! I'm so happy to see you. What brings you to Baral?" I asked as they followed me into our living room.

"This is Mr. Bhatti, my foreman. We're on our way to 'Pindi for a meeting. If it's okay, we'll stop by tomorrow on our return to Lahore when we have more time."

"Wonderful! Please, can you come for lunch tomorrow? Jim will be here, and I know he'll want to see you," I said. "Can I get you tea? Water? A soda?" I almost forgot to offer refreshments to a guest.

"No, thank you. *Inshallah* (God willing), we see you tomorrow when we return and Jim *sahib* is home."

Javed and Mr. Bhatti departed. His blue-black hair caught the sun's rays as he disappeared into the luxury car. The scar on the left cheek was more obvious in the daylight than in the dim lights of the cabaret where we had danced so many evenings. I sighed and went back inside. Javed reminded me of Lahore and the fun we had there. Dancing with him was one of the most enjoyable things about living in Lahore. I missed those evenings with the Faroukis.

The boys and I caught the bus to the store after their naps. I bought fresh beef, vegetables, and the ingredients Usef told me he needed for curry and *pulau* for tomorrow's lunch. By now, Usef had been working for us for a several weeks and had proved to be a good cook.

On the way back from the market, Kevin walked slower and cried, and his face flushed from the heat. Akbar, the gardener, ran to help me. He took Kevin in his arms and carried him the rest of the way home.

"*Baba, solar topi.*" Akbar gestured at Kevin's head and then pointed to his own turban wound around his head.

He was right. I'd need to find them sun hats for this brutal heat.

When Javed and Mr. Bhatti arrived the next day, Usef had prepared a wonderful meal of curry, *pulau*, and a rice and vegetable dish that I was proud to serve to our guests. It was good to have company and hear the news of Lahore.

"When will your wife be coming back from England?" I asked.

I wondered how this relationship worked, and I hoped to meet her someday. She was English, spent much of the year in her native country, and came to Pakistan only after the rains cooled the Punjab.

"When the monsoons come, probably early October," Javed said.

He missed his two sons and watched our boys playing on the carpet with their toy cars and trucks while we lingered over coffee. He smiled and tousled Mark's blond hair as he said good-bye.

"I'll be ready in a few minutes and can take you on a tour of the dam." Jim disappeared into the bathroom.

I had a moment to speak to Javed. "We looked for you at Falletti's the last Saturday night we were in Lahore. I'm sorry we didn't have a chance to say good-bye." I looked at Javed. His smoldering eyes barely hid his feelings.

"I missed you the next time I went. I've not found a good dance partner. Then I heard you'd moved to Baral, and I wanted to see you and Jim," he added, his manners intact.

I felt sorry for this lonely man. He had money and came from a prestigious Pakistani family, but his wife preferred to spend half the year away from him. We had seen him at Falletti's every time we'd gone there except that last time. I think he came to Baral to see that we were living in a decent place, probably considered the wilderness to someone like Javed.

Jim went back to work, taking Javed and Mr. Bhatti with him. He told me about their visit later that evening. Jim introduced them to his boss who recognized the name of their company. He told Jim to take them on a tour of the job. Like all visitors, they were impressed at the scope of the project and how rapidly the company had made progress carving a high-tech dam out of the wilderness. They thanked Jim and returned to Lahore.

I'd never get the chance to go on a *shikar* and learn what the hunt was all about.

⬦⬦⬦⬦⬦

REGISTRATION FOR SCHOOL CAME IN late August. I took Mark with his passport and immunization card to sign up. School would start in a few more weeks. Dawn Armstrong had invited us to go to Sunday school where the minister we'd met was the pastor. I dressed the boys and took them one hot Sunday morning. Mark enjoyed Sunday school. He thought it was real school and took it seriously. He got up and dressed, hurrying me along so we wouldn't be late. Dawn and Otis Armstrong picked us up on Sunday mornings where the three of us squeezed in the backseat of the white Ford sedan with their two boys. I liked church, and it was a way of getting acquainted in our new town. Jim listened to Mark's experi-

ences when we returned, grinning at Mark's version of the Bible stories he
recounted for his dad.

◇◇◇◇◇

I RETURNED HOME AFTER DANCE class one day to find Jim home in the middle
of the day.

"Are you okay?" I was concerned.

"Well, yes, but they sent me home to rest for a few hours," he said.

This was most unusual for Jim, my workaholic husband. "Why do you
need to rest?" I didn't see any signs of injury. Had there been an accident?

"Adeline Archibald was in trouble today. She needed a blood transfusion. They looked up people in the blood bank, and I was the first one
they could find with Type A negative blood. I've been at the hospital all
morning. The doctors put me in her room with a curtain between us and
gave her a direct blood transfusion from my arm." I noticed his forearm had
a bandage wrapped around it. "She's going to make it."

"Jim, that's wonderful you could help her. Do you feel lightheaded?
Are you weak? Was this the first direct transfusion they did? You must be a
hero!" I was amazed at his news.

"Anyone would have done it," he said. "I just happened to be the first
they found with Type A negative blood, and I was available. She lost quite
a bit of blood from internal bleeding."

How casual Jim was about his contribution in saving Adeline Archibald's
life!

"They said it was the first direct transfusion. Dr. Frewing was pleased
that his idea of having a living blood bank proved to be successful, especially
for Adeline," Jim said.

"Well, I'm proud of you, and I'm happy that Adeline will be all right."
Jim was casual about his contribution.

After resting most of the afternoon, Jim decided his basketball team
needed him, so he donned his shorts and left for the game. He came home
a little tired a couple hours later, but he had played the whole game. Twice,
he had to put his head between his knees when he felt lightheaded. His
team won the game, and he was pleased. Adeline Archibald survived her
ordeal and wrote Jim a heartfelt note of thanks after she was released from
the hospital.

36

Exploring in the Salt Mountains

JIM'S RELATIVELY NORMAL HOURS CAME to a screeching halt when his Pakistani assistant came down with malaria, and Jim had to work extra hours. Burnell Ambrose took over as warehouse manager when John Cardosa was reassigned to the London office. Jim was happy to see Burnell, who had been his first boss at the company's main office in South San Francisco when he was first hired in 1959.

Burnell's first change was to require sharing of the vehicles assigned to the warehouse personnel at the central supply department. Jim now had a Land Rover assigned to him every third night and every fourth Sunday. This was a great help for our family to have a vehicle for shopping and errands. Now we had a way to visit the project and observe the progress of the dam. Seeing the progress made the everyday inconveniences seem smaller when we could take pride in the magnitude of the project. Each time I saw the site, I marveled at the changes as the men reshaped the land and dug the long trench for the impervious clay core of the dam.

Jim and I were eager to explore more of this ancient part of the world. We had always loved visiting old mining towns in Nevada. We knew treasures waited for us here, too. One weekend, Jim reserved a company car from the fleet of white Ford sedans the company had available to rent.

Ghulam, the driver, arrived early. Jim sat in the front seat with him. Our plan was to visit a cement plant, a salt mine, and an ancient fort at Rohtas for starters. Jim had read of a huge salt mine at Khwera in Pakistan's Salt Range, about a thirty-mile drive from Baral Colony, which was on the way to a cement plant he wanted to check out. An article about the salt mine gave driving directions and distances along with the story. We decided to see the salt mine on the way to the cement plant. The article said the road was *kutcha* (jeepable), meaning not paved or "carpeted."

Khwera was Asia's oldest salt mine and the second-largest salt mine in the world after the Wieliczka mine in Poland. Khwera's wealth of pink and orange crystalline salt had been mined for hundreds of years. Over eighty miles of underground electric railroad tracks wove through the seventeen levels of the mine, twelve of them underground. The largest and most impressive chamber, deep within the mine, was 350 feet long. It contained the mine's greatest treasure, a mosque carved of pink crystalline salt. The pictures of the intricately carved mosque sparkling in pink splendor made it an attraction I was eager to visit. To get there, we'd have to take the trains or walk through the maze of tunnels dug by laborers using hand-cranked drills and gunpowder to blast away the rock salt. These laborers earned a little over a dollar a day for this tedious work.

In recent years, the British had granted hereditary rights to a mining job at Khwera to the descendants of the original fourteen local families. The Pakistani enterprise that now managed the mine when the British relinquished control in 1947 kept up this tradition.

Legend tells that Pakistan's Salt Range deposits were discovered in 327 BC when Alexander the Great defeated a local king nearby. Stories told that Alexander traveled as far east as the Mangla Fort and the S curve of the Jhelum River, where his view of the formidable mountains ahead turned him back, discouraged, to rest his troops and begin the trip back to Macedonia. His army's tired horses were resting in the cool air of the caves. The horses found the salt on the cavern walls to their liking, and licking the salt is rumored to have restored their strength. Asthma sufferers have also found curative powers by staying in the salt-filled chambers deep inside the caves. The underground chamber could accommodate up to twenty asthma patients in the subterranean rooms.

Our information said there was a rest house available for overnight guests, but we would need to bring bedding, mattresses, cooking utensils, and provisions. We decided a day's trip was enough so we packed a picnic and brought water and snacks.

We left the green fields of the Punjab and drove on paved roads that soon became gravel, bumpy roads west of the Grand Trunk Road. The road got steeper, and we wound up and over the hills. The forty miles or so took nearly two hours, but the directions brought us right to the entrance of the Khwera Salt Mine.

To our disappointment, the guard told Ghulam that the mine was closed for a festival at a village just over the hill. We were so close, yet we could only see a little sparkle as the sunlight hit the glistening pink rock salt that surround the entrance. Perhaps those were the very rock walls Alexander's horses had licked so many centuries ago. Even the air from the entrance smelled salty. We were disappointed, but we decided we would return another day.

Ghulam turned the car around and started toward the cement plant a few miles further west, the next site Jim decided was within driving distance for this day. At least he could check out the cement that had been such a problem to them at the dam. Most Pakistani cement was not up to the specifications required. The contractor was importing cement from Japan at great cost.

Halfway up the barren hill, a lone horseman riding a beautiful sorrel stallion came from the opposite direction. His gold and white outfit, fanned turban, and side sword made him look like a professional rider from a circus or performing group. As we got closer, I recognized him as one of the riders who had performed at the Lahore horse show in March. I was sure of it, and I was eager to see his magnificent horse up close. The horse's martingale and saddle blanket were bright red and gold. The gold tassels swished in rhythm with his strides.

"*Bas* (stop)! Please, Ghulam." I got out of the car and walked over to talk to the mounted horseman. He stopped the horse, waiting.

"*A Salaam alekum* (Hello, peace)," I said to him with a smile. "*Bahut acha* (Very nice)." I gestured to his horse and tack.

"*Alekum salaam* (Hello, peace)," he replied with a nod of his head.

I realized I was being a little brazen, but I wanted to see his magnificent horse up close. "Were you in the Lahore Horse Show?" I asked him.

He smiled. His wizened face expanded into a smile of pride as he nodded his assent. It was the horse I had seen.

"Oh, please, show my family your beautiful dancing horse!" I pointed to my wide-eyed sons watching me from the sedan.

Jim and Kevin had missed the horse show, and here we had a chance to see one of the stars of that event. I stepped back, curbing my desire to touch his beautiful horse. The rider saw my eyes shining with admiration. He smiled and turned the horse sidewise in the road. I leaned on the sedan, watching him.

He touched his heels to the stallion's belly, sawed ever so slightly on the reins, and the horse pranced in a quick step, almost like a mechanical horse. He kept up the dancing pace for about twenty feet, turned, and stood the horse on his hind legs. Then, to signal his impromptu exhibition was over, he touched the horse's head and leaned forward in the saddle. The stallion bent his left knee and extended his right leg, taking a gracious bow. I clapped my hands in delight. Jim and the boys clapped their hands as he brought the horse back up to a standing position.

"*Bahut acha! Sukreah. Bahut sukreah* (Wonderful! Thank you. Thank you very much)." I marveled at the unexpected opportunity for Jim to see a fraction of what we had seen.

He waved his hand, turned his mount, and continued on his way. The stallion's tail swished as they disappeared from view.

"Is that the horse we saw at the show, Mom?" Mark asked.

"Yes." I nodded. "That was the horse who stole the show in Lahore!"

"Dad, you missed the horse before, and now you got to see it." Mark was pleased.

Mark had liked the horse show, but now we had this was a special memory of a private performance on a back road chance meeting. How extraordinary!

Turning south from Khwera, we came to Kellar Kehar, a salt lake. We stopped to stretch our legs. Mark and Kevin chased the ducks and geese. Peacocks strutted, backing away as the boys approached. The male peacock spread his blue and green plumage in a wide fan behind his body. Kevin wanted to touch the feathers, but I pulled him back. Peacocks could be aggressive and territorial. We walked through the fragrant floral garden and found a shady spot by the lake. We opened our picnic cooler, and I offered sandwiches to everyone.

Ghulam looked at the wrapped sandwich. "What kind meat, *memsahib*?"

Muslim food laws were strict with pork or any pork products forbidden. Any food cooked in a pan that had been used for pork could not be used for cooking meat for a Muslim.

"It is chicken baked in foil, not in any pans, Ghulam."

Thankfully, he didn't ask if it were cut with a knife used for pork. Sliced meats from a butcher who might use the same knife or slicer would also have been considered contaminated. This satisfied him that it was safe. We all enjoyed our lunch in this remote paradise and watched the birds and lake while we rested.

"It's only a little farther to the cement plant. Are you up to more driving?" Jim asked.

"If we're that close, let's go," I said.

Kevin soon fell asleep while Mark stood watching the road ahead between the shoulders of Ghulam and Jim in the front. This road was "ironed" or paved, not rough. We climbed a few more hills and dipped into valleys with nothing but a few weeds and scraggly bushes growing. Finally, we drove over some railroad tracks and turned right and up an incline to the offices of the cement plant. Jim was interested in finding out what quality of cement they produced at Garawal's plant.

Jim introduced himself to the manager, who offered us tea. He was gracious with unexpected guests as were most Pakistanis. Hospitality was the golden rule in this part of the world. We declined the tea, and I took advantage of the restroom facilities at the cement plant office.

Jim asked a few questions about the cement, which was excavated from a pit over the hill behind the office. After loading it on railcars, gravity pulled the loaded cars down the hill to the shipping area near the office.

Jim's interest in their operation swelled the manager's chest with pride. He was eager to show Jim around and offered him a ride on the railcars to go to the top of the mountain and return. First, however, Jim must sign a paper, a waiver of liability, to ride as a passenger in a mine railcar. It had no safety features or a seat for a passenger. Wisely, Jim declined. We thanked the mine manager and said our good-byes.

We left the cement plant behind and started the long drive back to Baral. By following the directions we'd been given, we made a triangle of our visit, returned to the Grand Trunk Road until we reached Dina, our landmark to turn right toward the mountains and home.

"We'll go back to the salt mine before the monsoons or next spring," Jim said.

By now, we were discussing staying for a second thirty-month contract. The three-week vacation before the start of a second contract was attractive. For today, the boys were tired and needed a break from our back road explorations. And so did I.

"Next time we have the Land Rover on a Sunday, we can go to Rohtas Fort. It's just a few miles on the other side of Dina," Jim said as we passed the security gates at Baral. "Or we can try the salt mine again. You can take your choice."

The driver turned into our street where several maintenance trucks were parked. One was across the street. The others were in front of our next-door neighbor's home. Kevin was asleep, so Jim carried him into the house.

"What's happening?" I asked my neighbor.

"The lady across the street, Mrs. Smith, noticed a brick had dropped out of the back of her house. When she looked into the hole, a snake slithered out of sight inside the wall. The crew is deciding what to do. It was a small cobra." She shuddered.

"Why are they digging in your yard?" I asked. Our street was crawling with workers.

Pakistani workers dug with shovels, piling the dirt in a mound from the house to the drainage ditch in front.

"Our drain hasn't been working very well. Today, it stopped completely. We couldn't flush a toilet, and the drains from the sinks backed up. The maintenance crew decided they had to dig up the main sewer line when reaming the lines didn't work. Could I use your bathroom?"

"Of course, come right in," I said. "Let's make some tea until they finish."

She followed Mark and me into our house. Jim handed me a stack of mail we had picked up at the post office on the way home. On top were a letter from his parents and a postcard from San Francisco where they were visiting before school started again for Grace. A long envelope with a Washington DC postmark caught my eye, too. I could hardly wait for my neighbor to leave so I could read what was happening at home.

"We're going to a movie tonight. They're showing *Breakfast at Tiffany's* with Audrey Hepburn. John wants to get there early to get a good seat." She grinned. "Why don't you and Jim come with us?"

The company flew in movies twice a week and showed them in the

680-seat theater free to the employees and their families. I liked going on Wednesday afternoons with the boys when an appropriate movie was playing. Two showings, at two in the afternoon and one at seven in the evening, accommodated men on either day or swing shift. If we weren't so tired, I'd like to see that movie.

"We gave Usef the day off, and the boys are too tired to go tonight, but thanks for asking," I said.

The maintenance crew foreman came over and talked to Jim. We followed him outside and looked into the trench. The four-inch sewer line lay open like a severed artery.

"Look at this!" The foreman held up half a brick. Behind it in the sewer pipe were many flat rocks and, about two feet further along, another half a brick. "The Pakistanis were so impressed with the flush system that they thought anything and everything would magically disappear if they just put it in the sewer line. This is the seventh one we've had to dig up and remove rocks. The local construction crews thought they'd save time and toss all their debris into the toilet's sewer pipe. They filled some of them so good that we had to take them out all the way into the house." He shook his head in disbelief. "At least they didn't put as much in this one."

"Why did they put all the flat rocks in there?"

That wasn't part of the construction materials.

The foreman turned to talk to the workers, and Jim took me aside. "The Pakistanis use flat rocks. You don't see any toilet paper around, do you?"

I was stunned. The crew replaced the section of sewer pipe, tested it, and then filled in the trench with dirt around the sewer line.

"We'll send the landscape guys over to patch up the grass," he said to the neighbor.

"See you later." My neighbor waved as they left for the movie.

I went inside and sat on the living room sofa, eager to read the mail. Jim's parents had enjoyed San Francisco, but Grace was most happy to be with her twin brother, Chuck. The loss of his wife Peggy a few months ago had been devastating to him. Chuck and Peggy had no children, and they had always been close to Jim, and treated him like the son they never had.

A note from Dorothy Ziemer said she had seen Sherif. He wasn't happy with his new job, and wished he had come to Mangla with us. He asked Dorothy to let me know he was available.

The next letter was from my friend Pat who lived in Washington DC. She wrote of watching the Freedom March on Washington DC, where her husband worked for George McGovern from South Dakota. Pat had taken me to pass out campaign literature for John F. Kennedy in small towns of South Dakota. She was dynamic and bright, loving the political scene. I couldn't have a better pair of eyes to tell me what was happening in America. Her letter grabbed me at the first sentence:

> They came by trains, airplane, bus, and too many cars to count. People started marching at the Washington Monument and ended at the Lincoln Memorial. Music and speakers kept the crowd of over 250,000 people peaceful and united in one cause: freedom and equality regardless of color or race. They wanted segregation in schools to end and all Americans to have the same rights and freedoms. The strains of Joan Baez singing "We Shall Overcome," Peter, Paul, and Mary strumming the emotional folk song, "If I Had a Hammer," and "Blowing in the Wind" by Bob Dylan, which still rings in my head and heart. I felt like I watched history being made as Martin Luther King Jr. gave a rousing speech not soon forgotten that ended with his dream for America. I think we all felt it on the packed Mall that day. Surely, "the times they are a changin'."

I reread the letter and wondered how much of what was happening in America we were missing. My friend Pat was an example of American grassroots fundamentalism of the 1960s. I closed her letter, and a wave of longing for America washed over me. We were missing out on so much being so far from home.

◇◇◇◇◇

JIM HAD BEEN ALONE ON his birthday last year when we were still in the States, so I invited a few couples for dinner to celebrate his birthday in September. Otis and Dawn Armstrong had become good friends, along with our neighbors from the South Dakota job, Dora and Ray Haugen. I had to invite the angel who brought my groceries to Lahore, Ken and his wife Lovelle. Fida Shaw and Hamid Alvi, two educated, charming Pakistani bachelors, rounded out the dinner party. Usef did a remarkable job with a cake, and we put together a dinner using his skills and mine. Everyone enjoyed the evening, though late that afternoon Ken had to fly the boss to Lahore and missed the early part of the dinner.

Usef had been with us for about six weeks and was hinting that he needed a bicycle and a raise. I listened but didn't respond, considering his inconsistent work lately. He often left dirty pans and dishes in the sink when he left.

Ray and Dora hadn't been to our house yet, so they were looking around when they recognized Akbar as he swept the patio.

"Irene, I hate to tell you this, but that gardener has TB. He was working for our neighbors. When they sent him for medical tests, the doctors found he had active tuberculosis just a few weeks ago."

Dora's news of Akbar's tuberculosis was a shock. He had showed me his medical card. I had to talk to Jim about it as soon as our guests left.

Ken arrived in time for a late dinner while we were still chatting.

"Ken, sorry you're late. For you, I made three kinds of cauliflower. I had marinated cauliflower, cauliflower au gratin, and we even had some cauliflower mixed with curry, which I've heard is your favorite."

Everyone laughed, especially Ken. He and Jim disliked cauliflower, and on meatless days at Falletti's, they were served this vegetable in all its possible variations. They both vowed never to eat cauliflower again. I couldn't resist teasing Ken.

The next day, we told Akbar that his medical tests had to be repeated. He protested, but Jim borrowed a vehicle, and we took him to the hospital. We told the doctors what Ray had told us about Akbar's illness. I felt sorry for Akbar and wondered if the doctors wouldn't treat him for the disease.

"This man's chest X-ray doesn't match the one on file. He has a bone spur from an old injury on the third rib that makes it easy to identify him." The doctor turned to question Akbar. "He says he sent in his nephew for the X-ray. He gave Akbar's name so he could get a clean bill of health and work here. We'll have to withdraw his identity card so he can't use it again in Baral Colony."

"Couldn't he be treated?" I was not familiar with the disease, but I had faith that doctors could cure anything with antibiotics. Akbar was a kind older man and I felt sorry for him.

The doctor was less sympathetic than I was. "If we treated every man who wants to work in the colony, we'd need a facility ten times the size of the eighty four beds we have. And who would pay for it?"

Apparently, the doctors were well aware of the practice of sending in a healthy, younger relative for the medical tests. The younger man got a clean bill of health. By using the older man's name, he made it possible for those with a known condition to circumvent the system. Our medical team had discovered these methods. They had seen more than one fraudulent X-ray.

The week after we had to let Akbar go, Usef came to me again for a raise, and reminded me that he also needed a bicycle.

"Lahore sahib very much want me, pay me more," Usef said one day. He pouted as he did his chores.

"Usef, I think you liked Lahore better, didn't you?" I asked, suspecting the remoteness of Baral Colony wasn't a place for a good looking young man to find much entertainment.

"Yes, memsahib, very much like Lahore," he said.

I wrote a note to Dorothy and sent money for Sherif's bus fare. Her answer came a few days later. Sherif would be here the following Monday.

Usef accepted his final pay with no hard feelings on either side. He was a city boy, and would be happier where he could hang out in tea stalls and go to movies with his friends. He was great while he lasted, but I was pleased Sherif was on the way. Sherif knew our boys and how to prioritize their care over some chores. What great timing this exchange of bearers turned out to be.

Rohtas Fort

THREE WEEKS LATER FOUND US on the road to the four hundred-year-old Rohtas Fort. We drove a few miles to Dina, where our directions said it was only four miles west across the GT Road. Jim's suntanned face glowed with eagerness. He smiled at me and reached over to pat my hand.

The road made a sharp left turn soon after we crossed the Grand Trunk Road and then dwindled from a paved road to a *kutcha* road.

"Rohtas was built in the mid fifteen hundreds to prevent invading tribes from reaching Lahore after they came through the Khyber Pass," Jim said. "The Afghan king who built it named it after his son."

"Did they live there?" I thought of the garrison forts in our western United States where the soldiers lived.

The huge fort loomed ahead, taller and wider the closer we drove and rose several hundred feet above the flat farmland.

"It was capable of housing thousands of soldiers. They built it over two streams with stairs going down to the water so they could survive a long time inside the walls. The far western wall is high above a big cliff so troops couldn't breach the walls." Jim had read the history of this area during the months before we came.

I was curious to see inside. The fort sat high above the fields below with gates built high enough to allow elephants with a *howdah* on top of their backs easy passage. To reach the closest entrance gate, the shortest way was across a stream or small river. It looked shallow but was about one hundred feet wide. As we debated the wisdom of crossing the water in the Land Rover, a man waded toward us from the opposite bank. He held his basket perched on his head with one hand and held his *dhoti* up past his knees with the other. The water level didn't reach his knees, so the water wasn't very deep. Jim made his decision.

"We can go across the river right here. It looks shorter than following that road all the way around," he said.

"I'm not sure, Jim. What if we get stuck in the river?" I didn't want to risk our boy's safety.

Jim eased the vehicle into the water, which was soon up to the hubcaps. The Land Rover kept going, and I turned and watched the man who had waded across. He stood and watched our progress. The river became deeper, and water was now lapping up to the floorboards and splashing beside my feet. Fingerling fish swam quickly away as we stirred up their environ-ment. The submerged rocks were larger than they looked from the side of the river. Jim steered a zigzag course through the riverbed to avoid hitting them. Finally, we reached the opposite bank, and Jim put the Land Rover in lowest gear, climbed the embankment, and then stopped on the opposite bank. Jim parked beside the tall gate we had seen from the distance.

We entered the high gate that faced to the northeast, which was called the Khwas Khani Gate, after Sher Shah Suri's greatest general. With tall gates and a variety of architecture, the fort was a blending of Afghan and Hindu styles. We walked inside and explored a huge level area. Then we chose a stairwell that took us up to the next level. Here we looked out over the walls to the farms below, the grasses green and golden in the late summer sun. The walls of the fort were more than three feet thick and crumbling in many areas. The decorative top of the fort ramparts had large, peaked stones with openings for shooting bow and arrows at an enemy. Other spaces between the ridges allowed molten lead to be poured on enemies below.

Kevin and Mark loved exploring. We found many sets of stairs to climb, all leading to yet another vantage point. Jim took Mark's hand. I held Kevin's as we helped them up each of the steps that were a variety of sizes, all too high for their short stride and small feet. I watched each crevice and shadow, wary of snakes that could be lurking nearby. Tiny lizards darted between the stones at the sound of our approach.

The fort was over three miles in circumference according to the travel pamphlet we brought along. I tried to imagine it full of soldiers, horses, or maybe elephants. We felt once more like we had stepped back in time to another world. Some evidence showed that Alexander the Great had stopped at the site of the Mangla Fort where the sight of the formidable mountains may have persuaded him to return to Greece or Macedonia. This lush valley with water would have made a good campsite for his troops.

Kevin made a dash for the stairway descending from the middle of the fort to the river below. We held his hand as we went to see the river. Here was a packed earth space beneath the fort with a stream from the north and one from the east joining in a hidden confluence. The ground was packed where centuries of soldiers had trod as they brought fresh water to the troops billeted above. It was a wise place to build the fort, and the cliffs beneath the walls made scaling that side impossible.

As we walked toward the Land Rover, again I had to deal with the fact that there were no toilet facilities for women. Men never seemed to have a problem relieving themselves anywhere, as the stench of urine in the corners of the fort had disclosed. As we approached the Land Rover, I grabbed a beach towel I brought for emergencies and asked Jim to watch the boys. I got the idea of the big towel when I remembered how my mother had encircled me with a towel around her arms when I was a small child so I could change into my bathing suit on the beach. There were no changing rooms on the beaches of Lake Tahoe.

I walked past the vehicle and saw a few bushes that would afford some privacy along with my beach towel tent. There was no one in sight as I wrapped the towel around myself, as I looked around the bushes for snakes. I felt I was not alone. I was adjusting my capri pants while juggling the beach towel when I noticed I had an audience of a half-dozen men who appeared out of nowhere. There hadn't been a soul in sight when we left the fort, yet here was a group of men watching me. Perhaps I was the first American woman these men had seen. They probably thought all American women had very red faces.

◇◇◇◇◇

We hadn't celebrated Halloween last year in Lahore, where our children begging would have been a mockery in a country with so many poor. This year, our neighbor's children had costumes, and they were planning to trick or treat. I made costumes for Mark and Kevin out of the fabric from my sewing box, decorated two paper bags for their treasures, and took them along our street to see what neighbors had for the children. Jim stayed home to distribute candy to those who came to our door. Four houses down the street from us, a Pakistani engineer lived with his family. They were outside with a small brazier, cooking *samosas* and small appetizers of delicious Pakistani delicacies. They thought the children were coming because they were hungry and needed a meal, I guess. Their generosity and kindness was a surprise to our little American beggars.

◇◇◇◇◇

JIM HAD BEEN ASKED TO choose the dates for his second week of vacation that the company management urged him to take soon. We had decided to go to India in mid-November to see the Taj Mahal and as much as we could in a week's time. With Mark now in kindergarten, we decided it would be wiser to travel without the boys. They were too young to appreciate the sights of India's crowded cities and ancient sites, and I was reluctant to expose them to diseases. With only one week, Jim had a fast-paced itinerary in mind, and it would have been difficult for children. Our explorations of Pakistan, which had been a small part of the huge subcontinent and had many similarities, had whetted our appetites to see more. The magazine photos of Jackie Kennedy at the Taj Mahal and the Amber Palace where the photos showed her riding an elephant came into my mind. After much pondering and discussion, we scheduled our vacation for the second week of November.

Now we needed to find someone reliable to take care of the boys. Sherif was wonderful but needed his nights off, and we preferred an American take charge of their primary care with us so far away. The solution came when a nineteen-year-old American girl came to visit her parents in Baral. She liked the boys and was experienced at babysitting. She had younger siblings and appeared to be quite reliable. She was available to stay with Mark and Kevin for the week we planned to be away. We agreed on her pay, and our friends all agreed to look in and be available should she need help. Sherif would be there every day, too. We would be gone for a week and arrive back at Baral Colony in time for Thanksgiving. We made reservations for India.

India, Land of the Hindu

WE BOARDED THE PLANE THE morning of November 17, 1963, with some trepidation. Relations between India and Pakistan weren't the best in 1963. Pakistani's president, Field Marshall Mohammed Ayub Khan, continued to use the military to rule his part of the subcontinent with a gentle but firm hand. Gandhi had mentored Prime Minister Nehru of India in the doctrine of nonviolence long before the 1947 partition of India and Pakistan. However, we often heard shots fired in Azad Kashmir across the river from the site of Mangla Dam. Our passports showed our long stay in Pakistan, and Jim had his work visa as a form of identification. We had hopes that India would welcome us as American tourists.

Our flight from Lahore to New Dehli took only a half hour. Three of Jim's coworkers, seated a few rows forward, made the passengers chuckle when, as the turbulence bounced the prop jet around, one man hollered to his friend, "We should send a D-9 Caterpillar out here and smooth this out." Some passengers laughed at the construction man's humor while others may have wondered at their informality. His humor probably confirmed the suspicion held by many that all "Ameree-cans" were a little crazy.

The New Delhi stop allowed passengers to board, and in another short flight, we arrived in Agra where we planned to stay for two days and see the Taj Mahal. We collected our luggage and easily found a taxi. The driver circled the city, drove past a local shopping areas and bazaars and he stopped twice to allow free-roaming cows to pass in front of his van. India's sacred cows had the right of way. We checked in at the Clark's Shiraz Hotel and asked the concierge to arrange a guide and driver for the next day. We paid for his recommended tour of the Taj Mahal and the Red Fort, which left early in the morning before the sun was hot.

Our room was comfortable, quite an upgrade from the hotels we had stayed in during our visit to northern Pakistan. Agra was geared for visitors from around the world who came to see the Taj Mahal, the spectacular mausoleum that was its crown jewel. From our sixth-floor room, I looked toward the Yamuna River to see if I could make out the Taj Mahal from our window. The sun was setting, and I was able to see the profile of the fairy-tale structure on the horizon. It was a tease for the tour we had booked for tomorrow.

After changing for dinner, Jim and I went to find the lounge to have a cocktail and wait for the dining room to open for dinner. We were relaxed and unhurried as we found the lounge off the lobby. Along the back wall, a bar with a huge mirror and stacked glasses reminded us of many bars in American hotels. Cocktail tables dotted the room with candles and bowls of nuts that invited guests to linger. A lone sitar player sat cross-legged in the corner on a platform opposite the bar. Bright blue silk curtains framed his tan skin, further enhanced by his embroidered vest and voluminous red pants. His music sounded strange at first in a minor key, but he was a superb musician, and I soon found I liked the music. High minor tones and varied tempo drew me into the spirit of the songs he played. Some melodies he sang in a lyrical, plaintive voice. I felt myself transported by the feeling that here the spiritual was most important.

We ordered a drink and noticed an Indian couple who appeared in the arched entry to the lounge. Framed against the light was a tall man with a barrel chest and a flowing black beard. He escorted a woman who was dressed in a cerise-colored *sari* with gold bangles tinkling on her arms. He wore a turban that looked formed, more like a beehive than the Pakistani ones. He spoke in Hindi to the barman while his wife looked around the room. He started to sit near the bar, but she tugged his sleeve and brought him to the table next to ours. She smiled at me and struck up a conversation.

"Are you Americans?" Her English had a British accent.

She looked at us with unabashed curiosity. Her luminous dark brown eyes sparked with interest. I nodded. My eyes were drawn to the red dot in the center of her forehead.

"Yes, we are." Jim smiled. "I'm working on the Mangla Dam project. We've been in Pakistan for about a year."

"My brother married an American girl. She is from Michigan. Have you been there?" She was eager to talk more.

"No, not exactly, but nearby," I said. "We lived in the western part of the States. Michigan gets very cold in winter. Does your brother still live there?"

"No, they live in New Delhi, not far from here," she said.

Her husband ordered drinks. After watching Muslims decline alcoholic beverages, the Indians' easy acceptance of cocktails surprised me. I remembered last winter when I'd noticed a bearded, turbaned man in the dining room of Falletti's Hotel. When I asked Jamal and Najma about him, Najma had explained to me that the man I saw was a Sikh. He had a long beard and wore a huge, formed turban that identified him as belonging to the devout religious group.

"Sikhs don't believe in cutting their hair since it is part of a living being," Jamal said. "Sikhs are often vegetarians. They don't kill any creature for their food."

Other than their strict food restrictions and revering all living things, I knew little about Sikhs. They remained enigmatic and mysterious to me. I summoned my most brazen questions so I could learn more about the Indians in general.

"Can you tell me about the red spot on your forehead?" I asked. "Are you Sikhs?"

"Yes, my husband is. You can tell by his turban and his beard." My questions didn't faze her. They were open and very easy to talk to. "The red spot is called a *bindi* and signifies that I'm a married woman. The *bindi* is what my grandmother called her third eye, which gave a woman insight and understanding of things not seen by our two eyes. In recent years, our *bindi* has become more of a fashion statement."

"How do you put it on so it's so perfect and round?" I asked.

She laughed. "My mother can make a perfect, round *bindi* with her finger by dipping into the red lipstick. I find it easier to use the head of a tack or nail. We buy a small tool for this purpose in any bazaar."

"So are Sikhs allowed to drink?" She was a wonderful source of information.

"Yes, many Indian people drink a little. Alcohol is not prohibited like it is for our Muslim neighbors. Most Sikhs do abstain from smoking."

While Jim and her husband were chatting away about business, she and

I discussed our children. She had three. Her parents lived with them, as was the custom in much of the subcontinent. She hoped to go back to school when the children were older, as I did. Soon we were laughing and exchanging opinions like old friends.

"You must come to our home," she said. "We want to take you to meet our family. My name is Jaspinder. You can call me Jas for short. What is your name?"

"What a lovely name. My name is Irene. This is my husband Jim. You are so kind, and I wish we had more time here to accept your invitation. We have booked a long tour for tomorrow, the Taj Mahal in the morning and then the Red Fort and Shish Mahal Palace in the afternoon. We leave early the next morning for Jaipur. We can't leave our two sons too long."

She smiled ruefully. I felt sad, too. We got along so well, and I'd love to have met her family. How would their children be different from the Muslim children? Would their parents always live with them? My curiosity was increasing, but a short, discreet shake of Jim's head told me we had to stick to our schedule. We hadn't allotted extra time, nor had we expected to meet new friends.

The next morning, we met our guide, Mr. Singh, who drove us to the Taj Mahal. He paid our entrance fees and then ushered us through the turnstile to a long sidewalk. We stood awestruck at our first view of the Taj Mahal. Long, narrow reflecting pools stretched for about a hundred yards between the pearlescent Taj Mahal and us. We saw it twice, once upright and once upside down as if by magic, reflected in the water that mirrored its image. We stood on the long walkway looking at the reflecting pools and the beautiful white structure with its bulbous, tear-shaped dome. Four tall minarets anchored each corner of the square, creating the pleasing, perfect balance of the structure's bulk and spindly minarets.

The Taj Mahal, named for the favorite wife of Emperor Shah Jahan, Mumtaz Mahal, was built after she died in childbirth. Shah Jahan was so bereft when she died that he built this tomb as a tribute to his everlasting love for her. The designer used a variation of the Middle Eastern onion-shaped dome made in the shape of his tears.

We gazed in amazement at the beauty of this magnificent white work of art as we walked along the reflecting pools to the Taj. At the entrance, two uniformed security guards pointed at our shoes and then at a basket of foot coverings. We removed our shoes and checked them, pulling the fabric foot coverings from the basket over our feet. Jim had to check his leather belt and his wallet. He was reluctant to check his wallet. He compromised by removing the cash and his ID, which he put into his pocket, and then handed the leather wallet to the guard. Next, he checked my purse and put our leather belongings in an open cubbyhole. He handed us a chit, or claim ticket, to retrieve them later.

"Leather is from cows, sacred animals in Hindu religion," Mr. Singh said. "They cannot be taken into a holy shrine."

Shah Jahan was Muslim, not Hindu, but to the keepers of this treasure, it was sacred, and the Hindu laws applied.

Mr. Singh led us off to the side of the entrance to tell us about the huge marble edifice. "Perhaps you already know that the Taj was built in 1632 and completed in 1653 as a mausoleum for Mumtaz Mahal, the third wife of Shah Jahan. She died in childbirth with their fourteenth child. She was his favorite and most beloved wife, so here he built this tomb so their love would always be remembered. When Shah Jahan died, he was buried in a crypt beside her."

We walked around the white marble structure to the minarets by the Yamuna River where Mr. Singh pointed out the footings of a black marble building. A black Taj was rumored to be planned to be an exact duplicate of the Taj Mahal, on the opposite bank of the river. They say Shah Jahan wanted his mausoleum to be a replica of the original."

"You notice everything is in perfect symmetry," Mr. Singh said. "The minarets are real and can be used for the call to prayer. Notice the herring-bone design carved into the marble." He showed us the geometric carvings that would have been easy to miss from a distance. "Also notice the minarets are spaced far enough from the dome so that, in case one fell, it would not fall on the Taj. The minarets are one hundred and thirty-five feet tall, and the dome is one hundred and fifteen feet high. The minarets are placed about one hundred and fifty feet from the Taj, so if they fall, nothing could mar its beauty."

We looked at the distance, and I could see Jim judging the length from the top of the minaret to the base of the main structure. The distance appeared to be at least ten feet more than the height of the minarets, so the architect showed great foresight as well as attention to detail.

"There are eight identical doors to the interior. Only the one facing the reflecting pools is used."

We walked back toward the door to admire the floral designs carved into the marble. Where the floral carvings stopped, borders of marble with inlaid precious and semiprecious stones were set into the marble. After the gems were fitted into the carved marble, they were sanded and polished flat and felt smooth to the touch.

"Where did the marble come from?" Jim asked.

"Makrana in Rajasthan Province. It took a thousand elephants to carry the materials to build the Taj."

"Where did they get all the gemstones?" I asked.

"The turquoise came from Tibet, the Lapis lazuli from Afghanistan, the jade and crystal from China, and jasper from Punjab. All parts of India and Asia contributed," Mr. Singh said with pride.

"Notice the calligraphy around the main arch." He pointed out as we stood before the main entry and looked up at the façade around the pointed arch. The beautiful scroll-like symbols, probably Arabic or Persian script, were written all around the arch. "Do you see the size of these?" Mr. Singh pointed to those at shoulder height.

"Yes."

We both nodded.

"If your eye goes slowly up the arch, the figures get a bit larger as you read upwards, so anyone can stand right here and read the highest ones with as much ease as the lower letters." He was pleased with his disclosure of something we might have missed.

"Who thought to do such wonderful graduation of sizes?" I asked.

"Calligraphers from Syria and Persia were brought in just for these verses adorning the entrance. They wanted anyone to be able to read the verses written there, even without glasses."

Finally, we entered the main door to the crypt area under the tall dome. There were two sarcophagi, one smaller than the other. The larger was the emperor's; the smaller was his wife, Mumtaz Mahal. Here, beneath the dome of the world's most beautiful building, side by side were the bodies of the couple whose love was immortalized by this incredible work of art.

"These are the false tombs," Mr. Singh said to my disappointment. "The real tombs are one level below. No one can go there. They are identical to these but not for public viewing."

We walked around the chamber, admiring the marble walls inlaid with gemstones and lacy cut marble screens around the crypt. I felt the cold marble floor through my foot coverings even though it was a hot day. We walked around the outside and reclaimed our leather goods on the way out.

Mr. Singh had another surprise for us. We drove a short distance to a bridge and then to a parking area at the Red Fort. We followed him and again surrendered our shoes, my purse, Jim's wallet and belt. We walked through the red sandstone structure that was similar in design to see the Taj Mahal from this vantage point.

Here, the local guide told us the story of Shah Jahan being kept captive here by one of his sons. The poor man was so bereft after the death of his wife that he became crazed with grief. From these rooms where he was imprisoned, he could look across the river and feel the presence of his deceased wife in the grace of the building he'd built as a tribute to her.

After seeing the grounds of the Red Fort, Mr. Singh took us to the Shish Mahal Palace inside the complex. Mr. Singh gestured for us to follow him, and we joined a small group of tourists with the guide who was part of the Red Fort's staff. He asked each visitor where they were from. When we told him we were Americans, he eyes opened wide, and he grinned, obviously pleased.

"Just here, right where you are standing, *memsahib*, your president's wife, Jackie Kennedy, stood. For her visit, this room was totally refurbished to the same splendor as it had been for Shah Jahan and Mumtaz Mahal four hundred years ago. They loved this place, and so did your president's wife. When she came last year, she watched me as I lit the candles for her, and she was very much pleased. She said this place was most enchanting. Just watch."

He nodded to the guard, who closed the door. As we stood in darkness, he struck a match and lit the candle in his hand. The flame reflected off the walls, which were embedded with thousands of tiny round mirrors. The room became light enough to see each others faces, and the glow from that single candle cast its reflection to every corner of the room. Jim and I stood silently, holding hands, surrounded by the magic of this moment. I felt a chill as I realized we were following the footsteps of Jackie Kennedy.

We were in awe on our first day in India. Some of the architecture looked familiar, like the Taj Mahal and the Red Fort since Shah Jahan had also built the Shalimar Gardens in Lahore. There, the focus of the garden was at the exact center, with all paths and reflecting pools going away from

the main building. The Taj Mahal was unique in that the structure was placed on the far end of the long reflecting pool with the river behind it. Perhaps the rumor of Shah Jahan's plan to add a mirror image of the Taj of black marble across the river for himself was true.

◇◇◇◇◇

THE NEXT MORNING, THE CAR and driver picked us up right after breakfast. Our next stop was Jaipur. We drove through the streets of Agra, very similar to Lahore with many trucks, bicycles, and scooters competing for space on the road and people overflowing the sidewalks. Within a few miles, we were in flat, fertile farmland on a two-lane paved road. A few miles outside Agra, as we drove through the Uttar Pradesh in the Agra District, the driver pointed to a town in the distance in the midst of grain fields. From the distance, it looked as large as Rohtas Fort. Jim asked the driver what it was.

"Is old city, built by Akbar many centuries ago for his son, Salim who became Emperor Jahengir. Many people lived there. Then no more water. Everyone move to Lahore or Agra," our driver said.

"What's this city called?" Jim asked, now quite interested.

"Fetehpur Sikri, *sahib*. "You want to have a look?"

"Yes, if we will still get to Jaipur late this afternoon," Jim said.

We drove about a mile on the road to Fetehpur Sikri, a long, straight road that turned abruptly into the courtyard. It was built on a ridge with the open side toward the dry lake. We went inside and walked around the old structure that resembled the architecture of many buildings in Lahore. On the floor of the courtyard, a large pattern was laid out with different colored inlaid stones.

"What are those patterns for?" Jim asked.

"Is Parcheesi game, *sahib*. You know how to play Parcheesi?" he asked.

"Yes, but we usually play on a table with a board. How is this one played?"

"Prince put harem girls in different color dresses, and they move when prince commands them," he said with a smile, enjoying our surprise.

Jim wandered off to look at the higher structure reached by a long stairway I decided not to climb in my flat dressy shoes. The driver and I wandered over to a square, lacy building to the side of the game board. It was built with solid panels on the bottom half of the walls and carved red marble on the top half. I asked him about this building with short minarets on each corner.

"This is the house of the prime minister, the *Diwan a Khas*. Every fort or structure has a place for the most important advisors to be close to the prince in case he needs an immediate consultation. Soldiers and other advisors were located in barracks farther away."

The work that went into this well-planned town must have been incredibly difficult, hauling materials up to the top of the ridge and constructing this town far outside Agra.

We finished exploring the deserted city and returned to the road to Jaipur. At midday, we stopped in a wooded area where wild monkeys swung through the trees, chattering loudly at the car as we parked. The driver offered us a Coke from the little roadside market. Soon monkeys surrounded us. Some were shy, but others were aggressive.

"Best get back in car, *memsahib*," our driver said.

I could see these untamed monkeys didn't have the manners or socialization of those we saw in circuses. The brazen monkeys swung through the trees, scolding us for not providing them with a meal. A few chased our car to the main road as we resumed our drive.

◇◇◇◇◇

OUR RESERVATION IN JAIPUR WAS at the Rumbagh Palace Hotel, once the home of an Indian prince, which offered the finest accommodations available in Jaipur in 1963. Jim and I joked about staying in a palace. I expected it would be elegant. The lobby retained its former glory, furnished with brocade and velvet chair coverings, crystal chandeliers, and Oriental rugs, old but excellent quality. The heavy wood paneling added to the illusion of elegance.

Our room was furnished a little less grandly with worn brocades, threadbare velvet covers on the chairs, and a tattered Oriental rug. It was clean, and I imagined elegant parties this old palace had hosted.

Jim headed for the shower. He now judged hotels by the water pressure and heat of the water coming from the faucet. The plumbing again disappointed him. The faucet wouldn't turn off when he finished his shower, and we had to call maintenance to fix it. While we went to dinner in the dining room, we hoped they would repair the drip, or sleep would be impossible for me.

When we were waiting for our dinner to arrive, I looked over the tours available on a brochure I picked up at the desk.

"Jim, the Amber Palace is on a hill, and there are elephant rides to the top. I think we should arrange one tonight."

I was thinking of how smoothly our day in Agra had been with the educated, affable Mr. Singh as our guide. We learned so much from him that he was well worth his fees.

"Nah, I don't want to ride some elephant up the hill," Jim declared.

He wasn't going to change his mind. Maybe he didn't want to spend the extra money. The magazines had shown Jackie Kennedy and her sister riding the elephant up to the Amber Palace. How else would we get there? Would there be a cart? Could our driver take the car to the fort perched high on the hill we saw in the photographs?

"Jim, I really want to ride an elephant. Everyone says that's half the fun of visiting the Amber Palace. The gates and roadway are all designed for them to make the trip up the hill."

I read the guidebook to him and showed him the photos of the decorated elephant entering by the tall, curved gate.

"No, we're not paying to ride some elephant up the hill," he said, ending the discussion.

I was disappointed and sad. Whatever the cost, we'd probably never come here again and have the opportunity to ride an elephant.

The next morning, we met our guide and driver. Within a few miles, we were looking up at the Amber Palace, sprawled across the crest of the hills. A road snaked up the hill with a series of switchbacks. I looked around for some sort of vehicle, but the herd of elephants decked out in their finest *howdahs* and headpieces were all I could see. We were early, and the heat was just beginning to warm the high desert. I looked up toward the main entrance, the Sun Gate that faced east.

"Best to take road, *sahib.*" Our guide parked the car at the bottom of the hill.

Jim looked at the hill and the road that climbed to the Amber Palace in a series of switchback turns. Jim had his own plan.

I spoke up one more time, still hoping to ride on an elephant. "It's a long way up that hill, and it's steep. I wish you would reconsider and rent an elephant."

The guide heard our discussion and finished my plans with his next question. "Did you reserve last night, *memsahib*? If you have no reservation, is not possible."

"We'll just go straight up. It will be shorter." Jim started to climb the steep hill.

Seething with anger, I followed Jim up the hill. He started out with energy and a quick pace, all upward. I carried my purse and our video camera, and my shoes were not well suited to walking in the loose, sandy dirt. As we climbed, the sun became hotter. Soon, pebbles and bits of dirt filled my shoes, making each step uncomfortable. We paused to wait for an elephant to pass us, his customers lounging in the *howdah*. I faked a smile at the pampered passengers as I cursed my shoes. I didn't have any kind words for Jim at this moment either.

We started upward again. Jim put his arm out in front of me.

"Wait. Don't step there." Jim pointed to a steaming heap of elephant dung.

I stepped around it, silently cursing my stubborn spouse. I dropped my purse. The guide picked it up and offered to carry it and my camera. I handed the camera to him, grateful for not having to carry that additional weight.

The climb became steeper as we neared the top. The heat increased as the sun climbed overhead. I wished we had brought water or a Coke. I was thirsty and perspiring now. Another elephant passed as we reached the crest of the hill. I watched his padded feet swooshing on the path with a one-two-three-four gait, and his tail gave a slight swish like a wave as he passed. There went my dream of riding an elephant in India.

I sat down on a bench just inside the entrance to catch my breath. I shook the dust out of my shoes and wiped my feet with a few tissues from my purse. Jim was already walking around the courtyard, snapping photographs with his still camera. I had little enthusiasm for the sprawling palace with numerous wings on each of the four levels.

An old Indian man wearing a *dhoti* and turban walked over and gave me bow of greeting, his folded hands touching his forehead and then his chest while bowing his head. I assumed he was a self-appointed guide looking for customers.

He pointed to the lacy, carved structure in the center of the courtyard. "*Diwan a khaus.*"

Yes. They put a house for the prime minister, or diwan, near the front of every fort and castle. I remembered the name of that building from our stop at Fatehpur Sikri. He hovered around for a few minutes and decided I wasn't the decision maker. He waited for Jim to finish snapping pictures and returned to where I was resting with the old man. Now he and I were trying to converse in his Hindi and my small knowledge of Urdu. He saw Jim and beamed at the prospect of a paying customer. He pointed toward the house of carved marble panels.

"*Diwan a khaus.*" He pointed to the structure in the courtyard he had just shown me.

Jim turned, not sure what he was trying to sell, but Jim wasn't buying whatever it was. "No, I don't want a horse either." Jim turned to talk to our official guide who waited beside him.

The guide who brought us from the hotel smiled at the exchange.

"Jim, he's telling you that is the house of the *diwan*," I said. "This is the special house used by the prime minister for meetings."

He laughed at his own mistake and put his arm around me. "I thought you wanted to hire horses to tour the palace. It's a lot of walking, but it's amazing. Let's go." He was eager to see it all.

We spent the next few hours exploring the many rooms of the Amber Palace. The gardens and courtyard, sheltered from outside view by the formidable fort on the outer perimeter, showed a gracious living of the wealthy Rajastan princes of centuries before. We wandered the labyrinth of corridors that took us to a shrine deep within the palace. We stopped at the magnificent doors embossed with squares of silver panels, each showing a story of people and animals.

The guard pointed to our shoes. We dutifully removed them and donned the foot coverings from the waiting basket. We surrendered all our leather goods, shoes, purse, camera, and wallet again and entered the Hindu shrine. Tucked deep inside the huge Amber Palace was an exquisite, ornate gem of a shrine with a few people praying silently as we sat and watched the flickering candles. The peace and tranquility of this hidden sanctuary was a welcome respite from the heat and tension of the earlier part of the day.

The walk downhill was easier than the trip up. I insisted on walking in the serpentine pathway for the elephants, stepping around their droppings. I'd have taken the old man's horse if he had one since I couldn't have an elephant.

Back at the hotel, we had lunch and then went to explore the Pink City of Jaipur. This lovely desert city was the capital of Rajistan and India's first planned city. All the downtown buildings were made of deep pink-colored sandstone.

Jaipur was famous for star sapphires. I wanted to look at these gemstones and perhaps buy one as a souvenir of India. We could afford it with the money saved by not riding the elephant.

The shops closed after lunch for the owners to have siesta and reopened around four. We saw lovely jewelry in one shop where the owner responded quickly to the bell. He opened the safe and showed us the fine points of the star sapphires that made Jaipur famous. I chose a light blue stone with a perfect six-point star. Years later, we finally had the stone set into a ring for our tenth anniversary. The lovely ring still reminds me of Jaipur.

Jim and I laughed over our travels as we lingered over an English-style dinner in the hotel dining room. It had been a fairy-tale trip so far.

"I'd better reconfirm our flight to Bombay for tomorrow before we go to bed." Jim went to check at the front desk.

Bombay. The very name sounded intriguing to me. We were both eager to see what the next few days would be like. I felt like we were following in the footsteps of Jacqueline Kennedy. It was November 20, 1963.

South to Bombay (Mumbai)

OUR FLIGHT FROM JAIPUR TO Bombay stopped in Ahmedabad to board passengers and then brought us to Bombay, India's busy port city on the Gulf of Arabia. The traffic from the airport to downtown Bombay was like Pakistan's melee but amplified by the larger population. The sheer numbers of people, bicycles, cars, scooters, and trucks swelled the roadways and clogged sidewalks to overflowing with a crowded bedlam of humanity. Pedestrians, crowded off the narrow sidewalks, walked between and among the cars. One striking difference I noticed immediately was that the women on the streets of Bombay showed their tan faces, often with a scarf of rich, vibrant colors tossed over their shoulder but not with the intent of covering their beautiful faces or shining black hair. Only the older people with gray or white hair broke the pattern of sameness.

"India is a melting pot of all cultures and religions, as are many places in India, but none so cosmopolitan as Bombay," the taxi driver who picked us up at the airport said with pride. He pointed to Malabar Hill, an exclusive residential area, as he drove along the Marine Drive. "You must take this drive at night." We neared the hotel. "All the lights of Bombay are like jewels sparkling on the edge of the water. We call it the Queen's Necklace." He was proud of this city of hills and lush tropical

310

greenery. "And in the bay, ruins of an ancient civilization, thousands of years old, was found."

He dropped us at the hotel, the Taj Mahal Hotel, at the far end of Marine Drive. The wedge-shaped building was like a fort surrounded by streets on two sides with the bay just beyond the entrance. We entered the grand lobby that had interior stairways as well as elevators to access the rooms. After climbing several flights of stairs, we located our room and freshened up.

"Let's find the concierge and arrange a tour for tomorrow. Then we'll look around the port area across the street," Jim said.

We found the concierge desk in the main lobby. He quickly arranged a car and driver for the next day. When Jim asked him for recommendations on restaurants, he gave us a printed list of several nearby.

"Our dining room is quite good and popular as well. If you wish any alcoholic beverage, you must have a permit," he said. "I have the forms you'll need right here if you wish to fill them out."

We filled out the required papers, and he issued us each a permit. We tipped him and thanked him for his service. We went outside and crossed the street where a promenade along the water gave us a view of the harbor area. A huge arch that resembled the Arc de Triomphe in Paris stood facing the water. The arch was about eighty-five feet tall and had a bronze plaque on the side. We walked closer to look.

"The Gateway to India," Jim read the plaque on the stone arch. "This was built to commemorate the visit of King George V and Queen Mary on their 1911 visit to India."

The arch jutted out into the bay on an island or spur of land and was built to honor the British monarch. The Gateway also served as an epithet to the British Raj as well when the last British troops left India following their independence from British rule. The First Battalion of the Somerset Light Infantry passed through the Gateway on their way home from service to the British Raj in a ceremony on February 28, 1948, after the partition.

Early the next morning, our guide, Mr. Patel, arrived. He greeted us warmly and took us to his car. As we drove through the downtown business area, he explained a little of the history of this ancient city.

"Early Persian traders found the harbor of Bombay. They quickly took over the lucrative spice and silk trade, which led to the prosperity of their descendants, the Parsees. Although vastly outnumbered in proportion to the population, the Parsees have always been a driving force in the political life and the commerce of India. They also own the most important businesses and control most of the real estate, far greater than any other group."

"How did the Parsees come to India?" Jim was also intrigued.

"When the Moguls invaded Persia, they had a choice to pay higher taxes or to convert to Muslim religion. They fled and sailed to India. They settled here and in Gugerat Province in what is now Pakistan."

That was a new piece of history to both of us.

Our morning tour included a Jain temple, then a Catholic church, and even a Jewish synagogue. For a primarily Hindu country, this certainly was a cosmopolitan community.

Mr. Patel saw my surprise. "India has room for all religions. No problem. The Parsees have a large temple in the city. We cannot go in, but from the hilltop, we can have a view of the Towers of Silence from above."

He drove us up the road through the beautiful neighborhoods of Malabar Hill where he parked the car. We stood at a vista point overlooking the harbor in the distance. Below us in the thick undergrowth, scraggly trees partially obscured our view of the water. We could make out the rooftops of two buildings with flat, screened roofs, just visible through the trees. A squawking of birds and flapping of heavy wings could be heard nearby, yet none could be seen.

"These are the Towers of Silence where the Parsees put their dead. Since they believe that fire, earth, and water are all sacred, they cannot use cremation or burial for their dead. Instead, they let nature and the vultures who are so plentiful take care of the dead bodies. They wish to keep those elements free from contamination by the dead to make sure of preserving the earth."

"I knew the Parsees were Zoroastrian, the first monotheistic religion," I said. "But I didn't know about that practice. Is that how all dead people are taken care of?"

"Yes, a short time after death, the body of the deceased is placed on screens on the Towers below. The family offers prayers and allows the body to return to nature. The vultures and birds of prey strip the bodies of flesh, usually within a day or two. The bones are left to dry and are then removed to an ossuary."

We looked around at the beauty and peace of this hilltop with a glimpse of the screened rooftops visible through the trees below. The process of caring for the dead in this manner was strange to us, and we weren't sure what to think or say. Zoroastrians predated both Christ and Mohammed as the first monotheistic religion. I thought their practices bordered on more primitive cultures.

At the hotel bar that night, we used our permits to have a cocktail before dinner. The bartender put a bowl of large cashews on our table. We marveled at our experiences of the day. This big city cocktail lounge was more formal with a few Europeans as well as some Indian businessmen in Western clothing. I looked around, hoping to find a friendly face like the delightful Jaspinder I'd enjoyed in Agra. Here, no other women were in the cocktail lounge. We were ready when they called our names for dinner in the dining room.

The next morning, Mr. Patel took us to see the community laundry where *dhobis* worked in rented spaces with tiered pools of clean water. Each *dhobi* had a space where he could wash clothing first with soap. The second pool contained the popular bluing solution to whiten the clothing. A third pool was for rinsing. We watched from a bridge over the open-air laundry and saw barefooted men pound, beat, and wring the clothing. The hundreds of *dhobis were* doing laundry with huge baskets of clothing piled at the end of the washing pools. Faucets with running water made this a plush operation compared to the canal-side washing I had watched the *dhobis* doing in Lahore. The sky clouded over, and a few showers made us open our umbrellas. We stopped for lunch, and with the rain, we decided this was a good day to shop.

I'd promised my mother-in-law, Grace, I'd buy her a *sari* or some silk fabric. Looking for the right selection kept us busy much of the afternoon. We finally selected silk shirts for Jim and his father Am, and two lengths of raw silk, one for Grace and one for me to make a suit or jacket. I later discovered that the fabric was not as wide as I'd expected, only thirty-six inches, so a dress was the most I could make. The raw silk was a beautiful, tweedy fabric that could have passed for wool with the nubby texture. The silk mixed with wool was light as a feather. I bought Grace a sari embellished in silver that would be lovely with her white hair, and a blue green sari for myself. We bought as much as we dared, knowing we'd have to pay customs duty on our treasures. We decided to ship the items for Grace.

Could they possibly arrive in time for Christmas since we were at a port city?

"When will the package arrive in the States?" I asked the shopkeeper.

"Six to eight weeks, sea freight," he said.

The gifts wouldn't make it for Christmas but hopefully would please them early next year. She had shipped so many books and necessities to us that I felt we owed her a wonderful gift for all her trouble.

On our way back to the hotel that night, the lights on Marine Drive were glittering like thousands of white diamonds. So this was the Queen's Necklace. Bombay had been an experience in the exotic and very diverse character of India. We could see the beauty of the location, the greenery, and the water, but we had to overlook the hordes of people, teeming masses of humanity jammed into a space where even half of their number would be overcrowded. Bombay was unique, full of intriguing places and stories, but also dirty and full of poverty stricken people.

We boarded the airplane the next morning, November 22, 1963, to New Delhi, where we would stay for one or two nights, and then fly home to our children. I missed my sons, and I was ready to go home. India was a marvelous adventure, but I'd had enough for this trip.

Jim hailed a taxi at the New Delhi airport. I had ordered two more Indian dancer collages from Vera Chatterjee, and she had promised in her last letter that they would be ready to pick up when we passed through New Dehli and save customs duty and all the paperwork. The driver took us to the address I gave him. Her home was on the way into town and not much of a detour.

Mrs. Chatterjee greeted us at the door and invited us into her studio. I looked around at the lovely art work in progress and saw her stacks of fabric and neatly organized bowls of different sizes of jewelry. Her husband, a bent and frail-looking Hindu in a turban, western shirt, and trousers, came and greeted us warmly.

"Come sit. Would you like a cup of tea?" He was eager for company.

I was tempted to visit and learn more about his man who had quite a reputation as a scholar. He was now retired and not in good health. Jim looked at his watch, reminding me that we had to check into the hotel. He wanted to see some sights in New Delhi while we were here. I paid Mrs. Chatterjee and watched her wrap each burlap piece, a dancer and an elephant, in muslin cloth, tied the ends, and handed them to me with a smile. I paid her, and she walked us out to the waiting taxi.

"Perhaps I can come to Mangla next spring before the heat." She was eager for sales.

The taxi driver was willing to give us a short tour of the area. He drove us around the Red Fort, and we saw a city very similar to Lahore but drier and without the charming fringe of greenery. Less than one hundred miles separated the two cities, and the Punjabi influence stamped in Lahore was also noticeable in Dehli's architecture. Handsome red sandstone structures of the Moguls interspersed with modern office buildings showed little difference between the two cities.

That night, we noticed a somber atmosphere in the hotel's dining room. People held newspapers at their tables. The serious tones of their subdued conversations sounded like something had happened, but we couldn't quite hear what was going on.

We finally asked the waiter if he had heard any important news. The newsstand was sold out, so we couldn't buy a paper.

"Oh, yes, is terrible. A helicopter crash has killed four generals of the Indian army while they patrolled the Kashmiri border. The country is in mourning for the loss of the top army officers in the country," he told us.

Jim and I looked at each other. Would this cause an international incident and make travel between the two countries difficult? Would Pakistan be blamed for the crash of the Indian helicopter? Was it flying over the disputed area of Kashmir? Suddenly, the miles between here and our home in Pakistan seemed farther than the 300 miles to our children. I was worried. Jim tried to hide his concern, but the set of his jaw told me he was as concerned as I was.

I slept little that night with sights and sounds of India racing through my mind. We had spent a magical week, but now I wanted to be home with my children. What would tomorrow bring? Would India and Pakistan see the deaths of the four generals as a reason to go to war? Did Pakistan have anything to do with their death? The Azad Kashmir border between India and Pakistan had been a source of conflict for years, and we had often heard gunfire at Baral Colony since the project straddled the border of Azad Kashmir. What impact would that helicopter crash have on travelers trying to enter Pakistan?

Jim slept better than I did, but we were both awake before the alarm clock went off. We showered and dressed. I opened the door to the hall and found an English language Delhi newspaper for us.

"PRESIDENT KENNEDY ASSASSINATED!" the paper's headline screamed. "John F. Kennedy and Governor Connelly both shot on motorcade in Dallas, Texas, by unknown assassin." Halfway down the page, another headline read, "FOUR TOP INDIAN GENERALS KILLED IN HELICOPTER CRASH."

My mind couldn't embrace what I was reading. There must be some mistake. Was there a President Kennedy in Ireland or some other country? Perhaps he was the one killed, not our president! Who would kill our president and leave our country without a leader? Impossible. I handed the paper to Jim, unable to voice my concerns.

"My God, President Kennedy assassinated? Four Indian generals were killed on the Kashmir border patrol? This is a huge loss to India. If they think Pakistan had anything to do with that crash, they may not let us back over the border to Pakistan!" Jim put my own unspoken fears into words.

Today, we had planned visit to Amritsar, an Indian town near the border of Pakistan to see the famous Sikh Golden Temple. The news left us no desire to go anywhere but home to our sons. We wasted no time as we packed our clothing in a haphazard rush, checked out, and took a taxi to the airport. Two airline employees with somber faces checked our luggage. They offered us condolences, tears filling their eyes as they talked about President Kennedy. At the boarding area, three more teary-eyed Indian customs officials checked our passports. Their huge brown eyes could not contain their tears.

One blew his nose and dabbed his eyes as he choked up before speaking to us. "Mrs. Kennedy came through this airport on her visit. What a lovely lady."

"We are so sorry to hear about the murder of your president. We cannot believe that an American could have done this. The man must have been a Soviet spy," the customs officer said.

He paid no attention to the contents of our suitcases, nor did he ask us what we had bought in India. He stamped our passports and extended his hand in heartfelt sympathy. I looked around at the other customs officials whose response was the same. They cared for our fallen leader.

We were stunned. The good news was that we were on the way home and the plane was on time. Crossing the border into Pakistan was not the problem we feared it might be. The grief of the Indian people made the news more real to us. They had heard of the tragedy earlier than we had. We were still trying to absorb the news we didn't want to believe.

We boarded the plane with relief, but with concern for the future of our country and the world. As the plane sped down the runway, I said a prayer for a safe journey back to our sons and for our deceased president's family.

"May God rest his soul."

Thoughts of our dead president, the radiant prince of Camelot, kept going through my mind. And Jackie, his beautiful wife, whose own travels had inspired me on this trip. I felt like we had walked in her footsteps during each magical stop. The Indian people had such a good impression of Americans after her visit that we were the recipients of an extra measure of goodwill. It was November 23, 1963.

After the short flight to Lahore, we inquired about a flight to Mangla. The plane still only flew twice a week, and the next flight was tomorrow morning. John Ziemer picked us up so we could spend the night with them. We telephoned Otis Armstrong in Mangla. He and Dawn were checking on our sons and the babysitter. Otis assured us that our sons were fine. He was relieved that we were back safely in Lahore.

"Pakistan shut down all businesses. Nothing is open in the country, so you were fortunate the airlines were flying on schedule," John said. "Management wanted to shut down the work in respect for the president, but with the schedule so tight, they decided to stop for fifteen minutes. All equipment and tools stopped working. They maintained silence during that time."

Earlier in March, when Mr. Harney died, the equipment and men had stopped for a five-minute tribute to the founder of that company, one of the partners of the consortium of partners of the Mangla Dam project.

Ziemer's doorbell rang and Pan Am's Lahore office manager, Jerome Fernandez, silently handed several U.S. newspapers to John and Dorothy. We were all finding it difficult to believe the story that unfolded in the papers. The motorcade with President and Mrs. Kennedy cruised slowly through Dallas when an assassin opened fire and shot President John F. Kennedy. Governor Connelly was wounded but would recover. The photo of Jackie's stricken face and her bloodstained pink suit as she reached to help the Secret Service agent board the limousine showed a far different expression than the happy, relaxed face of the beautiful woman who had toured India. The previous photos of that carefree visit that left her footprints on the hearts of the people of the subcontinent were a sad contrast with the tragic photo of her in the car in Dallas.

America had lost a president. We stared at the black-and-white photographs of an event the people of America and much of the world would never forget.

Holidays in the Wake of Tragedy

THE SHOCK AND GRIEF FOLLOWING the assassination of President Kennedy hung like morning ground fog in the Indus River Valley over the enclave of Americans at Baral Colony. The rapid transition of government from Kennedy to President Lyndon Johnson was seamless, and our country continued without missing a beat. How rare that would be in many other parts of the world.

President Kennedy had spoken with a strong voice for civil rights. Some people in our American community voiced concern over the pending civil rights legislation. The fact that Johnson was a Southerner gave people concern about the passage of the Civil Rights Bill. Many of us felt the equality promised was imperative to America's democratic principles. As it turned out, our concerns were unfounded because, under the Johnson administration, more civil rights legislation was passed than at any other time in history.

We watched the mail for news from home with a greater intensity than ever. We subscribed to *Time*, *Life*, and *Reader's Digest* that were a month old when they arrived by sea mail in Pakistan. Jack Ruby's killing of Lee Harvey Oswald left us with more questions than answers. We wanted more details and for someone to explain why and how this could have happened in America. We felt in a vacuum with news trickling in at such a time delay.

The fear I felt that day in New Delhi when we learned of Kennedy's assassination and the physical separation from our boys by international borders convinced me that no travel was worth being separated from them. We'd been fortunate to have no problems this time, but the danger was not worth tempting again. My resolve was to take them with us or not venture out on any more trips. Our thanksgiving prayer that year was our safe return to our children.

Thanksgiving Day was subdued with the shadow of grief hovering over the holiday. We bought a turkey flown in from the States and laughed at the memory of last year's gift turkey cooked with feathers, entrails and all. The sights and sounds of the trip to India paled with the news from home that now dominated our thoughts. Television was not common in Pakistan in those years. Even if we'd had a radio, local news was broadcast in Urdu. The company flew in newsreels for important sports and news events that were shown before the featured attraction at the movie theater. These newsreels as our most reliable information source from America.

Within a week, the first newsreels arrived at Mangla. We squeezed into the packed theater to see the newsreel that none of us wanted to believe. The lights dimmed, and the theater played the Pakistani national anthem, as our entertainment license required before every movie shown. We watched in horror as the events of November 22 in Dallas were replayed on the screen in front of us. When the lights came back on, we filed out of the theater. The only sounds were a few sniffles. Hardened construction men left the theater with wet handkerchiefs and tear-swollen eyes. Our communal loss was heavy, and we all felt helpless so far from America. The reality of the assassination finally hit us with the visual evidence on that newsreel. We grieved alone, and we grieved as a group of Americans far from home.

Mail from the States took between seven and ten days by air. We received newspapers from Jim's parents, Aunt Isabel, and Uncle Frank each from their hometown papers, which we devoured as they arrived. We now had several accounts of the events on that fateful day, but all told the same horrible story.

◇◇◇◇◇

As DECEMBER BEGAN, I UNPACKED our Christmas ornaments that had been in a container on the sea in December 1962. Old family ornaments, Snoopy and Disney ornaments I'd bought for each boy, all those decorations that symbolized the season, helped us find a way to go on. This year's cedar tree was larger and needed more decorations than last year's smaller tree had required. Mark contributed construction paper chains from his kindergarten class. Kevin moved it around on the tree and helped place the ornaments, using great care not to touch the lights after I showed him they were hot. This word and demonstration had worked to keep him away from the stove, too.

The *Baral Town Crier* featured some suggestions for Christmas decorations made from tin can lids, folded construction or colored paper, and a variety of homemade ornaments. One day, I visited my neighbor, Lennie, who was an artist as well as an ardent crafter. She was making a glass tree from broken green beer bottles. It was glued to a Styrofoam cone she'd had the foresight to bring from home. She explained to me how she tempered the glass. I stayed and watched the process as she explained it to me.

"I heat the oven to four hundred degrees and then put the green Heineken beer bottles in the oven for about twenty minutes. Then I take them out with a long tined fork inserted into the mouth of the bottle and plunge them into ice water in the sink. Like this."

She spun the bottle with a quick twist of the fork into the water in her sink filled partly with water and a few ice cubes. A hissing noise came from the water as the glass cooled and crackled into a lovely pattern. She moved the crackled glass bottles to a towel on the counter to cool while she removed several other bottles, one by one, and repeated the process.

"Next, I tap the bottle to make pieces the sizes I want."

She wrapped the first bottle in a rag, tapped it with a hammer, and held up a curved piece of the bottle. The shard had the shape of a pine branch. I touched her curved glass branches. They looked sharp, but the edges felt smooth. The heat and plunge into ice water tempered the glass and made handling it safe.

Next, she selected pieces of glass the sizes she wanted, added glue, and held them on the silver foil she had wrapped around the styrofoam tree-shaped frame. The pieces created the effect of the layered branches of a pine tree. It was beautiful. *Okay. I can make that.*

That night, I explained to Jim what I had in mind. I cleared a spot in the pantry to stash the green beer bottles until I had enough. A few days later, he came home with a metal frame of a Christmas tree the size I'd requested, about two feet tall and fifteen inches across the bottom tapering to a triangle at the top. It was like a tree sawed in half from top to bottom, perfect for the decoration I had in mind for the brick fireplace. He also brought some fine wire, which he helped me wrap around the frame. Then I glued heavy-duty aluminum foil over the entire structure. Now I had a frame for my glass tree. When completed, this would be the focal point of the living room hanging above the fire on the red brick fireplace.

Each day, I scrubbed off the beer company's labels, put a half-dozen bottles in the preheated four hundred-degree oven, and then plunged them into ice water in the sink. I broke and glued the glass chips to the tree. I worked from the bottom up, using empty beer bottles I begged from our friends and neighbors before the servants took them away to sell. Finally, it was finished. Jim pounded a nail between the bricks at just the right height. My tree sparkled in the light as it hung in the center of the red brick fireplace. The repetitive work of creating a symbol of Christmas for our home helped me climb out of deep grief we all dealt with that season.

Lennie stopped by to pick up her two younger children who often played with Mark and Kevin. She examined the tree. "It's lovely, Irene. You did a great job."

I glowed at her praise. It was her idea, and she'd showed me how to make something out of what would have become trash. Pakistani people let nothing go to waste that could be reused. I had been there long enough to follow their example. I was proud of the tree that cost nothing but our efforts.

In early December, the electrical department erected a twenty-foot-tall frame for the community Christmas tree. They strung it with colored lights, and it sat overlooking the town from Hospital Hill, where it was visible from all over town. The four letters, NOEL, perched on top of the hospital's roof completed the town's decorations.

Santa Claus arrived in Baral Colony during the second week of December. Many families braved the cold so their children could see his arrival and the lighting of the Christmas tree. Santa arrived on the back of a camel, causing the children to gasp and point in wonder. The camel knelt down. Santa dismounted and distributed candy from his sack to the eager children. American children had never seen Santa arrive on a camel, so this novel entrance brought laughter and joy to them. Their shouts and laughter caused the camel to sidestep, scattering people who were in the beast's path. We laughed and hurried home for hot chocolate. Mark remembered the camel carrying Santa from the party last year in Lahore, but I wasn't sure if Kevin did.

Our Christmas program was a success with songs and dances by the high school choir and dancers as well as the adult singing group. I danced in a few simple routines I'd learned with our group of eight women dancers, and I sang in the adult choir. I found myself busier than ever when the women learned that I could sew. In the crunch of time, the tailor was overworked, so I helped make some of the costumes. In one way, I preferred fitting my own. The lecherous Muslim tailor who said he needed so many fittings had a way of being a little too familiar in his efforts to make sure each of our costumes had a good fit. We were beginning to wonder about our tailor, but he was one of the few who could fit women's clothing.

A few days before Christmas, someone knocked at our door. I opened it to see Alberta Wilcox. She and her husband Darrell and two teenage children had just arrived from the States. Her oldest child, Sharon, and I had been classmates at Reno High School.

"Hello! Come in! Welcome to Pakistan!"

I hugged her. It was wonderful to have someone from my hometown at Baral. We had talked on the phone once before I left last year. Her husband was considering the job in Pakistan. When Mr. Wilcox decided to accept the job and bring his family, Mrs. Wilcox had written me for my advice on what to bring. She asked if she could bring anything for us. I wrote back requesting the next size of shoes for the boys. I traced their footprints, gave her the size of the shoes they were wearing, and requested larger sizes. The local shoemaker's shoes were still too wide for their narrow feet.

Sherif made tea, and Alberta and I caught up with news from home. In my last letter to her, I had also asked her to bring a few toys for the boys. She had wisely left them outside our front door so the boys wouldn't see them. Sherif took Kevin into the bedroom while we opened the treasure trove of much-needed shoes, socks, and toys. Christmas looked brighter this year.

The gifts Mrs. Wilcox brought, along with the few things we had found earlier, were enough to bring smiles to the boys' faces on Christmas morning. After last year's invasion of unexpected guests at WAPDA Flats, we were happy to spend a quiet, peaceful Christmas Day at home alone.

We celebrated my twenty-fourth birthday quietly that Christmas Day with our own family.

To round out the holiday season, George and Adeline Archibald were hosting a year-end party on December 29 at their home. Adeline once again asked Jim and me to help her. They expected between eight hundred to one thousand people at the open house. We enjoyed introducing people we knew and meeting those we didn't. The party was a success, though I went home with sore feet from standing so long in high heels.

"Jim, I can never tell you how much I appreciate your blood donation. You saved my life," Adeline said, her eyes misting over. "I might not have seen this Christmas. I guess that makes us blood relatives."

This New Year's Eve in Baral Colony was a contrast to the celebratory events at the end of 1962 when families were jubilant at being reunited in time for Christmas. The end of 1963 left us with questions on how our country would fare with a new president while we still mourned the slain President Kennedy.

New Year's Day of 1964 brought the coldest weather on record to the foothills of the Hindu Kush. We turned up our heaters to keep warm, and Jim brought home scraps of lumber for the fireplace when they were available. We wore sweaters and winter coats whenever we went outside. I was glad I'd brought the winter wear from our two years in South Dakota. One day as I was walking to the washhouse in the rain with my basket of clothes, the cold wind blew right through my coat. The rain pelted down, bounced on the asphalt roadway, and turned white. It was snowing in Pakistan. Actually, for a few minutes, the snow became large balls of hail. We had joked when we lived in South Dakota that they had the hottest summers and the coldest winters on record when we lived there. Now we had snow in the Punjab. It hit the ground and stayed long enough for a few photos before it melted.

◇◇◇◇◇

JIM AND I DISCUSSED THE possibility of extending his contract for another thirty months. His first contract would be up in October, now ten months away. We would have three weeks of paid vacation and hoped to travel through Europe. We had discussed requesting a six-month extension, which we'd have preferred, but the company was not granting any short-term extensions. We would have to commit to an additional thirty-month contract. The company had few projects and not many new jobs to provide work in the States. Mangla Dam was their biggest and most important project. Jim might be without a job if we didn't agree to a second contract. Jim liked the Atkinson Company that treated employees like extended family. We had many good friends among his coworkers. There was plenty of time to decide as 1964 had just begun.

Jim signed up for bowling one night a week and now played basketball two nights a week. The adult choir practiced in the evening, and I signed up for Urdu lessons taught at the high school just two blocks away. We only needed to have Sherif work one night a week on the night we both had events outside. My morning dance classes continued, so life was full and busy.

◇◇◇◇◇

THE SAME WEEK AS THE rare snowstorm, another labor strike threatened to cripple the project. Work screeched to a halt, and tempers flared. Jim worked his shift and had to return to work until midnight to cover the swing shift. Extra guards were posted at the warehouse and other key buildings to prevent malicious mischief or fires being set to the precious materials stored there. The railroad spur from Dina to the job, a distance of eight miles, was critical for moving parts to the job. With no workers to run the train, needed materials sat on the boxcars. Meanwhile, the company negotiated with the labor leaders to end the strike.

One night, Jim went back to work at seven after working since early morning. I fell asleep after midnight, unable to stay awake by reading to await his return home. I was worried about the possibility of riots and demonstrations that could turn violent.

The next morning, he returned home as we were having breakfast.

"Did you have to work all night?" I was annoyed that he had to work such long hours.

"Yes, but we got the parts we needed from Dina to the warehouse." A satisfied smile crossed his tired face.

"I thought the railroad crew wasn't working."

"It wasn't. We cranked up the locomotive, drove it into the warehouse yard, unloaded it, and took it back to Dina," Jim said it like it was an everyday occurrence to drive a train.

"Who drove the locomotive?"

"Walt Butler drove it, but I went with him and rode shotgun."

"How did Walt know how to drive the locomotive?" I was astonished at their bravado.

"We had a mechanic figure out how to start it. He gave Walt a quick lesson, and we took off before anyone knew about it. There weren't any strikers around at two in the morning."

The labor dispute this time was over one man and his family, but it soon escalated into a full-fledged strike. The company had fired the man for incompetence, and the company gave him notice to vacate the company housing that he and his family occupied at Thill Labor Camp. He had a wife and several children, one an infant. They refused to move from the company quarters when he was fired, and the legal battle began. The eviction notice had the man's name and was intended to include all of his family. The fired man and his family remained in the Thill housing from August until January. The company moved them to a rental house in Jhelum even though the wife now had a five-day-old baby. The man complained that the company security officers moved them instead of the Jhelum police, the only ones who had legal jurisdiction to do so. His protest proved to be correct under Pakistani law. Workers sympathetic to the man and his family refused to work until he was reinstated.

Each day's delay cost the contractor time and enormous sums of money. Each delay in progress of the dam made the goal of early completion less feasible. The bonus for early completion was critically important to management, and this one man's dispute and the strike had ground the work to a stop. The company felt blackmailed but needed to stop the strike and labor dispute. They had no choice but to placate the man.

The company rehired the man they'd fired and issued an apology to him. The family was allowed to move back into their quarters at Thill Labor Camp. His previous misdeeds or incompetence was forgiven. He would be retrained to do another job and was back on the payroll.

With the strike over, work on the dam could now continue. There was less than two years until diversion of the Jhelum River planned for September 1965.

41

No Longer a Stranger

THE MONTH LONG FAST OF Ramadan followed the lunar calendar and began late in January. At the end of the fast, the Sweet Eid celebration came with the sighting of the *Hillal* moon. Later, the Meat Eid would restore the faithful with slaughtered lamb, goats, and meats. Sherif asked if he could take a few days off to visit his family in Kashmir. I knew this was important, and he wanted to see his family. We never knew Sherif's exact age but guessed he was about eighteen years old. The same week as his request for time off, we received a note from Dorothy Ziemer about Freddie and Florence's wedding, scheduled for early February in Lahore. Jim couldn't take time off work but encouraged me to attend. This would also give us a chance to visit the shoemaker in Lahore for the next shoes Mark and Kevin would soon need. I would take the American shoes that Mrs. Wilcox brought and show him how narrow their shoes must be. These would be a good pattern for the future. We decided to go, and Jim could enjoy the peace of a quiet house while we were away.

Jim arranged a rental car for the boys and me. I wrote our friends of our plans to attend the wedding of our Anglo Pakistani friends.

A tall, young man named Ahmed appeared with the rented Ford sedan that morning. He was eager and courteous, and he smiled as he stowed our suitcases in the trunk

Ahmed turned south at Dina, and I saw the Rohtas Fort to my right rising above the green fields. Men in fields were plowing with oxen yoked to their plows, preparing the soil for the early spring planting. Traffic wasn't heavy today, so we moved at nearly highway speed for miles at a time. The road still had flocks of flat-tailed sheep with their tails painted the identifying colors of the owners competing for space with oxcarts moving even slower than the sheep with their tall, wide loads of straw. Brightly painted trucks swerved around the animals, hurrying on their way. I still watched for oncoming traffic and twice told Ahmed when I could see that it was safe to pass. I saw the country from a different perspective as we traveled toward Lahore. This country, the traffic, and the people all seemed natural and a part of the landscape I knew. I settled back and enjoyed the ride with the sun pleasantly warm on my shoulder. The fields showed the pale green of early warmth in the Indus River Valley. The beauty of the contrasting colors of the wheat fields with the western mountains framing the view was a lovely scene.

We stopped at Gugranwala for a Coke and to stretch our legs for a few minutes. Ahmed chatted with a toy vendor in Urdu. I was beginning to notice the difference in the dialect from the Northwest Pushtu dialect and the Punjabi patterns of speech. Their conversation had a songlike quality of highs and lows. I heard the bass voice of the storekeeper coming from behind his graying beard. Mark liked the carved wooden toys, so I bought one for each boy bargaining in my Urdu that was probably mixed with the Pushtu words Bashir taught me on our trip last May.

On the next section of roadway, Ahmed told me he was from Sialkot, a town close to the Indian border. He liked working at Mangla and driving the Americans around his country.

"Did you know any Americans before this job?" I asked.

"No, *memsahib*, only just last year I started, and I meet many Amer-ee-kaans." He pronounced "Americans" the way many Pakistanis did.

"What does your family think about you working at Mangla Dam?"

"Oh, they very much happy. I make good pay. They think some Amer-ee-kaans have strange customs," Ahmed said.

"What kind of strange customs?" I was curious to know how they viewed us.

"My father and mother think it strange that American man marry his own mother. Not done by Muslims." He turned to explain to me what he had heard, paying little attention to the traffic.

"Ahmed, American men don't marry their mothers." I gasped in astonishment. "Where did you get that idea?"

"I heard it myself. Last fall, I drive American man, three children, and his wife to Lahore. He call his wife 'Mother' all the time. So he marry with his mother, right?"

"No, Ahmed."

How could I explain the title of "Mother" some men thought was appropriate to bestow on their spouses after they bore children? I wouldn't tolerate my husband referring to me as "Mother" even if he thought it was a compliment. Now these poor Pakistanis had a very wrong impression of Americans from that misused title.

"That man meant she was the mother of his children, not his own mother. No Christians would allow a man to marry his mother. That's against the law in America," I said.

Ahmed nodded, digesting what I'd told him. I wasn't sure he believed me. He had heard the man call his wife "Mother." How could we stop this wrong idea some Pakistanis believed was an American practice?

"Ahmed, perhaps you are thinking of Mongol tribes where man might marry his father's widow? I read in books where the man may marry to protect the widows in his clan? Americans don't do that," I explained. I wasn't sure Ahmed believed me.

When we reached Lahore, I asked Ahmed to stop at the shoemaker on the Mall. Our favorite shoemaker greeted us with a big smile and a cup of tea. He measured the boy's feet and compared their measurements with the last ones from seven months ago. He examined the American shoes Mrs. Wilcox brought, and he was impressed with the narrow shoes. He tried them on each boy and saw what I'd been trying to explain. I left with high hopes that the next shoes would be narrow.

Outside the shoemaker's shop, Majid came running up to us. "*A Salaam alekum, memsahib.* I not see you too long time." He had grown but still had his impish charm.

Majid's effervescent smile greeted me like an old friend. I'd missed this hardworking, street-smart boy. His charm and sad eyes melted my heart. He had responsibility to hustle and earn enough to feed his family.

"*Babas* grow more big." He smiled at Mark and Kevin.

He walked with us to the car where Ahmed waited. I surveyed the wide boulevard, feeling right at home. We stopped at the Mangla Dam Contractor's office where the men stood to greet me, John Ziemer, Jamal Farouki, and Freddie, whose wedding was tomorrow.

"You must come to dinner at the Punjab Club with the Ziemers, Najma, and me," Jamal said.

"If you are all going, I'd love to. Perhaps Alam can stay with the boys," I said.

"Bring the boys. They behave very well, and Najma would love to see them," he said.

The next day, the Ziemers and I arrived a little early for the wedding, so we went inside the Catholic church and found seats two rows back on the groom's side. At least John, Dorothy, and I figured the right side was for the groom in America so a Catholic church in Lahore was probably the same. Time passed, and no one else arrived. I was glad that we had come. How sad that they had such a small turnout for this wedding they had planned for a year. Barely a dozen people were in the church. Perhaps the attendees would be the men who worked with Freddie and close friends. I recognized Freddie's parents, who were already occupying the front pew on the right.

The music of the wedding march began as the clock chimed the hour. We looked toward the back of the church. The tall doors opened, and the two bridesmaids led the procession with the bride on her father's arm following them down the aisle. Florence smiled with a shy sidewise glance toward us as she passed. She looked radiant with her shiny, dark hair and cocoa-colored skin in a gown that was lacy and delicate As she joined Freddie at the altar, a crowd of people filed into the church and took their seats, shuffling and making noise as they settled themselves. I was astonished. Had we been mistaken to enter the church to wait for the bride? Was this a custom that we didn't know? We knew the Anglo Pakistanis tried to emulate everything British and ignored their Pakistani heritage. People continued to fill the church until about 150 guests found their seats, the bridal party standing and waiting until they were seated.

Freddie wore a dark tailored suit and had his black, straight hair slicked back like a movie star of the thirties. The bride and groom stood silently, though the groom shifted his weight from one foot to another. When the music stopped, everyone's attention turned to the priest and the couple.

The priest read the traditional wedding vows that always brought tears to my eyes. As the couple said their vows and the priest reached out for the ring, the groomsman fumbled in his pockets. The ring was given, the vows were exchanged, and the priest said, "You may now kiss your bride."

Now the bridesmaid lifted the bride's veil so she could receive the husband's first kiss, accompanied by a chuckle of nervous relief from the assembled people. The recessional music began, and the couple walked down the aisle together, smiling to their friends and family as they led us to the reception in the rectory.

John Ziemer introduced me to Art Cotter, the man who took Jim's job in Lahore. He was a tall, blond Nordic looking man with a wide set of shoulders. Jamal told me he had served some years in the Royal Canadian Mounted Police.

"Jim must have worked day and night to keep up with all the shipments. Going to the customs office alone takes most of every day." I knew Jim had worked long hours. "I like Lahore, but you must find Mangla much better for families."

I agreed, but this visit to Lahore was a wonderful treat for me. I felt comfortable. I knew where to shop and to find household items that had been on my wish list for several months. Best of all, I had time to visit with Claire Keller, my dear friend. We laughed at our succession of mishaps involving local taxis. What fun we'd shared, and each time we got together, we laughed at our challenges.

"We really did have some of the best laughs of all time," Claire sighed. I'd missed her.

The year we lived in Lahore was special, learning about a new culture and the practices of the Muslim people. Baral Colony was like an American town created in the middle of the Punjab with all the recreational facilities and conveniences Americans wanted. Lahore teemed with energy with exotic sights, smells, and sounds around every corner. Life in Lahore was comparable to university or urban cities anywhere with art, music, and the finest example of the culture of the country. Lahore deserved its nickname, the "Paris of the East."

Back at Baral Colony the day after the wedding, Ahmed helped me take the suitcases into the house. The boys were running around the front yard, happy to escape the car after hours on the road. A neighbor walked by with a monkey on a leash. I'd never seen anyone with a monkey, and after the wild, vicious ones Jim and I saw in India, I hurried back outside. Kevin was running toward the woman with the monkey, eager to see the animal. The woman stopped and picked up the monkey, who perched on her shoulder. She brought the monkey close so Kevin could pet the animal. As he reached to pet the monkey, the creature moved with lightning speed and bit Kevin's arm.

Kevin howled in surprise and pain. I picked him up and saw the teeth marks on his forearm. A little blood oozed through the skin. I was concerned about rabies or other diseases. *I've got to take him to the doctor.*

"Has the monkey had shots?" I asked the owner.

She was already walking away, unconcerned. I hadn't met her before, but she was going toward the houses further down the street. Ahmed came to see why Kevin was crying.

"Ahmed, I need you to take us to the hospital right away, please. I'll give you more *baksheesh.*"

I put both boys in the car, and Ahmed drove us to the hospital.

The doctor looked at Kevin's arm and checked his immunization cards. "He's up-to-date on his shots, including tetanus. Keep the wound clean, and bring him back if he has any red streaks. I'll look into it and let you know if any further treatment is recommended."

Few people at Baral Colony had dogs, much less exotic wild animals. Kevin suffered no ill effects, but I was determined to keep my boys away from that woman and her monkey.

◇◇◇◇◇

MARK THRIVED IN HIS KINDERGARTEN class under the dynamic tutelage of Marge Miller. Pakistanis looked twice at Mrs. Miller, whose heritage was Mexican American. She had dark skin, dark hair, and soft brown eyes. People thought she might be Goa, the Portuguese colony on the West Coast of India. No one could tell a story or chastise a willful child with the unspoken drama Mrs. Miller could bring with her eyes and gestures. Her twenty kindergarten students adored her, and she delighted them with an elastic face and eyes that made expressive question marks. She controlled the class with her arms crossed over her chest and an expression that stopped the class's worst mischief-makers in their tracks. She loved children, and they loved her.

Shortly after our trip to Lahore, parent-teacher conferences were held at the Mangla International School. Mrs. Miller met me for the conference. I was curious to know how Mark was doing in kindergarten. He loved going to school, got up, and dressed himself each morning, needing only a little help with buttons and *dherzi*-made shirts with buttonholes that weren't always the right size for the buttons.

Mrs. Miller greeted me with a warm smile. "Mark is doing well in school. He's adjusted well to the class and gets along well with his classmates."

"He gets up each morning, eager to go to school. He dresses himself, too," I said.

"There are times that Mark seems a bit nervous and is afraid to make mistakes," she said toward the end of the conference.

"Do you think we're too harsh with discipline at home? Jim recently took away all the crayons when he slipped and left marks on the coffee table." Jim expected military discipline from the boys, and they were so young. We had heated discussions about that subject.

"All children make mistakes. That's how they learn," she said with a sympathetic smile.

Jim, an only child, was twenty-nine years old when Mark was born and never spent much time with children. I'd always helped my mother with my two sisters, who were seven and nine years younger.

As we walked home, I thought about Mrs. Miller's observation about Mark's nervousness. He'd been upset when Jim took away the crayons, and a few days later, with his five-year-old artistic impulse, he drew figures on the wall of their bedroom with a pencil. Pencils were also banished when Jim discovered the transgression, or budding artistic talent. I felt torn, not wanting to stifle Mark's eagerness to draw while keeping the house in the perfect state Jim expected. Jim's hours left little time to play or interact with the boys, so his fatherhood role was to bark instructions and expect us to follow them. I wondered how other fathers handled setting boundaries yet offered some kind of encouragement, too. I was in the middle as the enforcer of his rules for the boys.

I found the forbidden crayons and laid a sheet from a newspaper on the coffee table, along with instructions to Sherif to watch for marks on the table and clean them if Mark's hand slipped again. There was more than one way to sidestep Jim's rules.

◇◇◇◇◇

THE LAHORE HORSE SHOW WAS scheduled for early March. We received an invitation that read:

PATRON-IN-CHIEF
FIELD MARSHAL MOHAMMAD AYUB KHAN, N.Pk., H.J.
PRESIDENT OF PAKISTAN
NATIONAL HORSE & CATTLE SHOW, 4TH TO 9TH MARCH 1964
FORTRESS STADIUM, LAHORE CANTONMENT
MR. & MRS. JAMES AYLWORTH AND TWO CHILDREN
YOU ARE REQUESTED TO GRACE THE OCCASION.

I looked at the invitation, and the memory of the last year's horse show flashed through my mind. Mark was now five and would enjoy the pageantry. Kevin, though only two years old, was walking better, rarely took naps, and would be entertained by the horses and excitement of the horse show. I showed the invitation to Jim with hopes that he could go with us. My imagination was focused on events of Fortress Stadium and the horse show. I'd missed some events last year with all the social activities and entertainment of that weekend.

Jim could not take time off work but encouraged me to go. Lahore was now an easy trip of three or more hours by car. The cost for the car and driver were reasonable. Our friends at WAPDA Flats invited us to stay with them. I sent an acceptance letter to our friends, and Jim reserved our rental car.

A few weeks later on a misty morning in March, the boys and I set out in a holiday spirit. Horse Show Week in Lahore was exciting. I compared it to my childhood when the Reno Rodeo attracted people from Nevada's small towns who all turned out to see the action. The Lahore Horse Show attracted pedigree horses and cattle from all over Pakistan, and the event sparked the season's most exciting social events.

We arrived in Lahore at midday and made our usual stop at the shoemaker's shop on the Mall. The shoes we'd ordered for Mark and Kevin were finished and fit well. The shoemaker finally made them narrow enough for their feet. We did a little shopping and arrived at the Bennett's home at WAPDA Flats in time for the boys to find their old friends at the playground.

Helen Bennett greeted me with warmth and enthusiasm. "Come in. You're just in time for cocktails."

We settled in to talk as if no time had passed.

"Are you still riding your friend's jumper?" I asked.

Helen, an expert rider, was happy to exercise the horse that got little attention from its owner. "Yes, I still take him out for a ride as often as I can, usually twice a week. He's such a fine horse. He could use more work to keep him in shape." She smiled at the mention of the horse. "Did you know they wanted to make another movie here this year?"

"Really? What did the WAPDA people say about that?" I asked.

"When the Bollywood crew asked to film here this year, WAPDA decided that, after so many things were missing last year, they turned them down," she said.

I remembered our stolen movie camera. Other residents reported wallets, jewelry, as well as cash and other valuables missing after the crew and cast left last year. Helen's cook served us dinner as we caught up with our news. I told Helen about our Christmas show and my dance class.

On the opening day of the horse show, we caught a taxi to Fortress Stadium. We watched the opening ceremony and parade and then individual bands marching to a tattoo of drums for the soldiers on parade.

Next came my favorite events, the animals. Sleek-humped Brahmin cattle were docile and aristocratic as they entered the arena with their handlers. The Brahma bulls in the American West were wild bucking creatures used for bull riding competition. These animals who looked the same were pampered and gentle.

Dancing camels delighted us with their agility and grace. Kevin watched. His eyes fixed on the ungainly creatures decked out with red and gold tassels on their halters. Then the horses paraded in formation, breaking into two groups and then four and racing around the arena at a fast, precise thread-the-needle formation. The flying horses skipped as they changed leads on the sharp turns. The horse and rider moved as one, seamless and precise in every movement.

An event we had missed last year was the tent pegging contest that showed the skill of the desert tribesmen driving their tall tent pegs into the earth as they swung their mallets from horseback. Mark and Kevin both cheered as the teams drove tent pegs further into the ground.

The West Pakistan Rangers Mounted Patrol entered the stadium. I saw a white horse across the parade field. I wondered if that could be Corporal Akbar's stallion. He moved with smooth, magnificent poise. The horse's arched neck showed his pride at the crowd's attention. I was sure this was the same horse. How I loved those afternoons along the canals where life passed at the pace of the clip-clop of the horse's hooves. Those images would remain with me, the mental snapshots of *dhobis* washing clothes, children swimming in the canals, and life passing in slow motion as I viewed it from the back of a horse. I thought there was no better way to see the country.

My visit to Lahore restored my enthusiasm. I relished the activities in the city where I felt at home with my old friends and neighbors. The only person I missed was Claire, who was visiting her husband in the south where his company sent him on a project.

◇◇◇◇◇

BACK IN BARAL COLONY, WE had ten days until our spring show, "Where Have All the Flowers Gone." Jayne Coffey put the finishing touches on our dance numbers. We hurried the tailor with his last costume fittings, and we were ready for the sold-out event. People were eager for entertainment, and we were going to do our best to provide that one missing element in our American town.

42

Banned in Jhelum Province

THE BARAL PLAYERS WAS COMPRISED of American and British expatriates who lived in Baral Colony, all with a love of theater. Many members, especially the British residents, were skilled in lighting, sound, and acting. With no TV and movies shown two days a week, the shows they wrote and produced were something people looked forward to and relished. Last year's first endeavor was called "She Wore a Yellow Ribbon." The mention of that production still brought smiles to the faces of those who saw the show. The name came from the big plastic ribbon each dependent had been given upon departure from the South San Francisco office. Each person received a ribbon to wear and larger yellow ribbons for their luggage for easy identification. I didn't understand what the title meant at first. With Lahore as my destination, I guess no one felt that I needed a yellow ribbon to identify our luggage or us. Or maybe the Honeymoon Express brought them into use.

I joined the Baral Players group in January, even though I had no experience other than some writing efforts during high school. The meetings consisted of brainstorming ideas with suggestions tossed out, many of which became the lines of the play. Everyone brought his or her experiences and culture shock situations that we had heard others tell about.

"Did you hear about the lizard who fell from the ceiling into Mrs. Gui-terrez's frying pan when she was scrambling eggs?"

Howls of laughter and a few gasps filled the room.

"How about Margaret's *bearer* spraying ants with her imported hair spray?" another person suggested.

"I thought it was her perfume," a man chimed in. "Her *homal* used that for ant spray."

"Charlie was shocked to find his *bearer* perched with his feet on the toilet seat, using their toilet," another added. "That could be a hilarious scene."

Others booed him down.

"'Mad Dogs and Englishmen' is a great song that would work well," an Englishman said.

That song was a hit in the show as two men, wearing pith helmets and carrying butterfly nets, performed it in front of the curtain during scenery changes.

Early project workers swore they ate hot dogs that had turned green in the mess hall. They now jokingly called all hot dogs "green wienies." Their complaint became the inspiration for a ghoulish operating room scene. A screen on stage shielded the doctors as they operated on a stricken fellow who suffered from too many "green wienies." As the surgery progressed, the doctor tossed green prop hot dogs over the screen. Four of us dancers performed a cha-cha number to the tune of "Mack the Knife." We wore short doctor's coats with large red buttons, fishnet stockings, and red high heels. As we danced, we pantomimed sharpening two dagger-length knives in rhythm to the music. The cha-cha Javed had taught me on the dance floor at Falletti's made learning the choreography easy.

This year's show poked fun at ourselves and the surprises of living in a strange, new country. Jayne Coffey met with the Baral Players to plan dances to go with the script. The Mangla International School Choir directed by Mary Pearson would perform.

Rehearsals for the March show started late in January. Now the pace accelerated as the date approached. This show was called "Where Have All the Flowers Gone," named after an anti-war song. In the sad verses of the song, the flowers disappear, to the young girls, then the young men, and finally the old men go away, just as some employees found they were no longer needed due to the rapid progress on the dam and the elimination of jobs.

Another title considered was "Surplus Blues," a term management used to describe an employee whose job was no longer needed as "surplus." The humor wasn't as poignant as the "Flowers" song. For instance, in one scene, a man walked onstage and announced, "Look what they've got in the commissary. Nylons!" As he held up a pair of nylons, the table of bridge-playing women onstage ran off to buy nylons before the supply was gone.

Our dance group was to open the show with a chorus line dance to "California, Here I Come" with kicks in high heels made by a shoemaker in Rawalpindi. We wore fishnet stockings with sheer nylons under them so the thick threads in those early net stockings wouldn't cut our feet. The costume was a silver lamé jacket with purple lapels and a matching hat. Our *dherzi* who made the costumes took too much time and required many fittings to make a simple sleeveless coat jacket, but eventually the costumes were completed to our satisfaction.

Opening night arrived, and the excitement was palpable. Both performances were sold out. The cast call was an hour before the show, and I arrived early with my various shoes and costumes.

The show's directors were frantic. They had just received notice that Mr. Khan, the district commissioner of Jhelum, cancelled our entertainment permit for the theater. With an hour before the opening and the possibility of 680 unhappy paid customers, we were determined, in the best show business tradition, that the show must go on. But how?

"We could move the show to the school gymnasium," one cast member said.

"The tennis courts are closer. We could borrow chairs from the restaurant and the bowling alley coffee shop," another said.

Neither alternative location would have the curtain, lights, and professional venue of our lovely, comfortable theater. If we performed without a permit, Mr. Khan could close our theater, and we'd be unable to enjoy the biweekly movies so many families looked forward to seeing. We couldn't jeopardize our theater.

Otis Armstrong arrived with Dawn and his sons, David and Gary. When Otis heard what Mr. Khan had done, he took over as mayor and personnel manager to solve the problem. Otis located the nearest telephone and, in his best Oklahoma drawl, spoke to the disgruntled district commissioner of Jhelum.

"Commissioner Khan, what is the problem?" he asked. "How can I fix it?"

"We were not invited to this show that is to be produced this evening," Mr. Khan said. "I cannot let the show go on. What if it has objectionable materials in its contents?"

Otis immediately recognized that Mr. Khan's annoyance was because he hadn't been invited to opening night. Mr. Khan enjoyed the dining hall, the bowling alley, and the swimming pool when he visited Baral as a guest.

"Mr. Khan," Otis said, "I have tickets for you and your wife, if she is willing to come, for tomorrow night's performance. I didn't think you'd want to attend the first night when the actors and singers will surely make mistakes. We consider the first show more like a dress rehearsal, a time to work out the problems. I think you'll enjoy the second, more polished performance tomorrow evening."

"What about reviewing the content for obscenities?" Mr. Khan asked.

"Our minister reviewed the script, and so has the Catholic priest from Rawalpindi. They have both deemed it is acceptable to their strict Christian guidelines," Otis said in his soothing, former undertaker's voice.

"What time tomorrow night should I come?" Mr. Khan was placated.

Otis' invitation to the second night's performance worked. Mr. Khan restored our entertainment license fifteen minutes before the opening number. The show could go on in the theater. People began filing in. But the cast was more nervous than ever after this last-minute on-and-off again show. We all put our whole hearts into the show that had been banned in Jhelum Province.

Our opening number was to the music of "California, Here I Come." I was in the center of the chorus line of eight women from Jayne's dance class. We flashed our biggest smiles as the spotlights hit our eyes, nearly blinding us. We stepped and kicked in a copy of the Radio City Rockettes number, our arms stretched out, touching one another's shoulder. After two or three times back and forth with our chorus line kicks, I felt what must be a hole in the stage. My heel dropped, and I danced the rest of the number on my toes. When the song ended, we danced off stage. I discovered that my new high heels had one heel snapped off. The Rawalpindi shoemaker had put a wooden heel on the shoe with no inside metal spike like American-made shoes.

In the second act, as we danced the "Mack The Knife" cha-cha number, I noticed the familiar faces of Mr. Guy F. Atkinson and his wife Rachel in front row seats. Mr. Guy was laughing, and so was Rachel. They loved the show and applauded our efforts. I didn't know they were in town, and I was thrilled to see them. Imagine, the founder of the company was here to see our thespian efforts.

After the show, Mr. and Mrs. Atkinson congratulated the members of the cast, giving us all the praise due professional entertainers. He and Rachel remembered having dinner with the Ziemers and us in Lahore a little over a year ago. For many years, when Mr. Guy or Rachel saw Jim, they always asked him if his wife was still dancing.

"The show was wonderful," Rachel said, hugging me. "Are you now settled here after getting acquainted in Lahore?"

"Yes, we're settled, and finding our way around this area. Are you here just to check on the dam?" I marveled that these two octogenarians traveled so far.

"Yes, Guy wanted to see the Mole in operation. Can you believe they boosted him up on that monster of a machine just so he could see it from the top? I gave them the devil." She shook her head at her husband's bravado at his age.

Gary Davey walked by and heard our conversation. He walked with me toward the Mandamco Club where most people were headed for a drink.

"Whenever Mr. Guy visits the job, I'm the one who gets to show him around. He got his hard hat and was determined to climb that Mole. There are about 30 steps to the top, straight up. I got two strong men, one on each side, and two others at the top as they boosted him up the machine." He said, shaking his head in disbelief.

"Well, he's the boss, and pretty hard to say 'no' to, I guess," I said.

"You've got that right. He wouldn't take no for an answer, or 'too dangerous,' either. Then we caught hell from Rachel for letting him do it." Gary was in a tough spot, but no harm came to the boss.

"Where Have All the Flowers Gone?" gave everyone a much-needed lift after the somber holiday season. It was good to hear laughter and see the smiles on the faces of the people in the audience.

The next night, Otis and Dawn Armstrong creatively embellished all the errors the cast made during the opening night performance to the district commissioner of Jhelum. After he saw the second night's show, Mr. Khan told Otis, "I'm glad you advised us to come tonight. The show was wonderful. I didn't notice any mistakes. They must have worked them out during the first night, just as you said they would."

The cast party after the second show was in the ManDamCo lounge, packed to capacity with participants and audience, many who recognized their own blunders or cultural shocks in adapting to local ways that had been worked into the script. I joined in the jubilation with the feeling that I'd become a member of this community, able to contribute my sewing, singing, and newly discovered dancing ability. I still missed my friends in Lahore, but Baral Colony was so much like being in America, even though it was half a world away.

Jim visited with the men at the bar while I danced with some of the guys from the show, and found our bachelor friend, Fida Shaw, to be a fine ballroom dancer when he formally asked Jim's permission to dance with me. We danced several numbers.

I went to the lady's room and found one of the dancers from our class upset.

"What's wrong?" I asked her.

"I was dancing with some Pakistani who was invited to the show. He pushed himself against me and wanted me to go outside with him. I told him, 'No, I'm married,' and he said, 'You American women do it with anyone. Why not me?' I was so insistent and insulted that I wouldn't have anything to do with him. I thought he'd rape me. So I slapped him. He left, mad as hell."

She didn't want to tell her husband of the insulting behavior a man who had a very mistaken impression of American women. She was crying, trying to compose herself in the restroom.

"What a creep," I said. "He deserved to be slapped."

"Please don't say anything," she said. "My husband will kill him if he finds out. I don't want any trouble." She sniffed and dabbed at her smeared mascara.

I held her while the last of her tears dried in her eyes. "I won't say anything. Tell me if he bothers you again. I have some Pakistani friends who could set him straight. Or we'll get the women together and teach him some manners." I spoke with bravado, but I also knew we were in a foreign country and things weren't as they were at home. We might not be believed if we involved the authorities.

Not all Pakistanis were as honorable as the ones we knew.

Errol Platt's News

THE SHOW GAVE ME A chance to meet new friends. I now felt less isolated in this beautiful American community. The Urdu classes challenged me, the dance and singing groups were fun, and we had more friends. After nine months, I was beginning to like Baral Colony.

Jim was scheduled to meet with Errol Platt, Margaret's husband, who was the project's business manager who handled personnel matters. We expected that Errol wanted to discuss Jim signing up for an additional thirty-month contract. For some reason, he called Jim in early, just a few weeks after the show in April. The company had very little new work in the United States, and we were planning to accept that extension.

"Irene, where are you?" Jim called as he came home that evening.

"In the kitchen." I was cooking dinner.

A week ago, Sherif had told me that he wanted to go back to Lahore, and had quit. I missed him, but knew he, too, missed the excitement of Lahore. Since we were in the middle of the show, I postponed hiring another *bearer*. I was also experimenting to see if I could get by with the new *mali* doing the yard work and carrying the laundry for me. He seemed ambitious and might do some cleaning, too. It was more important to have the right *bearer* than to take just anyone who applied. I'd learned that a long time ago.

"You better sit down. I have some news," he said.

Oh, dear. Someone must have been hurt.

He took my hand as he pulled me down beside him on the sofa. He took a breath. "Errol Platt called me into his office and shut the door. He explained to me the problem they have. The man doing the purchasing in the South San Francisco office passed away from cancer. Another has a brain tumor and will be out for a long time. The company needs a man in South San Francisco to do the purchasing right away." Jim stopped and took a deep breath. "They want me there in three weeks."

"What about the contract you have now?" I'd heard of people who decided to quit before their contract was up and were required to pay their own way home, at a considerable expense.

"They'll release me from this contract so we can leave right away. The company will pay our expenses to go home. I tried to get them to agree to three weeks vacation. The office is in trouble, and they need me as soon as possible. I could only get two weeks of vacation. That's better than nothing, right?"

I was speechless. I had expected this meeting would mean that Jim was going to sign up for another thirty months. Now management wanted us on a plane within a week. This was a good opportunity for Jim. I missed my family and life in the United States. I had no objection to going home now. I would be happy to be anywhere in the States. I'd be able to have a telephone, buy clothing and shoes easily, and see my family. I was happier every time I thought about it. We'd be home in a month and have our trip through Europe on the way.

"Jim, it sounds wonderful. We need to get shots, make reservations and pack and ship our stuff home." My mind filled with the details that we'd have to do.

"So you're agreeable to leaving in a week?" That old transfer grin was twitching in the corners of his mouth.

"Yes, we can do it."

Jim hugged me and gave me a big kiss. We were so excited that I could hardly eat the dinner I'd prepared. I couldn't sleep that night thinking of all the things I needed to do. Shots came first.

The next morning, before I could make breakfast, someone knocked on the door. A woman I recognized from the supermarket stood there.

"Do you have an ironing board to sell? I really need one if you do," she said.

"How did you know we were being transferred?" I was shocked that this woman knew the news I'd learned the night before.

"I heard some women talking at the commissary. They said you were going back to the States," she said.

Another woman came right behind her. "Do you have a mixer to sell? I'll match anyone else's offer," the second woman said.

"You might as well sell the household items here. We can buy new ones back home, and it will help people who need them. And it will be that much less to pack," Jim said.

Jim left for work. A steady stream of women came to our door all that day. I made a list of items I sold, the name of the buyer, and the price we agreed on. I kept the ironing board for a few days so I could pack our clothes in wearable condition. I wouldn't have time to bake, so I let the woman leave with her prize, my mixer. By the end of the first day, most of our household items were sold. Pakistan's lack of consumer goods in the sixties made each thing in my closet an item that someone coveted. Dora loved my black coat with velvet trim, and it fit her well. She bought it immediately. Another woman needed a bathing suit. I had a new one with the tags still attached that I was saving for summer. She was elated and paid me full price plus sales tax, at her insistence. Many of my dresses were tailor-made and designed for my tall, lean frame, so few women could wear those, and I'd need them for the trip home. Two weeks in Europe shone like a beacon to me, a focal point while we prepared for departure.

My first priority was to get any shots we needed. I got our international shot cards and took Mark out of kindergarten. We boarded the jitney bus to the shopping center where we caught the next bus up the hill to the hospital.

"I need to get the tetanus shot today. The one I had in the States gave me a rash, and I was sick for nearly a week. We leave on April 29, and I need time to get over the tetanus shot," I told the nurse. "I suspect my son Kevin may also be allergic to either tetanus or penicillin." I told her about the lump on his buttocks and pain in his hip after the stitches last May.

She gave me a shocked look. "The reaction you had was probably because you're allergic to tetanus vaccine. I'm going to test you and see what happens." She brought a needle and injected a single drop under the skin of my forearm.

Within minutes, a red, swollen spot the size of a silver dollar appeared where the vaccine entered my system.

She returned about fifteen minutes later and looked at my arm. "You're allergic to tetanus. Don't ever let anyone give you a shot, even if you step on a rusty nail. We'll mark your international shot card that you've had it. All your other shots and the children's are up-to-date. You're good to go." She handed back our international health and immunization cards signed by the doctor. "Have a good trip home. I wish I were going with you." She smiled and hurried on.

I was relieved not to need another tetanus shot.

Dora and Ray Haugen invited us for dinner that night. We enjoyed this couple, and they loved our two sons. Dora and the women on the Oahe Dam job had taught me to play bridge. We had all talked together about the possibility of going to Mangla when the news first reached us in South Dakota in early 1962. How time had flown since then, and how much I had learned in this country. Dora settled in at Baral, happy with her garden, bridge, and occasional trips to Lahore. Life for her and many of the American women wasn't too different from the remote jobs they had been assigned to in America. Most of them could live happily far from towns. Big dams and hydroelectric projects weren't located in urban areas. The town at Baral satisfied the needs of the families better than many jobs where they had lived before this one, and Baral was a jewel of a place to live by comparison.

On Friday night, Shorty and Jim Wesson hosted a dinner party for eight of us. Shorty was as good a cook as she was at doing my hair. We enjoyed this congenial group of friends. Shorty, like Dora, had learned to adapt to wherever the company sent her husband. Adjusting to wherever they landed was the construction wife's most resilient quality.

Burnell Ambrose, Jim's boss in the warehouse, and his wife Jean hosted a dinner party for twelve on Saturday night, just three days after our transfer. The Ambrose's party was a special send-off from Pakistan when all the guests showed up in Pakistani clothes. Many of the Americans adopted the *shalwar kameez* outfit for the comfort and light fabrics. Some of the men had *karakul* hats of fine lamb's wool. Two or three of the women had elegant *sari*s wrapped around like a skirt and then draped over their left shoulder. The top worn with the *sari* was a matching sleeveless or short-sleeved blouse of matching fabric to complete the ensemble.

Each night, we were feted at another party, sometimes cocktails with one group and dinner with another. The Archibalds had us for cocktails, and it was sad to say good-bye to Adeline. Her health wasn't strong, and I felt it would be a blessing when they could go home, too. Once more, she thanked Jim for donating blood.

During the day, I packed our clothing and items to bring home. We were allowed two suitcases per person, but traveling with that much baggage would be burdensome. We settled on five suitcases, none very large. The warehouse sent boxes to pack our household items. The framed pictures I had bought, four jute-framed collages from India, our brass and copper lamps, some brass vases and decorative articles, a camel saddle with leather seat, a nest of carved tables and some tablecloths, and locally made cushions were most of what I was taking home. I packed the green glass Christmas tree, which would be a reminder of the time spent making a unique decoration that occupied me during the weeks when we all were filled with grief. My neighbors brought their old newspapers to pack breakable items for the long sea journey.

Out shipment home was lighter than the fifteen hundred pounds I had shipped in the fall of 1962 from Reno, a small shipment for a whole household. The women of Baral Colony had bought my treadle sewing machine, my mixer, iron, and all household appliances. There wasn't a great deal to pack since the furniture, kitchenware, and dishes belonged to the company.

On April 22, 1964, Jim's meeting with Errol Platt gave him the news of the job he was needed for in the States. One week later, on April 29, 1964, our family boarded PIA's morning flight. As we took off, the pilot circled the future Mangla Dam where the men and machines were hard at work. We looked at the open scars in the earth that were being transformed into the world's largest compacted earth fill dam.

The curve of the Jhelum River where Mangla Devi was said to grant wishes of those who asked bustled with activity. If there really was a god as generous as Mangla Devi, I hoped that she granted my wish for the early diversion of the river and the early completion of the dam.

I believed the wish would be granted. After all, this had been a part of India, the land of mystics and magic.

Conclusion

MANGLA DAM'S SCHEDULE WAS ON track for early diversion of the Jhelum River when we left for home in late April 1964. Workers who were hired to work on the project brought a higher employment rate to Pakistan. With the town completed, the farm producing food, and recreational activities available for the families, all efforts were now concentrated on the diversion of the river planned for the window of time between September and late October of 1965. Work accelerated to round-the-clock shifts in preparation for completing the tunnels to divert the Jhelum River.

Our trip to Europe began in Beirut where we rested for two days to recover from the whirlwind week of activities to depart on short notice. Even with small children, Europe was a memorable adventure, and we were grateful we saw as much of Europe as we could.

Back in California, Jim returned to work in mid-May 1964 at Columbia Service Company, the name given to the South San Francisco and London offices that supplied Mangla Dam Contractors. He flew from Paris, and I continued with the boys to Amsterdam, London, and Southampton, where we boarded the Holland American's *Statendam*. Traveling by sea to New York was a perfect way for the boys and me to adjust gradually to time changes. We visited relatives in Pennsylvania and bought a station wagon at Jim's suggestion. During the next five days, I drove across the country with my two small sons who were stellar travelers. By the time we arrived back in Reno in mid-June 1964, we had traveled around the world.

We kept up with the progress of the project through Jim's daily contacts, the company's newsletter with detailed articles and photographs, and letters from friends. From California, we could envision each problem more clearly since we had seen the project and terrain.

Mr. Guy F. Atkinson's ninetieth birthday party was celebrated in early 1965 at a spectacular party at the Biltmore Hotel in Los Angeles. The impressive invitation requested the pleasure of our company, and we attended with about six hundred company employees, partners, and the extensive Atkinson family. I fretted about what to wear for the formal occasion. The only appropriate thing I had was the *sari* I'd bought in Bombay. I hesitated to cut the delicate silk fabric, but I was uncomfortable wearing a *sari*. The lovely six yards of fabric had royal blue threads in one direction and emerald green in the other with a tiny fleur-de-lis pattern throughout. The wide *pelou* border at the end had a foot-wide highly embellished border. With a simple empire waist pattern, I cut the sheath dress with the wide border at the top, trimmed the side split with the narrower two-inch-wide side border of the fabric, and stitched the remaining fabric into a stole to cover my shoulders. Gold gloves, a gold evening bag and shoes, and earrings with blue-green beads set off the simple dress. Several other ladies wore dresses fashioned from colorful *saris* that evening. Each dress was unique, and I was pleased my homemade effort had turned out so well. The compliments we received on our dresses were like our badge of honor from our long journey and the bazaars where we had shopped. As we went through the receiving line, Rachel squeezed my hand.

"Your dress is exquisite. It is so nice to see you again. Don't stop dancing." She said.

The evening was a tribute to the patriarch of the Atkinson family who had started the company in Nevada in the 1920s. In the early days, the company did some work on the Boulder, later named Hoover Dam, and participated in some way on most of the dams on the Columbia River between Washington and Oregon. Mr. Guy and the company he founded had received numerous awards from the construction industry and earned the respect of his competitors and partners alike.

The team spirit of the company employees, the Atkinson family, and the outpouring of love to Mr. Guy, the respected and admired founder of the company, made it a gratifying evening. The company that carried his name had risen to the top of the construction industry.

Their greatest achievement to date was Mangla Dam, well on the way to early completion. We were all proud to celebrate with him on this magical evening.

Mangla Dam became the subject of many publications in the world press. Visitors came to view the job and visit the American colony. That February, President Mohammed Ayub Khan came to visit with the Shah of Iran. On March 22, 1965, His Royal Highness, Prince Phillip, the Duke of Edinburgh, came to visit on behalf of Her Majesty, Queen Elizabeth, landing at the Mangla Airport in his Avro airplane under the watchful eye of our own pilot, Ken. Ken's comment was, "Whatever else the British have to be proud of about their prince, they can certainly be proud of his flying."

The students of Mangla International School were elated at the visit of American's closest thing to royalty, movie actor Marlon Brando, who stopped to visit the school while touring Mangla.

◇◇◇◇◇

ON SEPTEMBER 6, 1965, INDIAN soldiers fired on West Pakistan, and the two countries were at war. Nearly half the workers departed immediately to rejoin their units in Pakistan's reserve army. The Pakistani army issued blackout and stop work orders, but management objected and kept working during daylight hours and shut down most of the night shift. Residents of Baral Colony were issued blackout curtains of heavy plastic to darken their homes at night. Streetlights were turned off, and a curfew was enforced, including no cigarette smoking outside after dark. Some equipment continued to work until the army called again and told the managers that their pinpoint lights were visible in New Dehli. Now they were limited to daylight hours, and the time for diversion was approaching. The contractor consulted with the Pakistan army and WAPDA, the agency in charge of the dam. To delay the diversion because of the war might prolong the construction by a full year. The window of opportunity was short, from early September until the winter monsoons began in mid-October. The Pakistani government and the army encouraged the Americans to proceed at their own risk.

On September 16, 1965, with the war still raging and shots being fired across the Jhelum River in Kashmir, a large dump truck dropped load after load of rocks into the remaining narrow channel. Four bulldozers pushed dirt on top of the huge rocks. American supervisors and the construction manager, Joe McNabb, stood on the opposite bank, watching the river shrink to a trickle. After a few more loads from the dump trucks, the bulldozers pushed the fill material right to the edge of the Jhelum, and the downstream water stopped. The Jhelum River now flowed through the tunnels and around the area where the dam would rise. Early diversion was accomplished on September 16, 1965.

The India-Pakistan war ended a few days later.

The first commercial electricity was online July 1, 1967, a full year ahead of schedule. Later in July 1967, the second power generator began production.

⬦⬦⬦⬦

THE DEDICATION OF MANGLA DAM took place on November 23, 1967, with dignitaries and government representatives from all the World Bank countries who had made this moment possible. Flags of the countries that were the World Bank partners and had financed the undertaking flew over the restored Mangla Fort, including Australia, Canada, Germany, Pakistan, India, the United Kingdom, and the United States. Mr. Guy F. Atkinson, now in a wheelchair, and his wife Rachel traveled to Pakistan for the dedication. Many Americans had been sent back to the United States, but those who remained felt enormous satisfaction. They had completed one of the world's most difficult construction projects a year ahead of a rigid schedule in a remote area eight hundred miles from the nearest port and around the world from the major suppliers, not to mention the uncertain temper of the river and unpredictable weather. The war interrupted progress on the dam for those two weeks, but the contractor managed to keep the schedule.

The company earned the $100 million-dollar bonus for early completion and paid the government of Pakistan $60 million of it in taxes. Government officials had cheered on the contractor, knowing they would enrich their treasury with the taxes the company would pay.

An Italian firm won the bid for the second dam of the Indus Basin Project, Tarbela Dam. Many workers who received training at Mangla Dam found employment there. The Americans shipped the equipment back to the United States.

Guy F. Atkinson died on September 12, 1968, but had lived to see the completion of the challenging project.

◇◇◇◇◇

AMERICANS LEFT A LEGACY TO Pakistan far greater than the multimillion-dollar dam to control floods and produce affordable electricity. About twenty-five thousand Pakistani employees worked at the dam during the six years of the project, many of whom received skilled training that they used to find jobs at Tarbela Dam, in Saudi Arabia's oil fields, and other projects in the Middle East.

The town of Baral Colony with all its facilities was turned over to the Pakistani army now responsible for operating the power station. The extensive buildings for the construction of the dam and Thill labor colony, its mosque, schools, clinics, and facilities remained and were left for the Pakistani people.

Mangla Lake, when filled, created a 100 square mile reservoir and has become a popular recreational area where people can fish, camp, and boat. Resorts have sprung up along the shores and hills around the lake, turning that bleak, arid land into a destination resort.

But perhaps the greatest legacy the American people left was on the human level, little known outside the Baral Colony. Americans are generous people who often saw a need and responded. American women formed church groups and reached out to help the villagers where they saw a need. Village girls learned to type on borrowed or donated typewriters the American women of the Dostian Group used to teach typing. "We'll teach you, and you can teach someone else." The TSA shop provided income for women who were encouraged to learn a skill by dedicated missionaries in Lahore. Their shop gave women fellowship and companionship as well as additional income for their families. Their beautifully embroidered table-cloths, napkins, and other articles sold by volunteer American women in the TSA shop brought one hundred thousand dollars to these women.

The women's clinic in Dina took a year for the American women to receive the Red Cross grant to provide supplies for the clinic. Village women who never had prenatal care were examined, given prenatal instruction, and now had the support of a doctor and midwife available for their labor and delivery.

The Americans went to build a dam but also contributed to the Pakistani people countless hours helping people with ideas and projects whose benefits remained long after the Americans departed.

◇◇◇◇◇

OUR DREAM OF TRAVEL AND adventure was fulfilled. Life was not easy in Pakistan, but with a sense of humor and friends to share the problems, we learned to conquer the obstacles and overcome the challenges. None of us who went there would trade the experience for an easy life. Several women told me, "This is the only place I ever lived that I cried when we left." *Bearers* became friends, we related to their problems, and tried to make life better when we saw need.

Many of the children who grew up in Baral Colony said, "The experience changed my life." Their education spilled outside the classroom, exploring the country on picnics and hikes, school trips, and their parents' vacations. Parents were happy to raise their children far from the drug and free-love society that prevailed in America during the sixties. The spirit of Mangla lives on with their frequent reunions, usually in the San Francisco Bay Area or the Pacific Northwest, when American women occasionally show up in *saris* with tales of their unique experiences growing up in the American town in the Punjab. Unlike many high school reunions, all parents and adults associated with the dam project are welcome.

The memorial issue of the Baral Town Crier was published on May 30, 1968, with 21 families remaining, all of whom had lived in Pakistan for six years. The Mangla International School's graduating class was small that year with 10 students graduating. During the years of operation, the school's highest attendance was 487. Now the last employees wrapped up the job and locked the doors with a few loyal Pakistani workers like Fida Shaw.

Rohtas Fort and the ghost town of Fetehpur Sikri were named World Heritage sites some years after our return.

When the equipment from Mangla was sold or shipped back to the United States, the Mole was sent to England where it was used to dig the Mersey Tunnel.

We returned with a greater empathy for people who live in poverty, a better understanding of the Muslim culture and people, and a greater appreciation for the freedom we enjoy in America. Our lives were forever changed by the sights and sounds, the people and places, who enriched our lives and gave us a glimpse of life behind the veil on the far side of the world.

The Early Days of Mangla Dam

Future site of Mangla Dam, 1962

Mangla Dam site below Sultanpura Rest House, 1962

Early 1962, beginning construction on Mangla Dam

Early construction of Baral Colony, 1962

*Tunnels and construction of Mangla Dam with the
Mangla Fort in the background*

Spillway nearly completed with batch plant on the left

Diverting the Jhelum River, September 16, 1965

Tunnel Boring Machine at work on tunnels

Nearly completed spillway and stilling basin

Aerial closeup of spillway

Aerial view of dam powerhouse

Aerial views of Mangla Lake as it is being filled

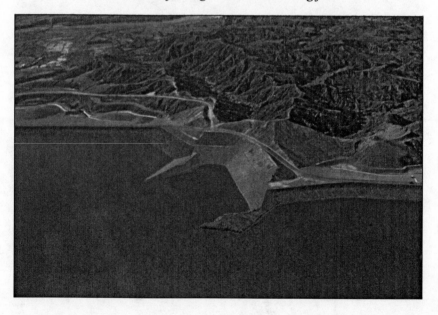

Completed Mangla Dam and powerhouse

View of Mangla Dam with restored Mangla Fort on the right

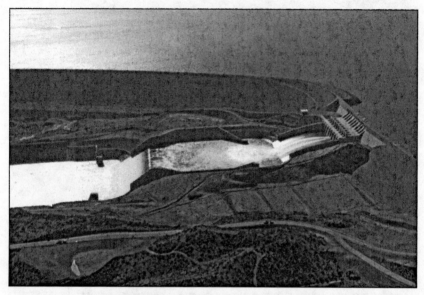

The Mangla Dam spillway after project completion

An aerial view of the competed dam and surrounding construction site

WORLDS LARGEST EARTH FILLED DAMS as of 1968
by Volume of Fill

Dam	Country	Year of Completion	Volume million Cu. Yd.
Tarbela	W. Pakistan	Projected	175
Mangla Project *Mangla Dam, Sukian Dam, Jari Dam*	W. Pakistan	1967	140
Fort Peck	USA	1940	125
Oahe	USA	1960	92
Oroville	USA	UC	81
San Luis	USA	UC	78
Garrison	USA	1954	67
Saiony	USSR	UC	63
Nurek	USSR	UC	59
Kiev	USSR	UC	59
Gorky	USSR	1955	58
High Aswan	UAR	UC	58
Portage Mountain	Canada	1967	57
Tabasqua	Syria	UC	52
Fort Randall	USA	1956	50
Kakhovka	USSR	1955	47
Tsimlyansk	USSR	1952	44
Volga (Lenin)	USSR	1955	44
Mica Creek	Canada	UC	42
Cochiti	USA	UC	41
South Saskatchewan	Canada	UC	40

UC = Under Construction

Mangla Dam, when raised by 40 feet to full development level (planned for the future), the total fill of Mangla Dam is estimated to be 200 million cu. yd.